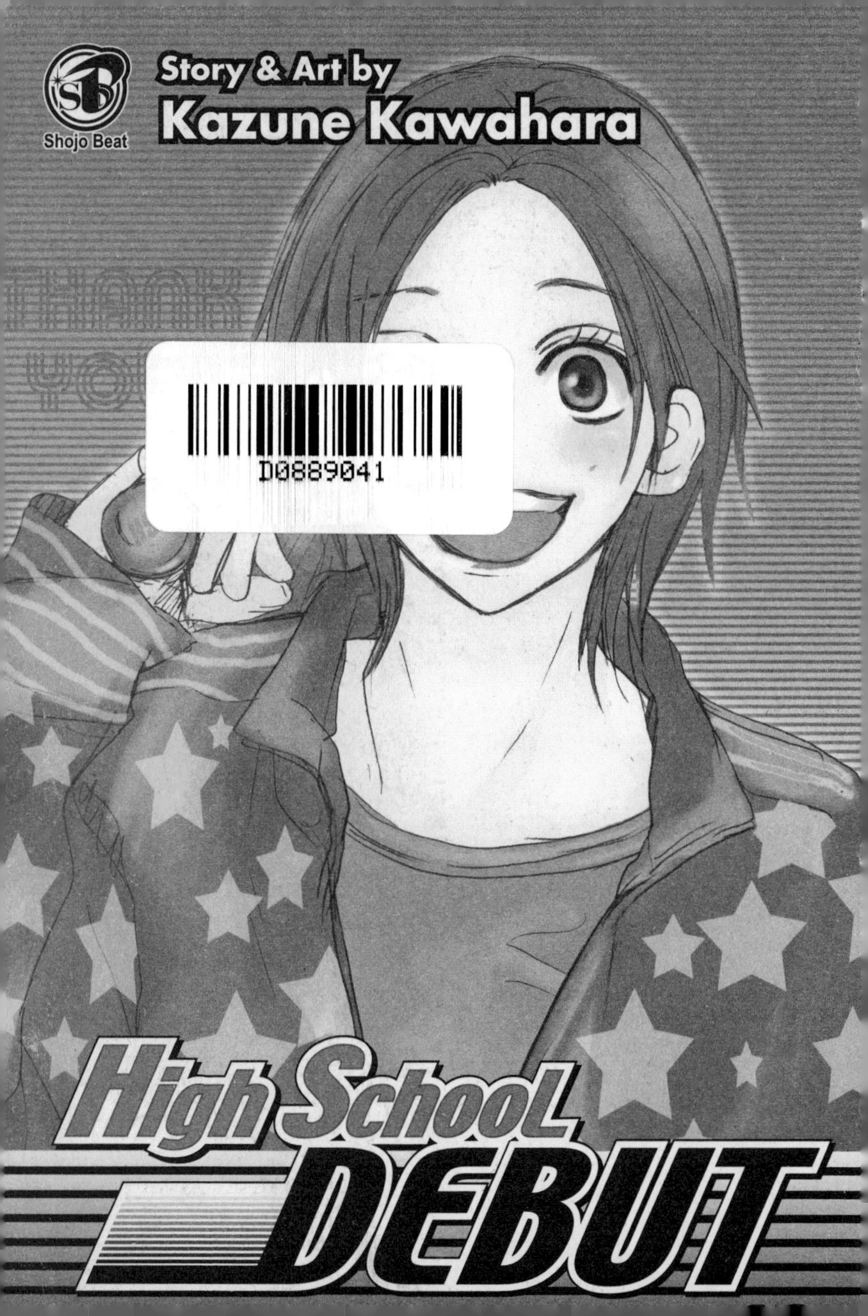
Shojo Beat
Story & Art by
Kazune Kawahara
High School
DEBUT

High School DEBUT

★★ Contents

Story Thus Far...

High school student Haruna used to spend all her time playing softball in junior high, but now she wants to give her all to finding true love instead! While her "love coach" Yoh is training her on how to be popular with guys, the two of them start dating.

During their second summer vacation together, Haruna books an away trip to celebrate Yoh's birthday. It's only after she makes the arrangements that she realizes what could happen between the two of them. Is she ready?! She decides that she is, but Asami and the others interrupt their private time. Their trip ends in chaos!

It's winter now and Yoh is thinking about what he wants to do after graduation. Haruna wants to help! While Haruna does some research, Yoh slowly works out what he wants to do and decides on a college. However, it's in Tokyo! The thought of a long-distance relationship is weighing heavily on Haruna's mind...

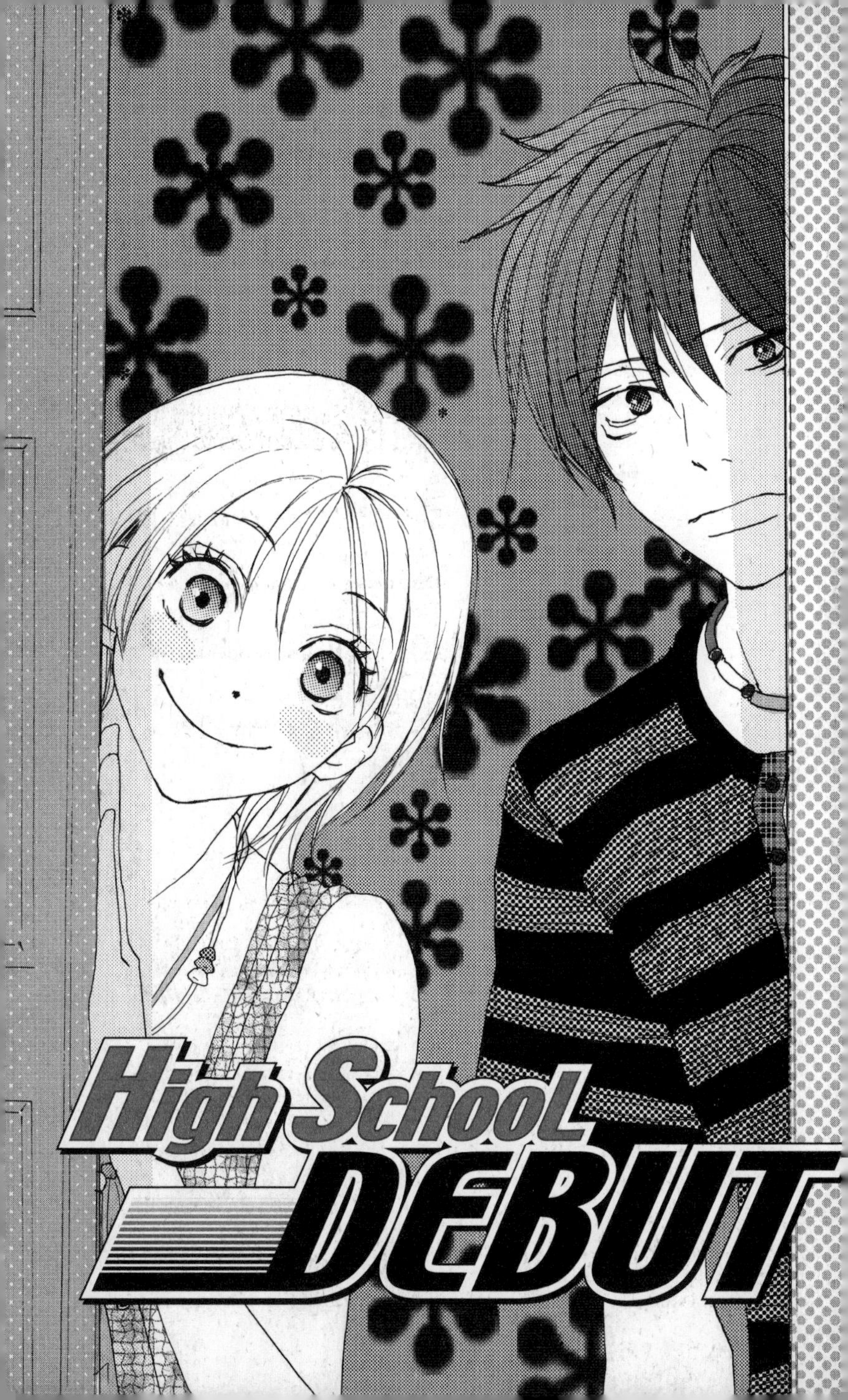
High School
DEBUT

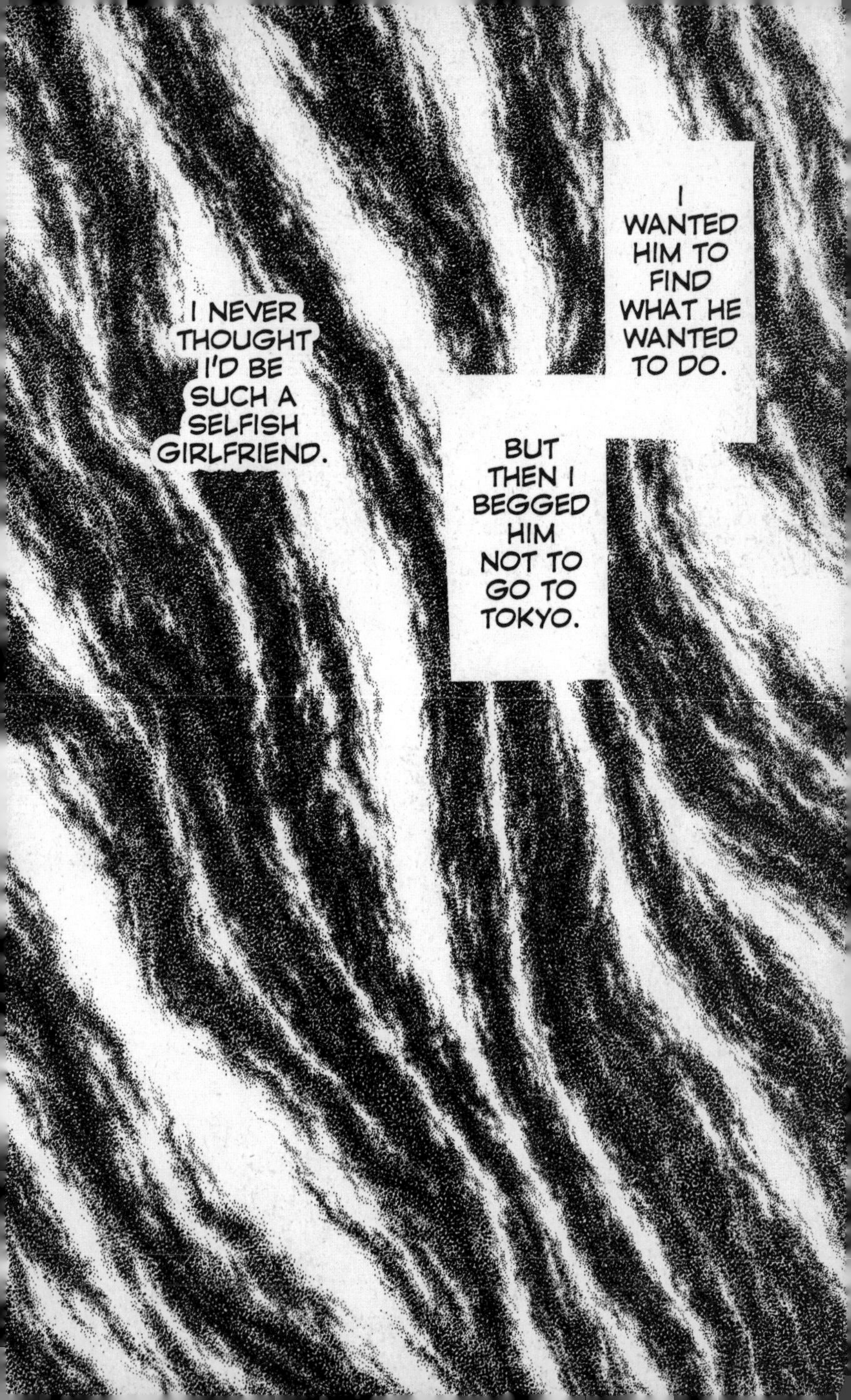
I WANTED HIM TO FIND WHAT HE WANTED TO DO.
BUT THEN I BEGGED HIM NOT TO GO TO TOKYO.
I NEVER THOUGHT I'D BE SUCH A SELFISH GIRLFRIEND.

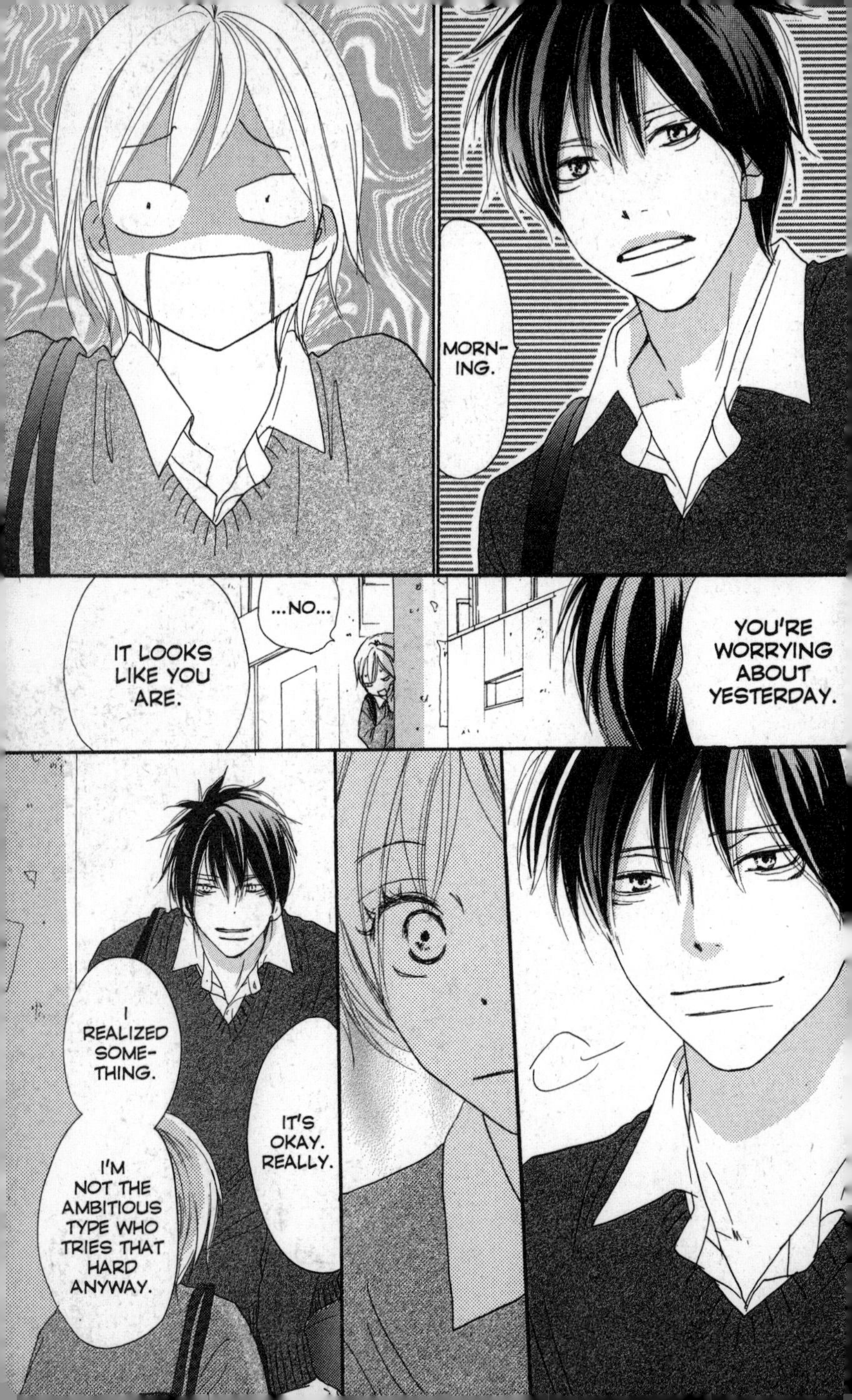
MORN-
ING.
YOU'RE WORRYING ABOUT YESTERDAY.
...NO...
IT LOOKS LIKE YOU ARE.
IT'S OKAY. REALLY.
I REALIZED SOME-THING.
I'M NOT THE AMBITIOUS TYPE WHO TRIES THAT HARD ANYWAY.

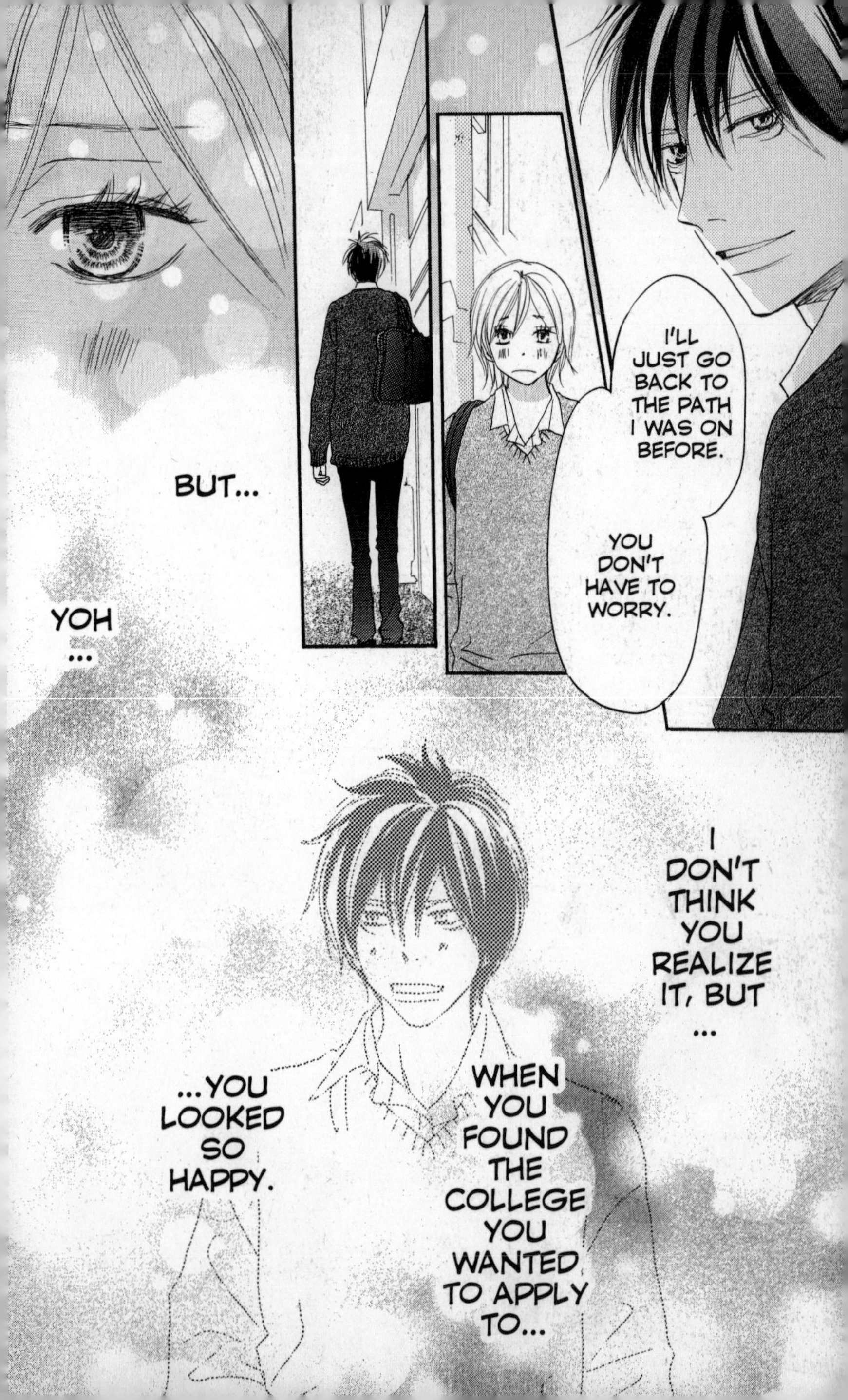
I'LL JUST GO BACK TO THE PATH I WAS ON BEFORE.
YOU DON'T HAVE TO WORRY.
BUT...
YOH ...
I DON'T THINK YOU REALIZE IT, BUT ...
WHEN YOU FOUND THE COLLEGE YOU WANTED TO APPLY TO...
...YOU LOOKED SO HAPPY.

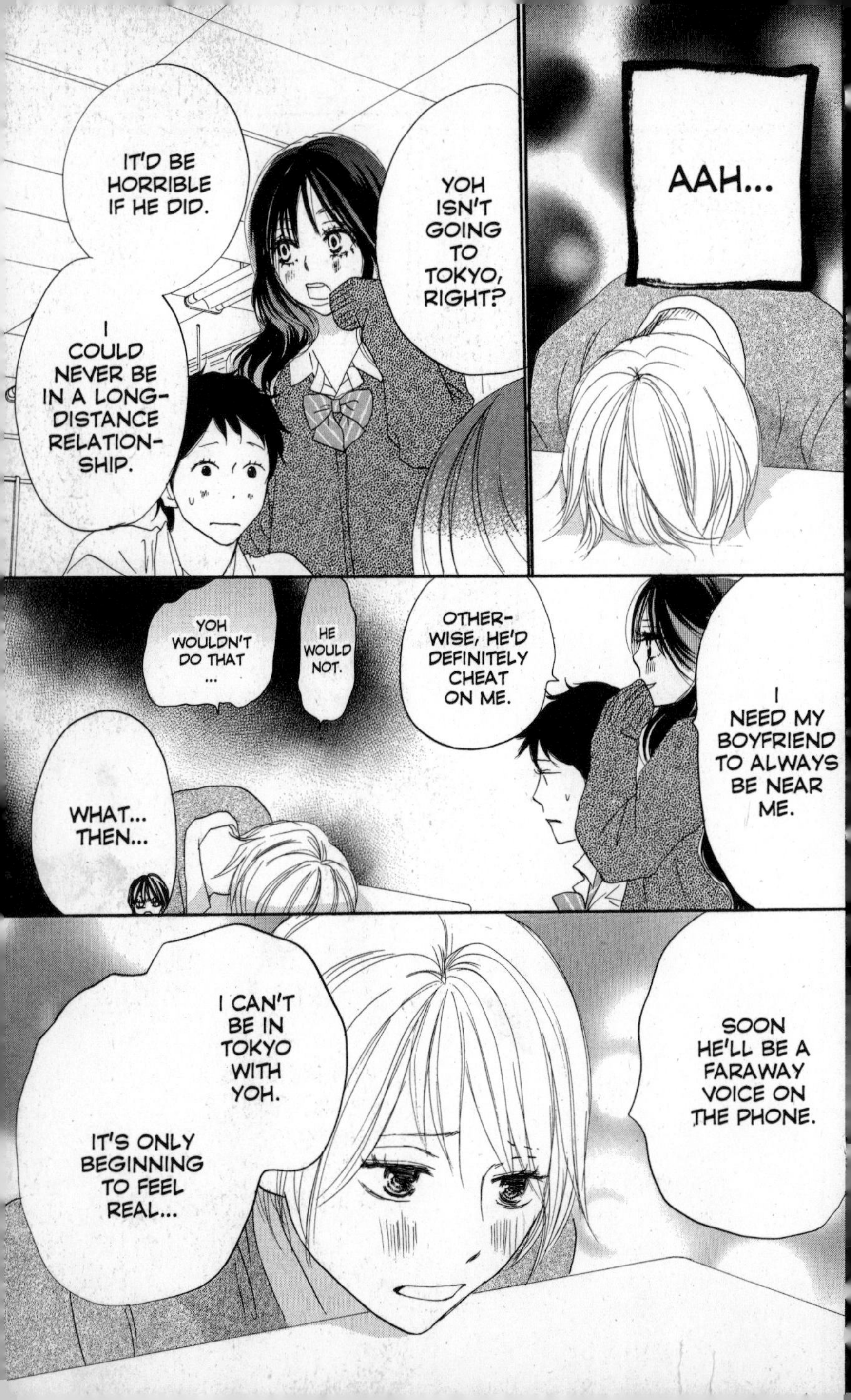
AAH...
YOH ISN'T GOING TO TOKYO, RIGHT?
IT'D BE HORRIBLE IF HE DID.
I COULD NEVER BE IN A LONG-DISTANCE RELATIONSHIP.
I NEED MY BOYFRIEND TO ALWAYS BE NEAR ME.
OTHERWISE, HE'D DEFINITELY CHEAT ON ME.
HE WOULD NOT.
YOH WOULDN'T DO THAT ...
WHAT... THEN...
SOON HE'LL BE A FARAWAY VOICE ON THE PHONE.
I CAN'T BE IN TOKYO WITH YOH.
IT'S ONLY BEGINNING TO FEEL REAL...

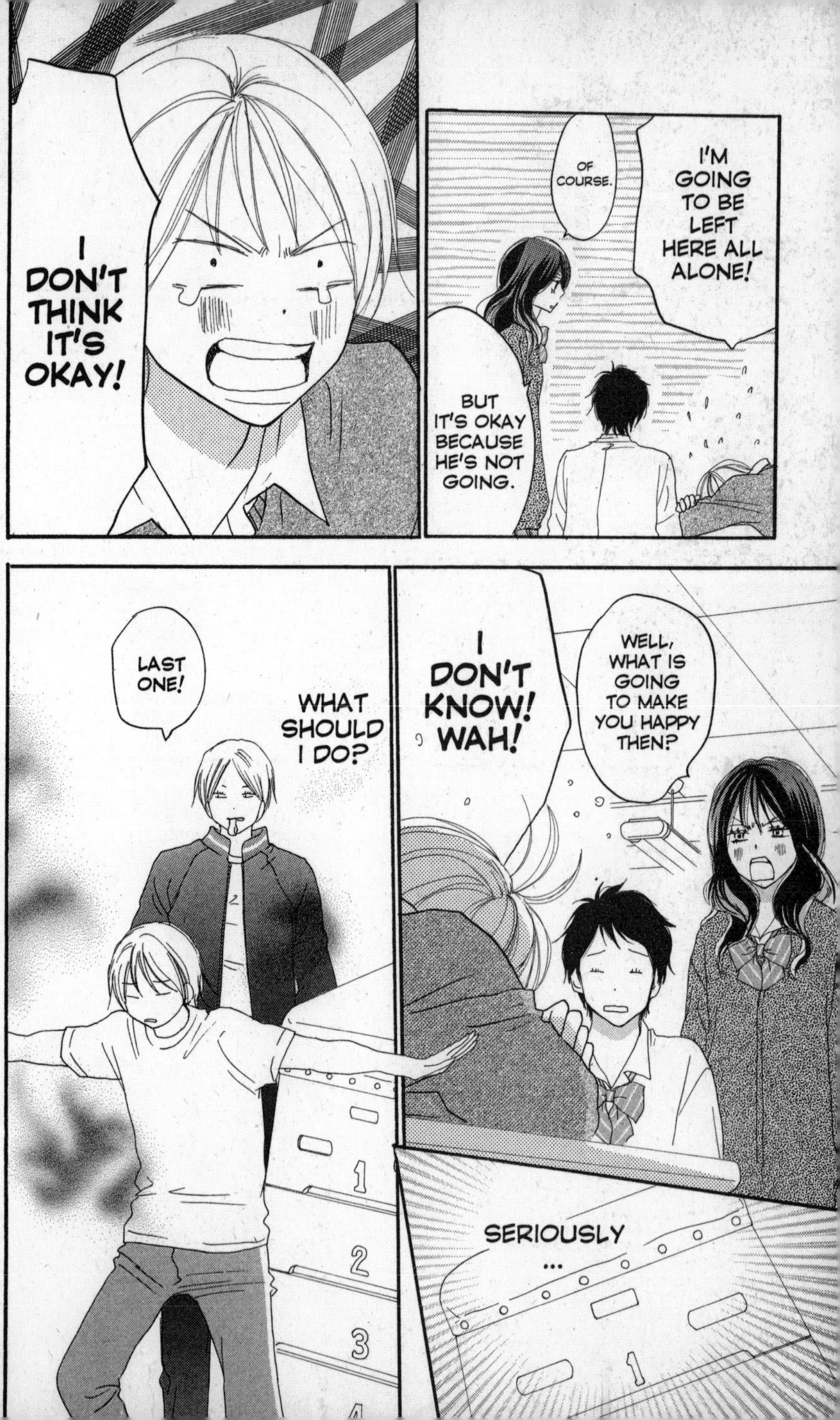
I'M GOING TO BE LEFT HERE ALL ALONE!
OF COURSE.
BUT IT'S OKAY BECAUSE HE'S NOT GOING.
I DON'T THINK IT'S OKAY!
WELL, WHAT IS GOING TO MAKE YOU HAPPY THEN?
I DON'T KNOW! WAH!
SERIOUSLY ...
WHAT SHOULD I DO?
LAST ONE!

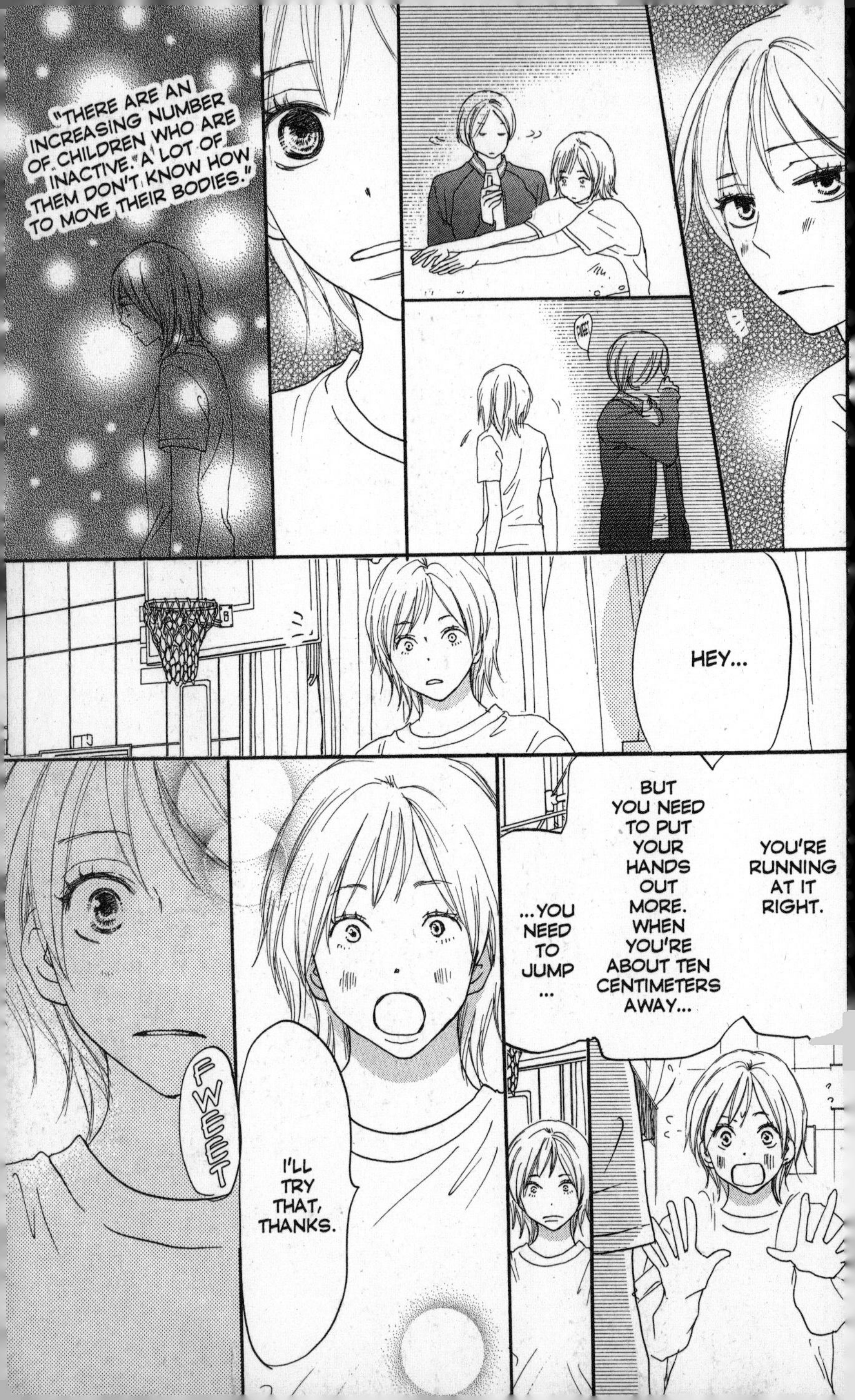
"THERE ARE AN INCREASING NUMBER OF CHILDREN WHO ARE INACTIVE." "A LOT OF THEM DON'T KNOW HOW TO MOVE THEIR BODIES."
HEY...
YOU'RE RUNNING AT IT RIGHT.
BUT YOU NEED TO PUT YOUR HANDS OUT MORE. WHEN YOU'RE ABOUT TEN CENTIMETERS AWAY...
...YOU NEED TO JUMP...
I'LL TRY THAT, THANKS.
FWEET

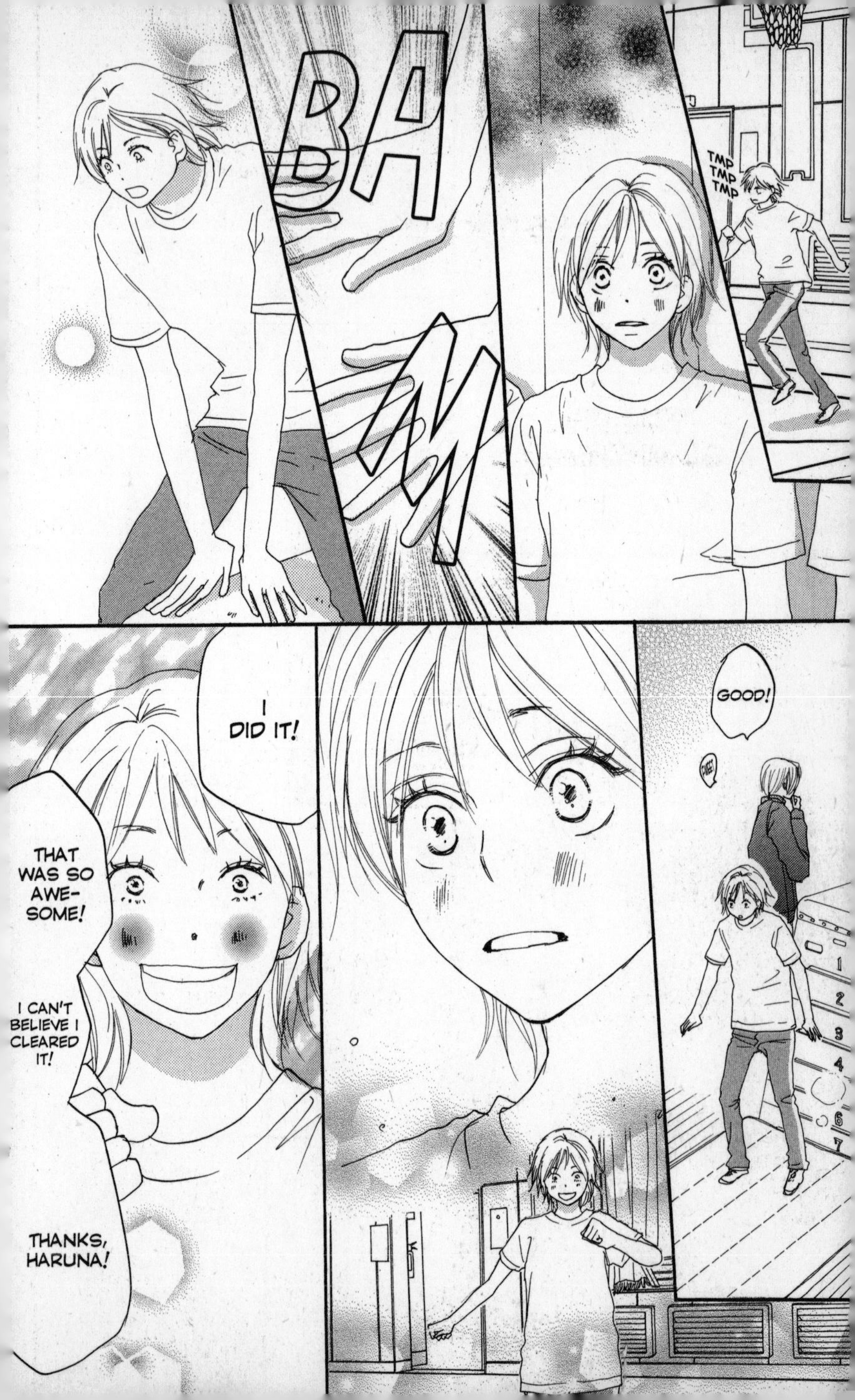
TMP TMP TMP
BAM
GOOD!
I DID IT!
THAT WAS SO AWE-SOME!
I CAN'T BELIEVE I CLEARED IT!
THANKS, HARUNA!

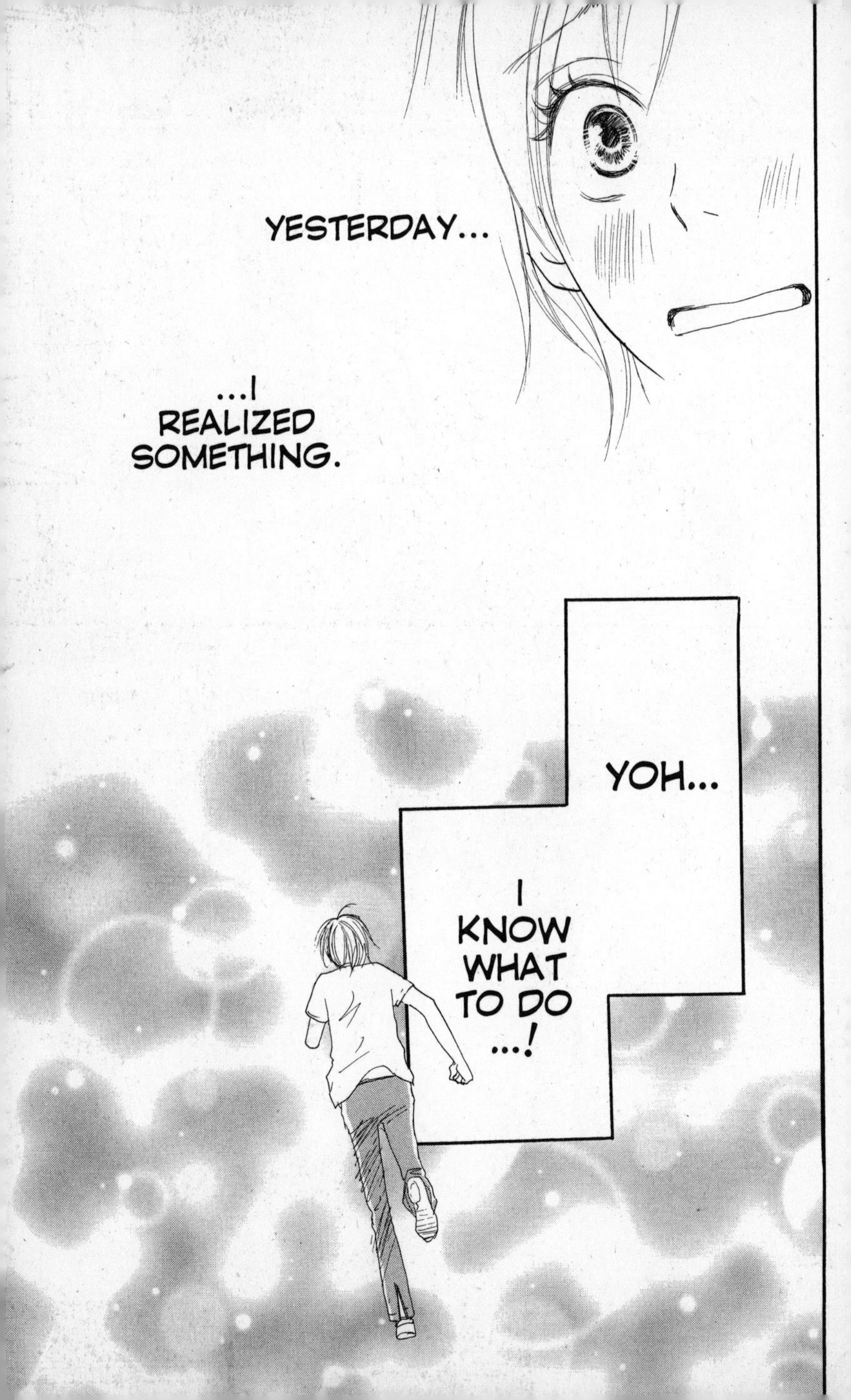
YESTERDAY...
...I REALIZED SOMETHING.
YOH...
I KNOW WHAT TO DO ...!

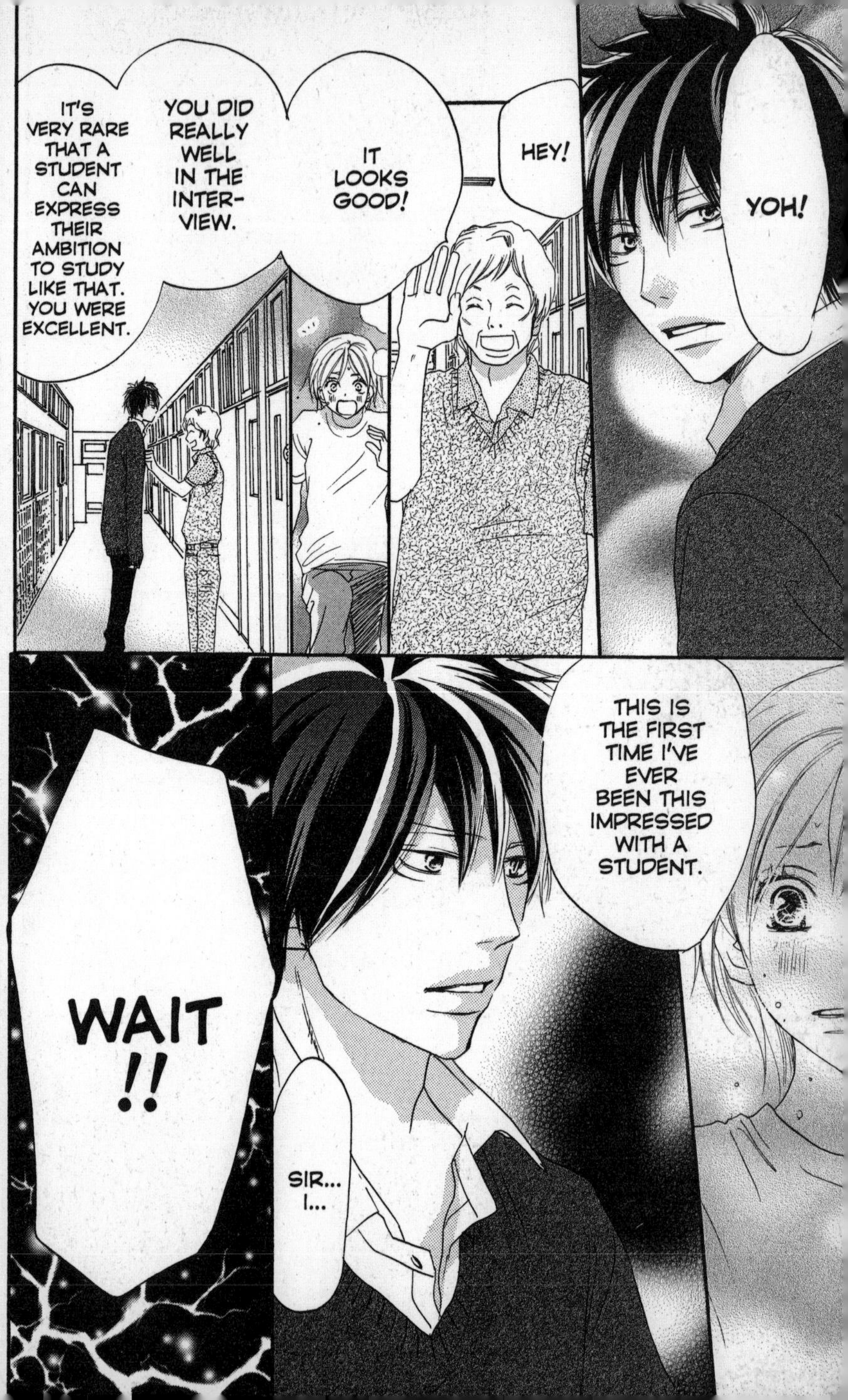
YOH!
HEY!
IT LOOKS GOOD!
YOU DID REALLY WELL IN THE INTER-VIEW.
IT'S VERY RARE THAT A STUDENT CAN EXPRESS THEIR AMBITION TO STUDY LIKE THAT. YOU WERE EXCELLENT.
THIS IS THE FIRST TIME I'VE EVER BEEN THIS IMPRESSED WITH A STUDENT.
SIR... I...
WAIT !!

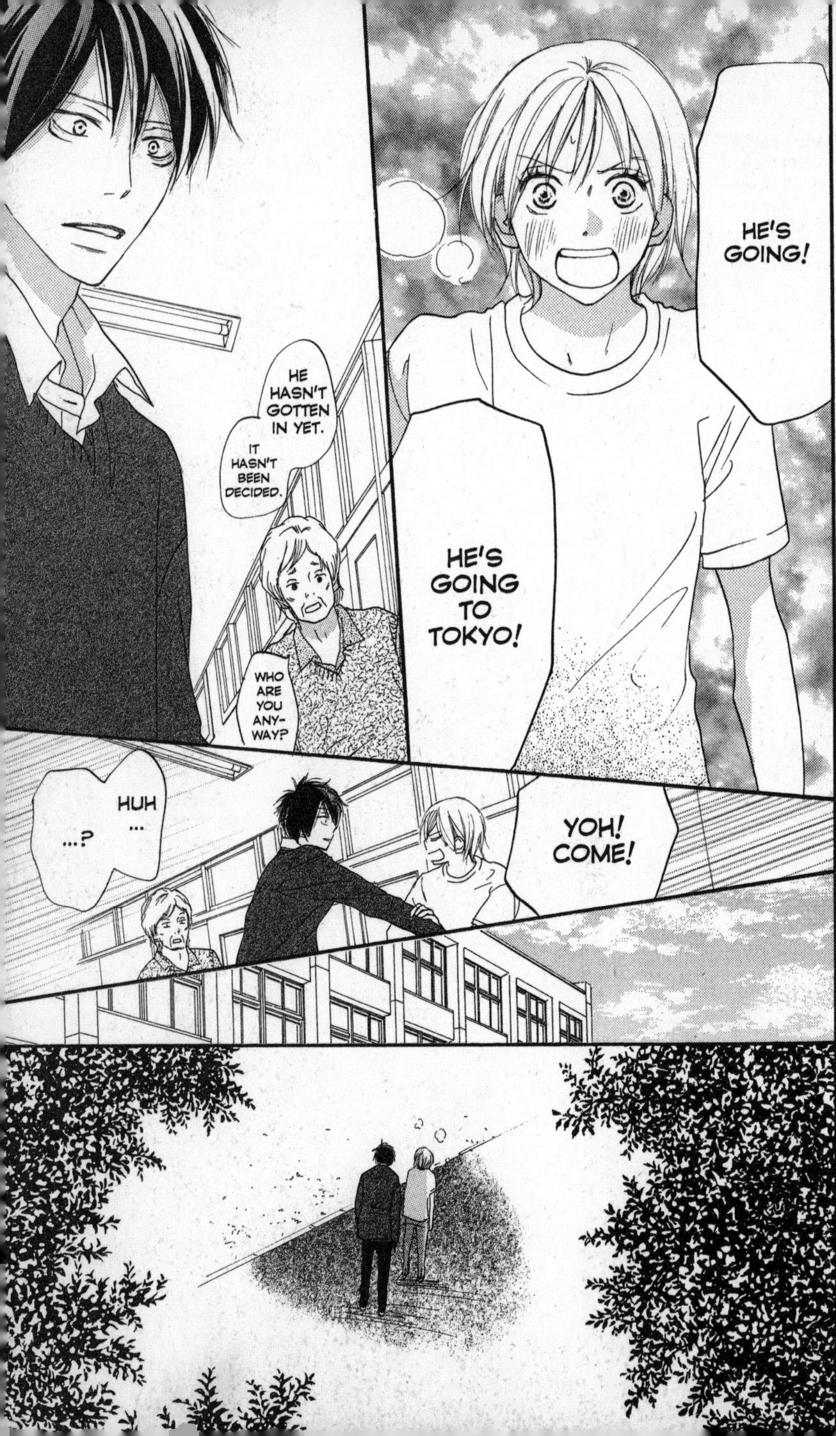
HE'S GOING!
HE'S GOING TO TOKYO!
HE HASN'T GOTTEN IN YET.
IT HASN'T BEEN DECIDED.
WHO ARE YOU ANY-WAY?
YOH! COME!
HUH ... ...?

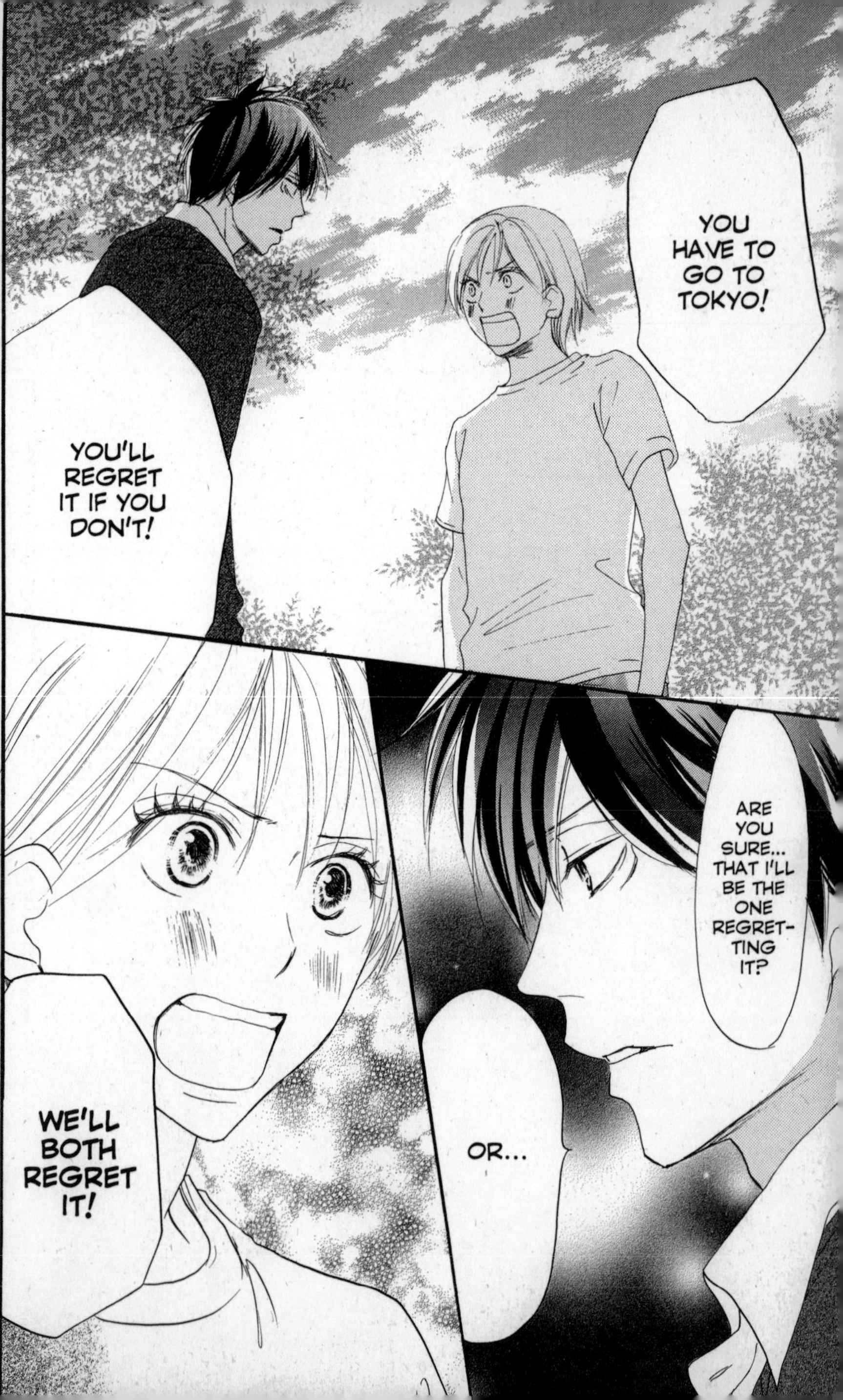
YOU HAVE TO GO TO TOKYO!
YOU'LL REGRET IT IF YOU DON'T!
ARE YOU SURE... THAT I'LL BE THE ONE REGRET-TING IT?
OR...
WE'LL BOTH REGRET IT!

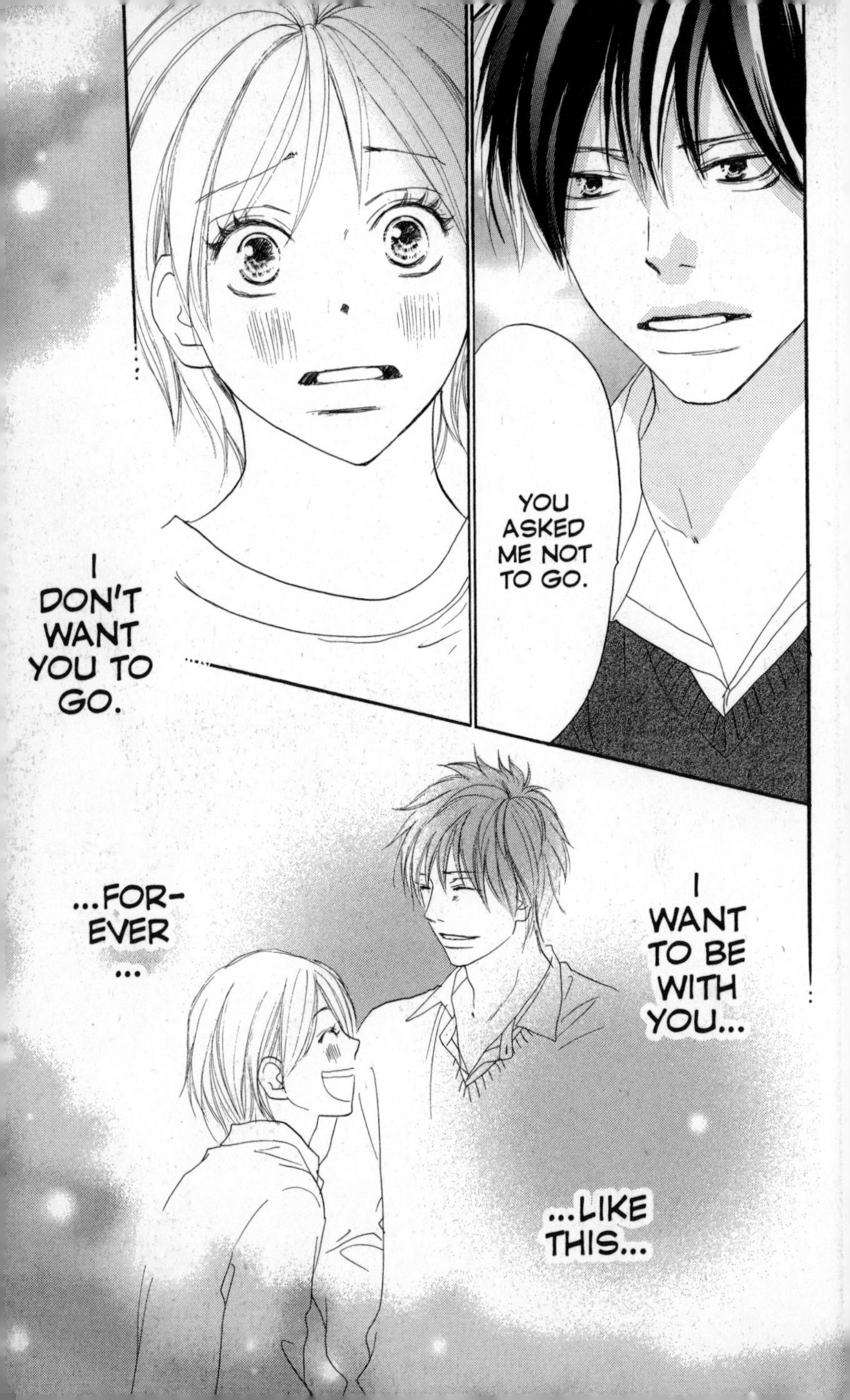
YOU ASKED ME NOT TO GO.
I DON'T WANT YOU TO GO.
I WANT TO BE WITH YOU...
...FOR-EVER...
...LIKE THIS...

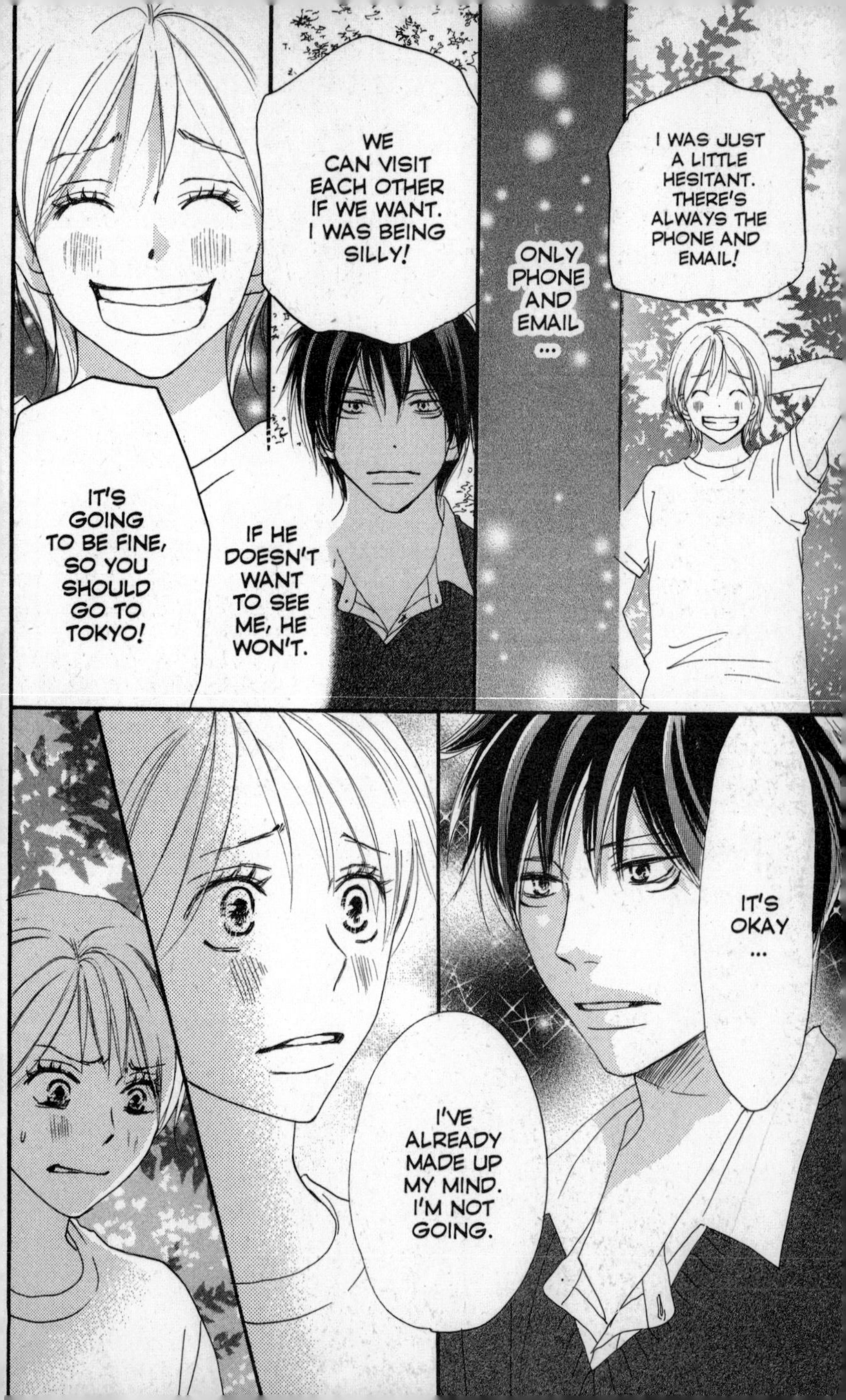
I WAS JUST A LITTLE HESITANT. THERE'S ALWAYS THE PHONE AND EMAIL!
ONLY PHONE AND EMAIL...
WE CAN VISIT EACH OTHER IF WE WANT. I WAS BEING SILLY!
IT'S GOING TO BE FINE, SO YOU SHOULD GO TO TOKYO!
IF HE DOESN'T WANT TO SEE ME, HE WON'T.
IT'S OKAY...
I'VE ALREADY MADE UP MY MIND. I'M NOT GOING.

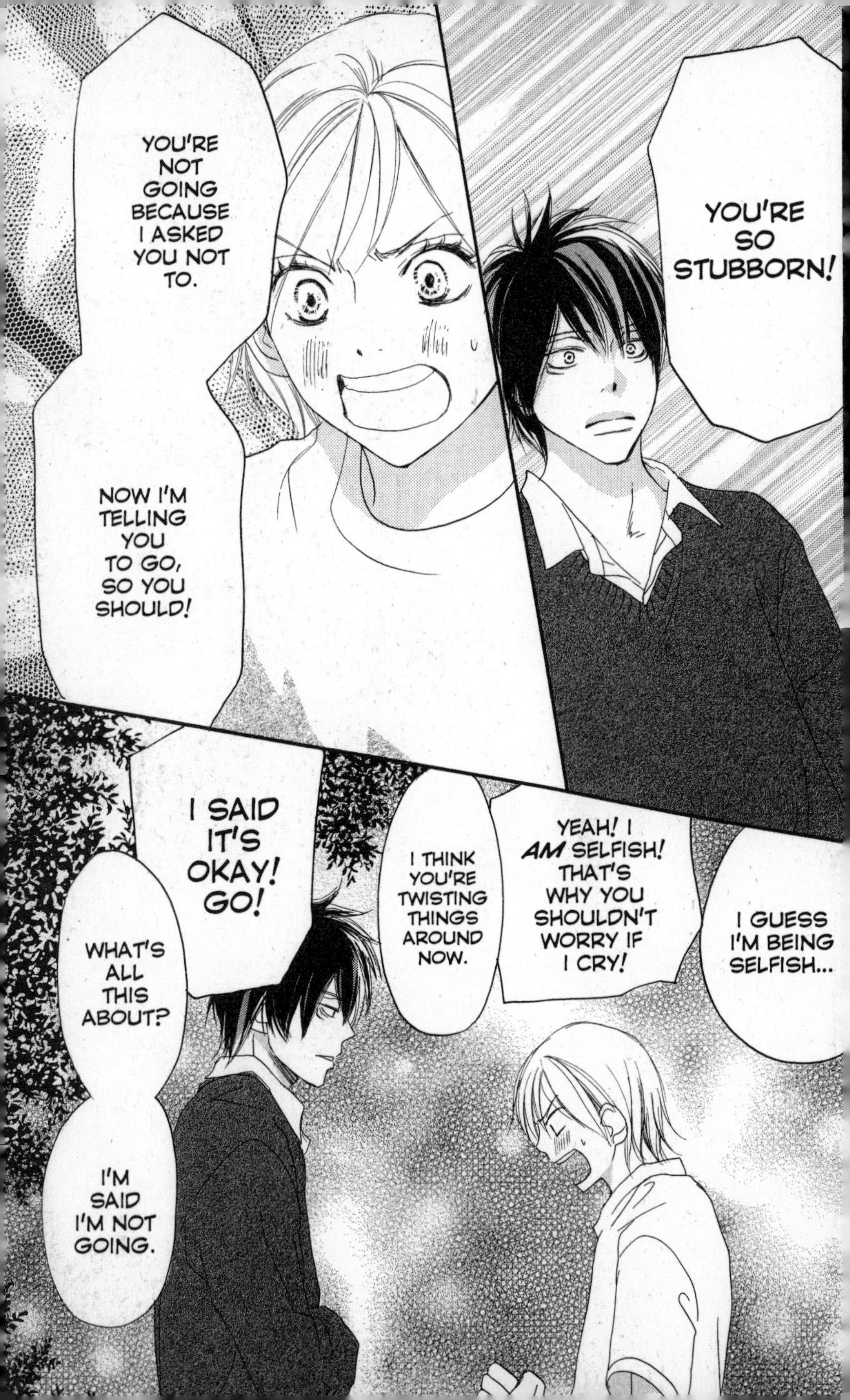
YOU'RE SO STUBBORN!
YOU'RE NOT GOING BECAUSE I ASKED YOU NOT TO.
NOW I'M TELLING YOU TO GO, SO YOU SHOULD!
I GUESS I'M BEING SELFISH...
YEAH! I *AM* SELFISH! THAT'S WHY YOU SHOULDN'T WORRY IF I CRY!
I THINK YOU'RE TWISTING THINGS AROUND NOW.
I SAID IT'S OKAY! GO!
WHAT'S ALL THIS ABOUT?
I'M SAID I'M NOT GOING.

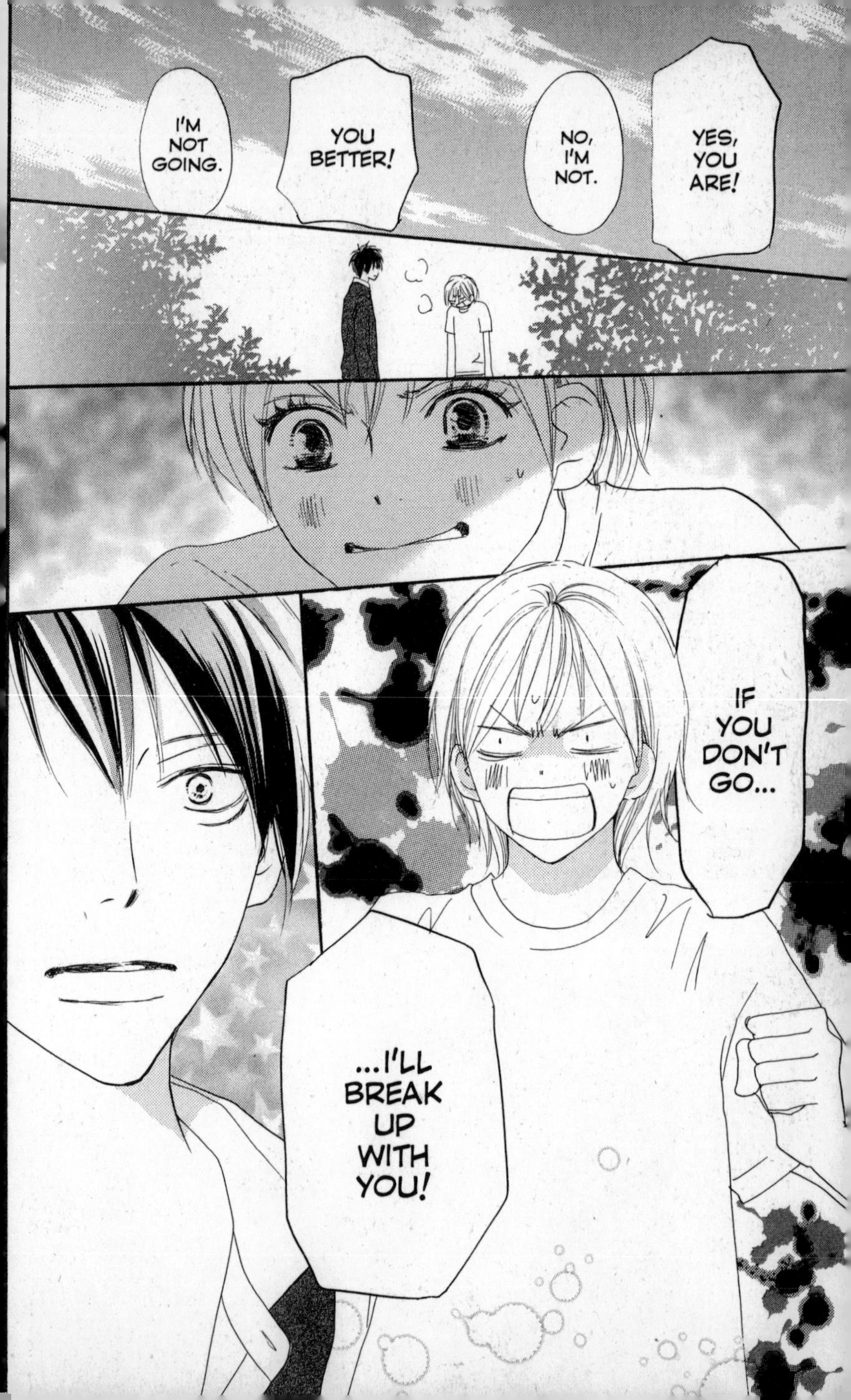
YES, YOU ARE!
NO, I'M NOT.
YOU BETTER!
I'M NOT GOING.
IF YOU DON'T GO...
...I'LL BREAK UP WITH YOU!

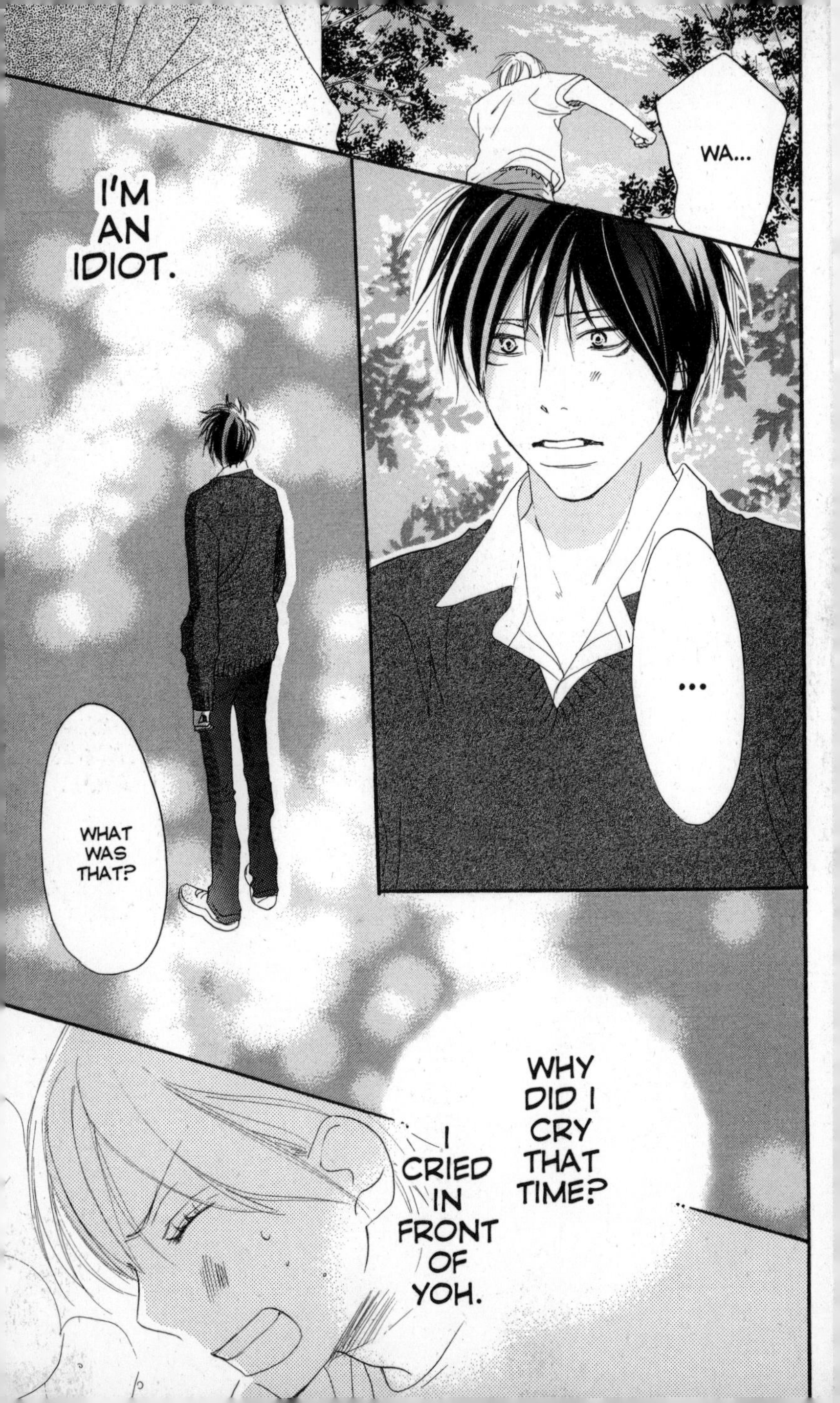
WA...
...
I'M AN IDIOT.
WHAT WAS THAT?
WHY DID I CRY THAT TIME?
I CRIED IN FRONT OF YOH.

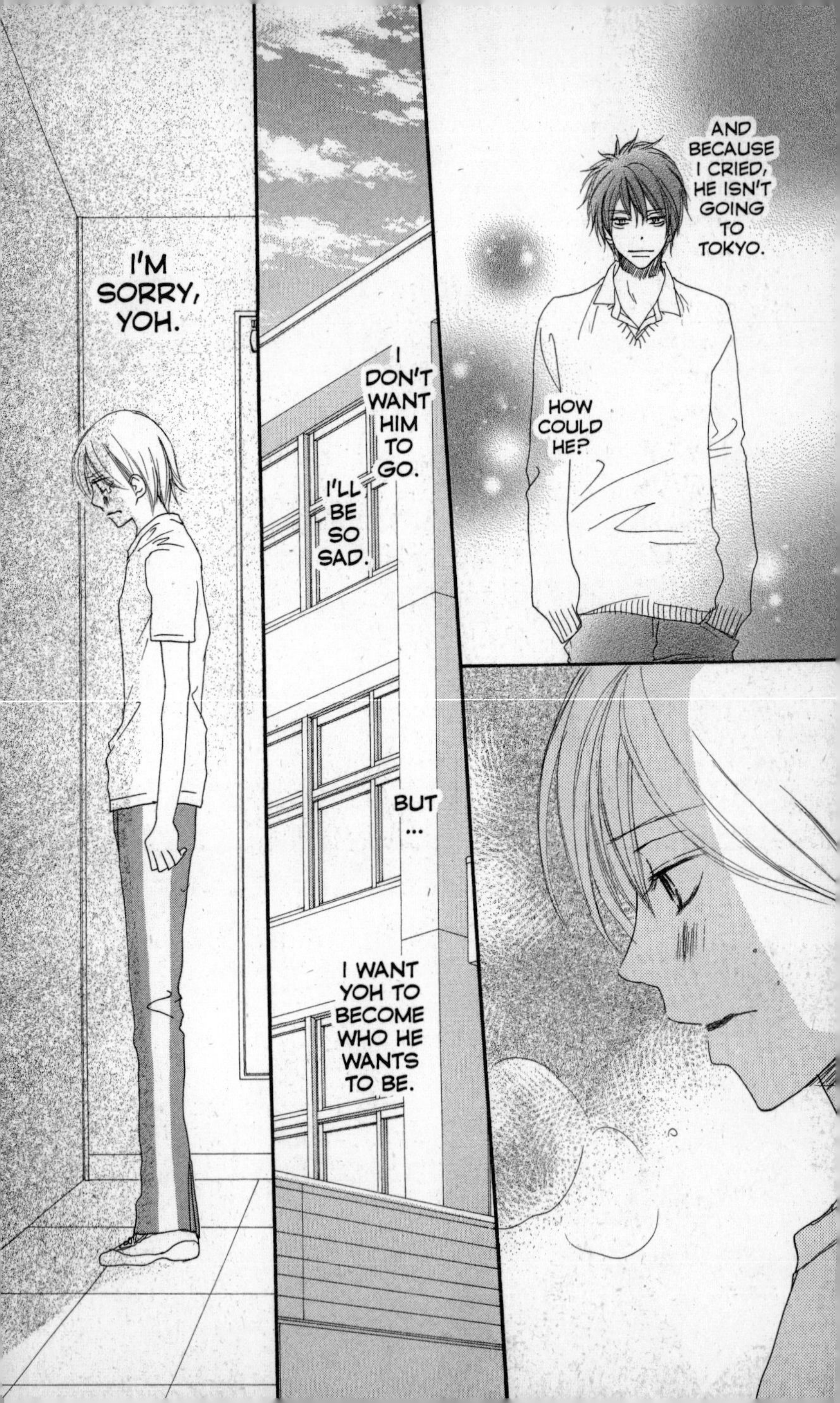
AND BECAUSE I CRIED, HE ISN'T GOING TO TOKYO.
HOW COULD HE?
I DON'T WANT HIM TO GO.
I'LL BE SO SAD.
BUT ...
I WANT YOH TO BECOME WHO HE WANTS TO BE.
I'M SORRY, YOH.

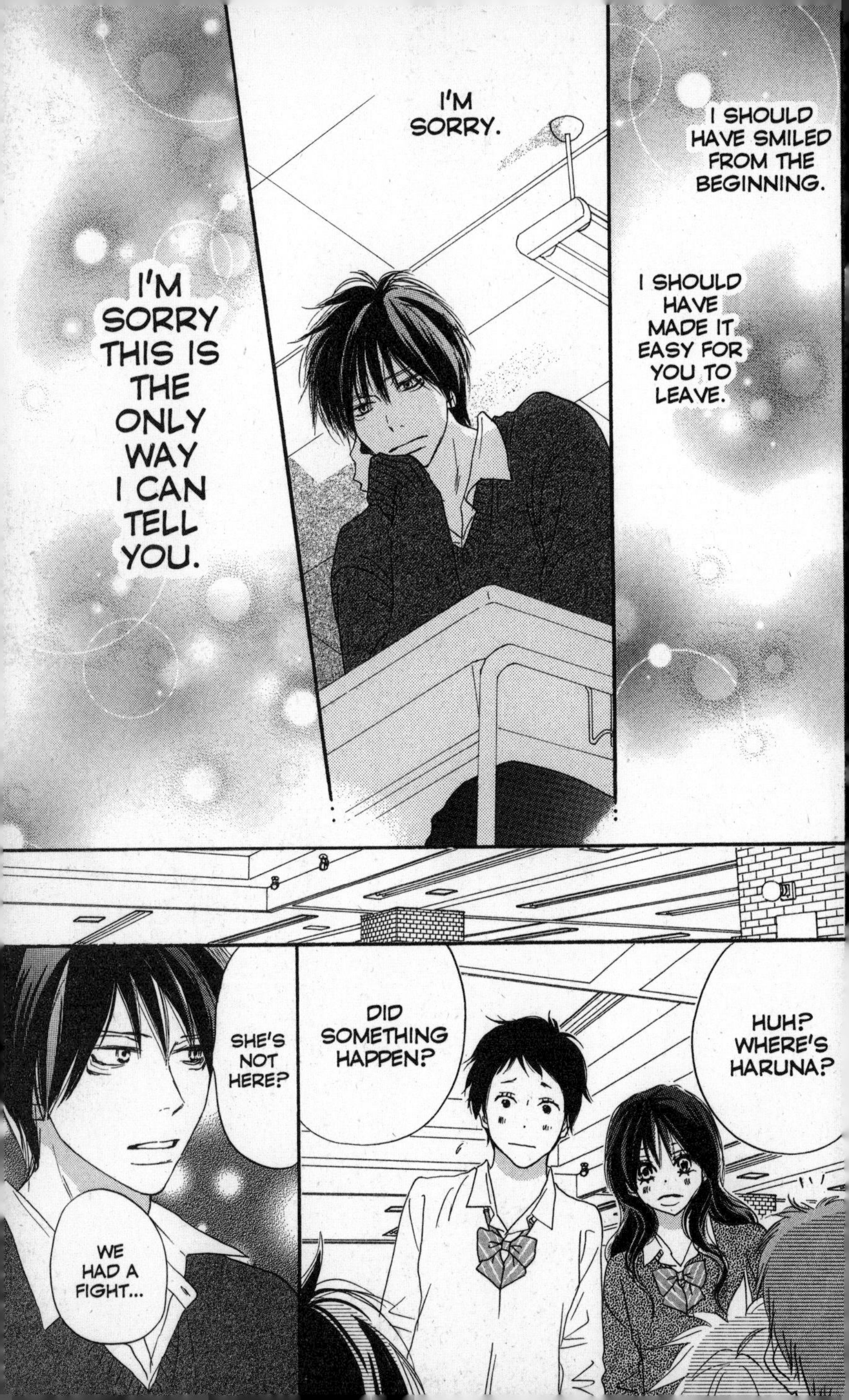
I SHOULD HAVE SMILED FROM THE BEGINNING.
I SHOULD HAVE MADE IT EASY FOR YOU TO LEAVE.
I'M SORRY.
I'M SORRY THIS IS THE ONLY WAY I CAN TELL YOU.
HUH? WHERE'S HARUNA?
DID SOMETHING HAPPEN?
SHE'S NOT HERE?
WE HAD A FIGHT...

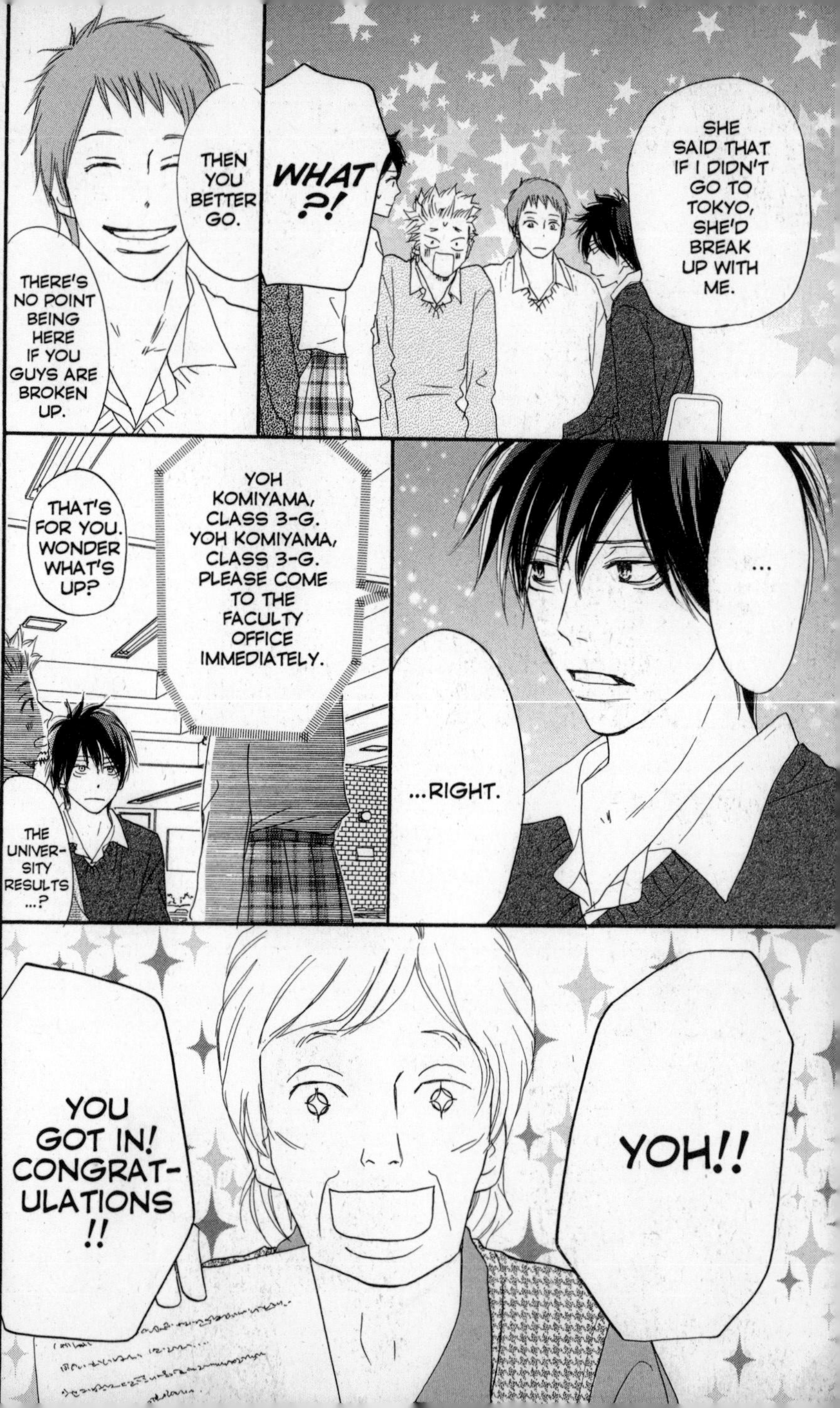
SHE SAID THAT IF I DIDN'T GO TO TOKYO, SHE'D BREAK UP WITH ME.
WHAT ?!
THEN YOU BETTER GO.
THERE'S NO POINT BEING HERE IF YOU GUYS ARE BROKEN UP.
...
...RIGHT.
YOH KOMIYAMA, CLASS 3-G. YOH KOMIYAMA, CLASS 3-G. PLEASE COME TO THE FACULTY OFFICE IMMEDIATELY.
THAT'S FOR YOU. WONDER WHAT'S UP?
THE UNIVER-SITY RESULTS ...?
YOH!!
YOU GOT IN! CONGRAT-ULATIONS !!

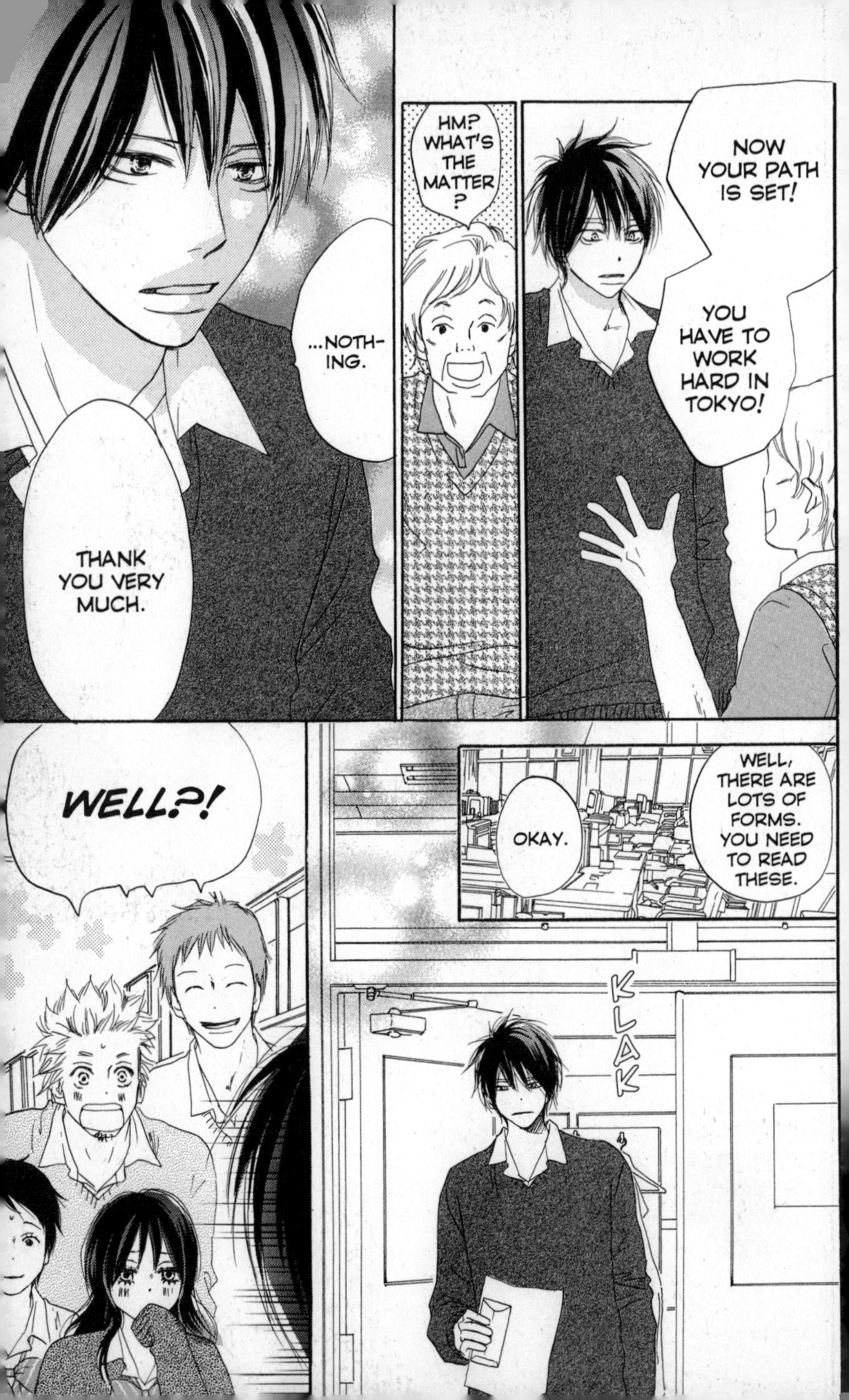
NOW YOUR PATH IS SET!
YOU HAVE TO WORK HARD IN TOKYO!
HM? WHAT'S THE MATTER?
...NOTH-ING.
THANK YOU VERY MUCH.
WELL, THERE ARE LOTS OF FORMS. YOU NEED TO READ THESE.
OKAY.
KLAK
WELL?!

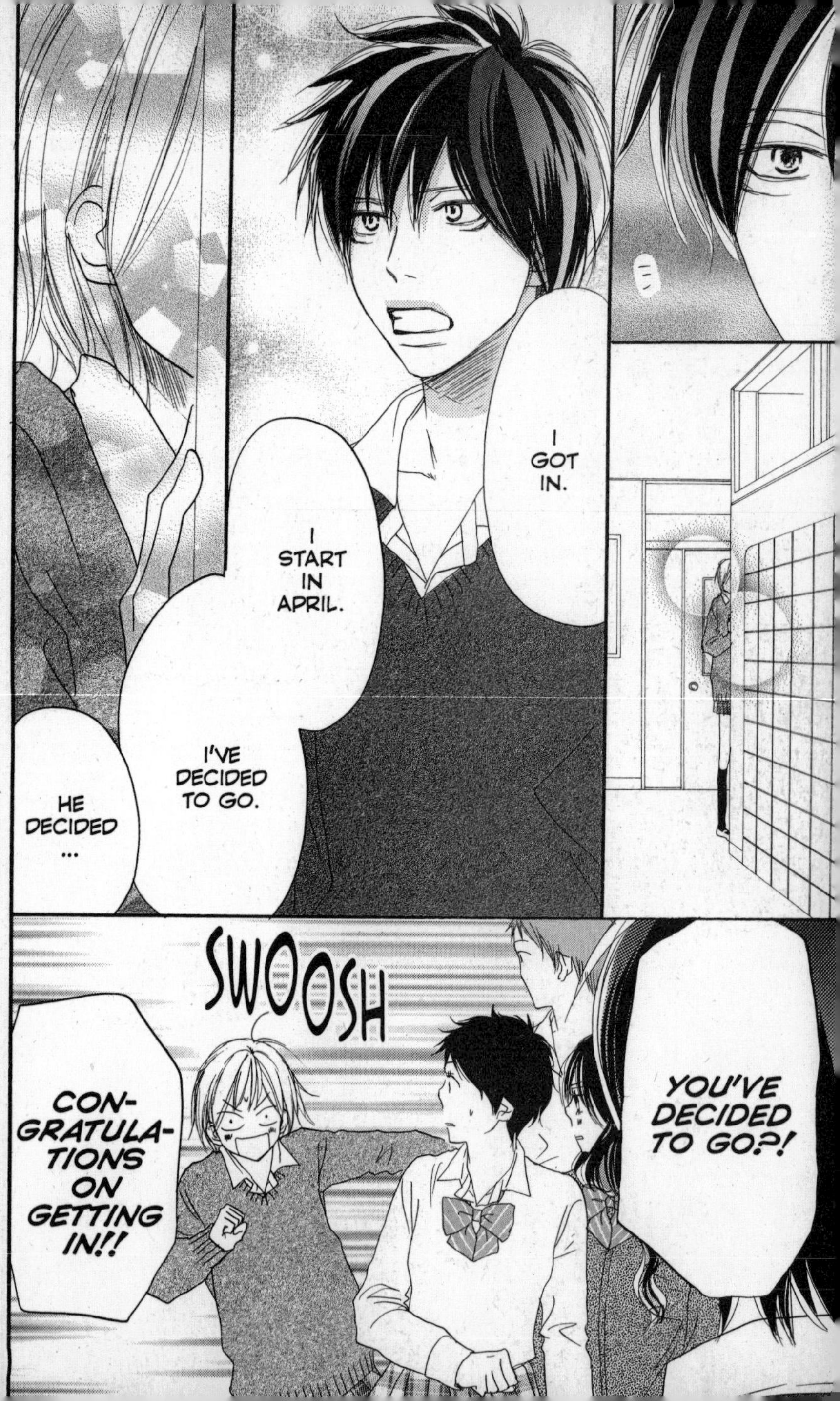
...
I GOT IN.
I START IN APRIL.
I'VE DECIDED TO GO.
HE DECIDED ...
YOU'VE DECIDED TO GO?!
SWOOSH
CON-GRATULA-TIONS ON GETTING IN!!

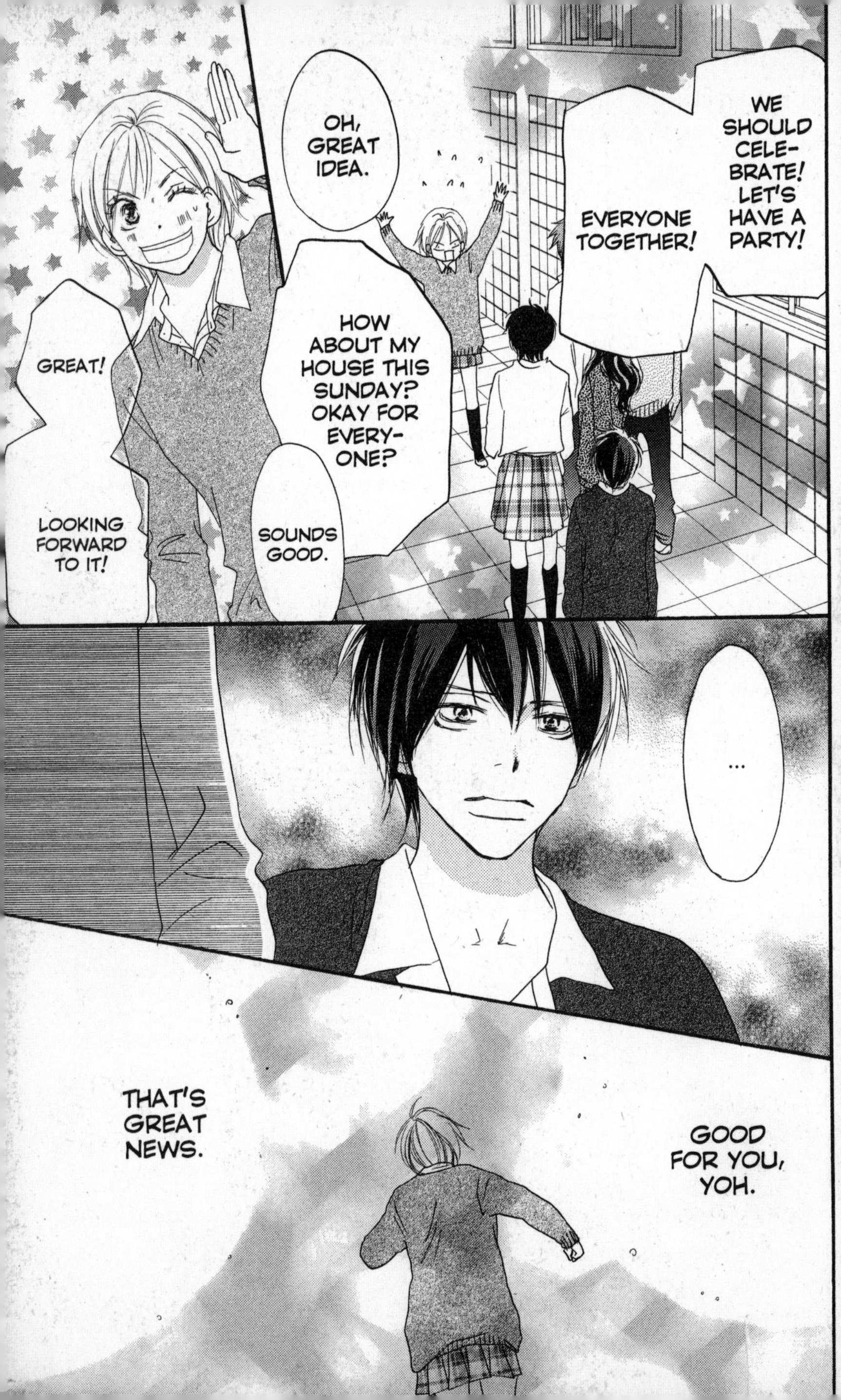
WE SHOULD CELEBRATE! LET'S HAVE A PARTY!
EVERYONE TOGETHER!
OH, GREAT IDEA.
HOW ABOUT MY HOUSE THIS SUNDAY? OKAY FOR EVERYONE?
SOUNDS GOOD.
GREAT!
LOOKING FORWARD TO IT!
...
GOOD FOR YOU, YOH.
THAT'S GREAT NEWS.

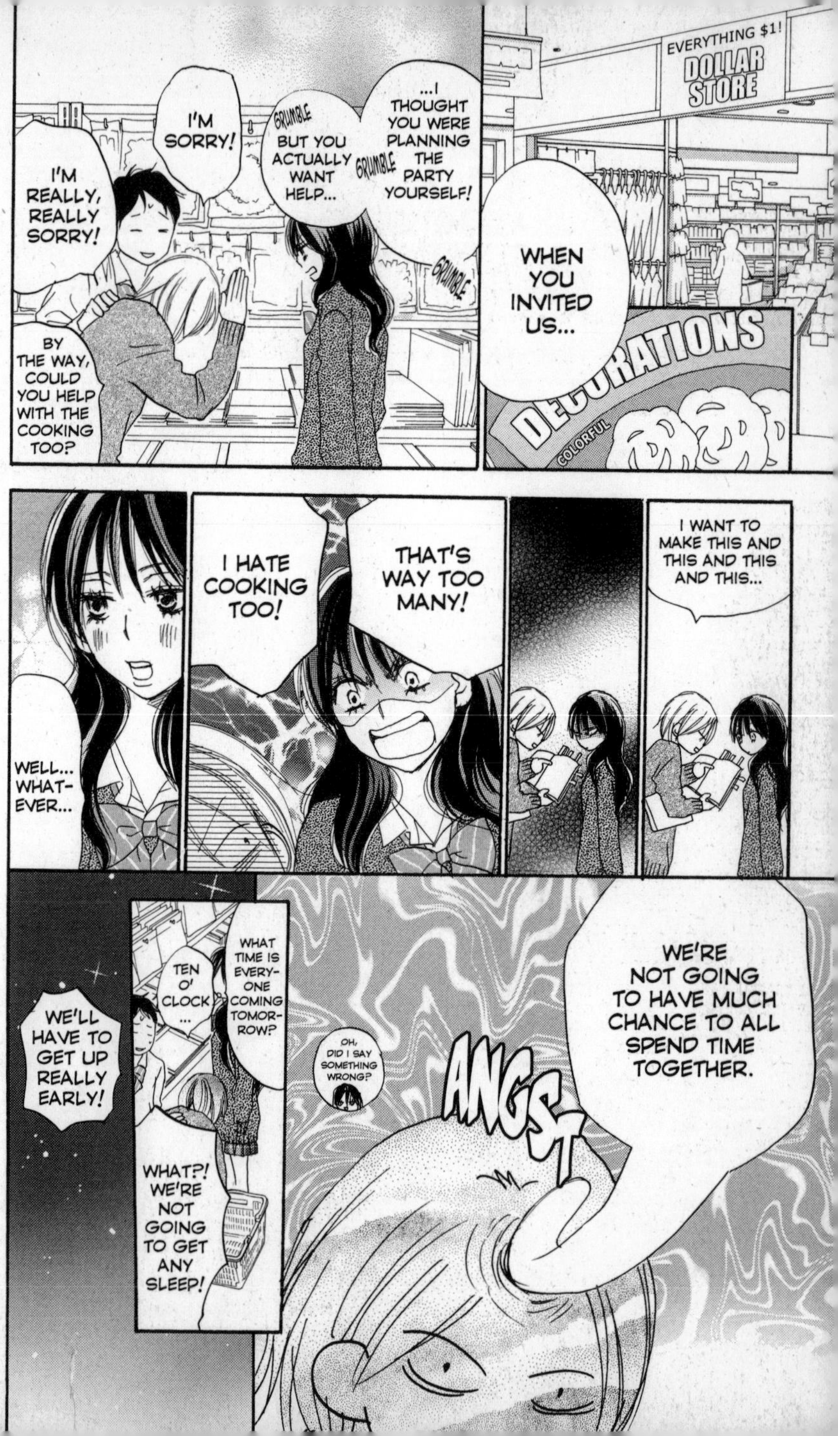
EVERYTHING $1!
DOLLAR STORE
WHEN YOU INVITED US...
DECORATIONS
COLORFUL
...I THOUGHT YOU WERE PLANNING THE PARTY YOURSELF!
GRUMBLE
BUT YOU ACTUALLY WANT HELP...
GRUMBLE
GRUMBLE
I'M SORRY!
I'M REALLY, REALLY SORRY!
BY THE WAY, COULD YOU HELP WITH THE COOKING TOO?
I WANT TO MAKE THIS AND THIS AND THIS AND THIS...
THAT'S WAY TOO MANY!
I HATE COOKING TOO!
WELL... WHATEVER...
WE'RE NOT GOING TO HAVE MUCH CHANCE TO ALL SPEND TIME TOGETHER.
ANGST
OH, DID I SAY SOMETHING WRONG?
WHAT TIME IS EVERYONE COMING TOMORROW?
TEN O' CLOCK ...
WHAT?! WE'RE NOT GOING TO GET ANY SLEEP!
WE'LL HAVE TO GET UP REALLY EARLY!

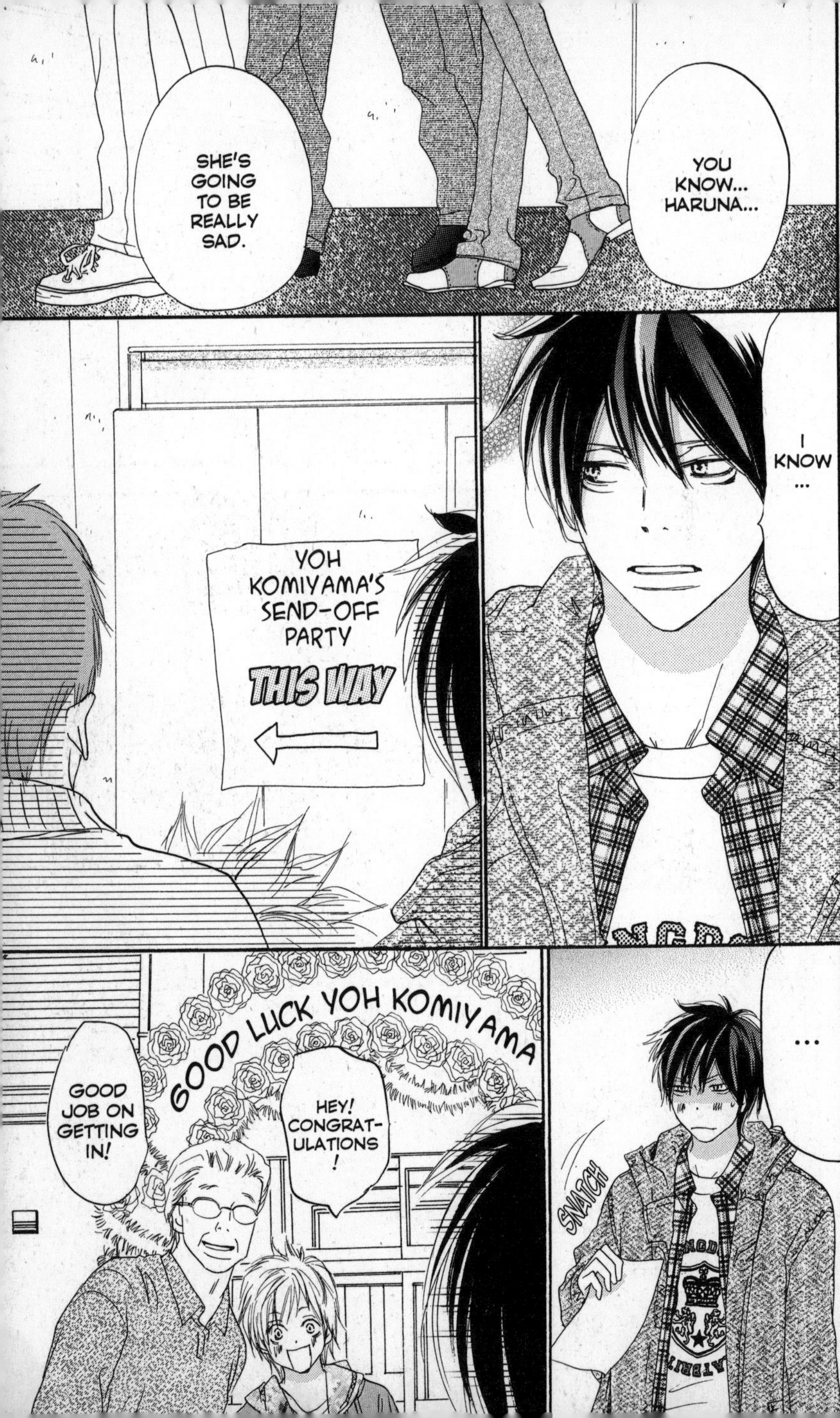
YOU KNOW... HARUNA...
SHE'S GOING TO BE REALLY SAD.
I KNOW ...
YOH KOMIYAMA'S SEND-OFF PARTY
THIS WAY
...
SNATCH
GOOD LUCK YOH KOMIYAMA
HEY! CONGRATULATIONS!
GOOD JOB ON GETTING IN!

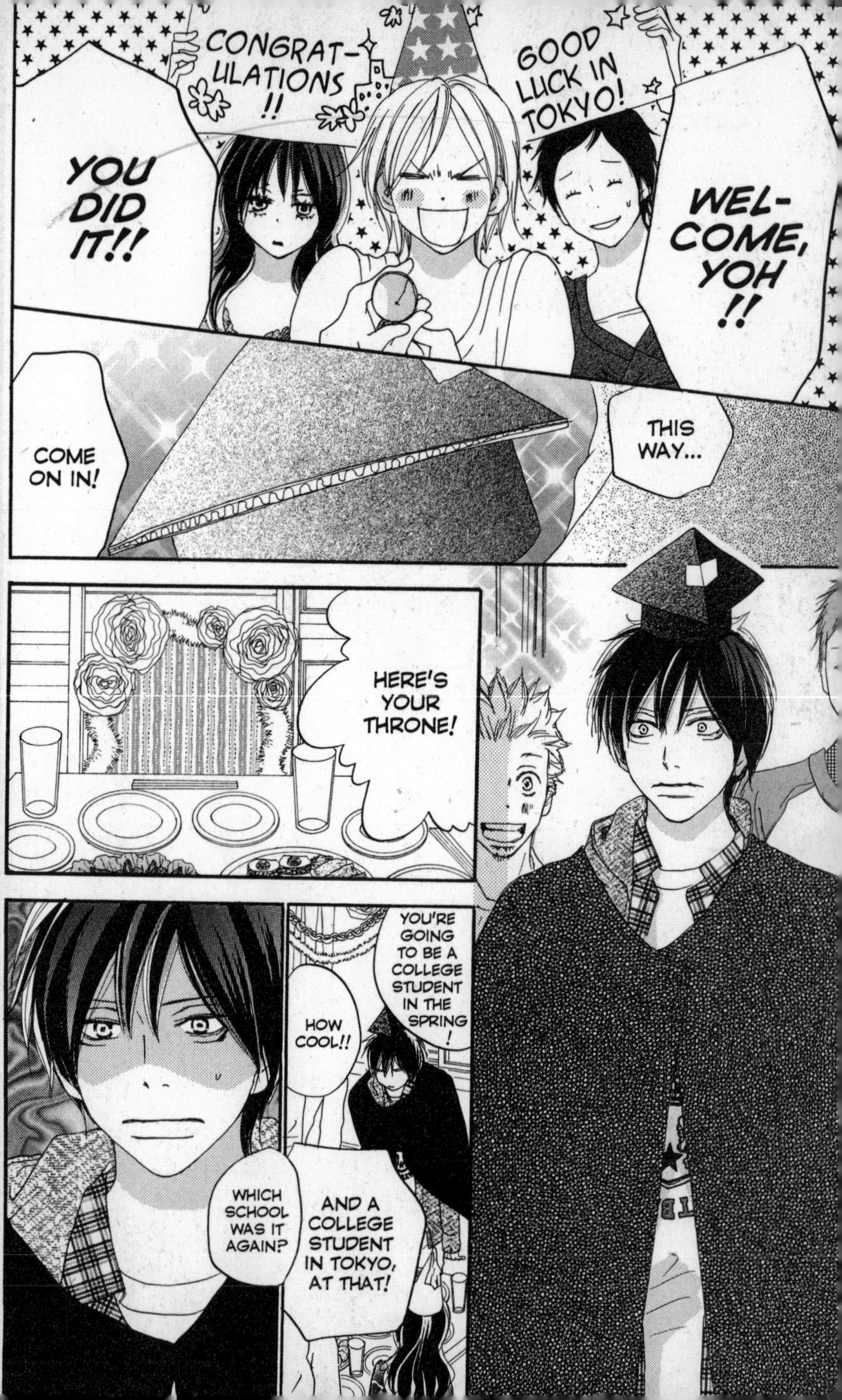
WELCOME, YOH!!
GOOD LUCK IN TOKYO!
CONGRATULATIONS!!
YOU DID IT!!
THIS WAY...
COME ON IN!
HERE'S YOUR THRONE!
YOU'RE GOING TO BE A COLLEGE STUDENT IN THE SPRING!
HOW COOL!!
AND A COLLEGE STUDENT IN TOKYO, AT THAT!
WHICH SCHOOL WAS IT AGAIN?

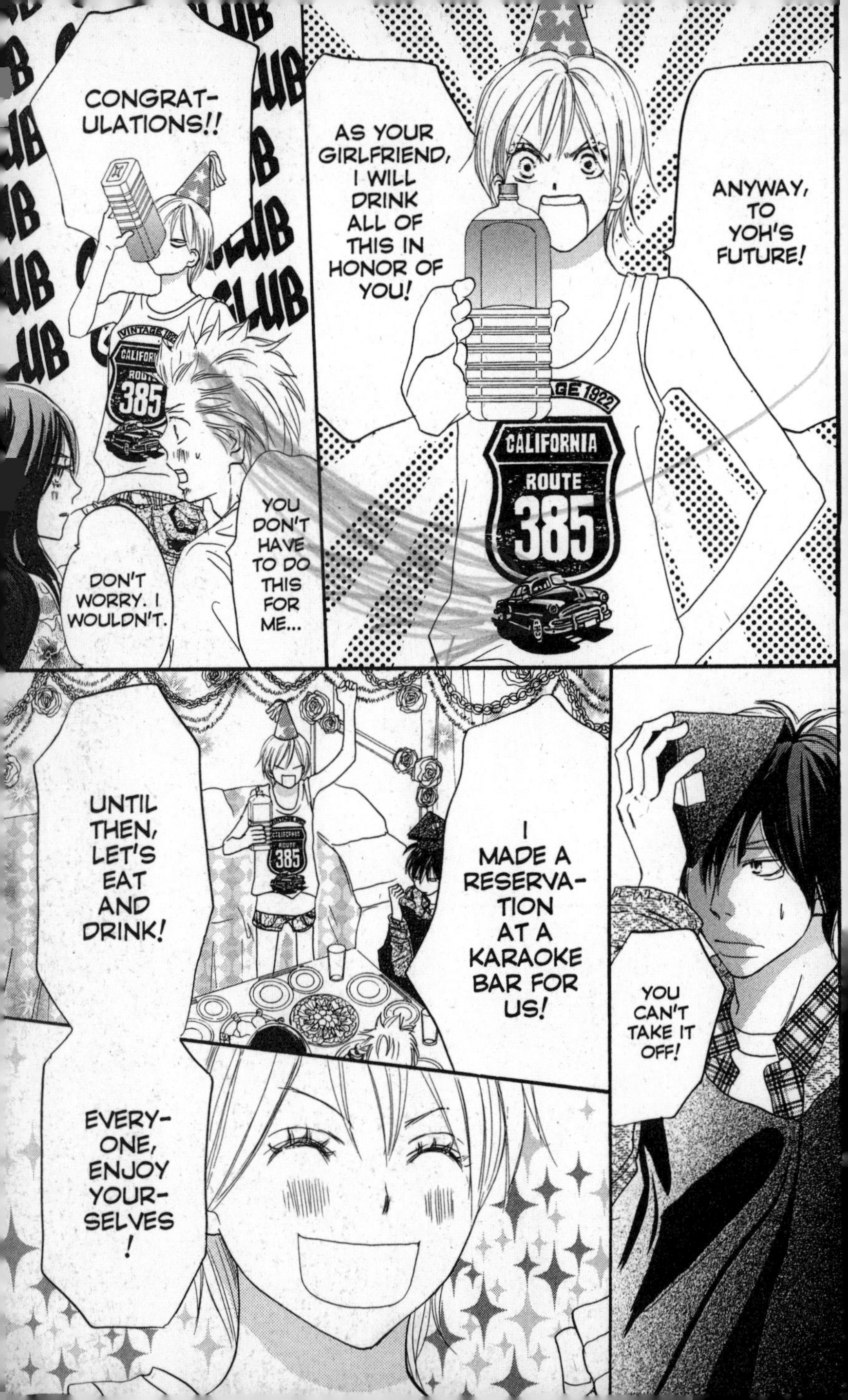
ANYWAY, TO YOH'S FUTURE!
AS YOUR GIRLFRIEND, I WILL DRINK ALL OF THIS IN HONOR OF YOU!
CALIFORNIA ROUTE 385
CONGRAT-ULATIONS!!
YOU DON'T HAVE TO DO THIS FOR ME...
DON'T WORRY. I WOULDN'T.
YOU CAN'T TAKE IT OFF!
I MADE A RESERVA-TION AT A KARAOKE BAR FOR US!
UNTIL THEN, LET'S EAT AND DRINK!
EVERY-ONE, ENJOY YOUR-SELVES!

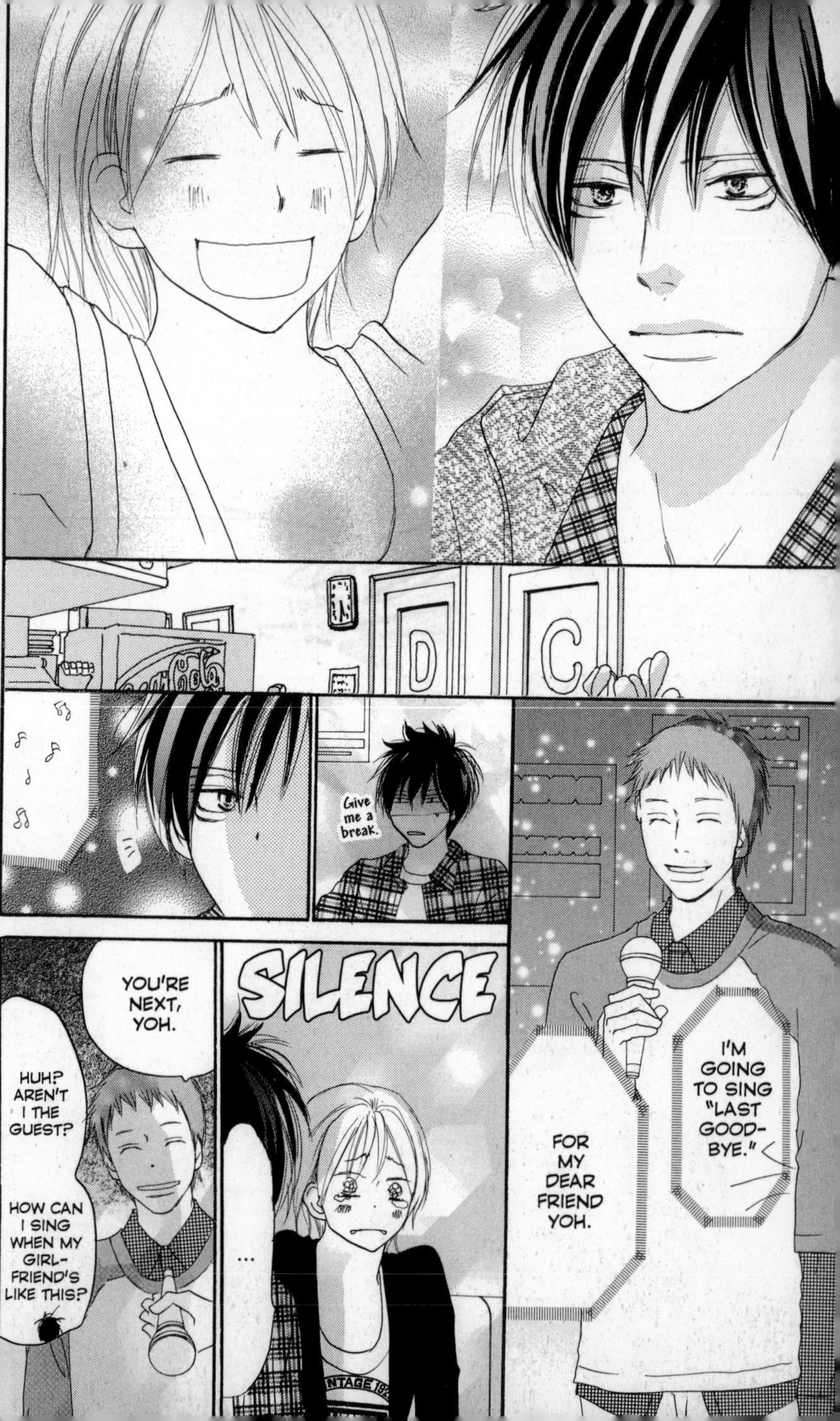
I'M GOING TO SING "LAST GOOD-BYE."
FOR MY DEAR FRIEND YOH.
Give me a break.
SILENCE
...
YOU'RE NEXT, YOH.
HUH? AREN'T I THE GUEST?
HOW CAN I SING WHEN MY GIRL-FRIEND'S LIKE THIS?

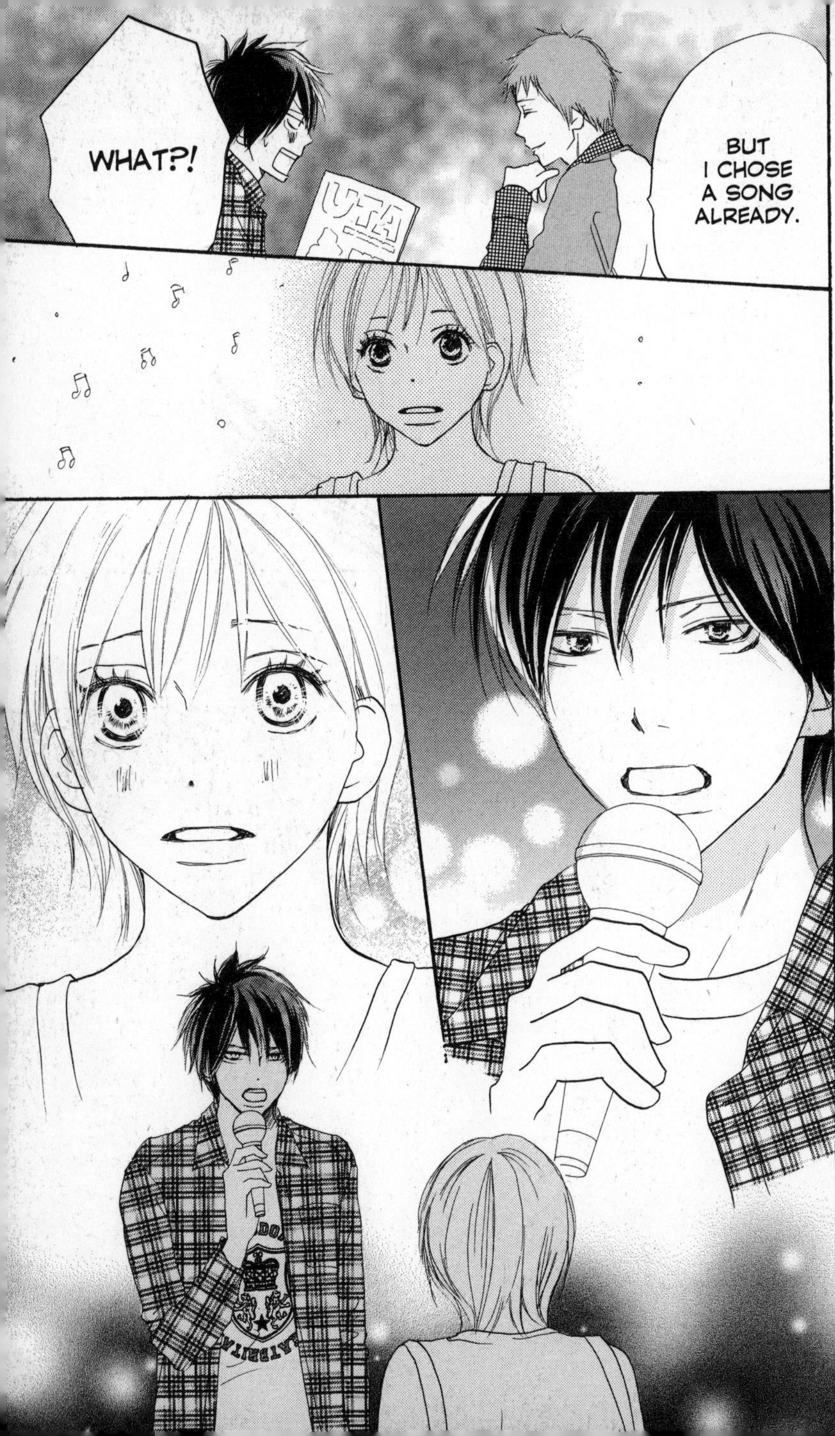
BUT I CHOSE A SONG ALREADY.
WHAT?!

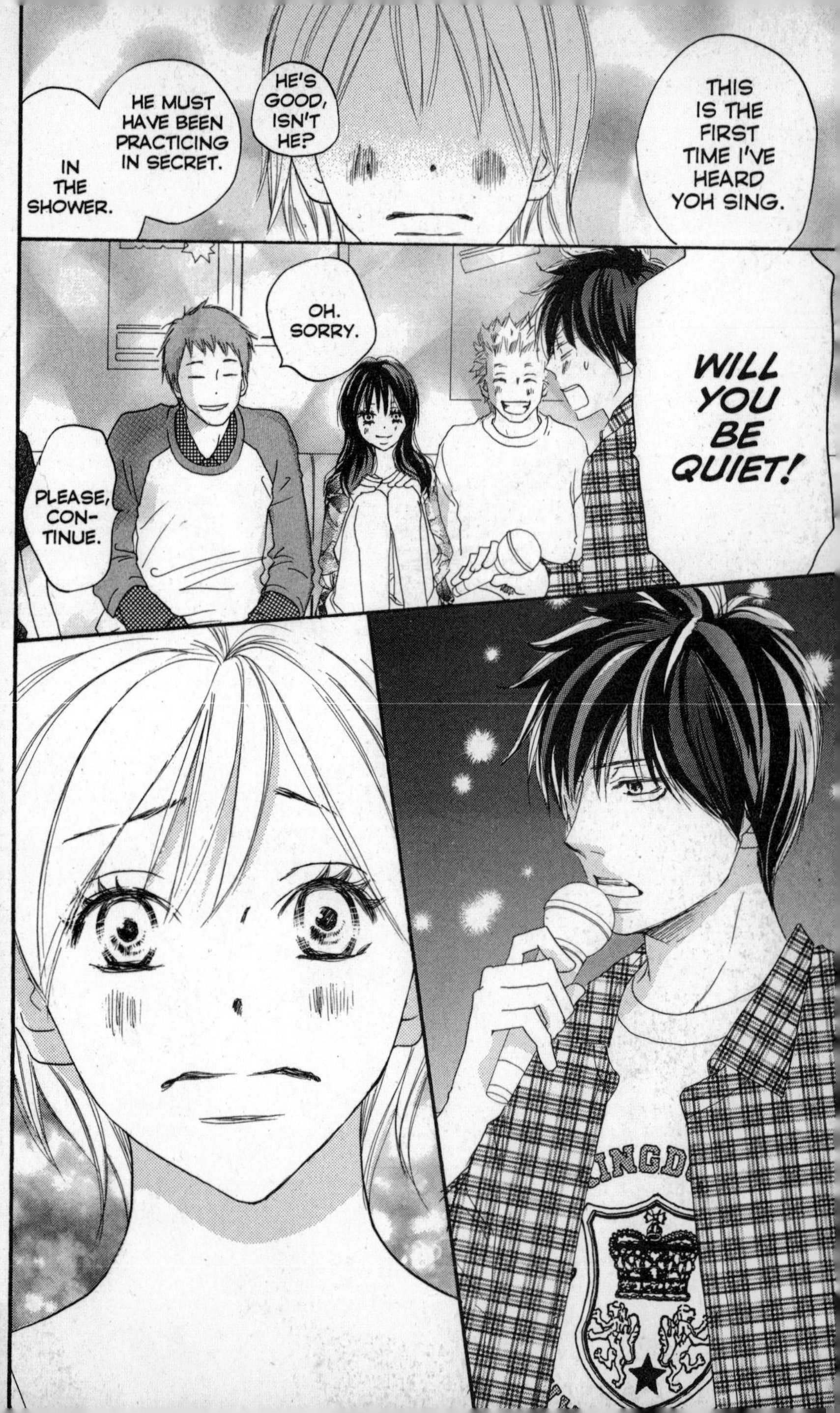
THIS IS THE FIRST TIME I'VE HEARD YOH SING.
HE'S GOOD, ISN'T HE?
HE MUST HAVE BEEN PRACTICING IN SECRET.
IN THE SHOWER.
WILL YOU BE QUIET!
OH. SORRY.
PLEASE, CON-TINUE.

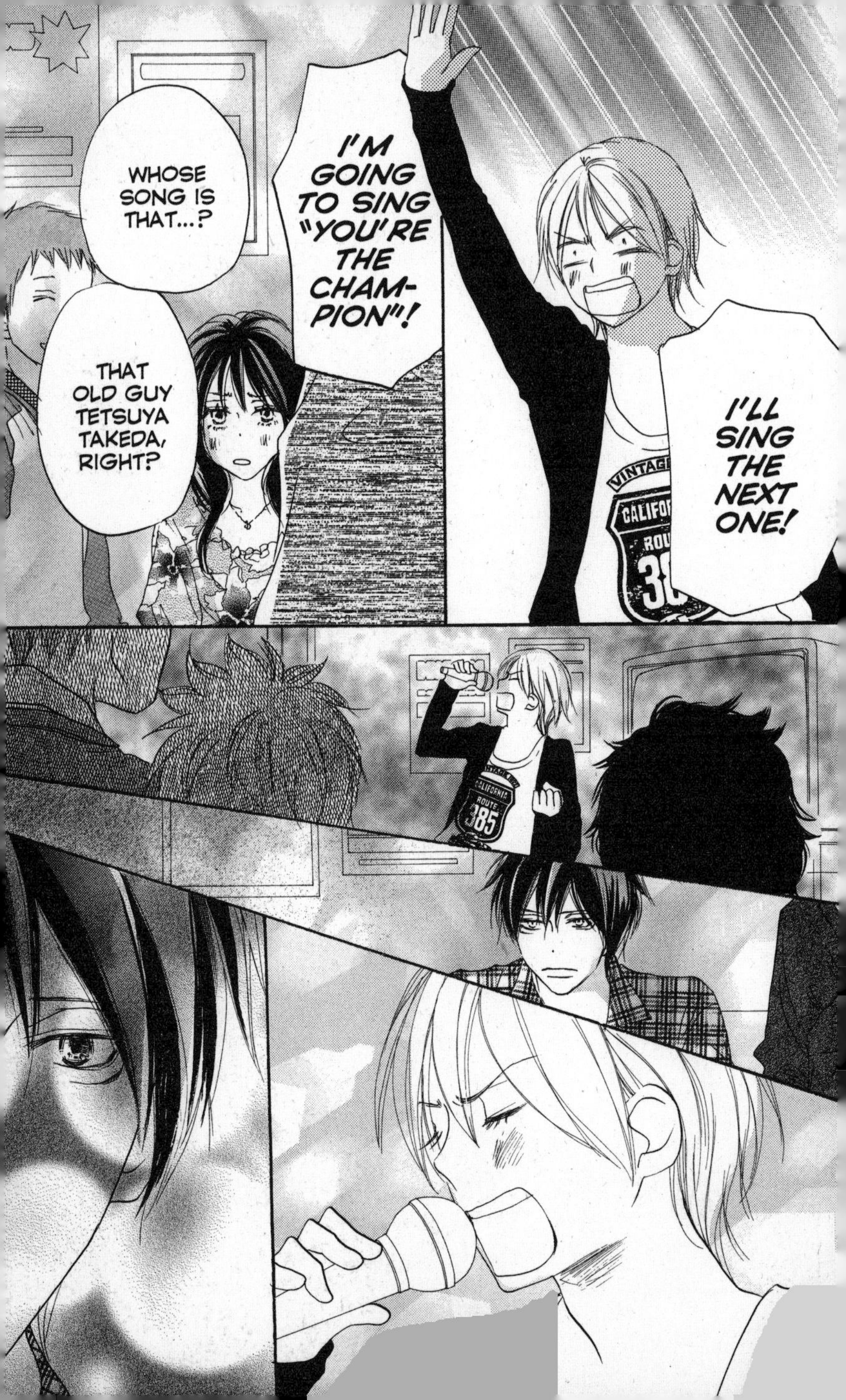
I'LL SING THE NEXT ONE!
I'M GOING TO SING "YOU'RE THE CHAMPION"!
WHOSE SONG IS THAT...?
THAT OLD GUY TETSUYA TAKEDA, RIGHT?

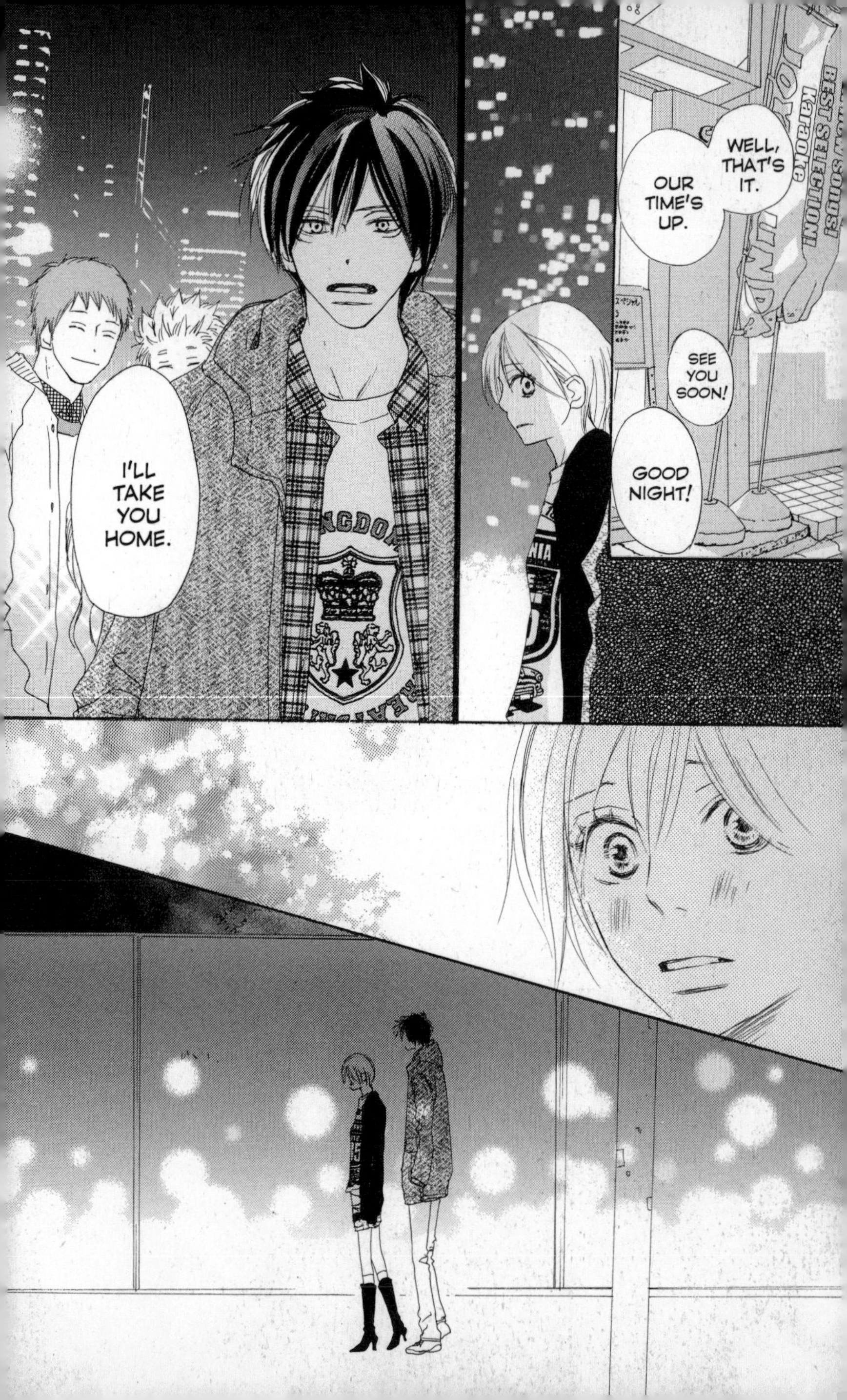
BEST SELECTION!
Karaoke
WELL, THAT'S IT.
OUR TIME'S UP.
SEE YOU SOON!
GOOD NIGHT!
I'LL TAKE YOU HOME.

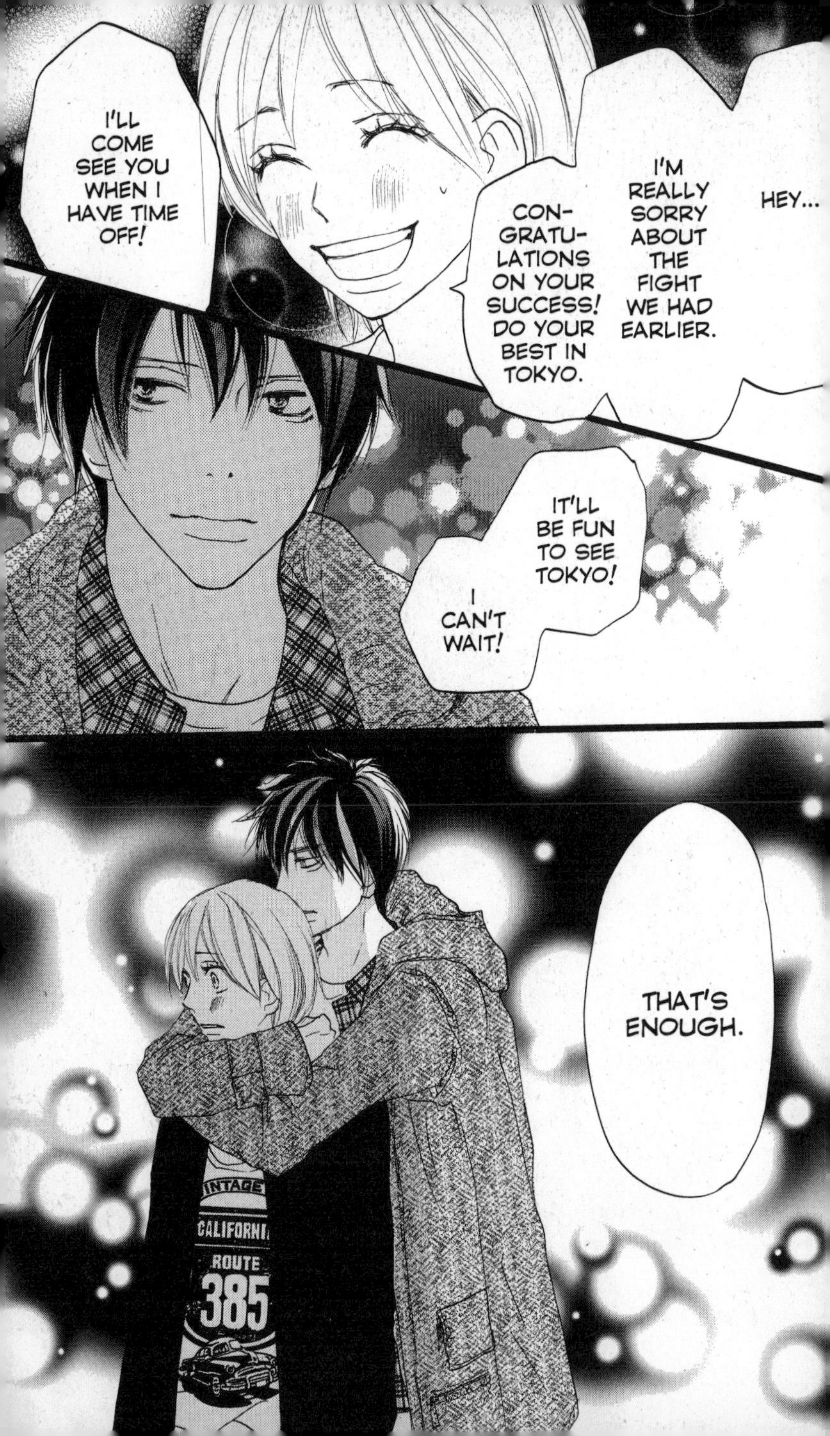
HEY...
I'M REALLY SORRY ABOUT THE FIGHT WE HAD EARLIER.
CON-GRATU-LATIONS ON YOUR SUCCESS! DO YOUR BEST IN TOKYO.
I'LL COME SEE YOU WHEN I HAVE TIME OFF!
IT'LL BE FUN TO SEE TOKYO!
I CAN'T WAIT!
THAT'S ENOUGH.
ROUTE
385

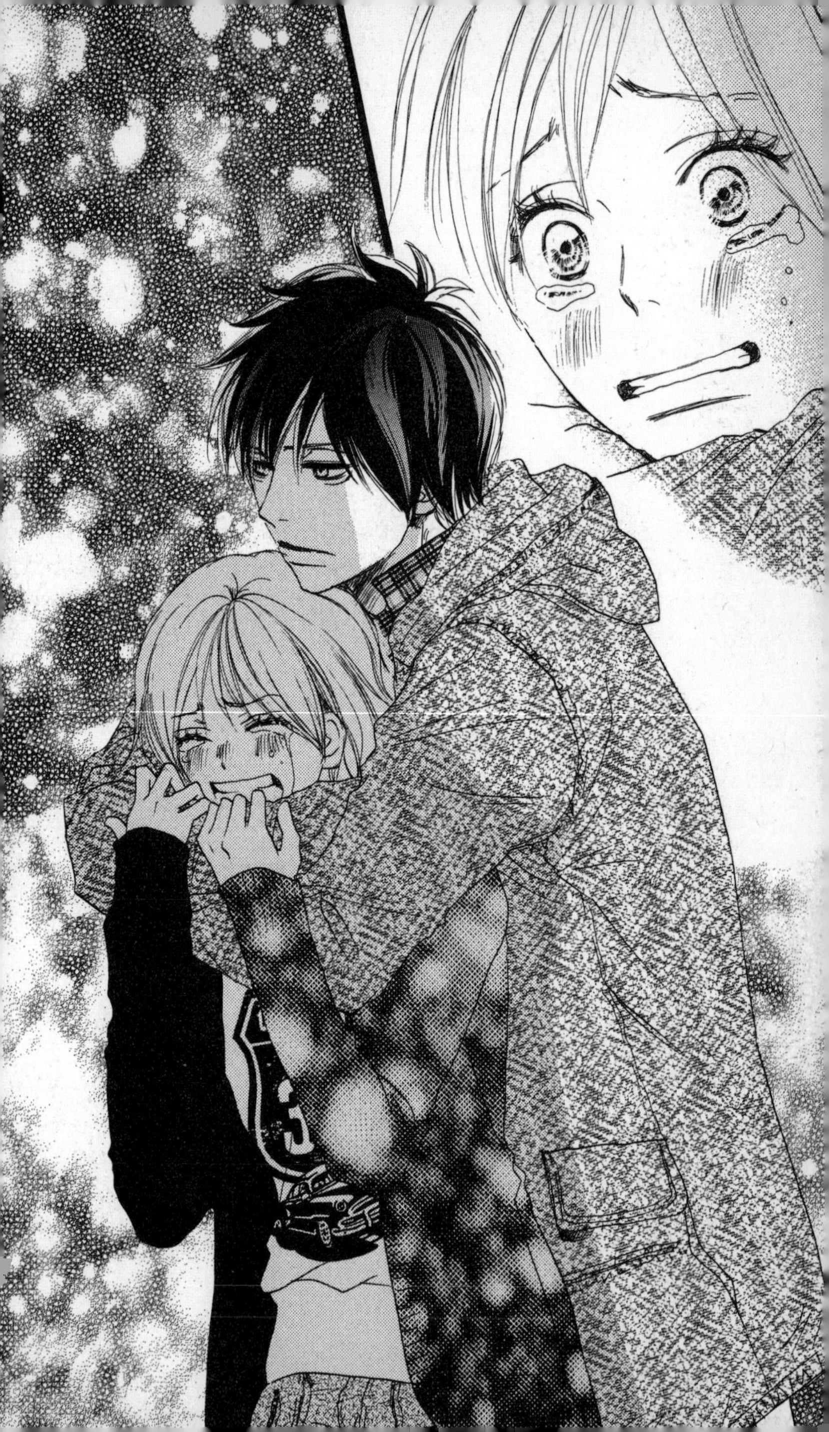

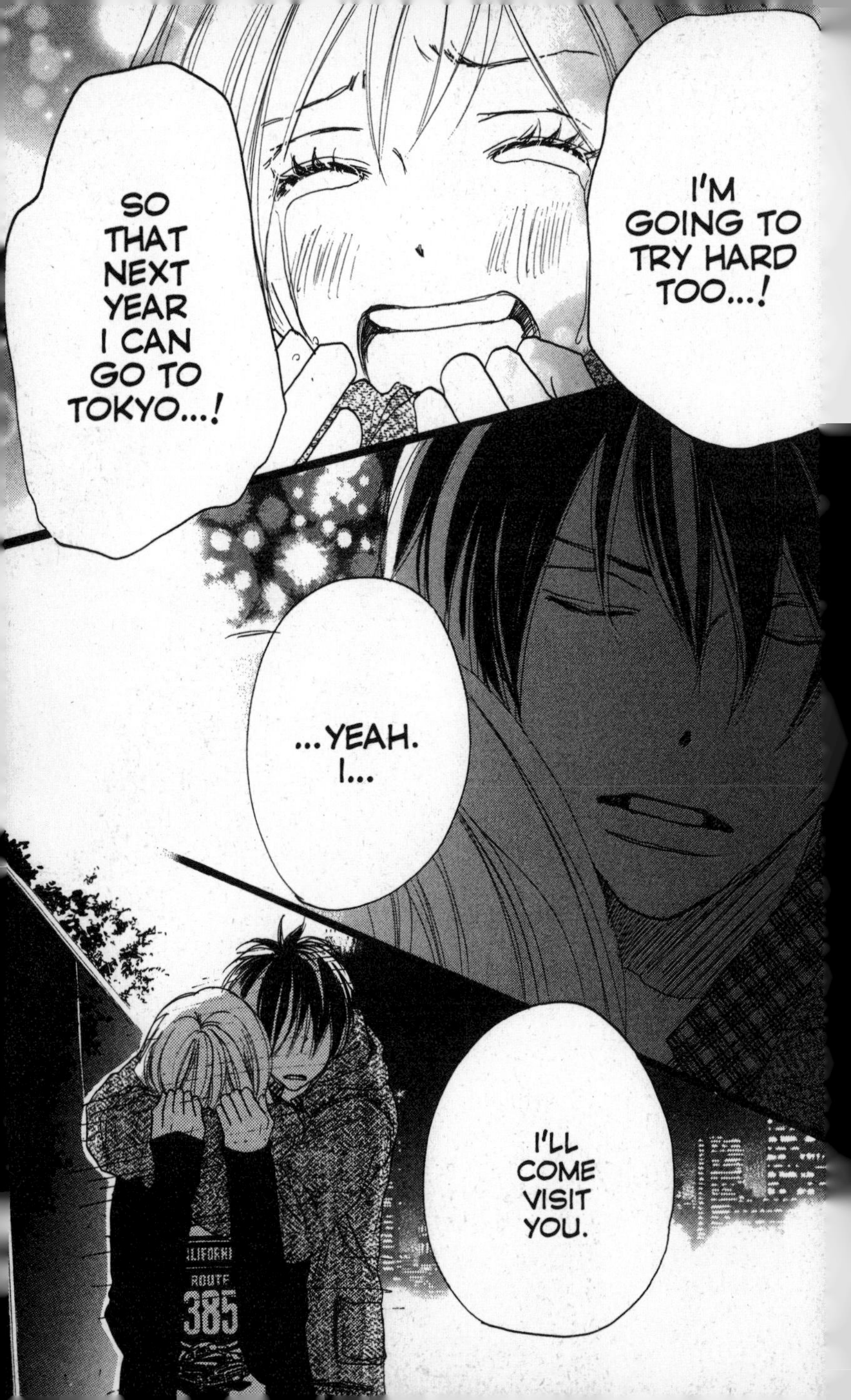
I'M GOING TO TRY HARD TOO...!
SO THAT NEXT YEAR I CAN GO TO TOKYO...!
...YEAH. I...
I'LL COME VISIT YOU.

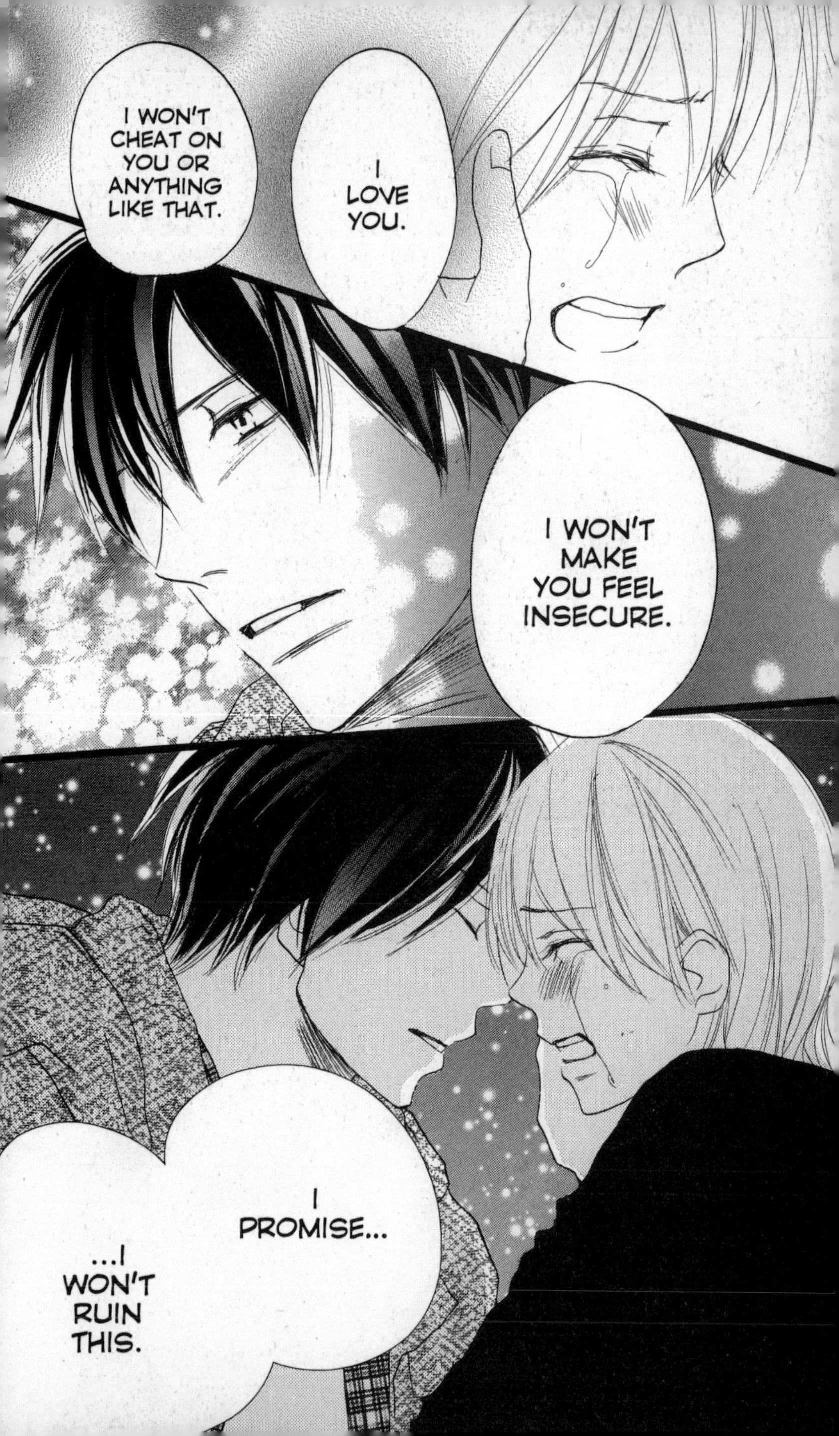
I LOVE YOU.
I WON'T CHEAT ON YOU OR ANYTHING LIKE THAT.
I WON'T MAKE YOU FEEL INSECURE.
I PROMISE...
...I WON'T RUIN THIS.

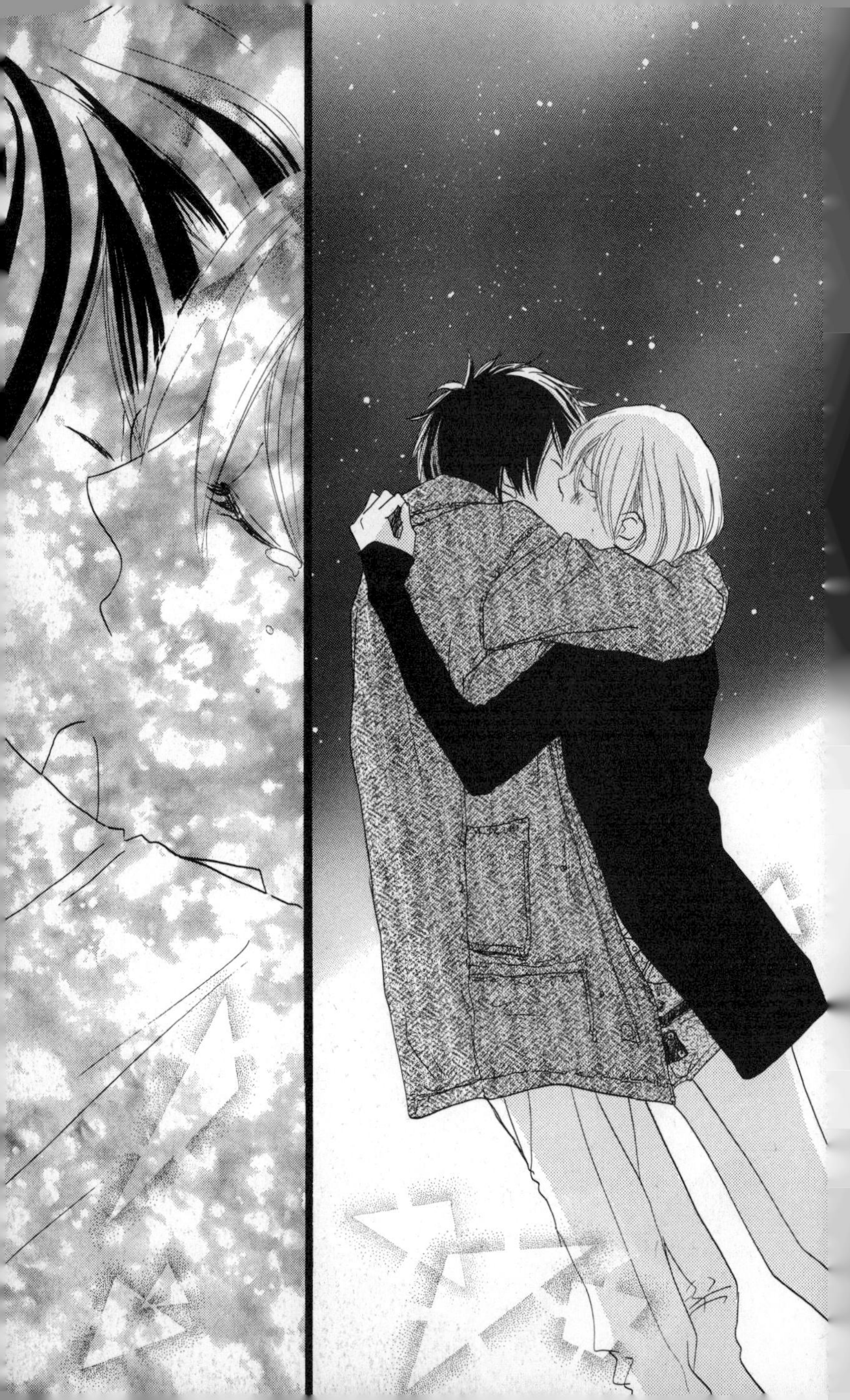

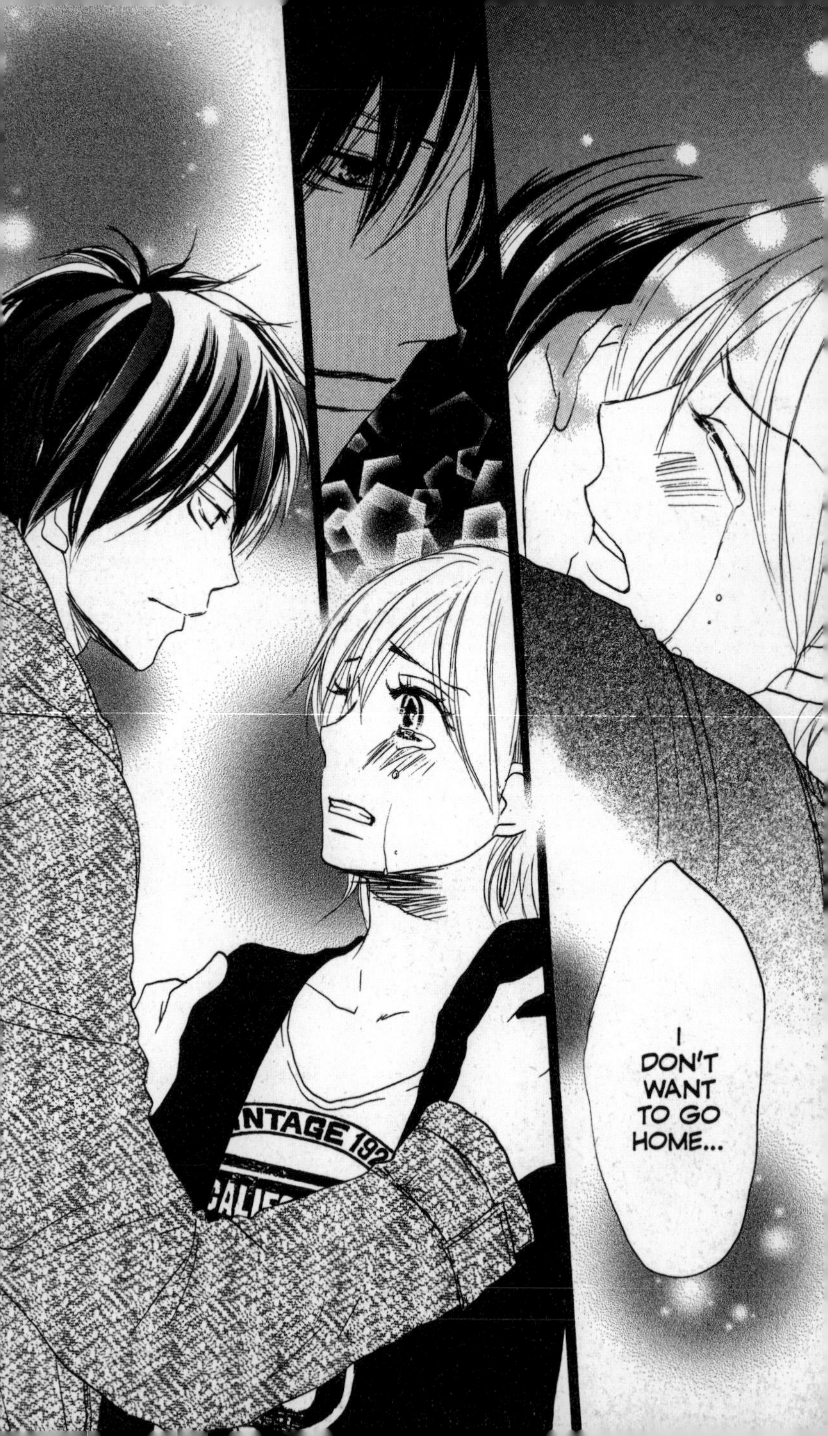
I DON'T WANT TO GO HOME...

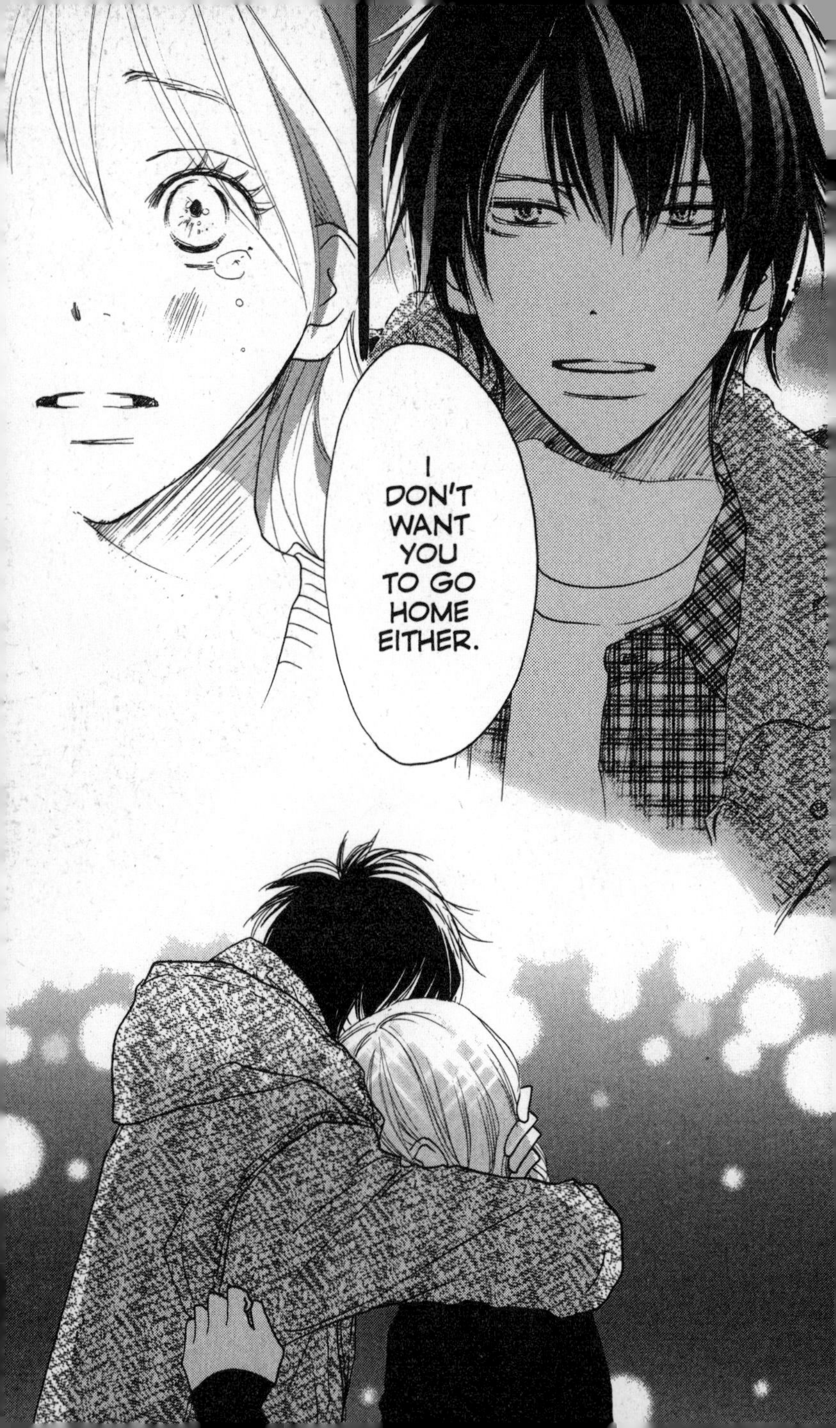
I DON'T WANT YOU TO GO HOME EITHER.

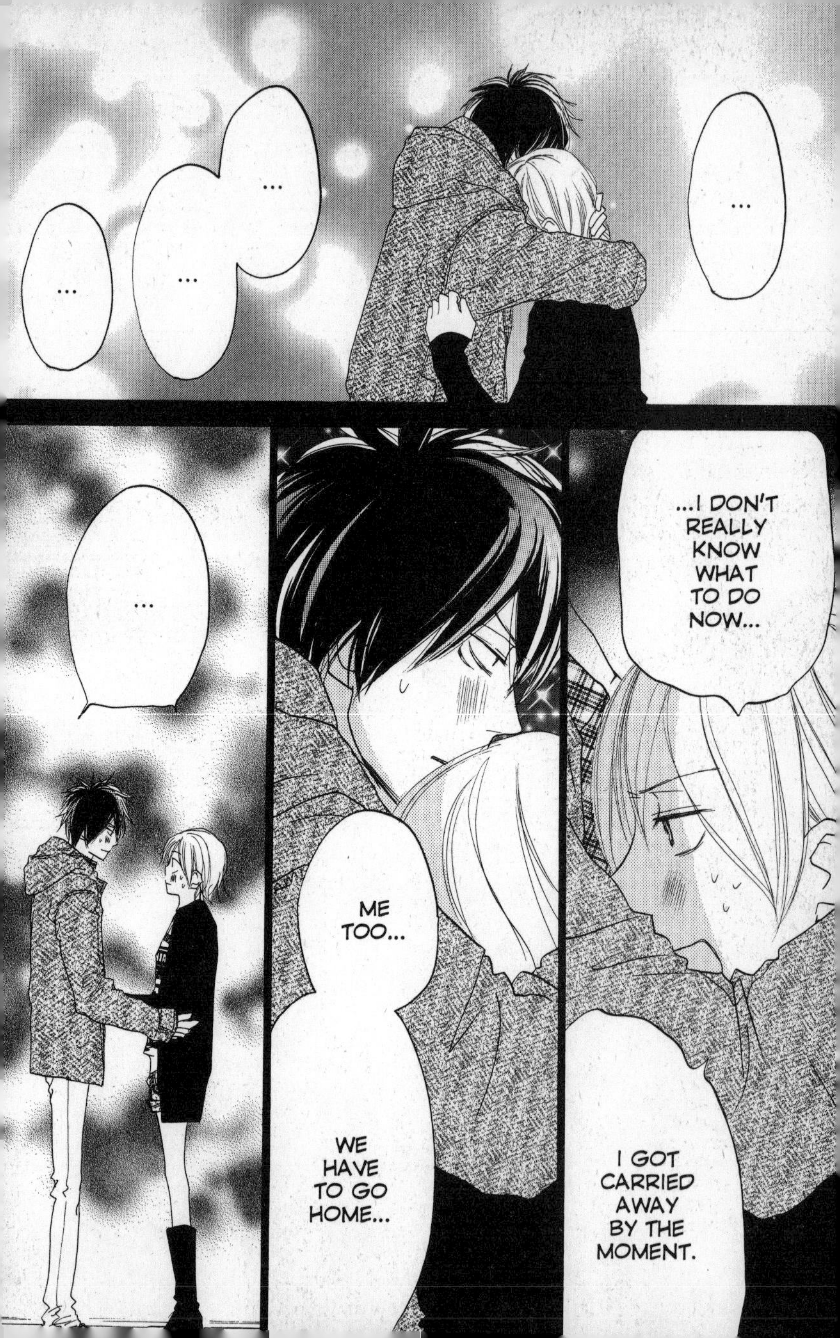
...
...
...
...
...I DON'T REALLY KNOW WHAT TO DO NOW...
I GOT CARRIED AWAY BY THE MOMENT.
ME TOO...
WE HAVE TO GO HOME...
...

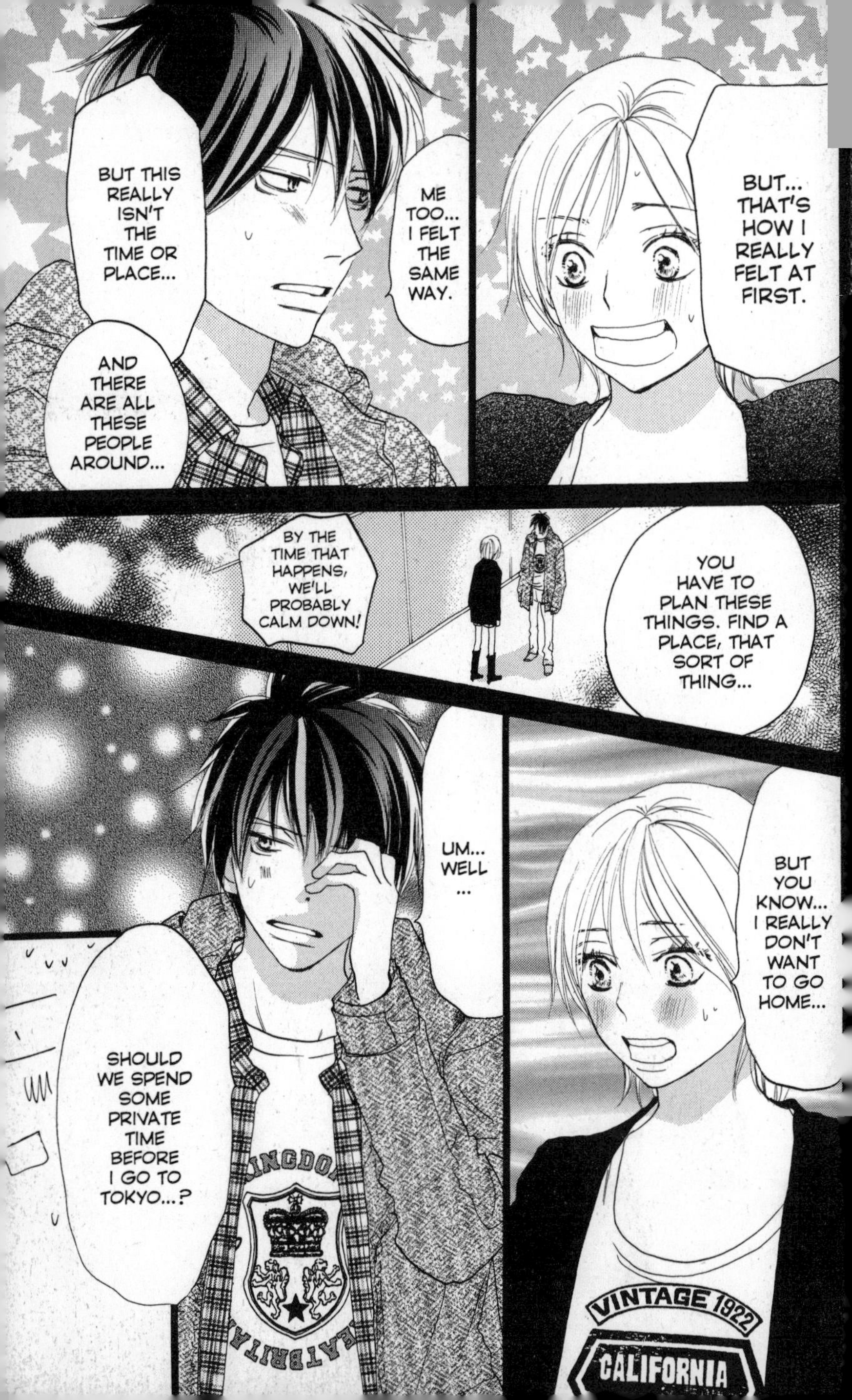
BUT... THAT'S HOW I REALLY FELT AT FIRST.
ME TOO... I FELT THE SAME WAY.
BUT THIS REALLY ISN'T THE TIME OR PLACE...
AND THERE ARE ALL THESE PEOPLE AROUND...
YOU HAVE TO PLAN THESE THINGS. FIND A PLACE, THAT SORT OF THING...
BY THE TIME THAT HAPPENS, WE'LL PROBABLY CALM DOWN!
BUT YOU KNOW... I REALLY DON'T WANT TO GO HOME...
VINTAGE 1922
CALIFORNIA
UM... WELL ...
SHOULD WE SPEND SOME PRIVATE TIME BEFORE I GO TO TOKYO...?

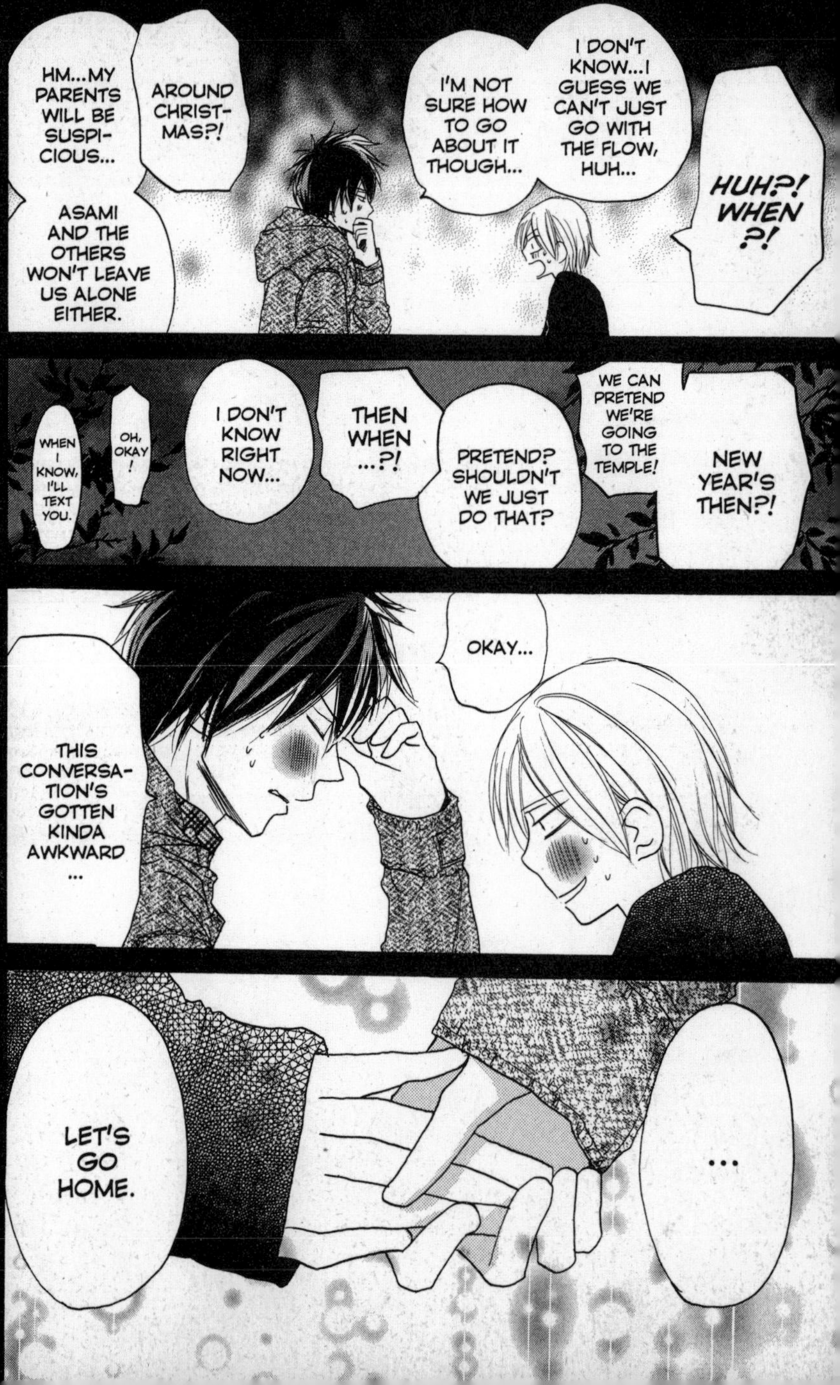
HUH?! WHEN?!
I DON'T KNOW...I GUESS WE CAN'T JUST GO WITH THE FLOW, HUH...
I'M NOT SURE HOW TO GO ABOUT IT THOUGH...
AROUND CHRIST-MAS?!
HM...MY PARENTS WILL BE SUSPI-CIOUS...
ASAMI AND THE OTHERS WON'T LEAVE US ALONE EITHER.
NEW YEAR'S THEN?!
WE CAN PRETEND WE'RE GOING TO THE TEMPLE!
PRETEND? SHOULDN'T WE JUST DO THAT?
THEN WHEN ...?!
I DON'T KNOW RIGHT NOW...
OH, OKAY!
WHEN I KNOW, I'LL TEXT YOU.
OKAY...
THIS CONVERSA-TION'S GOTTEN KINDA AWKWARD...
...
LET'S GO HOME.

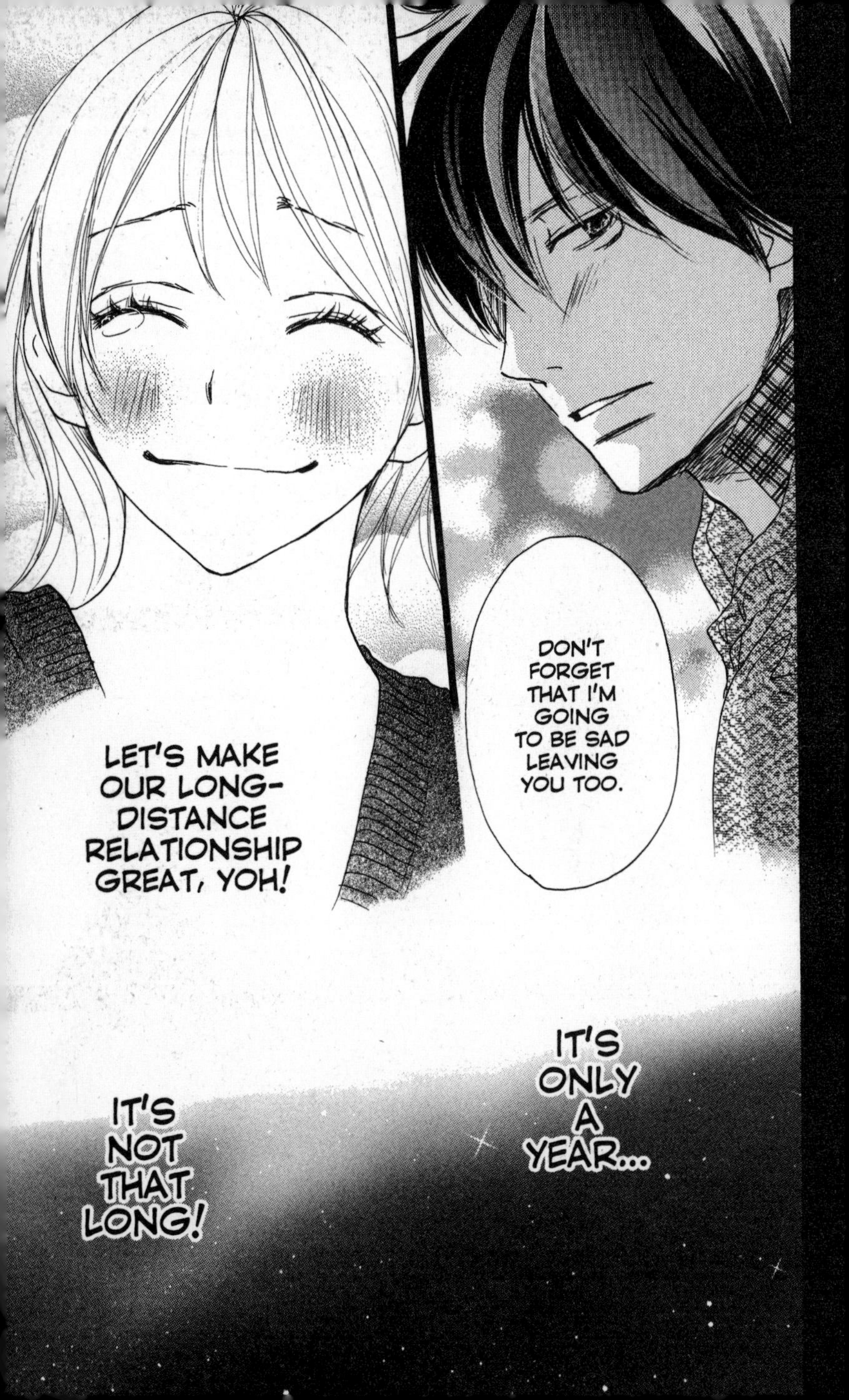
DON'T FORGET THAT I'M GOING TO BE SAD LEAVING YOU TOO.
LET'S MAKE OUR LONG-DISTANCE RELATIONSHIP GREAT, YOH!
IT'S ONLY A YEAR...
IT'S NOT THAT LONG!

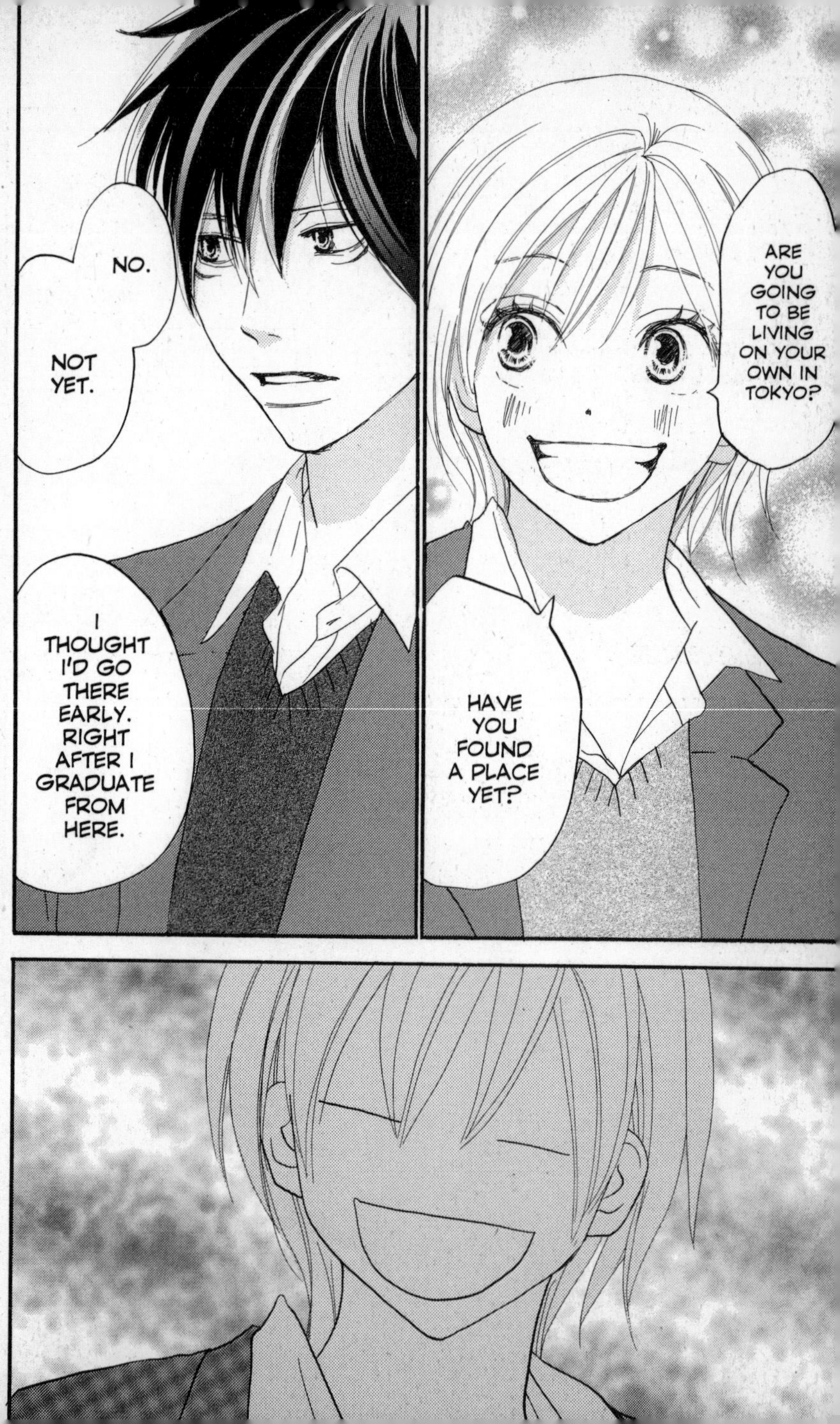
ARE YOU GOING TO BE LIVING ON YOUR OWN IN TOKYO?
HAVE YOU FOUND A PLACE YET?
NO.
NOT YET.
I THOUGHT I'D GO THERE EARLY. RIGHT AFTER I GRADUATE FROM HERE.

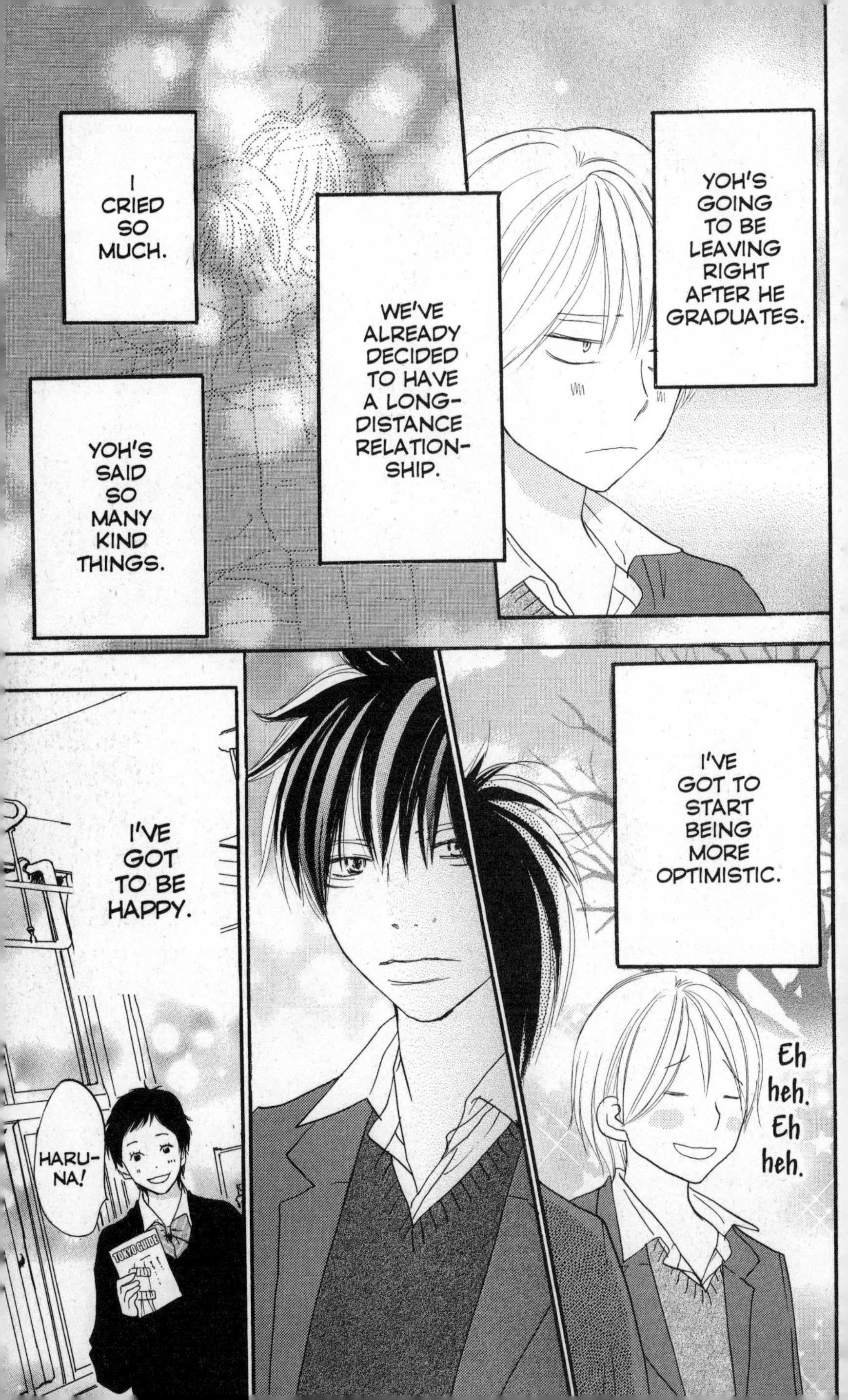
YOH'S GOING TO BE LEAVING RIGHT AFTER HE GRADUATES.
WE'VE ALREADY DECIDED TO HAVE A LONG-DISTANCE RELATION-SHIP.
I CRIED SO MUCH.
YOH'S SAID SO MANY KIND THINGS.
I'VE GOT TO START BEING MORE OPTIMISTIC.
Eh heh. Eh heh.
I'VE GOT TO BE HAPPY.
HARU-NA!
TOKYO GUIDE

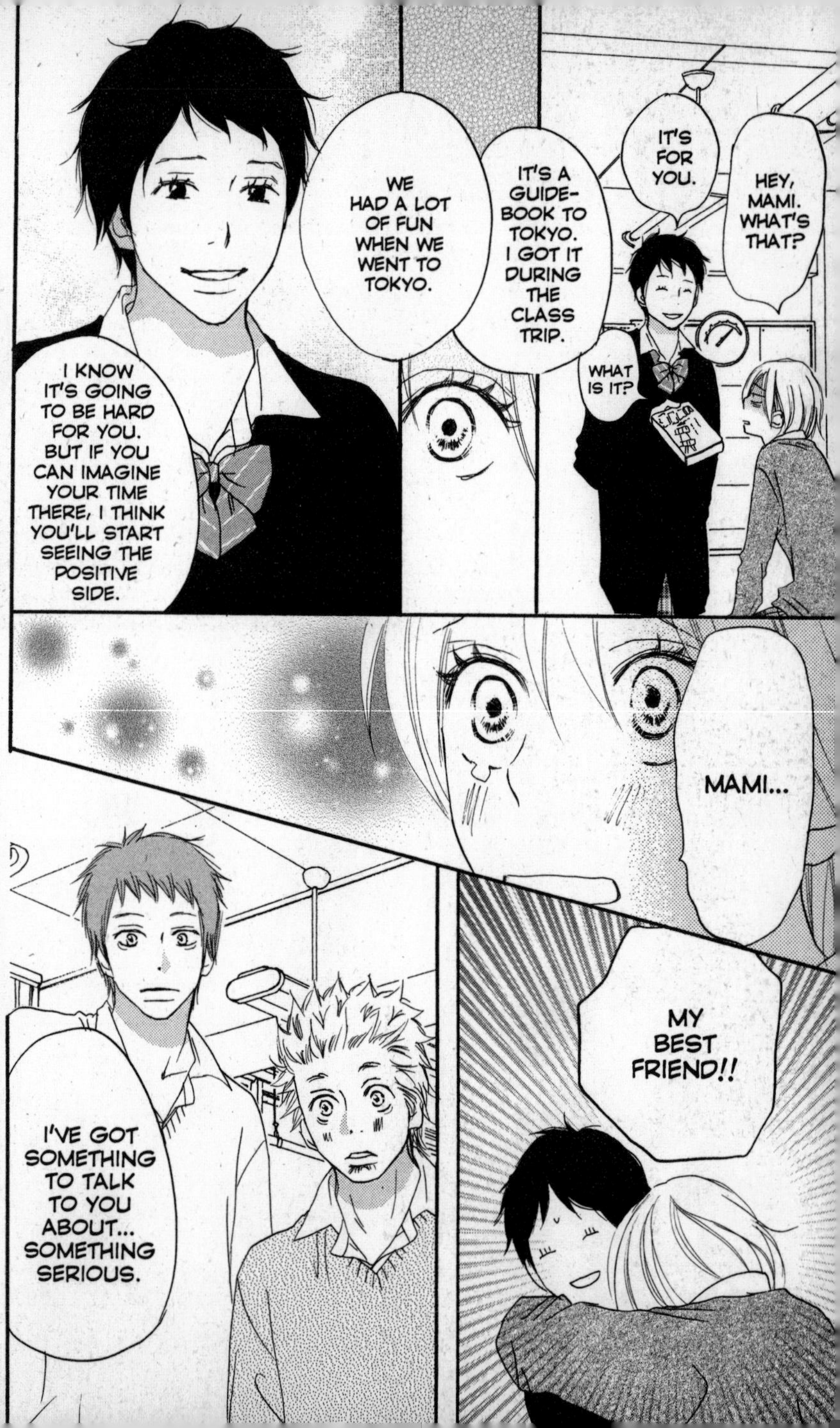
HEY, MAMI. WHAT'S THAT?
IT'S FOR YOU.
WHAT IS IT?
IT'S A GUIDE-BOOK TO TOKYO. I GOT IT DURING THE CLASS TRIP.
WE HAD A LOT OF FUN WHEN WE WENT TO TOKYO.
I KNOW IT'S GOING TO BE HARD FOR YOU. BUT IF YOU CAN IMAGINE YOUR TIME THERE, I THINK YOU'LL START SEEING THE POSITIVE SIDE.
MAMI...
MY BEST FRIEND!!
I'VE GOT SOMETHING TO TALK TO YOU ABOUT... SOMETHING SERIOUS.

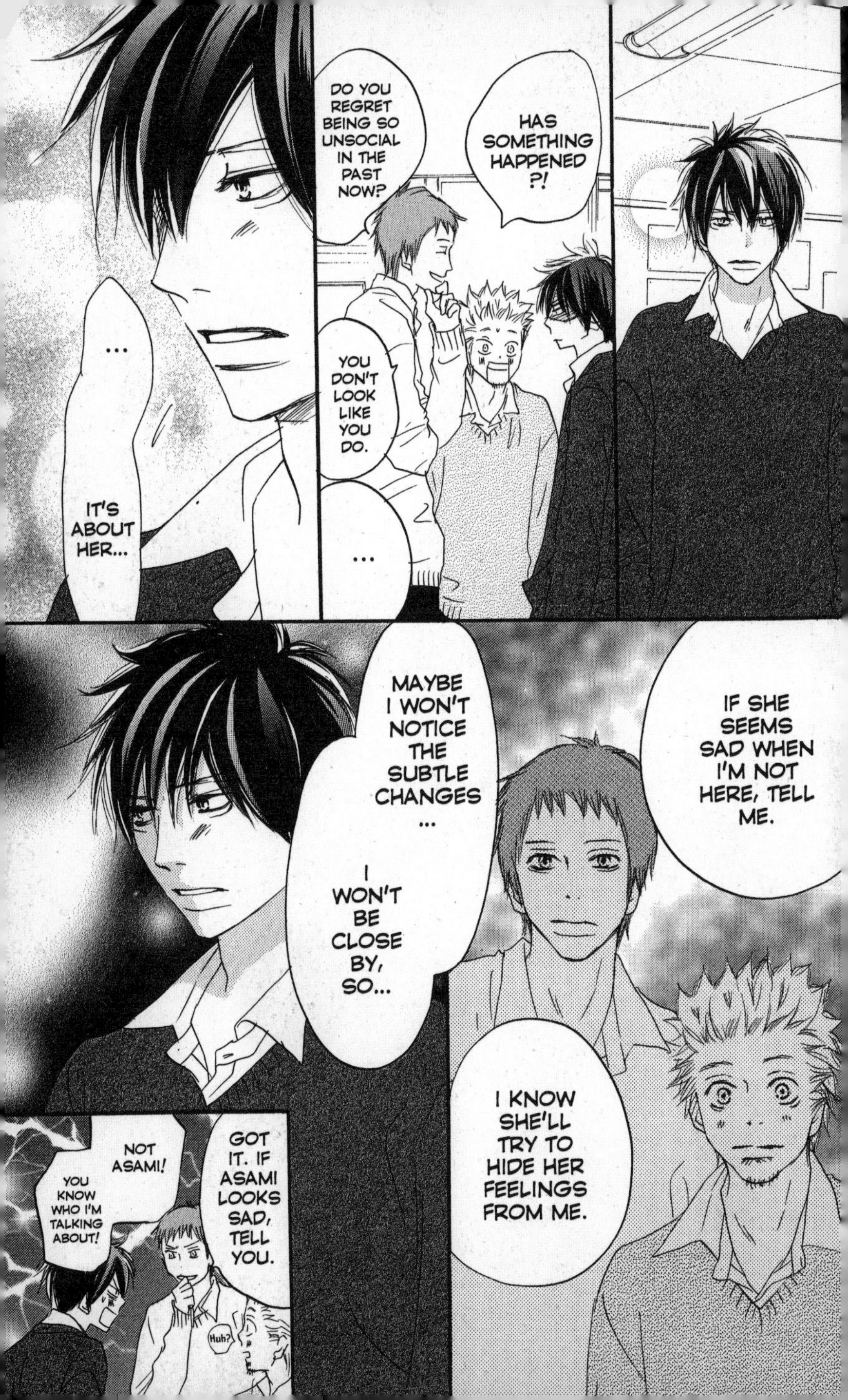
HAS SOMETHING HAPPENED ?!
DO YOU REGRET BEING SO UNSOCIAL IN THE PAST NOW?
YOU DON'T LOOK LIKE YOU DO.
...
...
IT'S ABOUT HER...
IF SHE SEEMS SAD WHEN I'M NOT HERE, TELL ME.
MAYBE I WON'T NOTICE THE SUBTLE CHANGES ...
I WON'T BE CLOSE BY, SO...
I KNOW SHE'LL TRY TO HIDE HER FEELINGS FROM ME.
GOT IT. IF ASAMI LOOKS SAD, TELL YOU.
NOT ASAMI!
YOU KNOW WHO I'M TALKING ABOUT!
Huh?

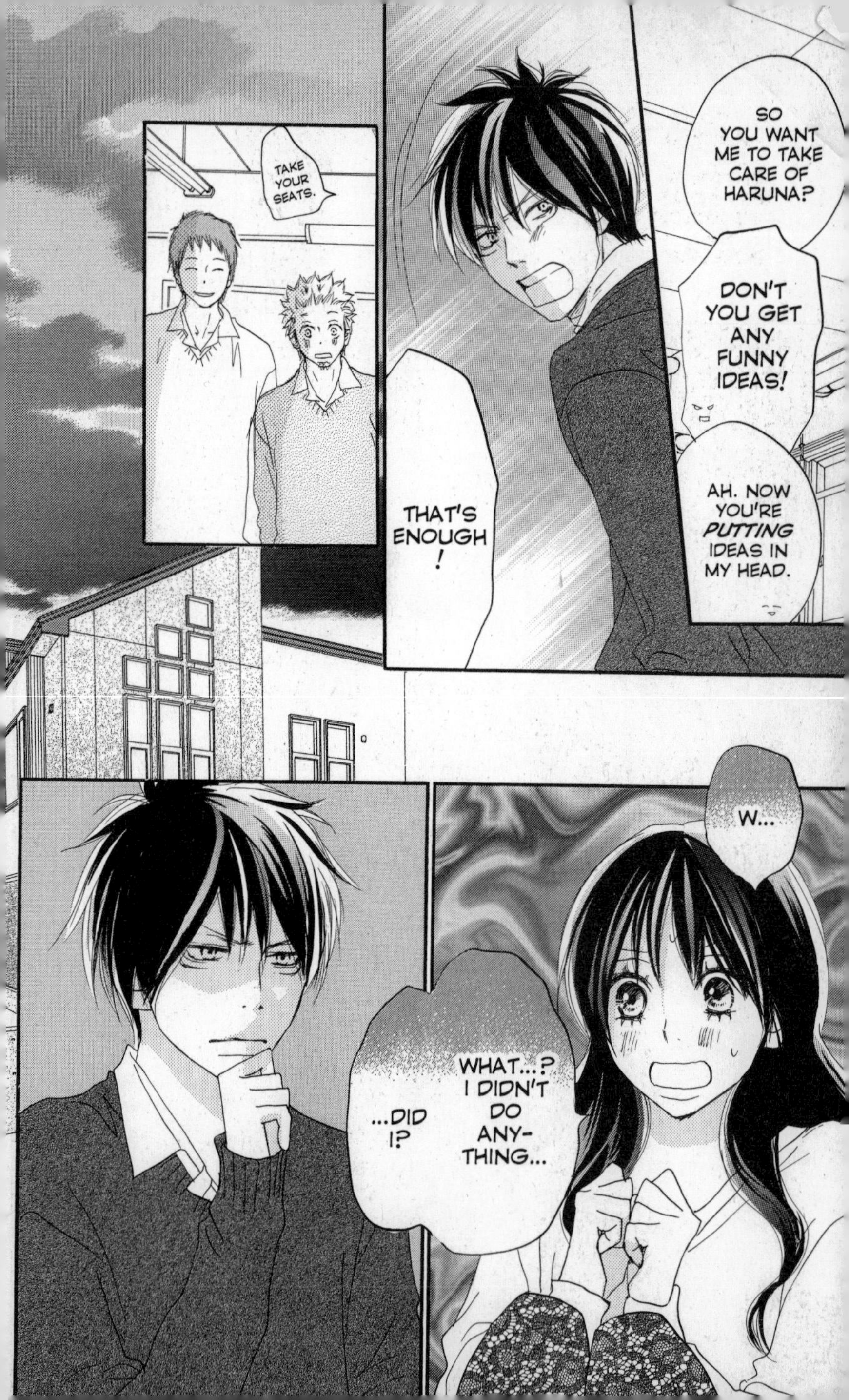
SO YOU WANT ME TO TAKE CARE OF HARUNA?
DON'T YOU GET ANY FUNNY IDEAS!
AH. NOW YOU'RE *PUTTING* IDEAS IN MY HEAD.
THAT'S ENOUGH!
TAKE YOUR SEATS.
W...
WHAT...? I DIDN'T DO ANYTHING...
...DID I?

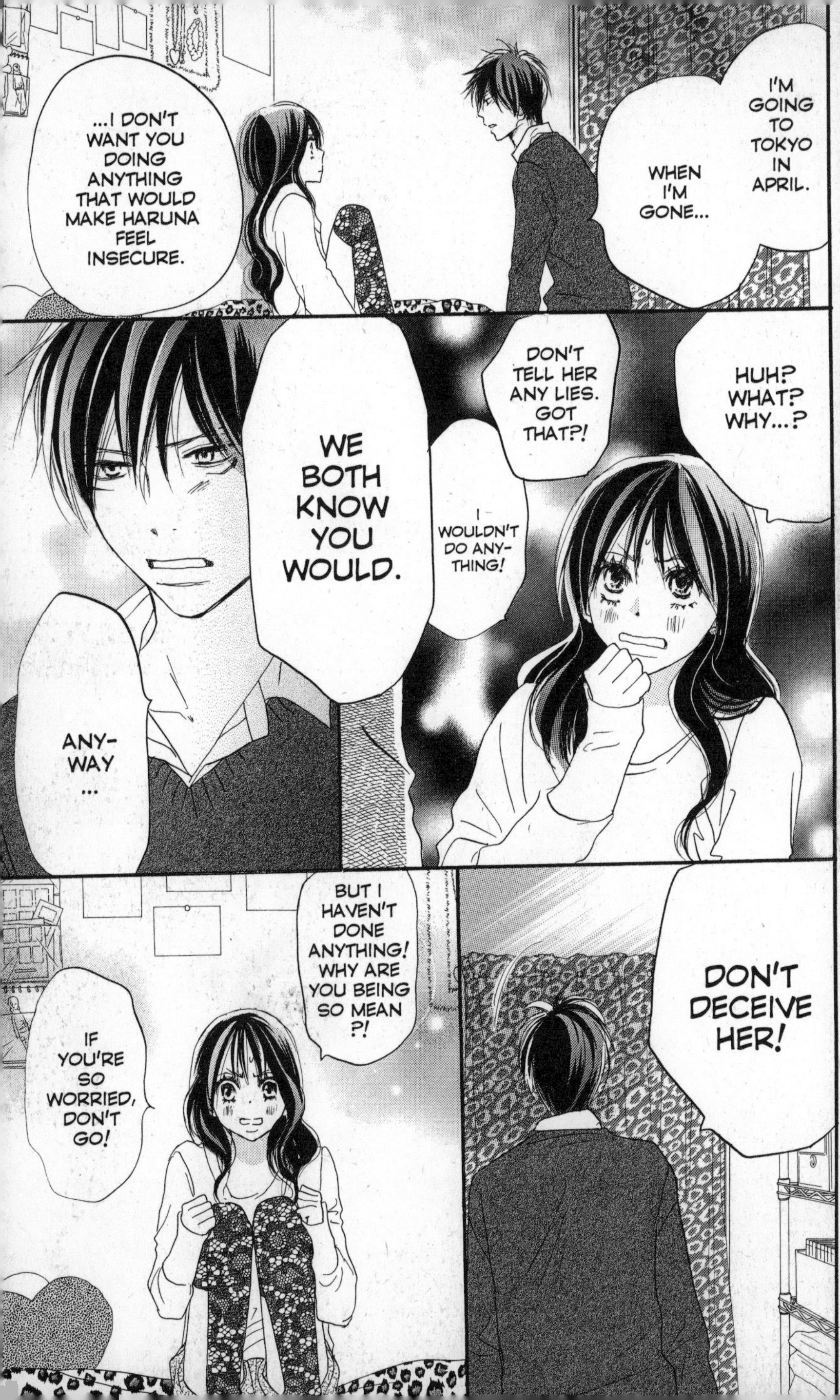
I'M GOING TO TOKYO IN APRIL.
WHEN I'M GONE...
...I DON'T WANT YOU DOING ANYTHING THAT WOULD MAKE HARUNA FEEL INSECURE.
HUH? WHAT? WHY...?
DON'T TELL HER ANY LIES. GOT THAT?!
I WOULDN'T DO ANY-THING!
WE BOTH KNOW YOU WOULD.
ANY-WAY...
DON'T DECEIVE HER!
BUT I HAVEN'T DONE ANYTHING! WHY ARE YOU BEING SO MEAN?!
IF YOU'RE SO WORRIED, DON'T GO!

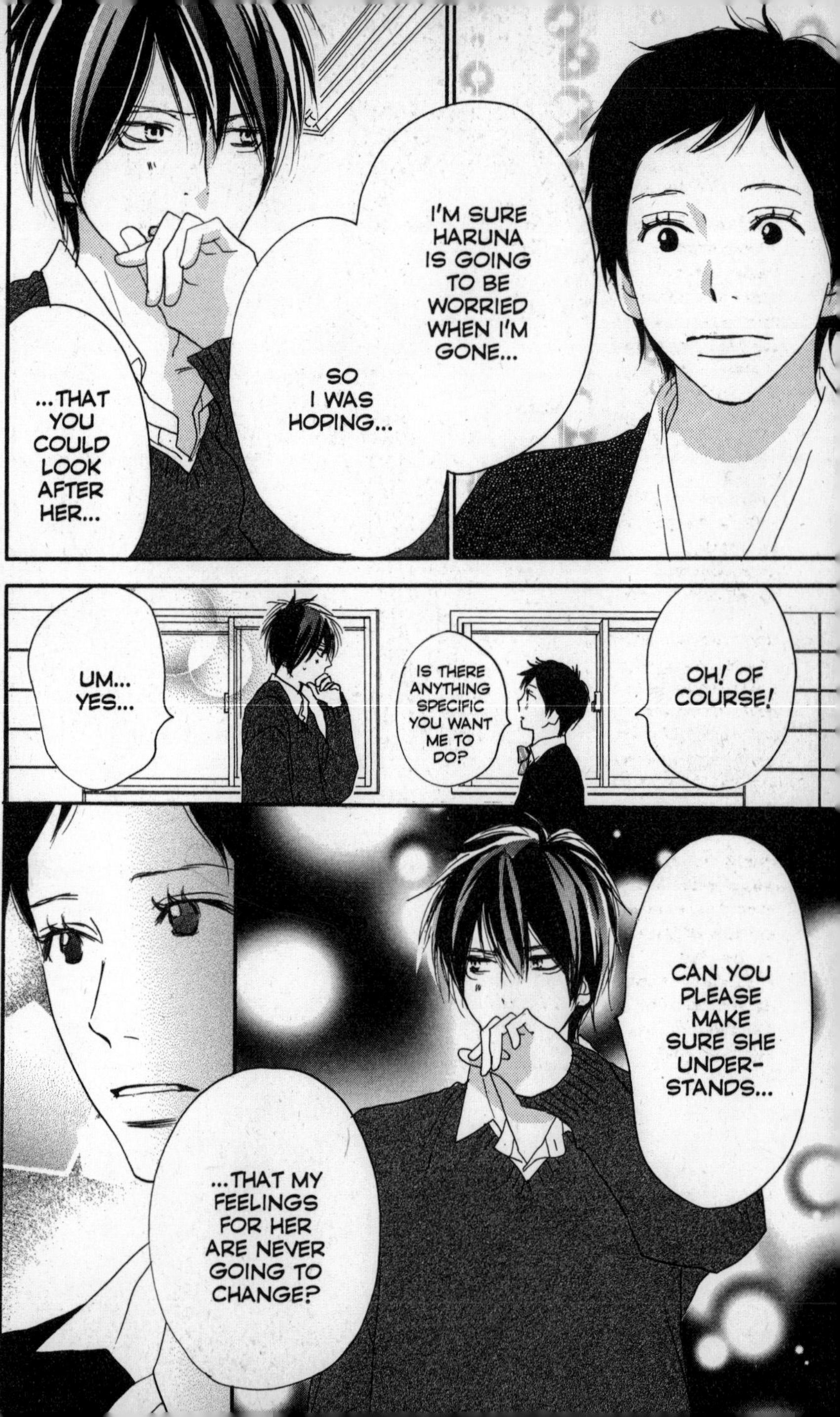
I'M SURE HARUNA IS GOING TO BE WORRIED WHEN I'M GONE...
SO I WAS HOPING...
...THAT YOU COULD LOOK AFTER HER...
OH! OF COURSE!
IS THERE ANYTHING SPECIFIC YOU WANT ME TO DO?
UM... YES...
CAN YOU PLEASE MAKE SURE SHE UNDER-STANDS...
...THAT MY FEELINGS FOR HER ARE NEVER GOING TO CHANGE?

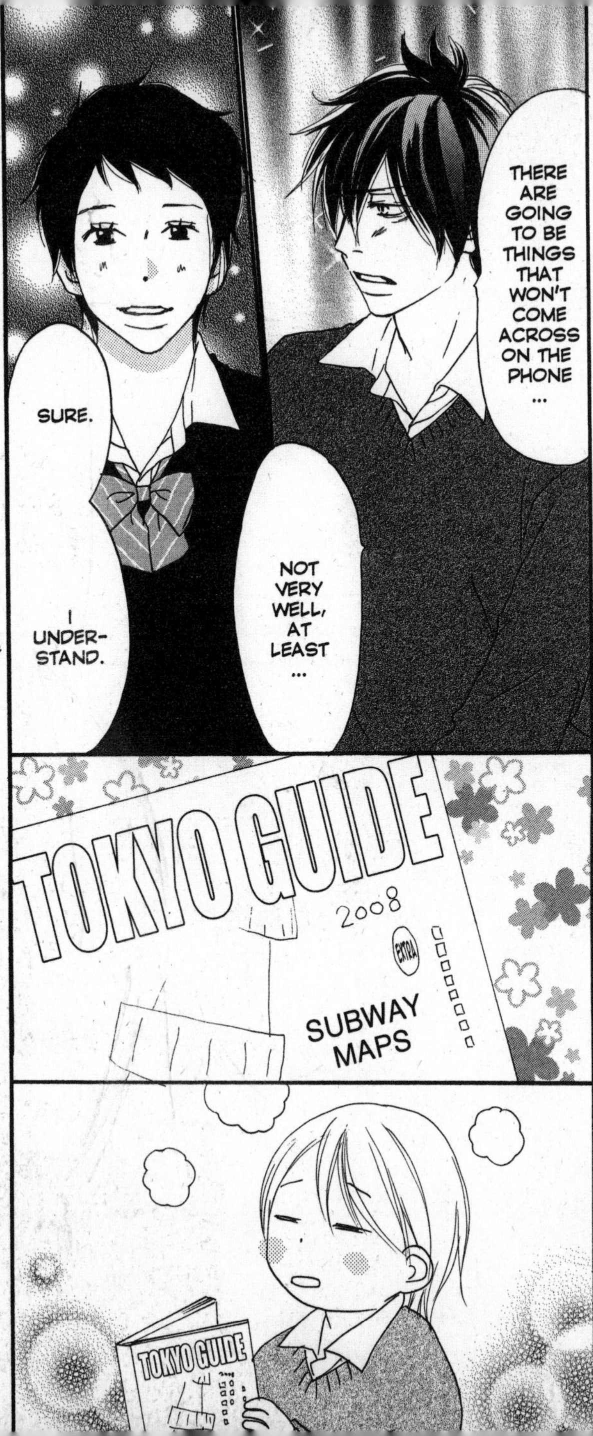
THERE ARE GOING TO BE THINGS THAT WON'T COME ACROSS ON THE PHONE ...
NOT VERY WELL, AT LEAST ...
SURE.
I UNDER-STAND.
TOKYO GUIDE
2008
EXTRA
SUBWAY MAPS
TOKYO GUIDE

1 There are only two notes in this volume.

Hello! This is the last volume! Thank you for sticking with me over such a long time. It's all because of you readers that this series reached 13 volumes. A really, really, really big

THANK YOU!

I'm not sure if I should write this here, but I'd like to thank my assistants who helped me out with this series!

Just about all of the nice backgrounds... (Not just about... All the pretty ones... Sorry, let me start again!) All of the pretty backgrounds were drawn by them. All the bad ones were by me.

I really don't know how manga works. Really! A lot of my friends who can draw well helped me out too. That's why I can still sleep ten hours a day even on a deadline... I'm sorry! What should I do with myself...?

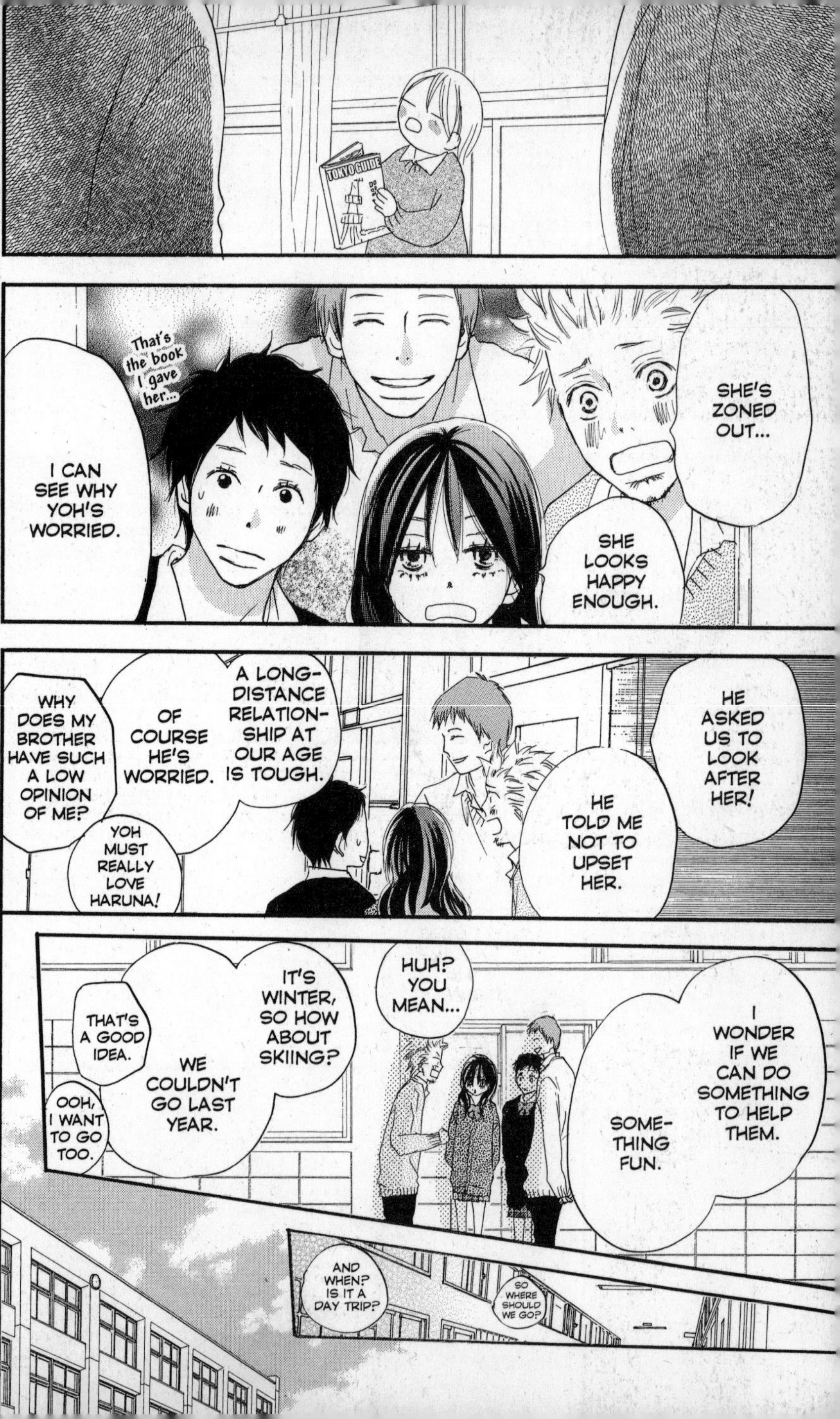
TOKYO GUIDE
SHE'S ZONED OUT...
SHE LOOKS HAPPY ENOUGH.
That's the book I gave her...
I CAN SEE WHY YOH'S WORRIED.
HE ASKED US TO LOOK AFTER HER!
HE TOLD ME NOT TO UPSET HER.
A LONG-DISTANCE RELATIONSHIP AT OUR AGE IS TOUGH.
OF COURSE HE'S WORRIED.
WHY DOES MY BROTHER HAVE SUCH A LOW OPINION OF ME?
YOH MUST REALLY LOVE HARUNA!
I WONDER IF WE CAN DO SOMETHING TO HELP THEM.
SOMETHING FUN.
HUH? YOU MEAN...
IT'S WINTER, SO HOW ABOUT SKIING?
WE COULDN'T GO LAST YEAR.
THAT'S A GOOD IDEA.
OOH, I WANT TO GO TOO.
SO WHERE SHOULD WE GO?
AND WHEN? IS IT A DAY TRIP?

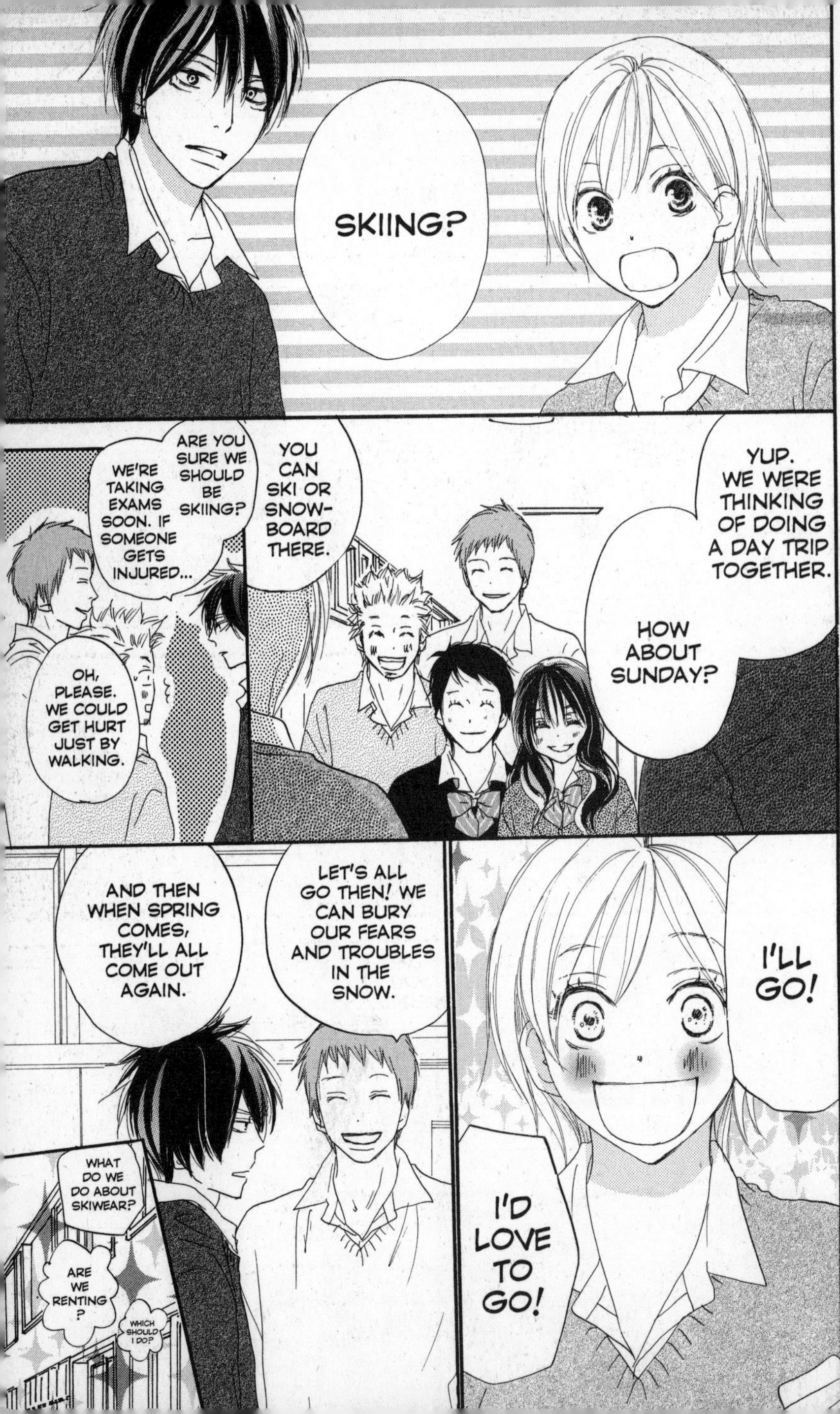
SKIING?
YUP. WE WERE THINKING OF DOING A DAY TRIP TOGETHER.
HOW ABOUT SUNDAY?
YOU CAN SKI OR SNOW-BOARD THERE.
ARE YOU SURE WE SHOULD BE SKIING?
WE'RE TAKING EXAMS SOON. IF SOMEONE GETS INJURED...
OH, PLEASE. WE COULD GET HURT JUST BY WALKING.
I'LL GO!
I'D LOVE TO GO!
LET'S ALL GO THEN! WE CAN BURY OUR FEARS AND TROUBLES IN THE SNOW.
AND THEN WHEN SPRING COMES, THEY'LL ALL COME OUT AGAIN.
WHAT DO WE DO ABOUT SKIWEAR?
ARE WE RENTING?
WHICH SHOULD I DO?

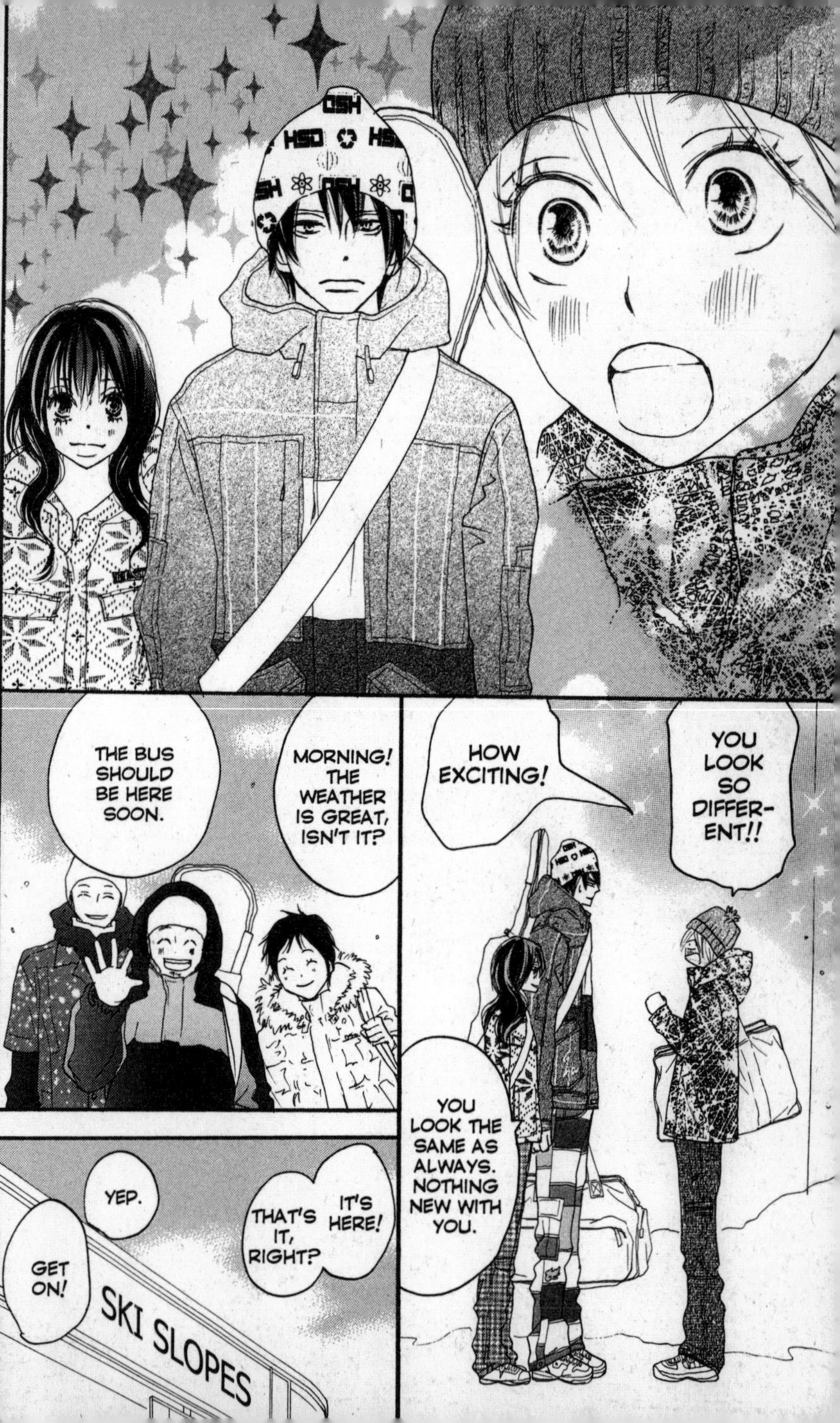
YOU LOOK SO DIFFER-ENT!!
HOW EXCITING!
YOU LOOK THE SAME AS ALWAYS. NOTHING NEW WITH YOU.
MORNING! THE WEATHER IS GREAT, ISN'T IT?
THE BUS SHOULD BE HERE SOON.
IT'S HERE!
THAT'S IT, RIGHT?
YEP.
GET ON!
SKI SLOPES

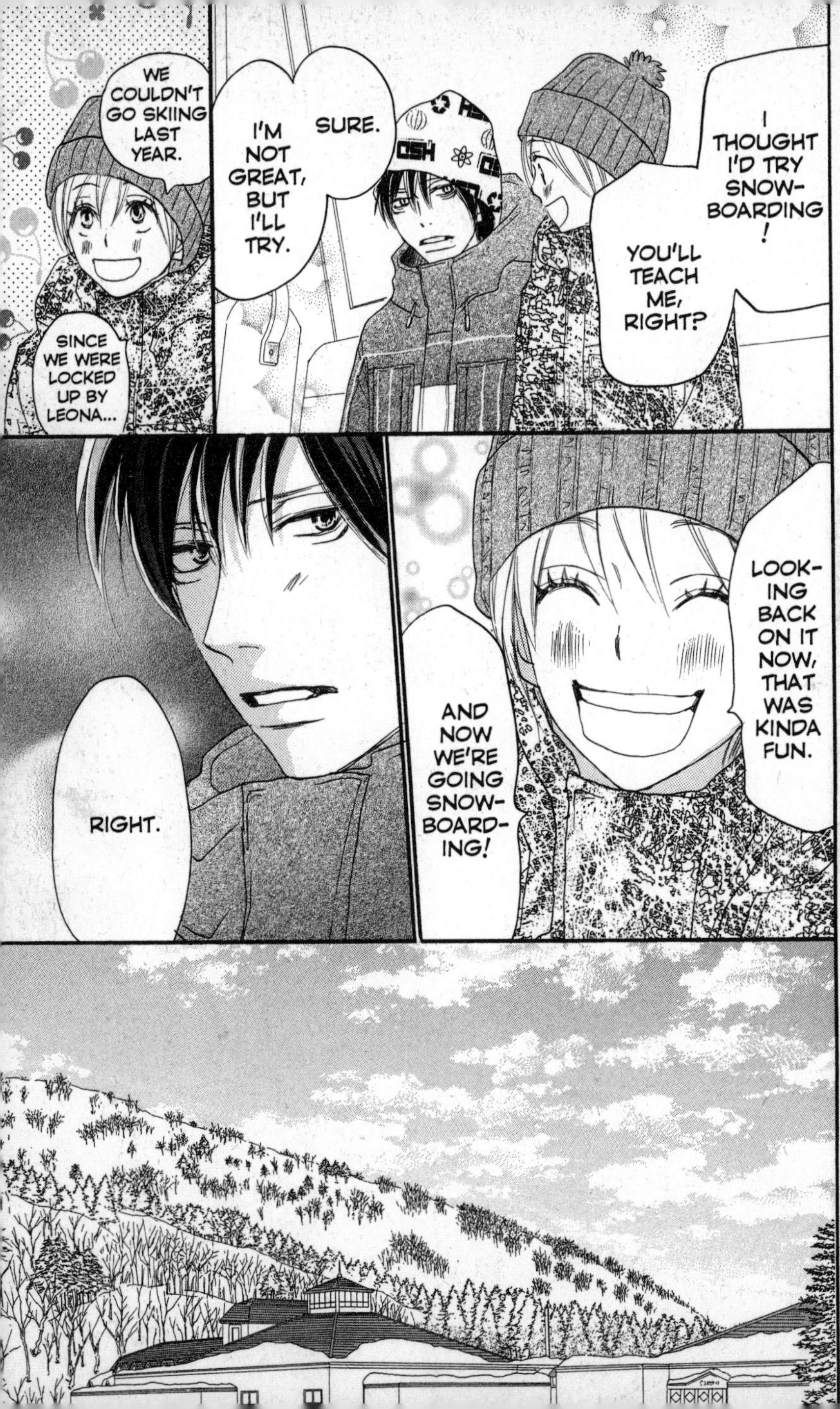
I THOUGHT I'D TRY SNOW-BOARDING!
YOU'LL TEACH ME, RIGHT?
SURE.
I'M NOT GREAT, BUT I'LL TRY.
WE COULDN'T GO SKIING LAST YEAR.
SINCE WE WERE LOCKED UP BY LEONA...
LOOK-ING BACK ON IT NOW, THAT WAS KINDA FUN.
AND NOW WE'RE GOING SNOW-BOARD-ING!
RIGHT.

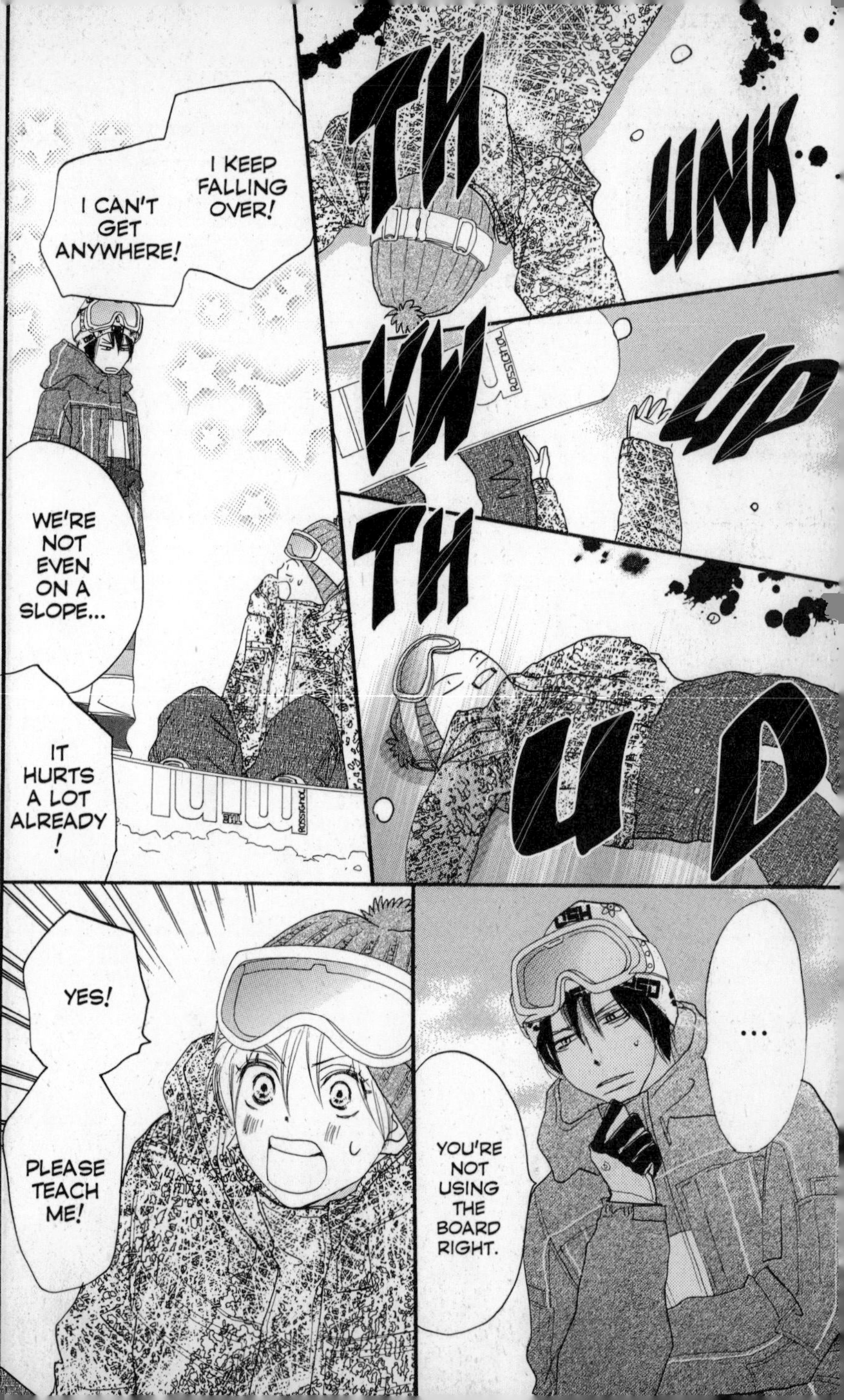
THUNK
WHUP
THUD
I KEEP FALLING OVER!
I CAN'T GET ANYWHERE!
WE'RE NOT EVEN ON A SLOPE...
IT HURTS A LOT ALREADY!
...
YOU'RE NOT USING THE BOARD RIGHT.
YES!
PLEASE TEACH ME!

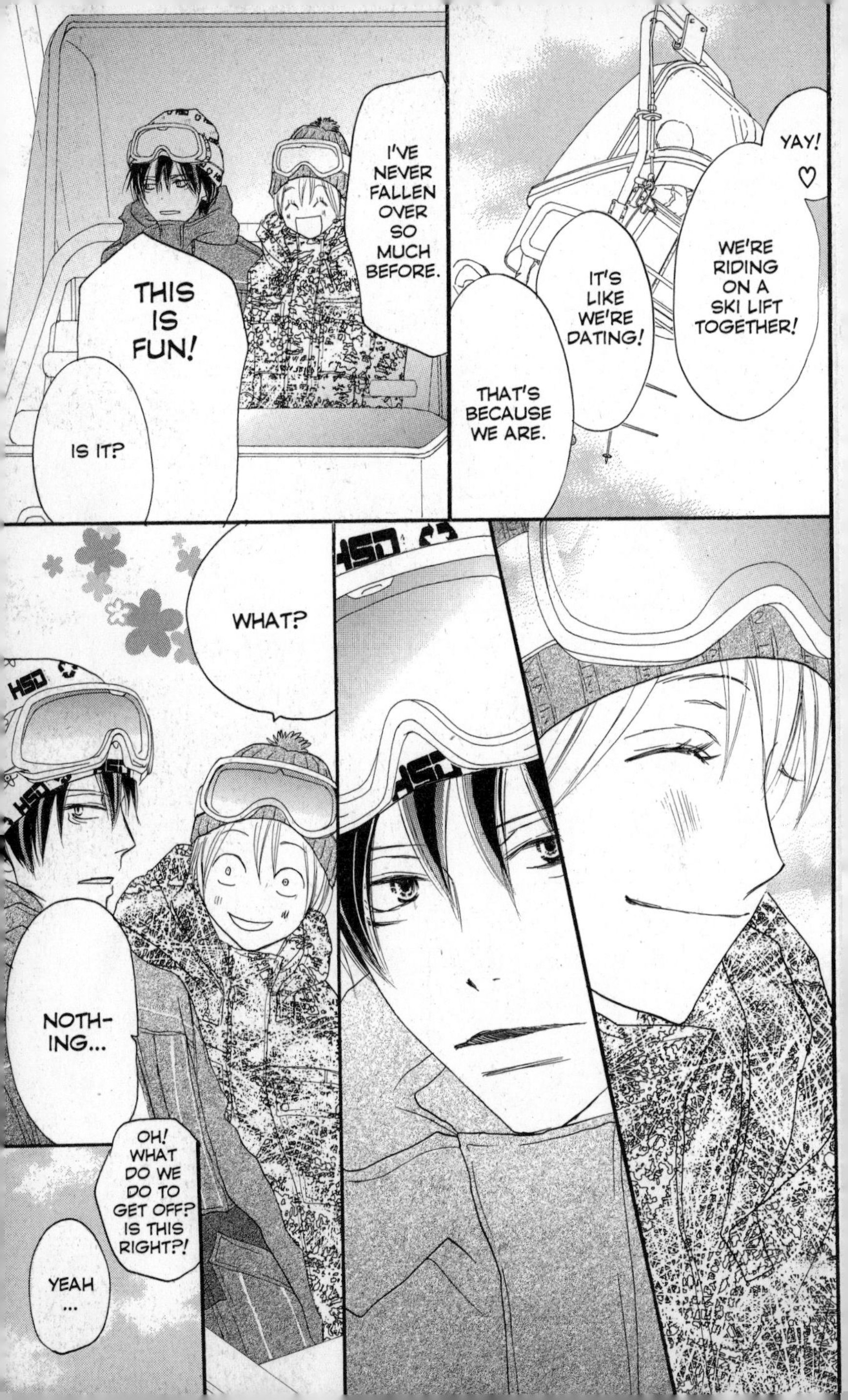
YAY! ♡
WE'RE RIDING ON A SKI LIFT TOGETHER!
IT'S LIKE WE'RE DATING!
THAT'S BECAUSE WE ARE.
I'VE NEVER FALLEN OVER SO MUCH BEFORE.
THIS IS FUN!
IS IT?
WHAT?
NOTH-ING...
OH! WHAT DO WE DO TO GET OFF? IS THIS RIGHT?!
YEAH ...

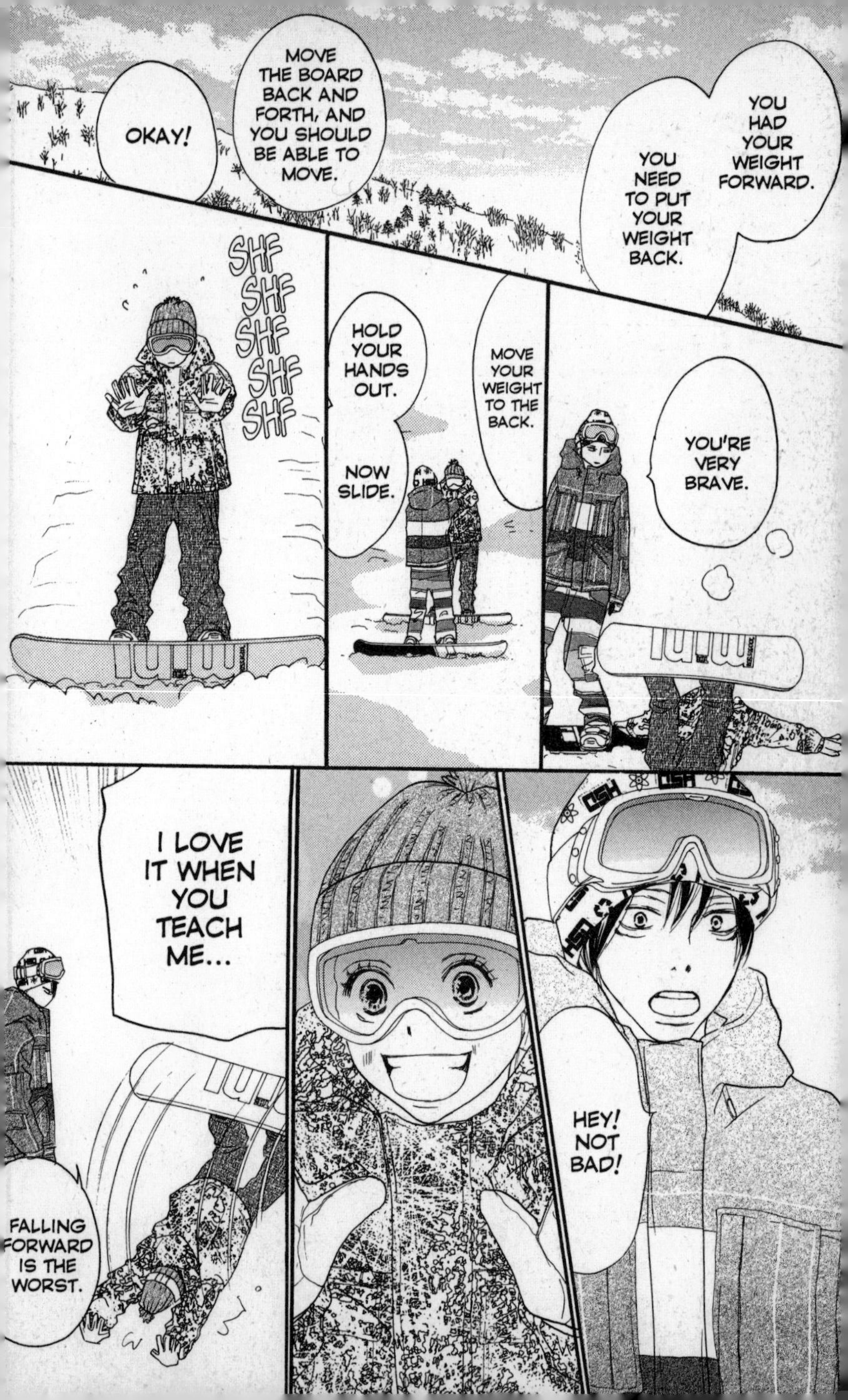
YOU HAD YOUR WEIGHT FORWARD.
YOU NEED TO PUT YOUR WEIGHT BACK.
MOVE THE BOARD BACK AND FORTH, AND YOU SHOULD BE ABLE TO MOVE.
OKAY!
YOU'RE VERY BRAVE.
MOVE YOUR WEIGHT TO THE BACK.
HOLD YOUR HANDS OUT.
NOW SLIDE.
SHF SHF SHF SHF SHF
HEY! NOT BAD!
I LOVE IT WHEN YOU TEACH ME...
FALLING FORWARD IS THE WORST.

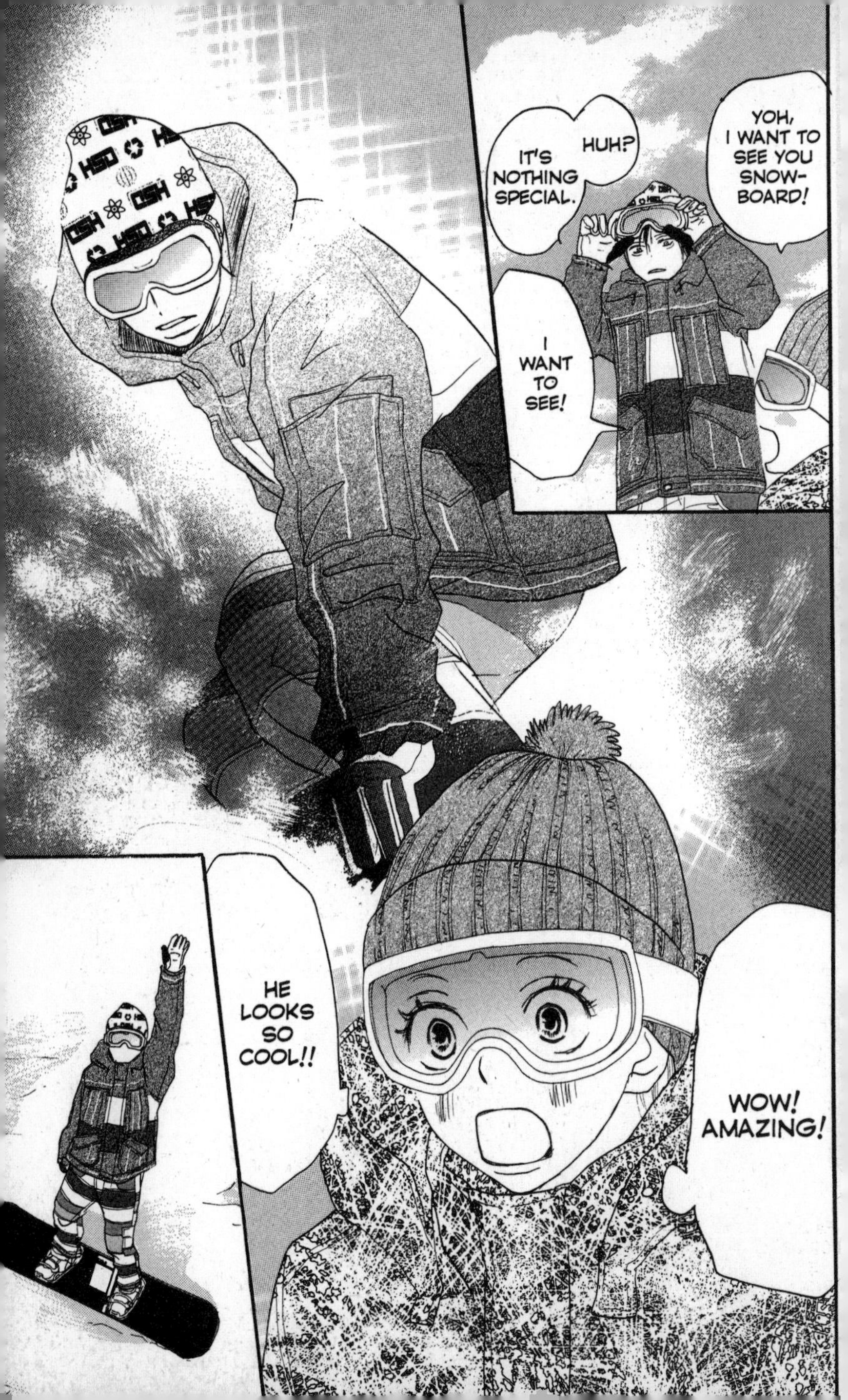
YOH, I WANT TO SEE YOU SNOWBOARD!
HUH?
IT'S NOTHING SPECIAL.
I WANT TO SEE!
WOW! AMAZING!
HE LOOKS SO COOL!!

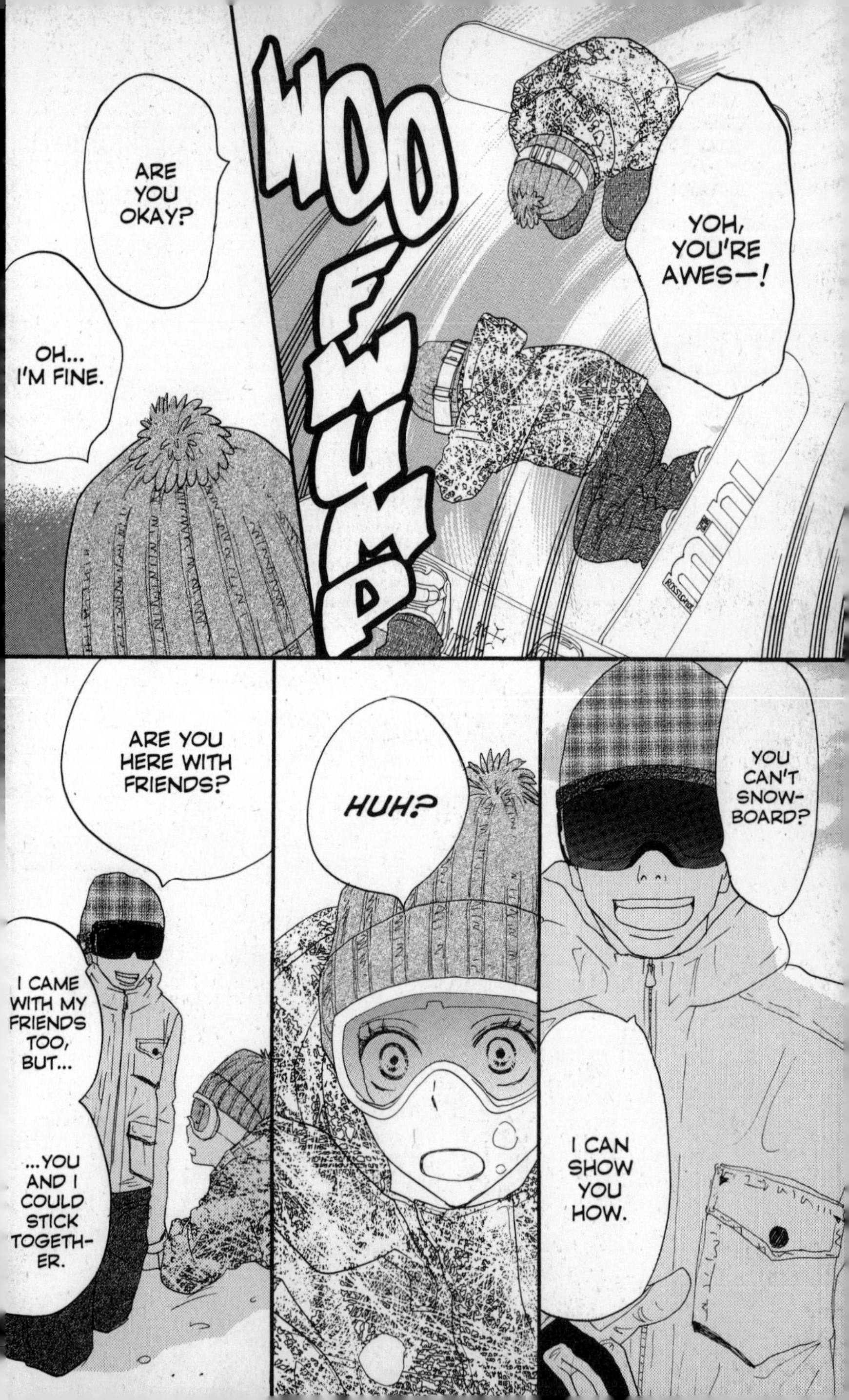
YOH, YOU'RE AWES—!
WOOFWUMP
mini
ARE YOU OKAY?
OH... I'M FINE.
YOU CAN'T SNOWBOARD?
I CAN SHOW YOU HOW.
HUH?
ARE YOU HERE WITH FRIENDS?
I CAME WITH MY FRIENDS TOO, BUT...
...YOU AND I COULD STICK TOGETHER.

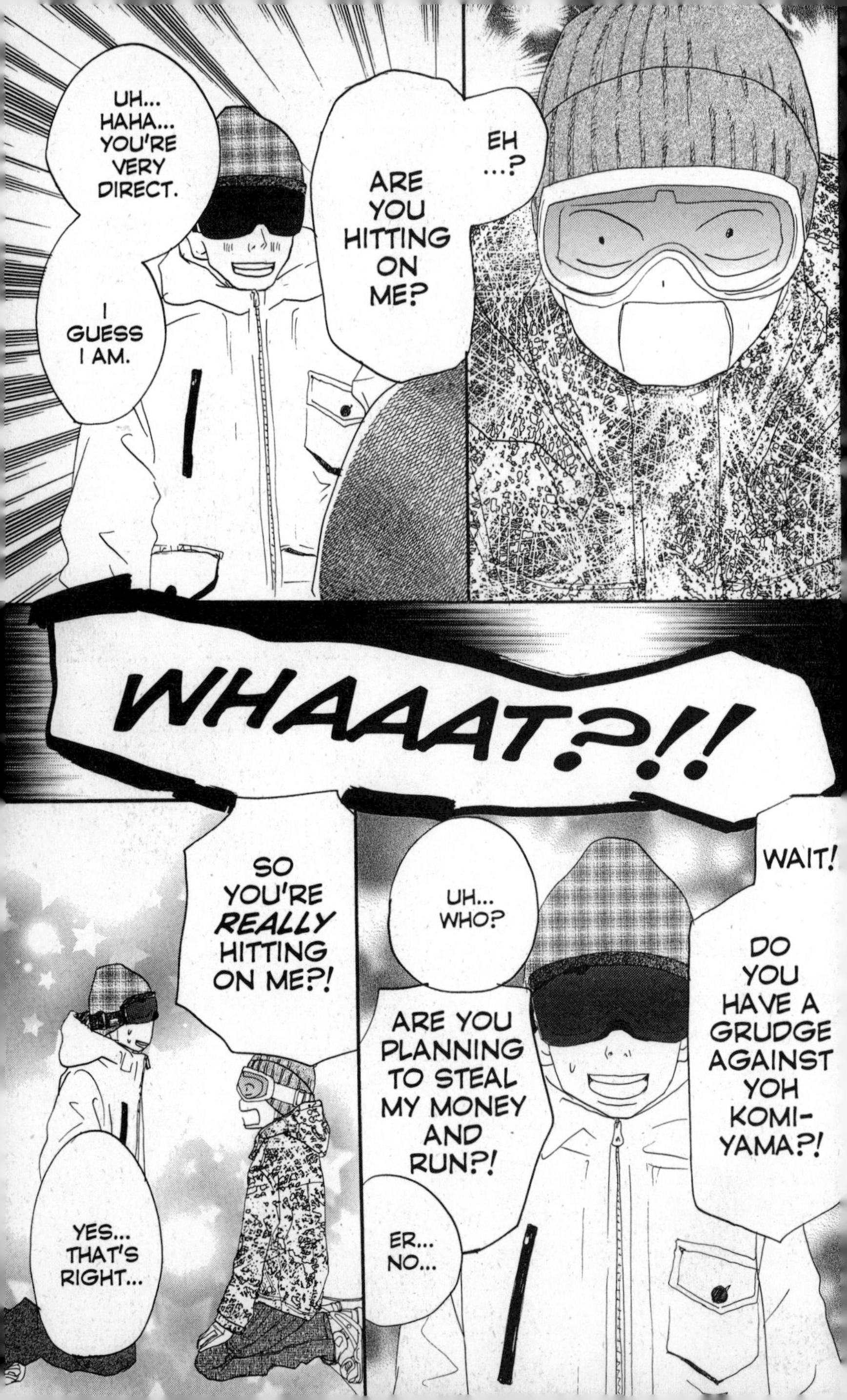
EH ...?
ARE YOU HITTING ON ME?
UH... HAHA... YOU'RE VERY DIRECT.
I GUESS I AM.
WHAAAT?!!
WAIT!
DO YOU HAVE A GRUDGE AGAINST YOH KOMI-YAMA?!
UH... WHO?
ARE YOU PLANNING TO STEAL MY MONEY AND RUN?!
ER... NO...
SO YOU'RE *REALLY* HITTING ON ME?!
YES... THAT'S RIGHT...

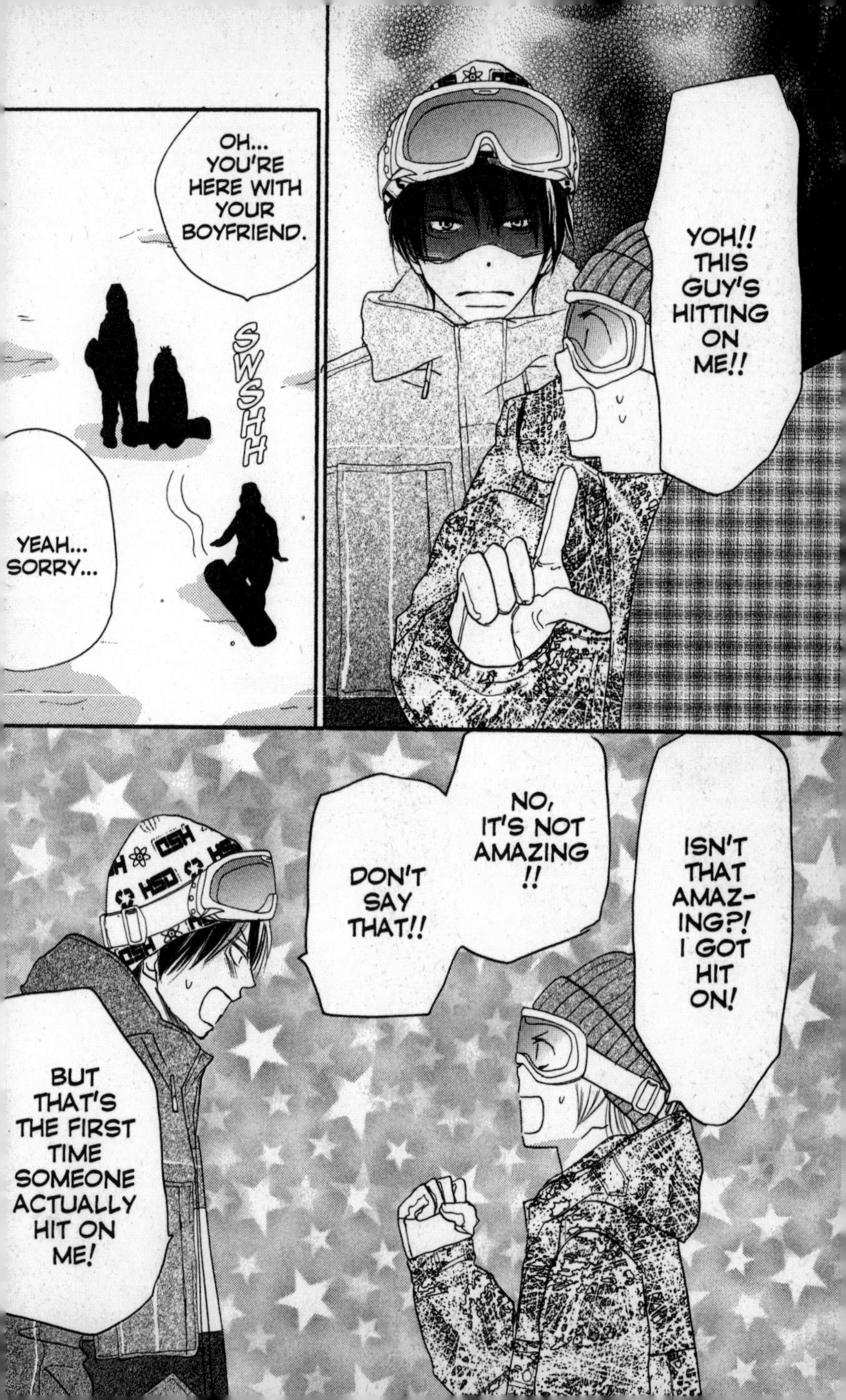
YOH!! THIS GUY'S HITTING ON ME!!
OH... YOU'RE HERE WITH YOUR BOYFRIEND.
SWSHH
YEAH... SORRY...
ISN'T THAT AMAZ-ING?! I GOT HIT ON!
NO, IT'S NOT AMAZING!!
DON'T SAY THAT!!
BUT THAT'S THE FIRST TIME SOMEONE ACTUALLY HIT ON ME!

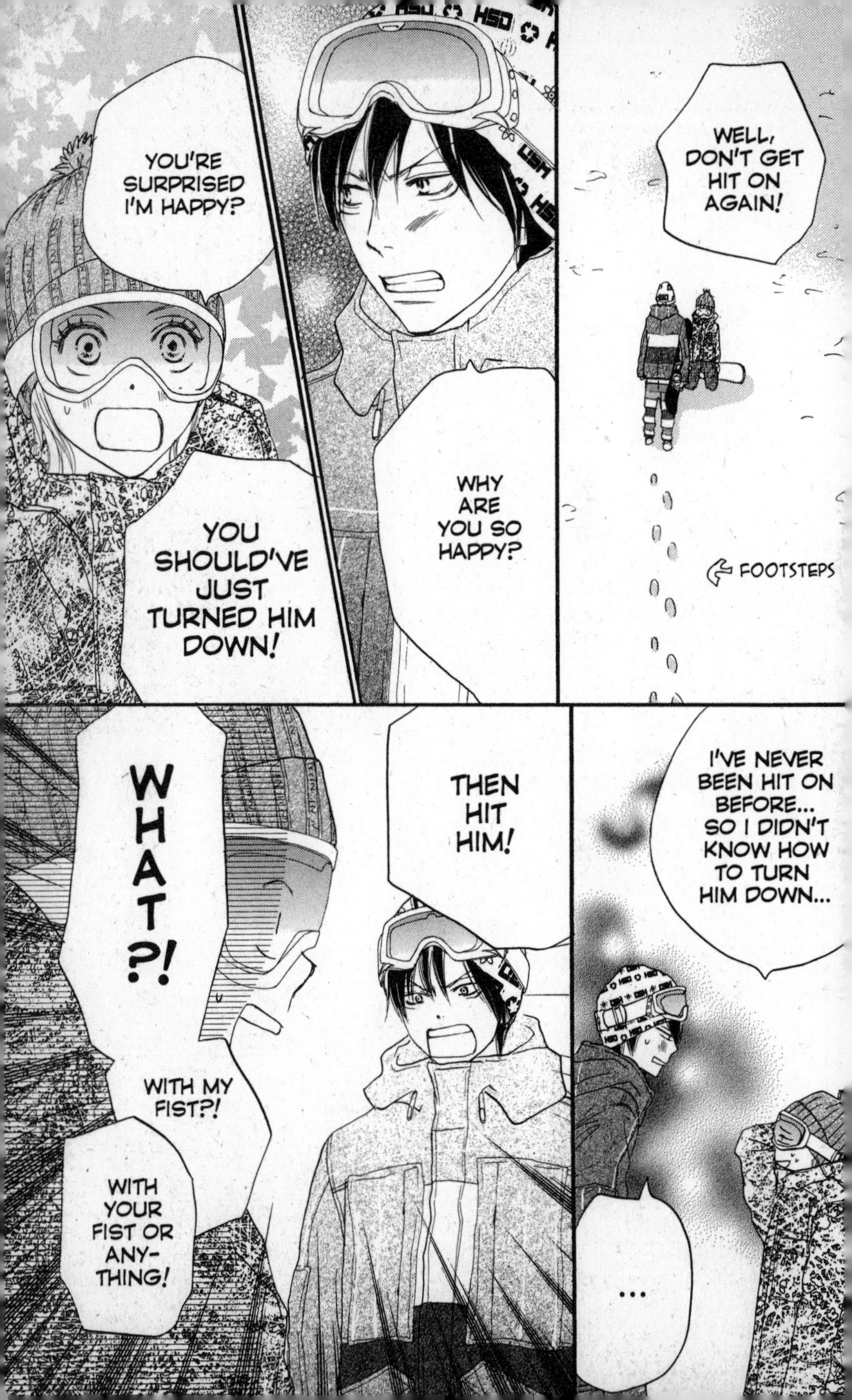
WELL, DON'T GET HIT ON AGAIN!
FOOTSTEPS
WHY ARE YOU SO HAPPY?
YOU'RE SURPRISED I'M HAPPY?
YOU SHOULD'VE JUST TURNED HIM DOWN!
I'VE NEVER BEEN HIT ON BEFORE... SO I DIDN'T KNOW HOW TO TURN HIM DOWN...
...
THEN HIT HIM!
WHAT?!
WITH MY FIST?!
WITH YOUR FIST OR ANYTHING!

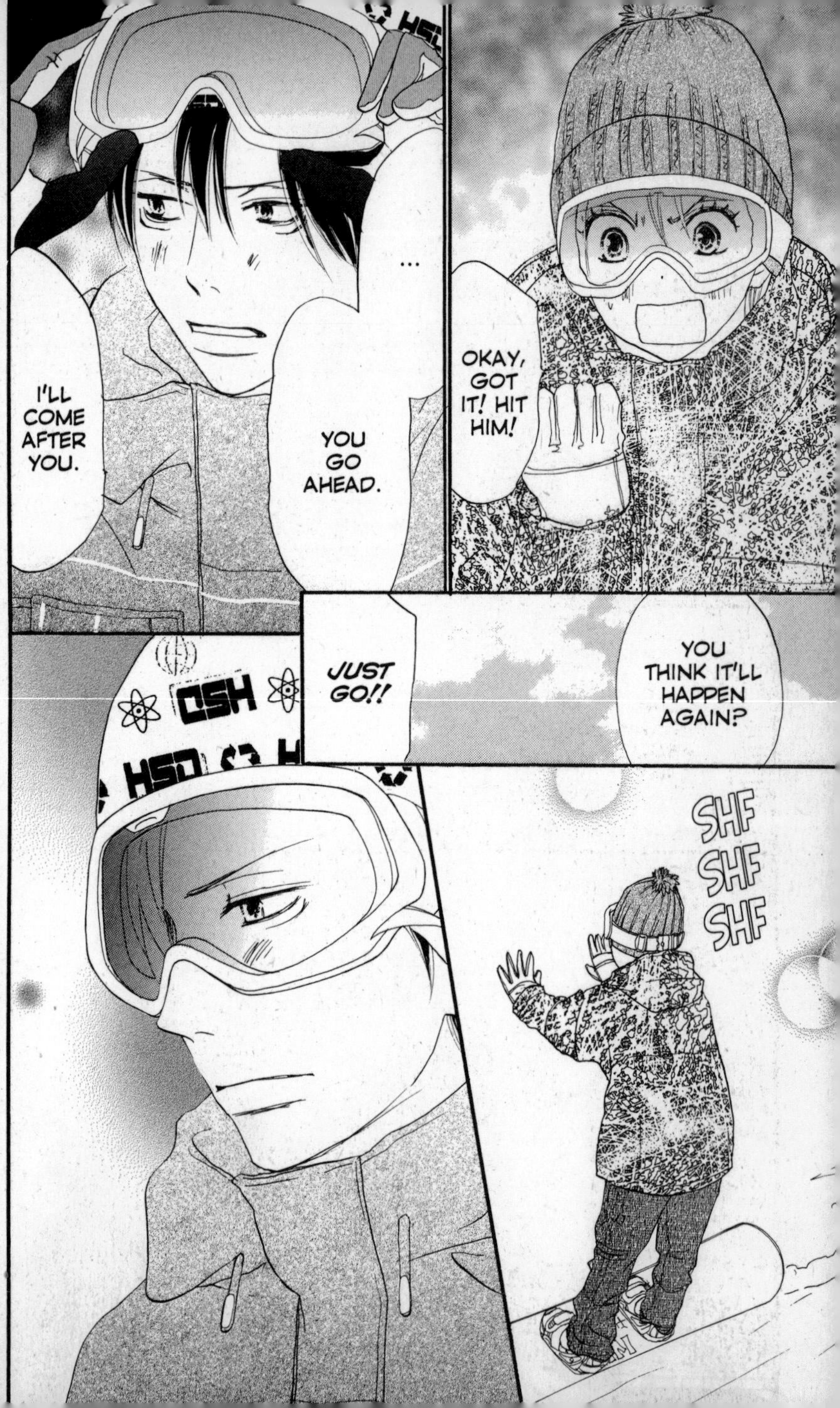
OKAY, GOT IT! HIT HIM!
...
YOU GO AHEAD.
I'LL COME AFTER YOU.
YOU THINK IT'LL HAPPEN AGAIN?
JUST GO!!
SHF SHF SHF

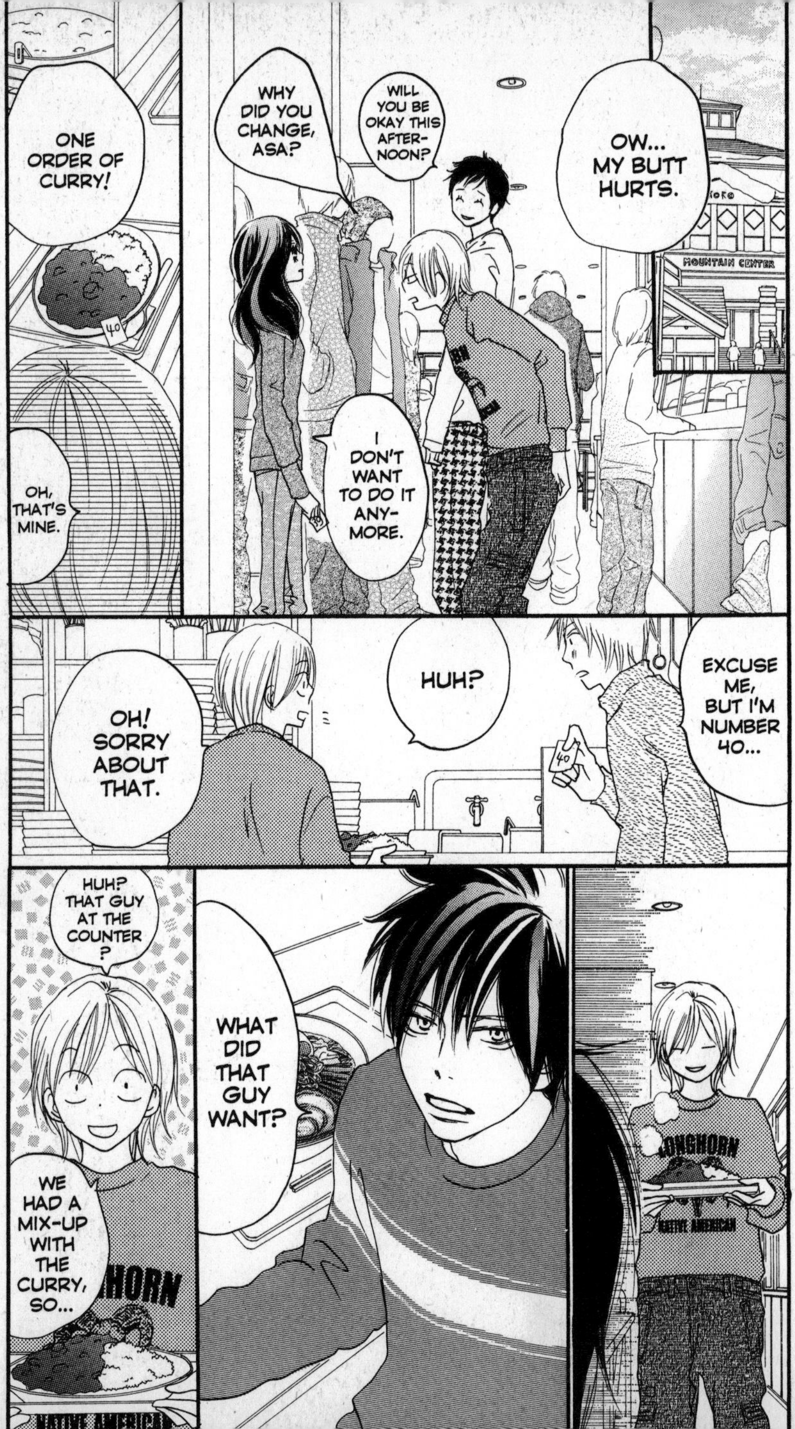

OW... MY BUTT HURTS.
MOUNTAIN CENTER
WILL YOU BE OKAY THIS AFTERNOON?
WHY DID YOU CHANGE, ASA?
I DON'T WANT TO DO IT ANYMORE.
ONE ORDER OF CURRY!
OH, THAT'S MINE.
EXCUSE ME, BUT I'M NUMBER 40...
HUH?
OH! SORRY ABOUT THAT.
LONGHORN
NATIVE AMERICAN
WHAT DID THAT GUY WANT?
HUH? THAT GUY AT THE COUNTER?
WE HAD A MIX-UP WITH THE CURRY, SO...

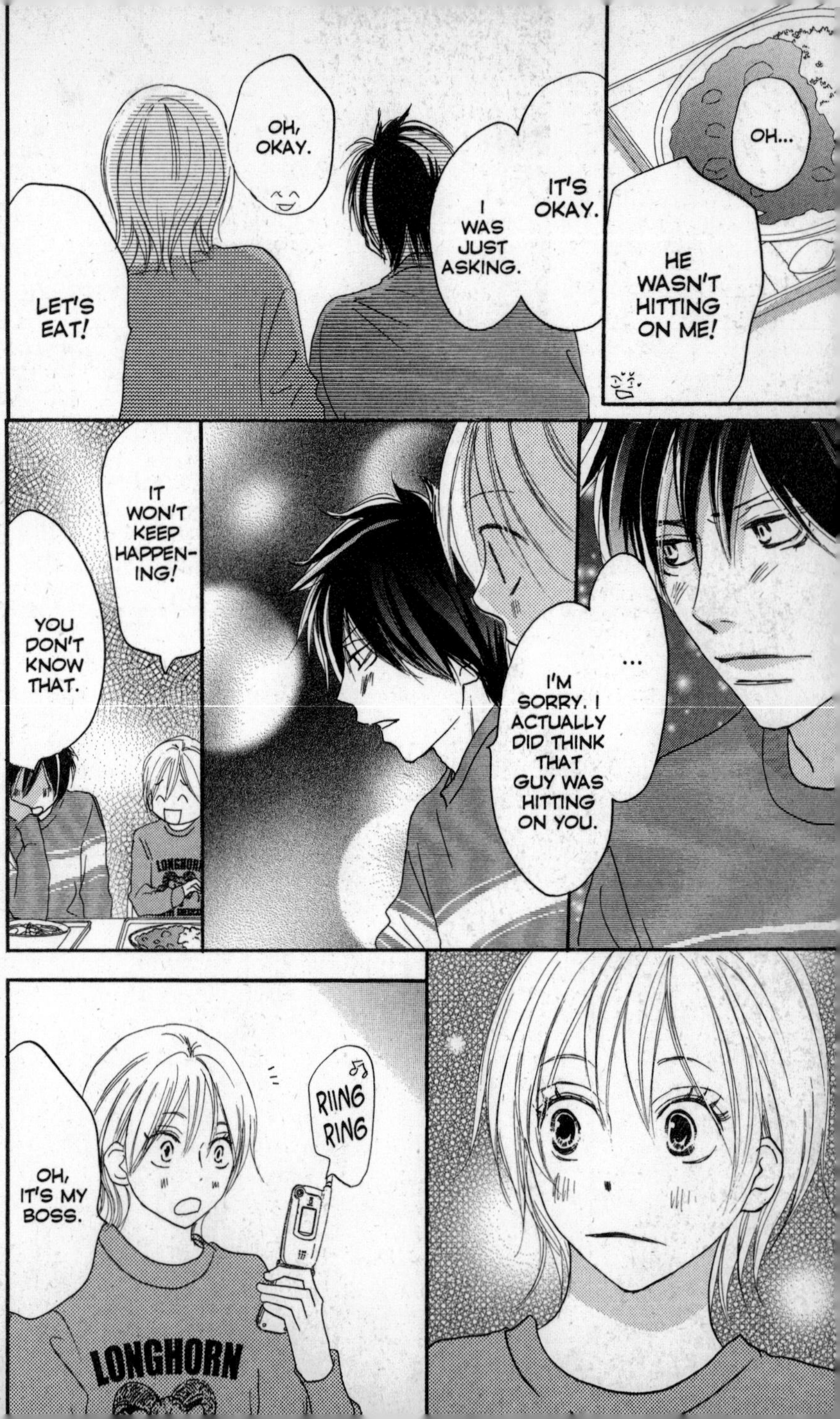
OH...
HE WASN'T HITTING ON ME!
IT'S OKAY. I WAS JUST ASKING.
OH, OKAY.
LET'S EAT!
...
I'M SORRY. I ACTUALLY DID THINK THAT GUY WAS HITTING ON YOU.
IT WON'T KEEP HAPPENING!
YOU DON'T KNOW THAT.
RIING RING
OH, IT'S MY BOSS.
LONGHORN

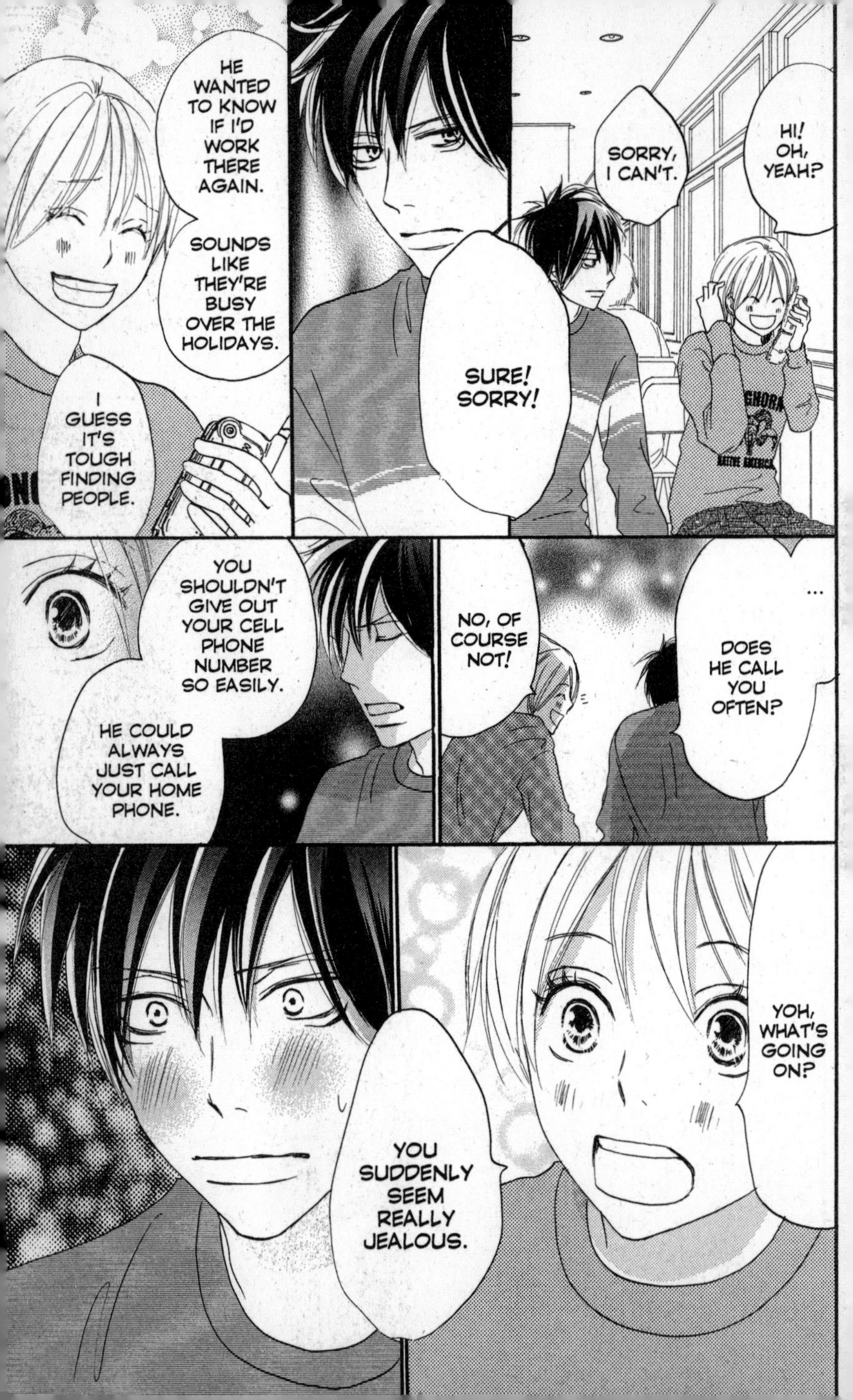
HI! OH, YEAH?
SORRY, I CAN'T.
SURE! SORRY!
HE WANTED TO KNOW IF I'D WORK THERE AGAIN.
SOUNDS LIKE THEY'RE BUSY OVER THE HOLIDAYS.
I GUESS IT'S TOUGH FINDING PEOPLE.
...
DOES HE CALL YOU OFTEN?
NO, OF COURSE NOT!
YOU SHOULDN'T GIVE OUT YOUR CELL PHONE NUMBER SO EASILY.
HE COULD ALWAYS JUST CALL YOUR HOME PHONE.
YOH, WHAT'S GOING ON?
YOU SUDDENLY SEEM REALLY JEALOUS.

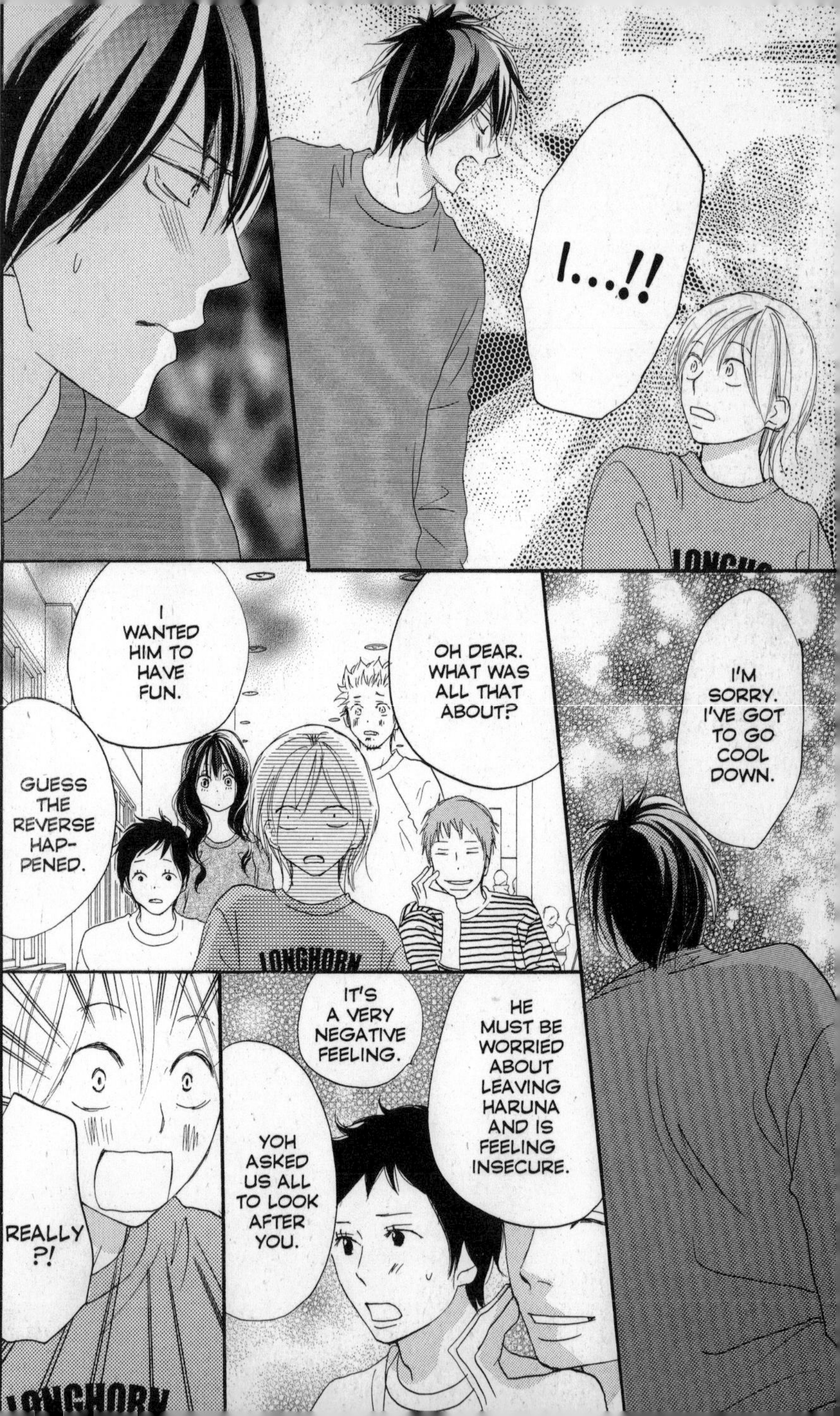
I...!!
I'M SORRY. I'VE GOT TO GO COOL DOWN.
OH DEAR. WHAT WAS ALL THAT ABOUT?
I WANTED HIM TO HAVE FUN.
GUESS THE REVERSE HAP-PENED.
HE MUST BE WORRIED ABOUT LEAVING HARUNA AND IS FEELING INSECURE.
IT'S A VERY NEGATIVE FEELING.
YOH ASKED US ALL TO LOOK AFTER YOU.
REALLY?!

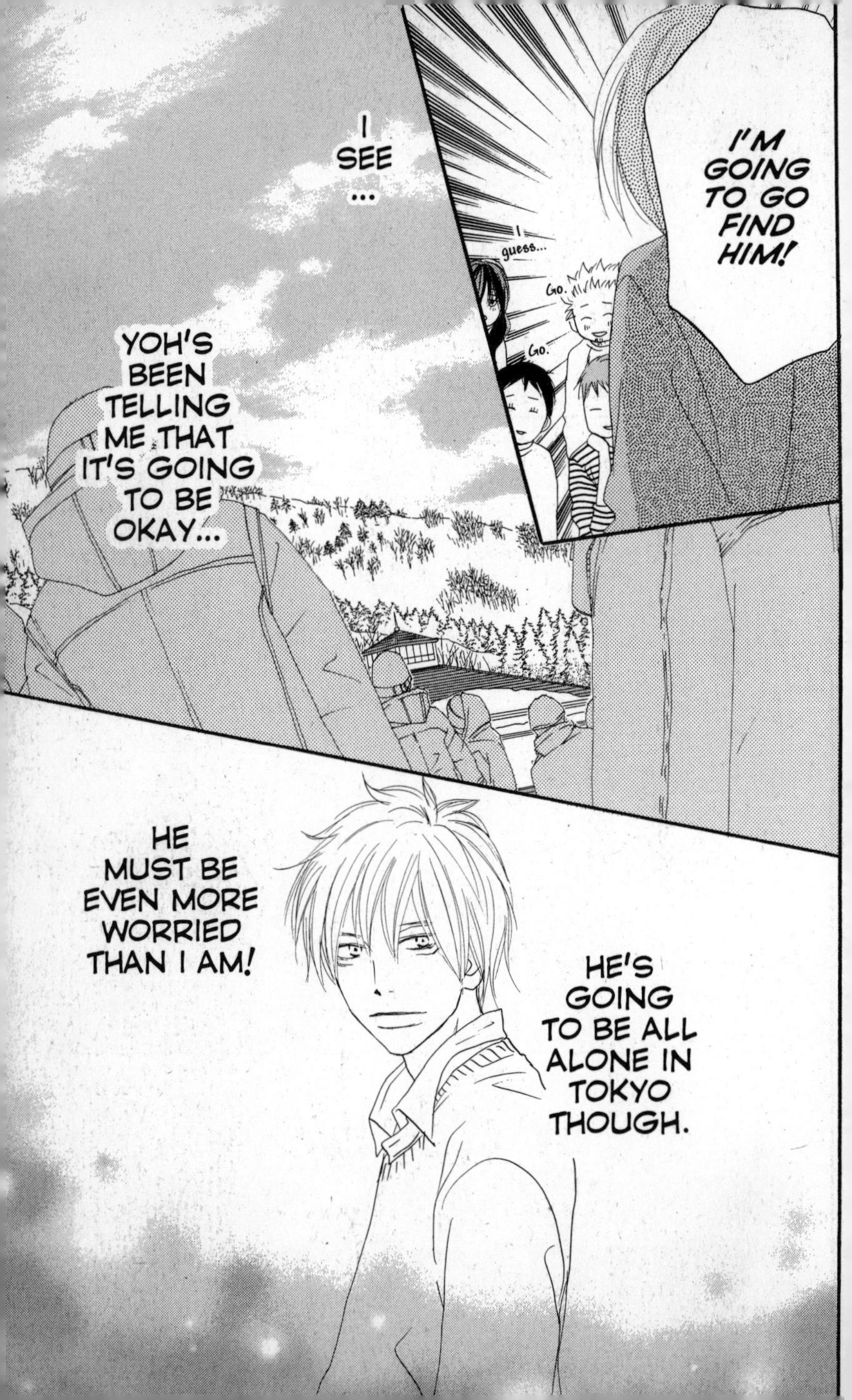
I'M GOING TO GO FIND HIM!
I guess...
Go.
Go.
I SEE...
YOH'S BEEN TELLING ME THAT IT'S GOING TO BE OKAY...
HE'S GOING TO BE ALL ALONE IN TOKYO THOUGH.
HE MUST BE EVEN MORE WORRIED THAN I AM!

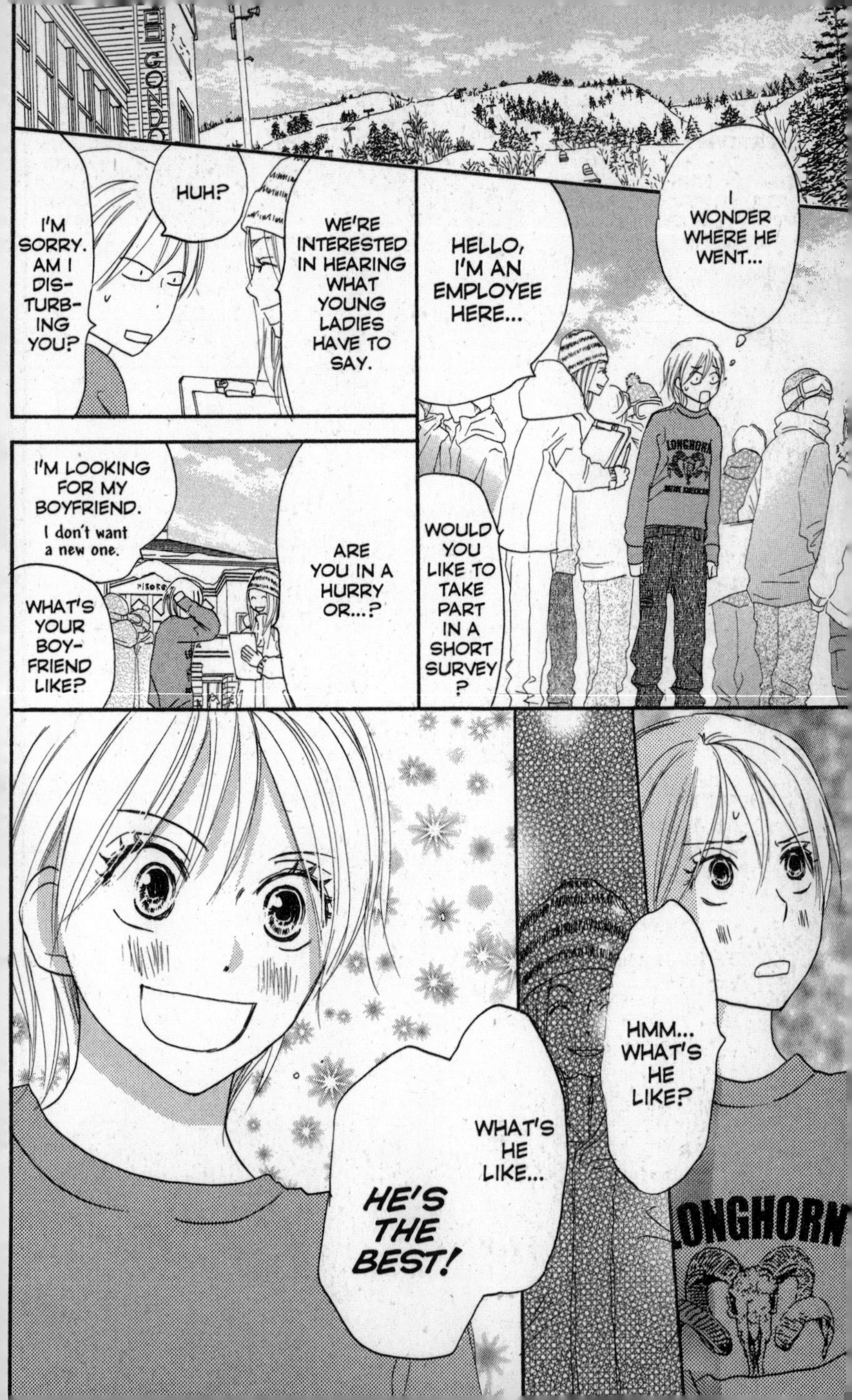

I WONDER WHERE HE WENT...
HELLO, I'M AN EMPLOYEE HERE...
WOULD YOU LIKE TO TAKE PART IN A SHORT SURVEY?
LONGHORN
WE'RE INTERESTED IN HEARING WHAT YOUNG LADIES HAVE TO SAY.
HUH?
I'M SORRY. AM I DISTURBING YOU?
ARE YOU IN A HURRY OR...?
I'M LOOKING FOR MY BOYFRIEND.
I don't want a new one.
WHAT'S YOUR BOYFRIEND LIKE?
HMM... WHAT'S HE LIKE?
LONGHORN
WHAT'S HE LIKE...
HE'S THE BEST!

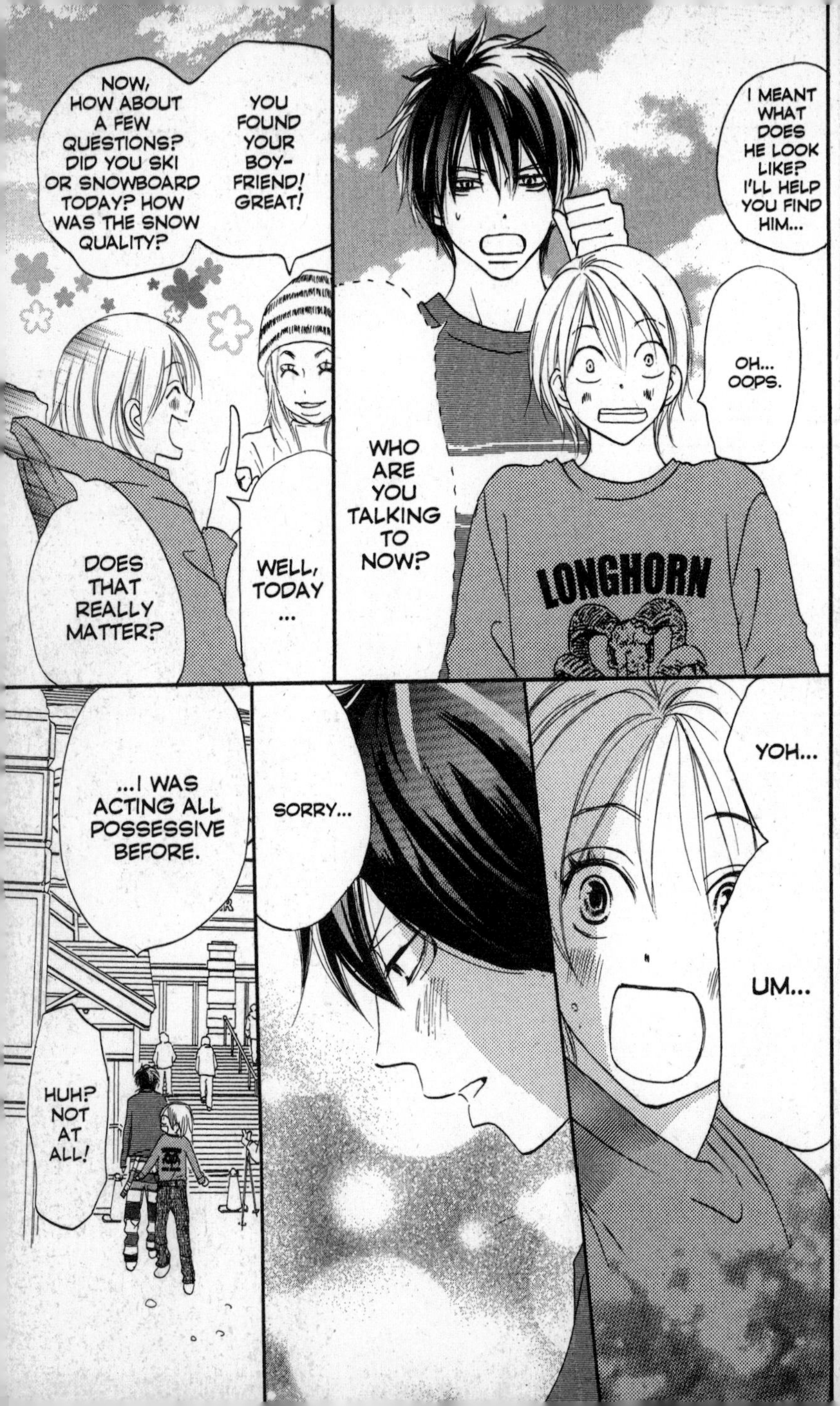
I MEANT WHAT DOES HE LOOK LIKE? I'LL HELP YOU FIND HIM...
OH... OOPS.
WHO ARE YOU TALKING TO NOW?
YOU FOUND YOUR BOY-FRIEND! GREAT!
NOW, HOW ABOUT A FEW QUESTIONS? DID YOU SKI OR SNOWBOARD TODAY? HOW WAS THE SNOW QUALITY?
WELL, TODAY ...
DOES THAT REALLY MATTER?
LONGHORN
YOH...
UM...
SORRY...
...I WAS ACTING ALL POSSESSIVE BEFORE.
HUH? NOT AT ALL!

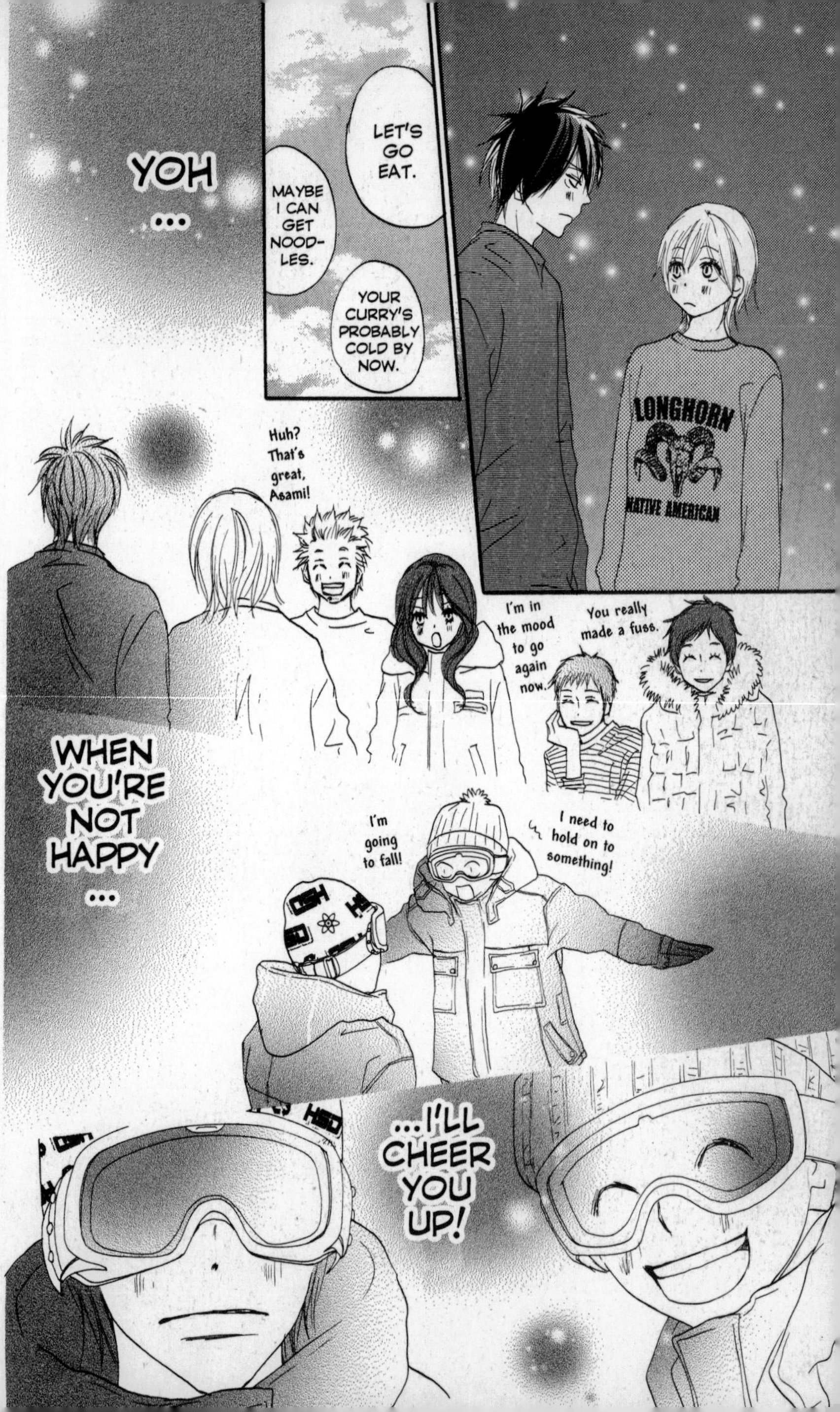
LET'S GO EAT.
YOUR CURRY'S PROBABLY COLD BY NOW.
MAYBE I CAN GET NOOD-LES.
YOH ...
You really made a fuss.
I'm in the mood to go again now.
Huh? That's great, Asami!
I need to hold on to something!
I'm going to fall!
WHEN YOU'RE NOT HAPPY ...
...I'LL CHEER YOU UP!

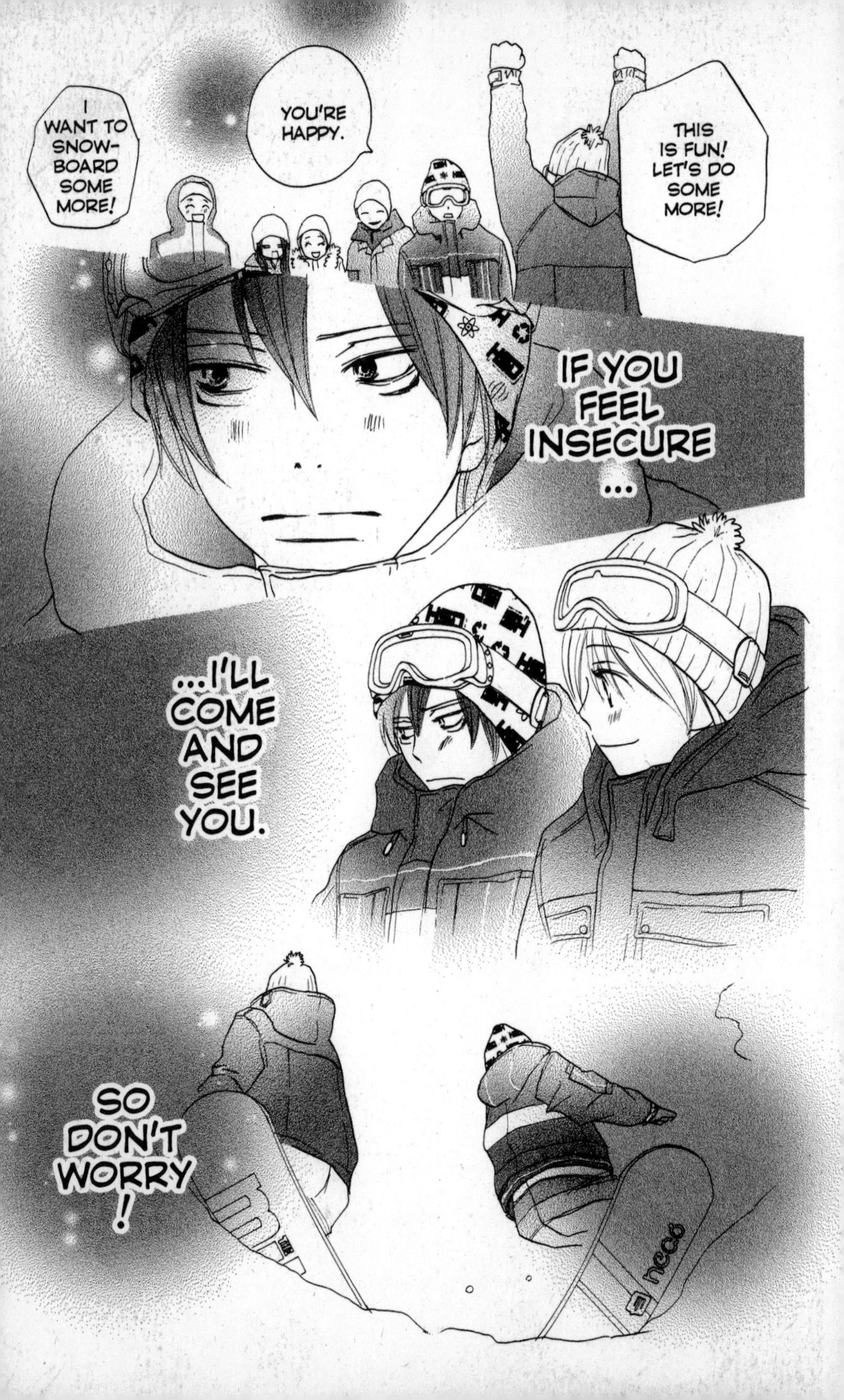
THIS IS FUN! LET'S DO SOME MORE!
YOU'RE HAPPY.
I WANT TO SNOW-BOARD SOME MORE!
IF YOU FEEL INSECURE ...
...I'LL COME AND SEE YOU.
SO DON'T WORRY!

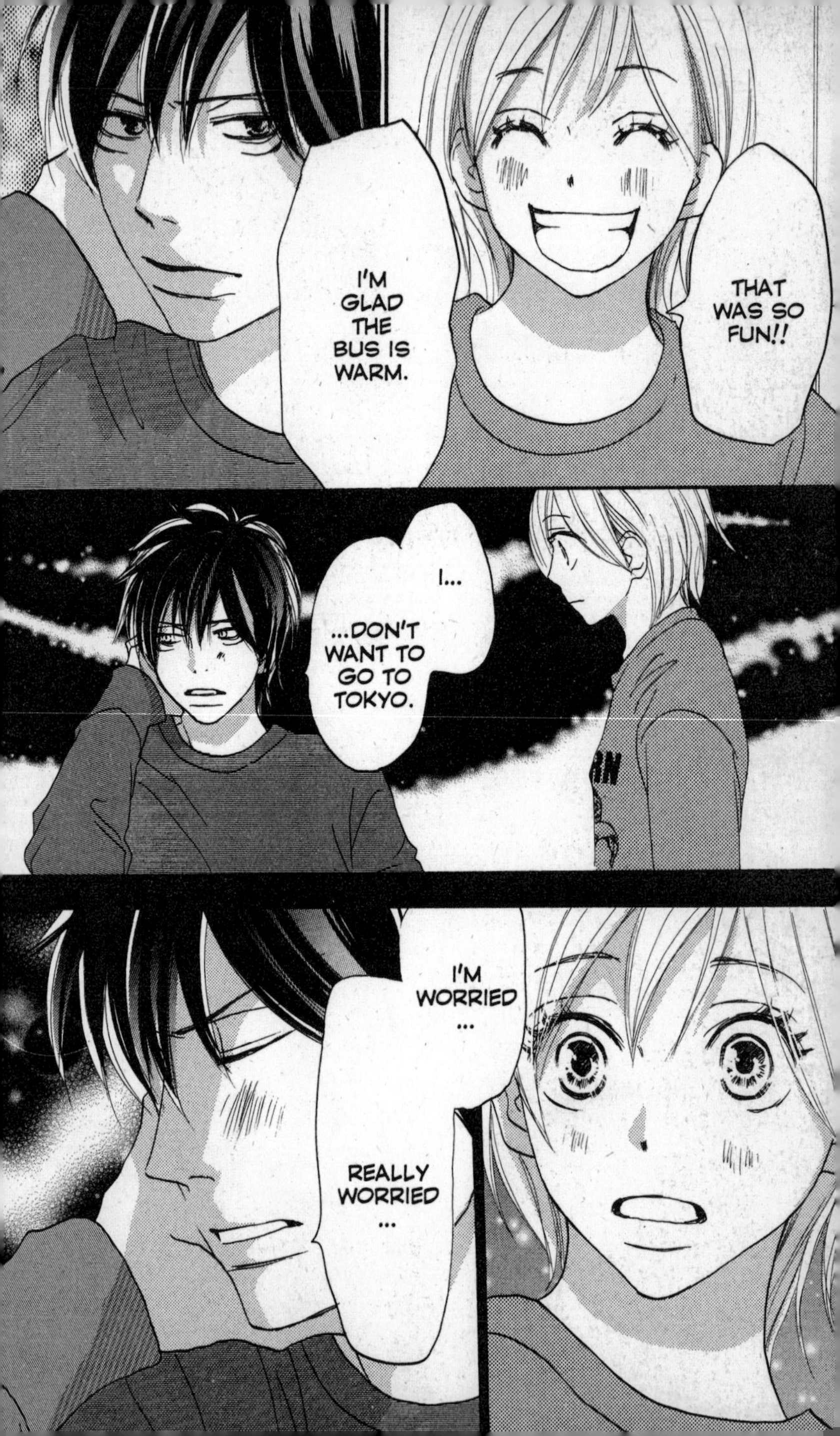
THAT WAS SO FUN!!
I'M GLAD THE BUS IS WARM.
I...
...DON'T WANT TO GO TO TOKYO.
I'M WORRIED ...
REALLY WORRIED ...

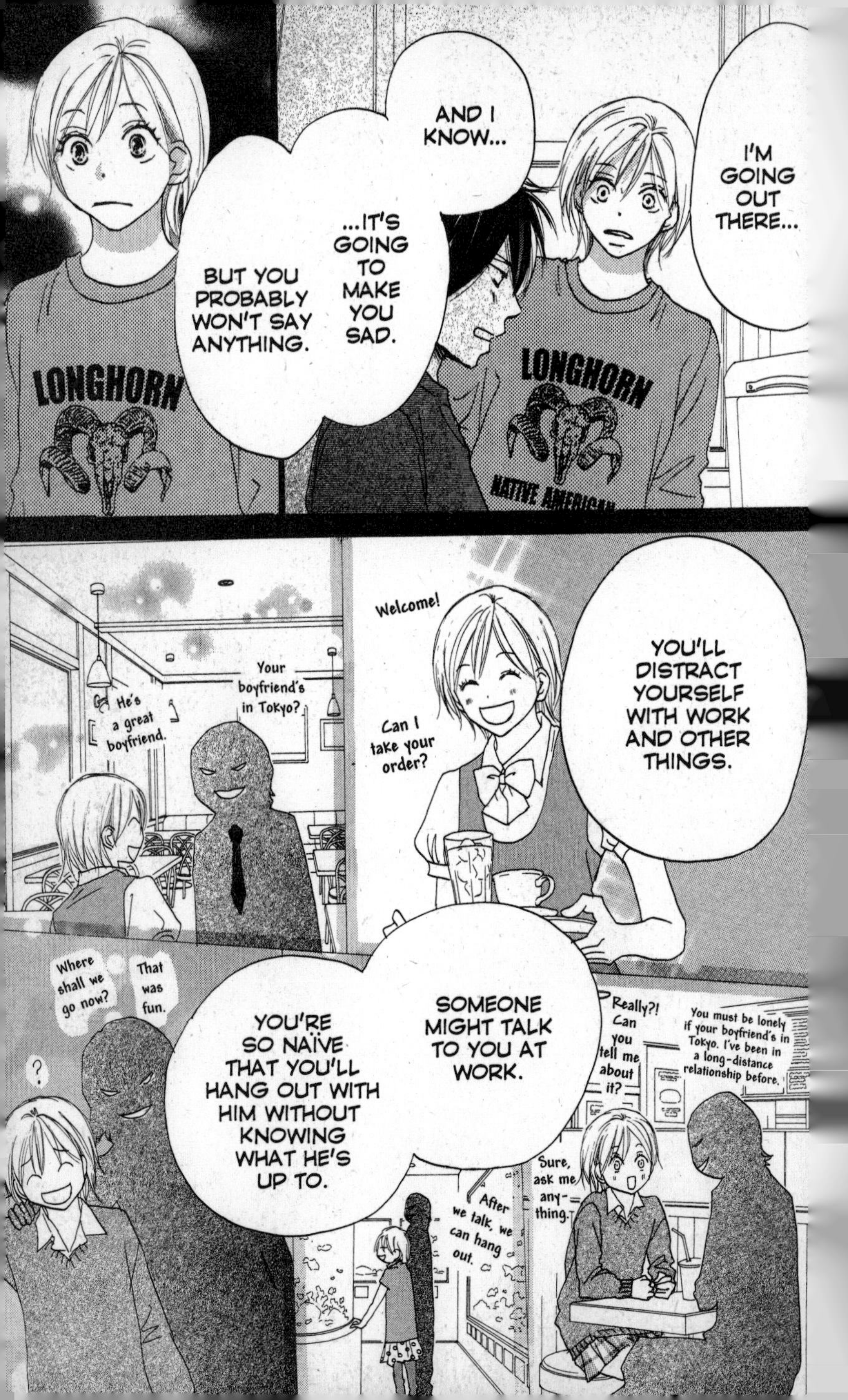
I'M GOING OUT THERE...
AND I KNOW...
...IT'S GOING TO MAKE YOU SAD.
BUT YOU PROBABLY WON'T SAY ANYTHING.
LONGHORN
LONGHORN
YOU'LL DISTRACT YOURSELF WITH WORK AND OTHER THINGS.
Welcome!
Can I take your order?
Your boyfriend's in Tokyo?
He's a great boyfriend.
SOMEONE MIGHT TALK TO YOU AT WORK.
You must be lonely if your boyfriend's in Tokyo. I've been in a long-distance relationship before.
Really?! Can you tell me about it?
Sure, ask me anything.
After we talk, we can hang out.
YOU'RE SO NAÏVE THAT YOU'LL HANG OUT WITH HIM WITHOUT KNOWING WHAT HE'S UP TO.
That was fun.
Where shall we go now?
?

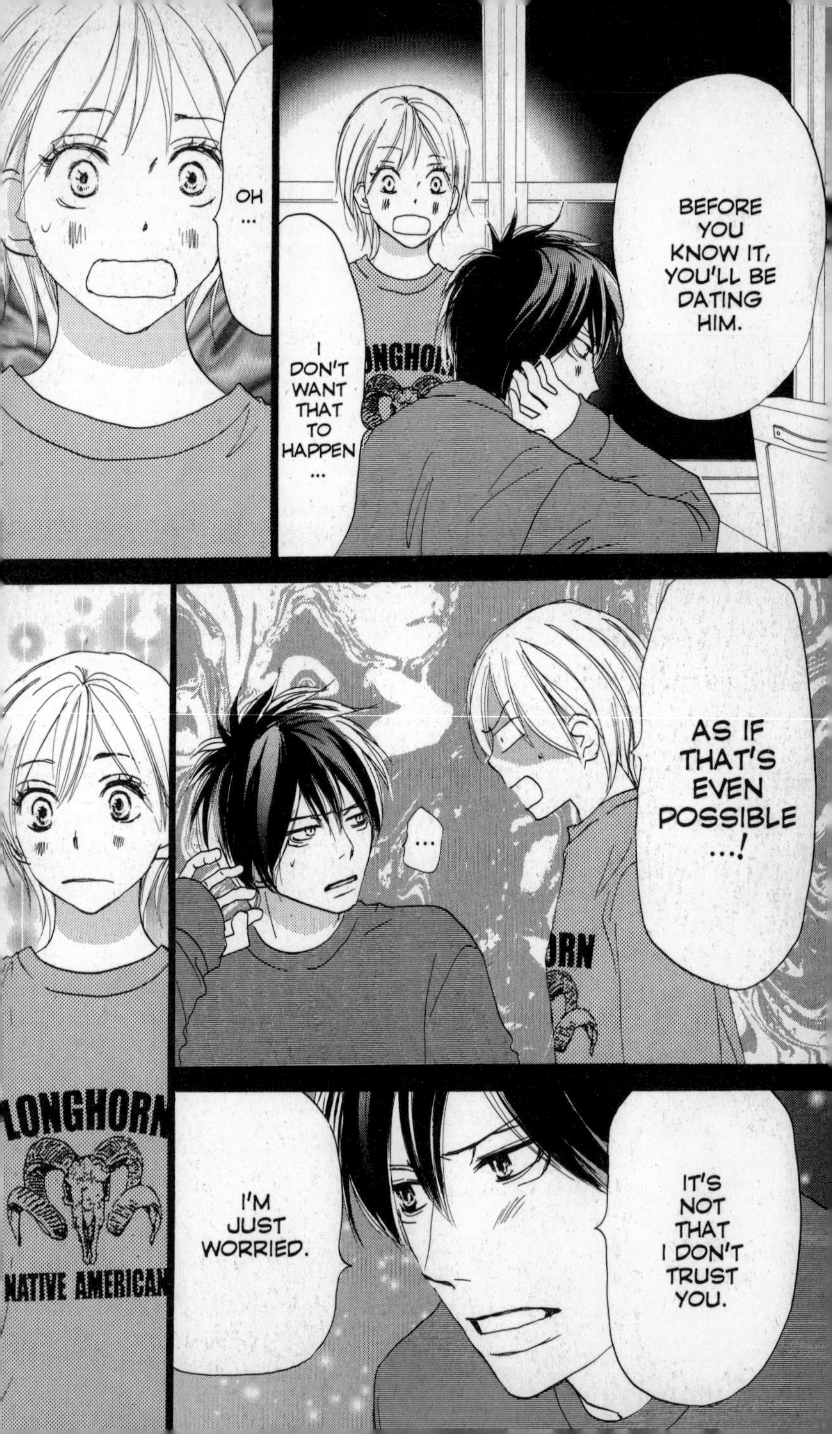
BEFORE YOU KNOW IT, YOU'LL BE DATING HIM.
I DON'T WANT THAT TO HAPPEN ...
OH ...
AS IF THAT'S EVEN POSSIBLE ...!
...
IT'S NOT THAT I DON'T TRUST YOU.
I'M JUST WORRIED.
LONGHORN
NATIVE AMERICAN

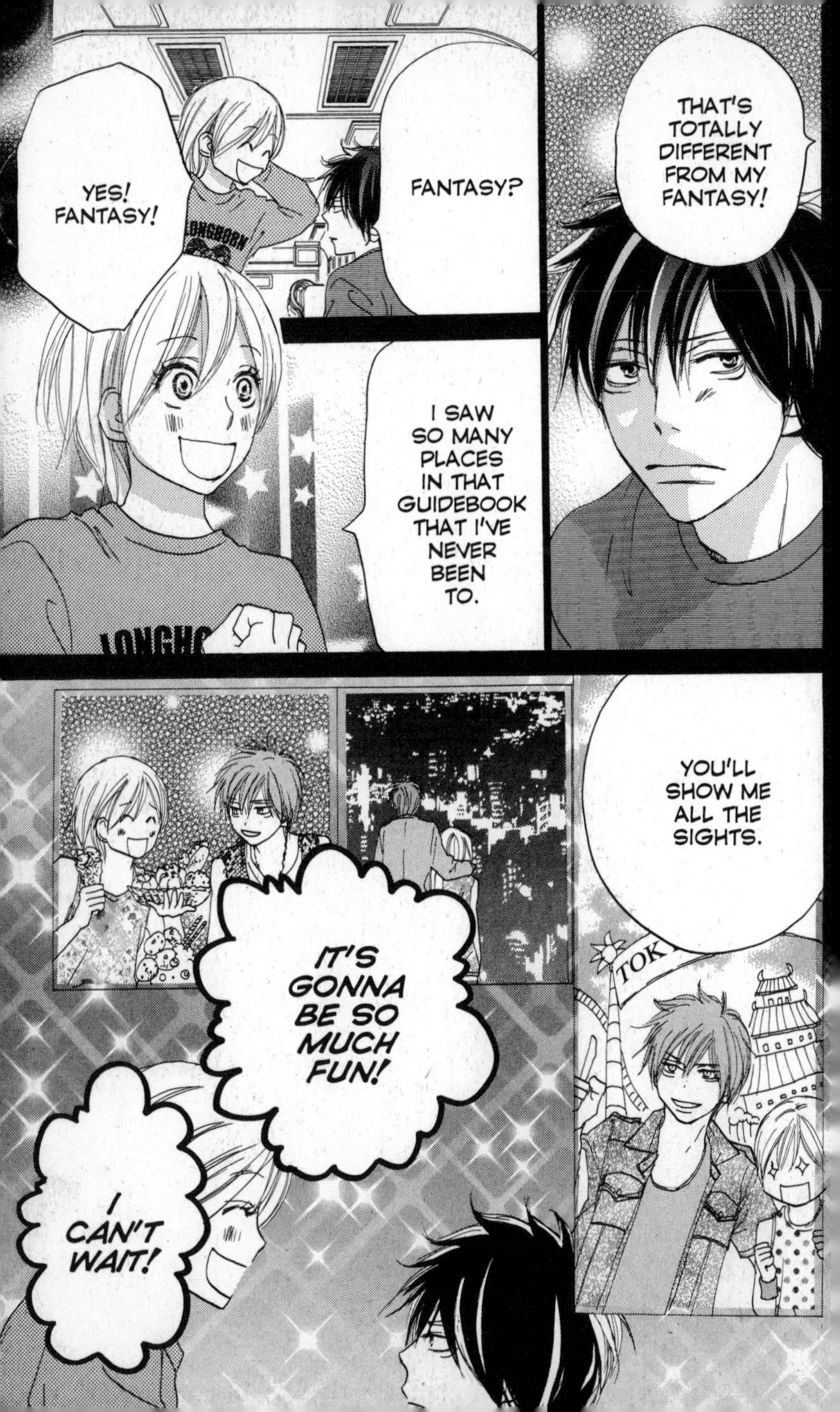

THAT'S TOTALLY DIFFERENT FROM MY FANTASY!
FANTASY?
YES! FANTASY!
LONGHORN
I SAW SO MANY PLACES IN THAT GUIDEBOOK THAT I'VE NEVER BEEN TO.
YOU'LL SHOW ME ALL THE SIGHTS.
IT'S GONNA BE SO MUCH FUN!
I CAN'T WAIT!

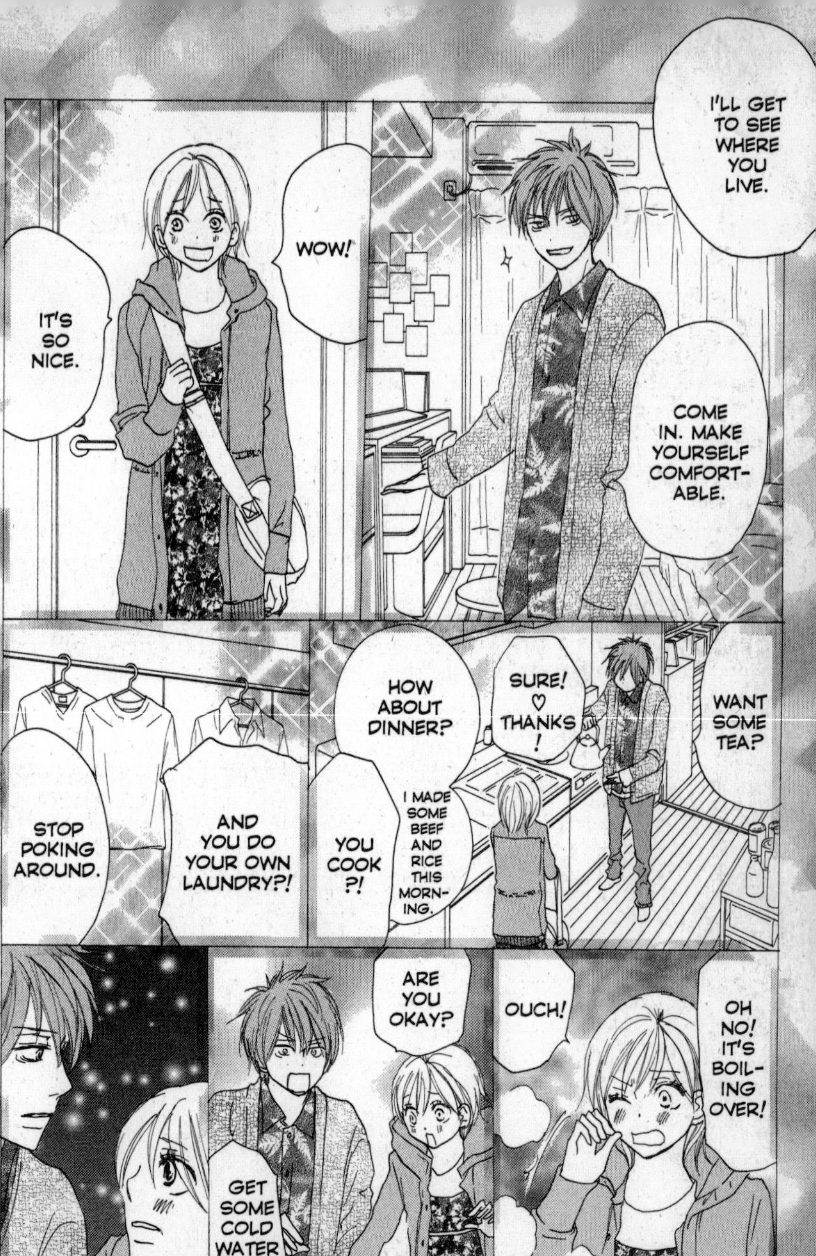
I'LL GET TO SEE WHERE YOU LIVE.
COME IN. MAKE YOURSELF COMFORT-ABLE.
WOW!
IT'S SO NICE.
WANT SOME TEA?
SURE! ♡ THANKS!
HOW ABOUT DINNER?
I MADE SOME BEEF AND RICE THIS MORN-ING.
YOU COOK?!
AND YOU DO YOUR OWN LAUNDRY?!
STOP POKING AROUND.
OH NO! IT'S BOIL-ING OVER!
OUCH!
ARE YOU OKAY?
GET SOME COLD WATER ON IT!

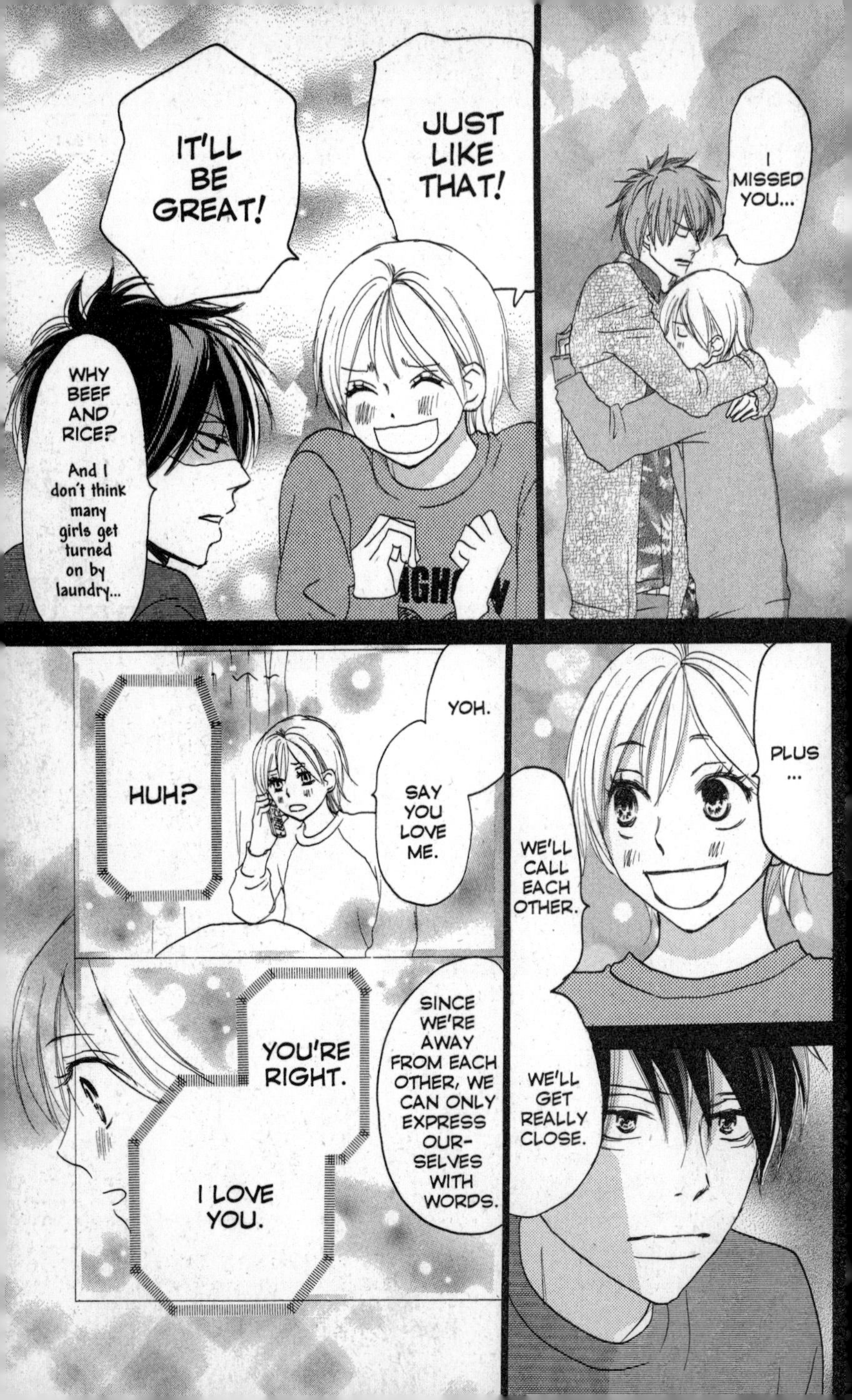
I MISSED YOU...
JUST LIKE THAT!
IT'LL BE GREAT!
WHY BEEF AND RICE?
And I don't think many girls get turned on by laundry...
PLUS ...
WE'LL CALL EACH OTHER.
WE'LL GET REALLY CLOSE.
YOH.
SAY YOU LOVE ME.
HUH?
SINCE WE'RE AWAY FROM EACH OTHER, WE CAN ONLY EXPRESS OUR-SELVES WITH WORDS.
YOU'RE RIGHT.
I LOVE YOU.

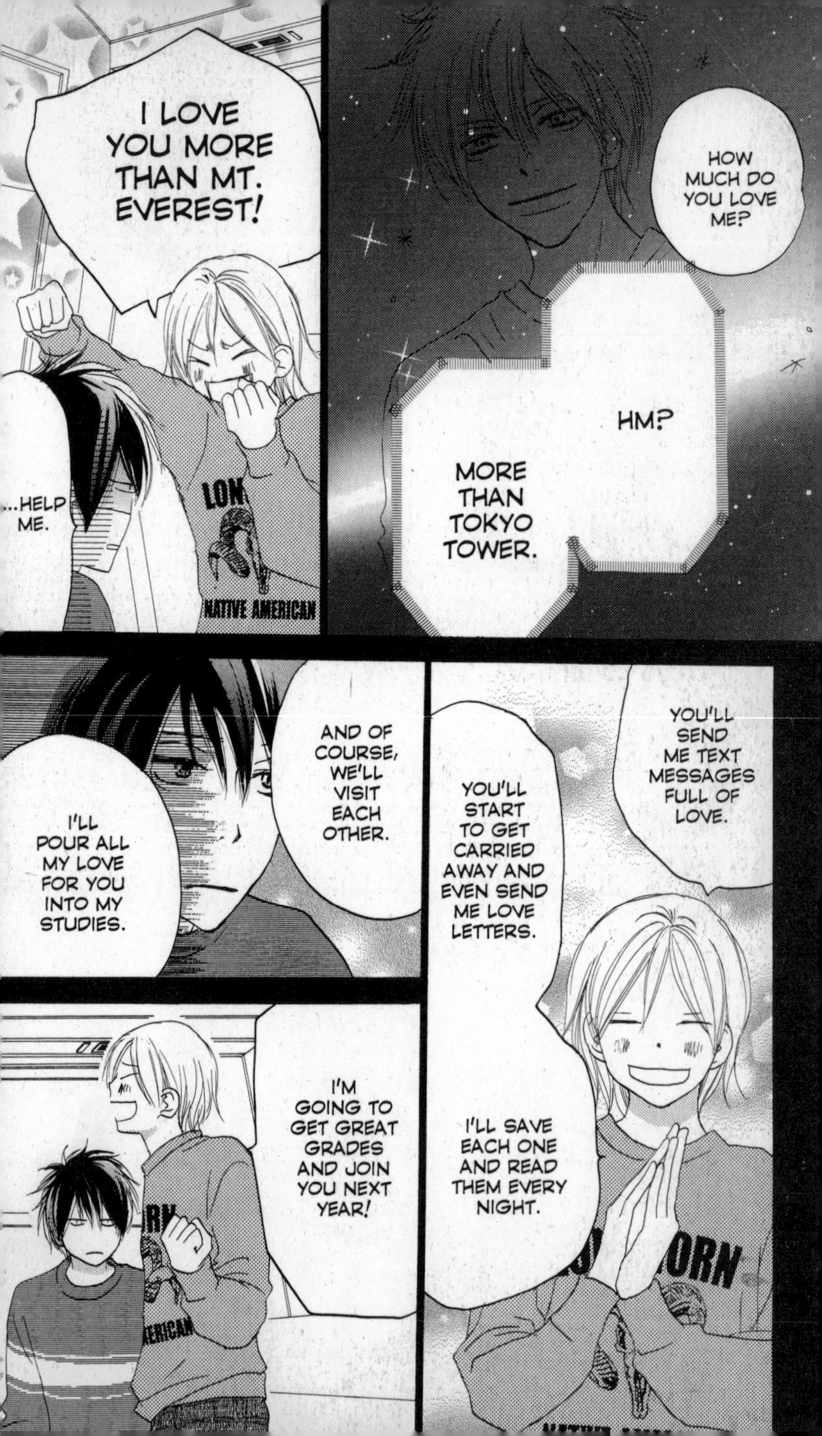
HOW MUCH DO YOU LOVE ME?
HM?
MORE THAN TOKYO TOWER.
I LOVE YOU MORE THAN MT. EVEREST!
...HELP ME.
NATIVE AMERICAN
YOU'LL SEND ME TEXT MESSAGES FULL OF LOVE.
YOU'LL START TO GET CARRIED AWAY AND EVEN SEND ME LOVE LETTERS.
I'LL SAVE EACH ONE AND READ THEM EVERY NIGHT.
AND OF COURSE, WE'LL VISIT EACH OTHER.
I'LL POUR ALL MY LOVE FOR YOU INTO MY STUDIES.
I'M GOING TO GET GREAT GRADES AND JOIN YOU NEXT YEAR!

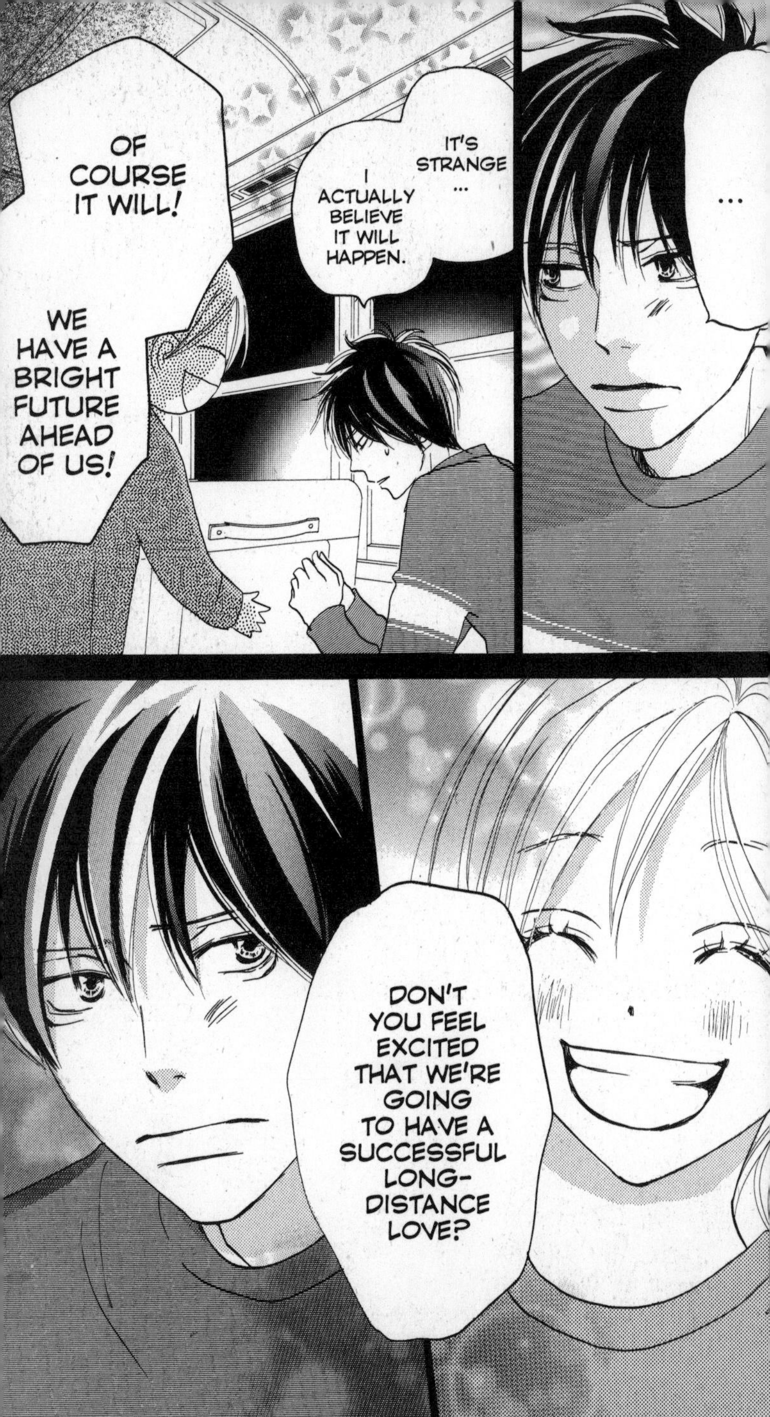
...
IT'S STRANGE...
I ACTUALLY BELIEVE IT WILL HAPPEN.
OF COURSE IT WILL!
WE HAVE A BRIGHT FUTURE AHEAD OF US!
DON'T YOU FEEL EXCITED THAT WE'RE GOING TO HAVE A SUCCESSFUL LONG-DISTANCE LOVE?

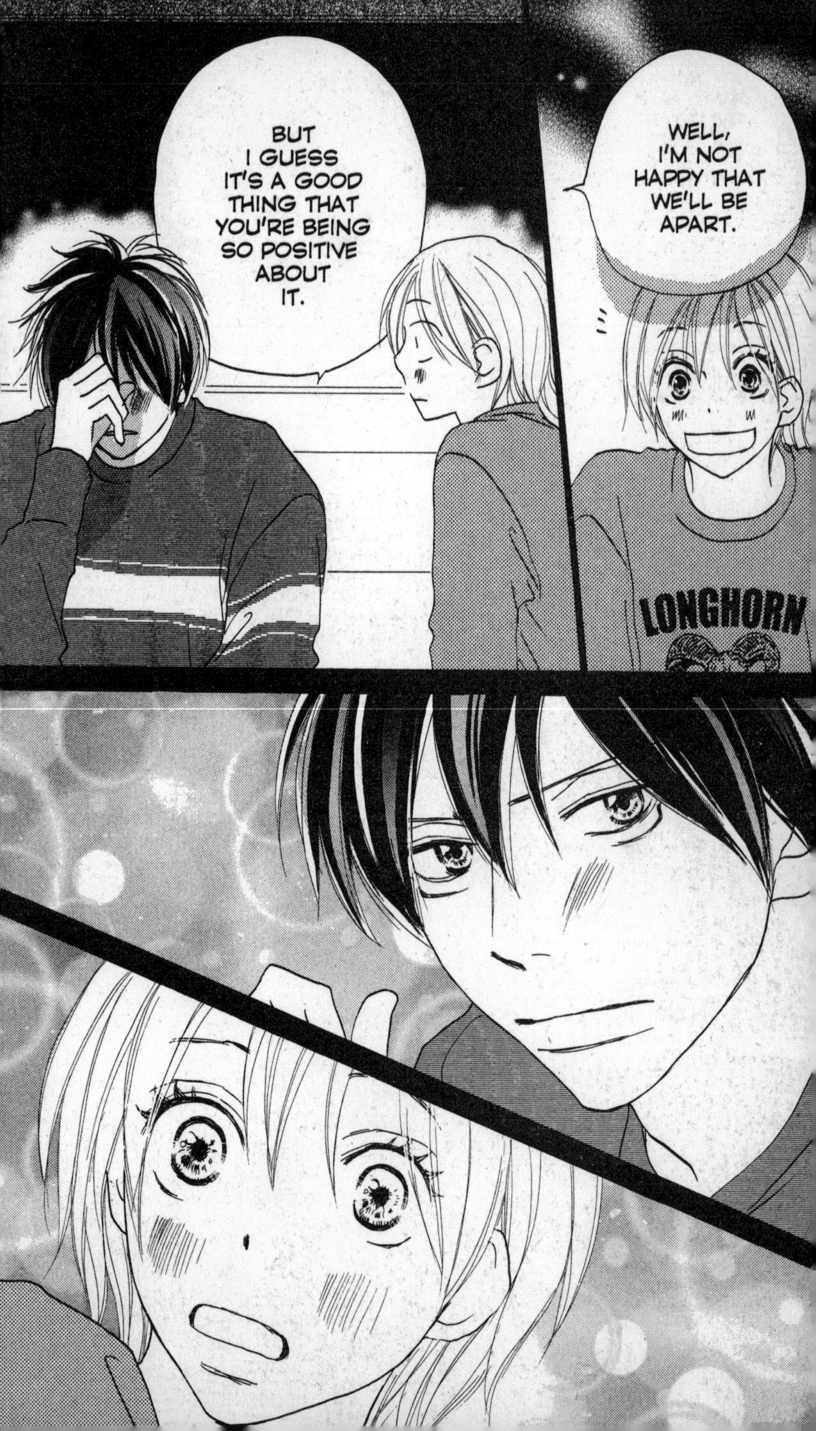
WELL, I'M NOT HAPPY THAT WE'LL BE APART.
LONGHORN
BUT I GUESS IT'S A GOOD THING THAT YOU'RE BEING SO POSITIVE ABOUT IT.

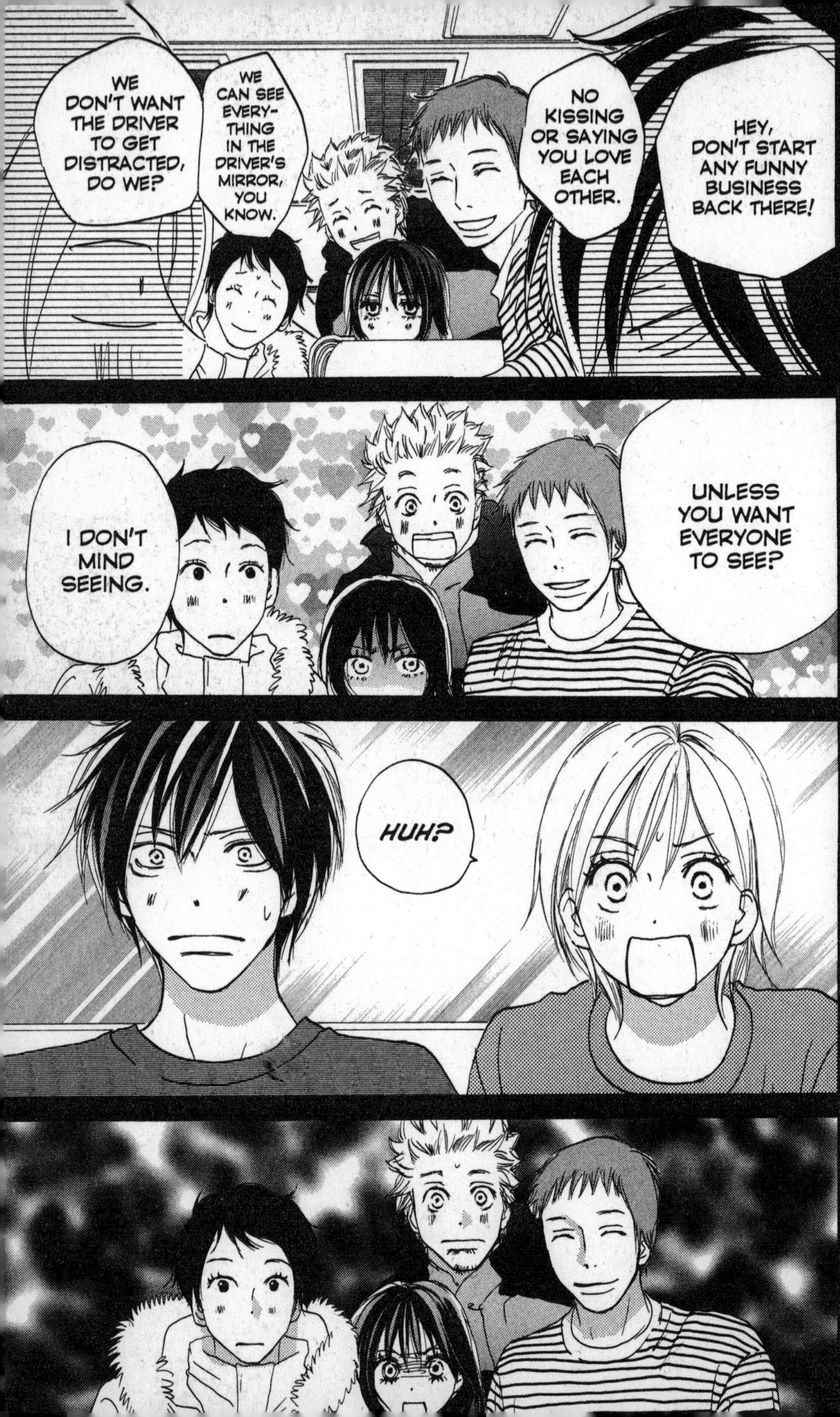
HEY, DON'T START ANY FUNNY BUSINESS BACK THERE!
NO KISSING OR SAYING YOU LOVE EACH OTHER.
WE CAN SEE EVERY-THING IN THE DRIVER'S MIRROR, YOU KNOW.
WE DON'T WANT THE DRIVER TO GET DISTRACTED, DO WE?
UNLESS YOU WANT EVERYONE TO SEE?
I DON'T MIND SEEING.
HUH?

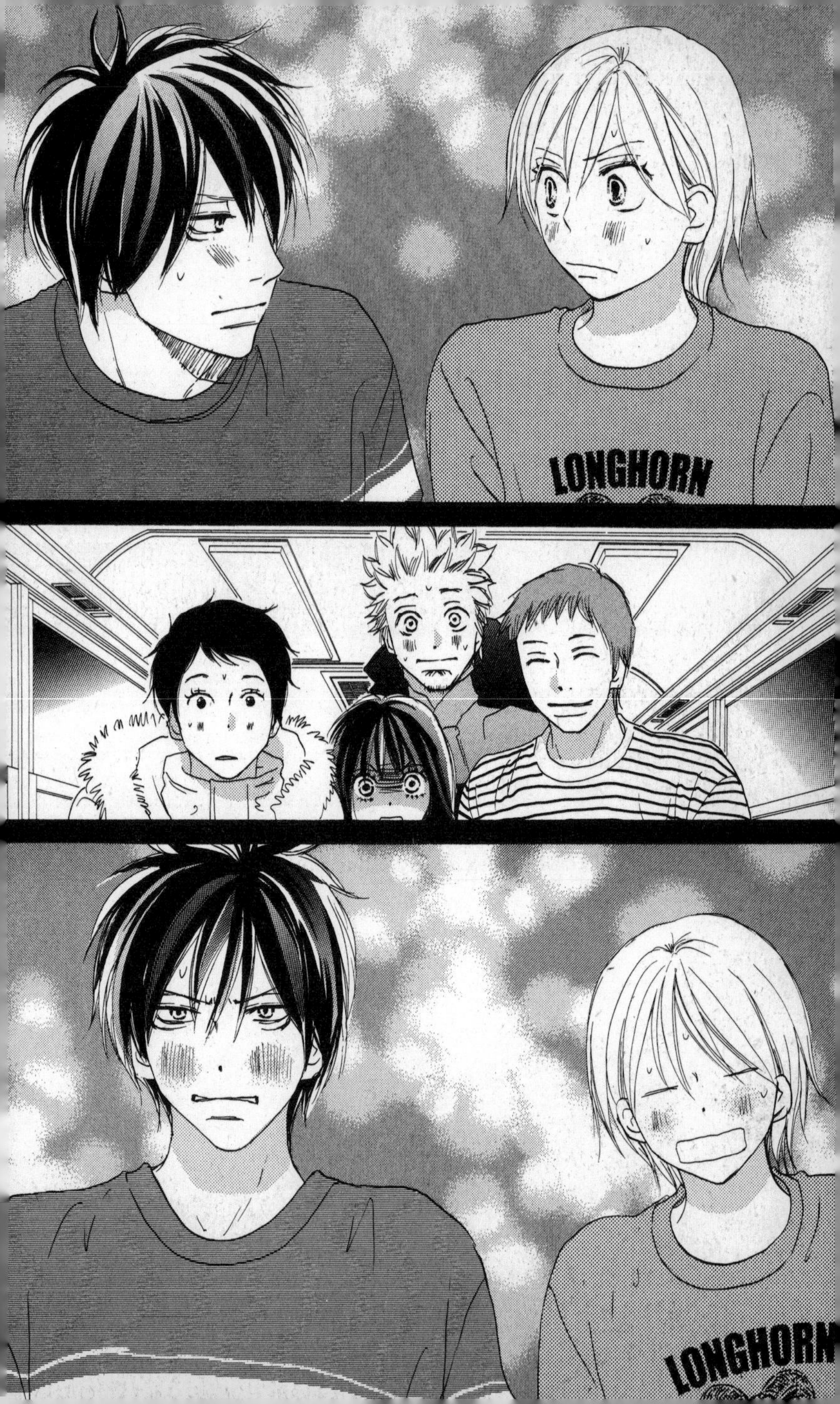
LONGHORN
LONGHORN

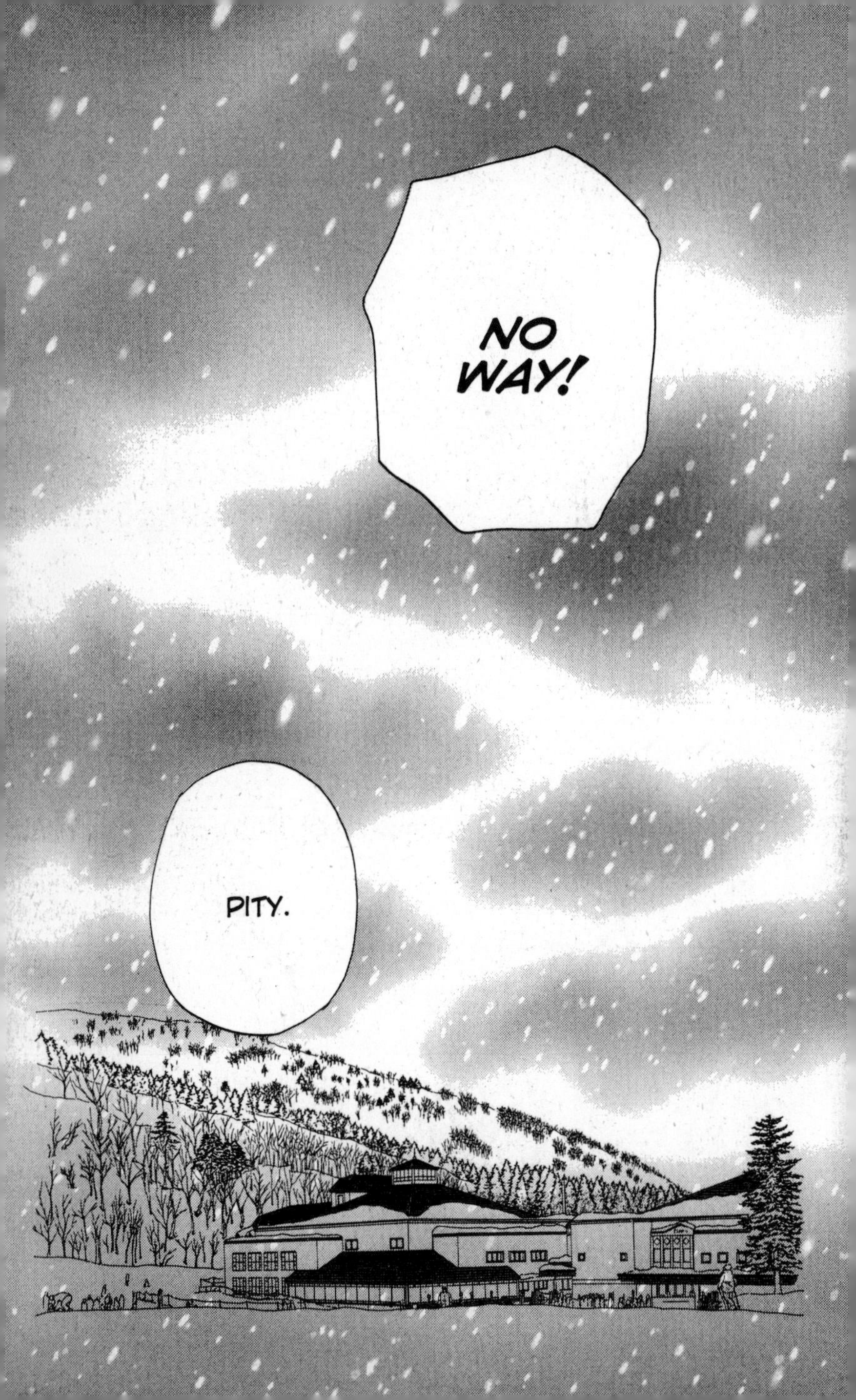
NO WAY!
PITY.

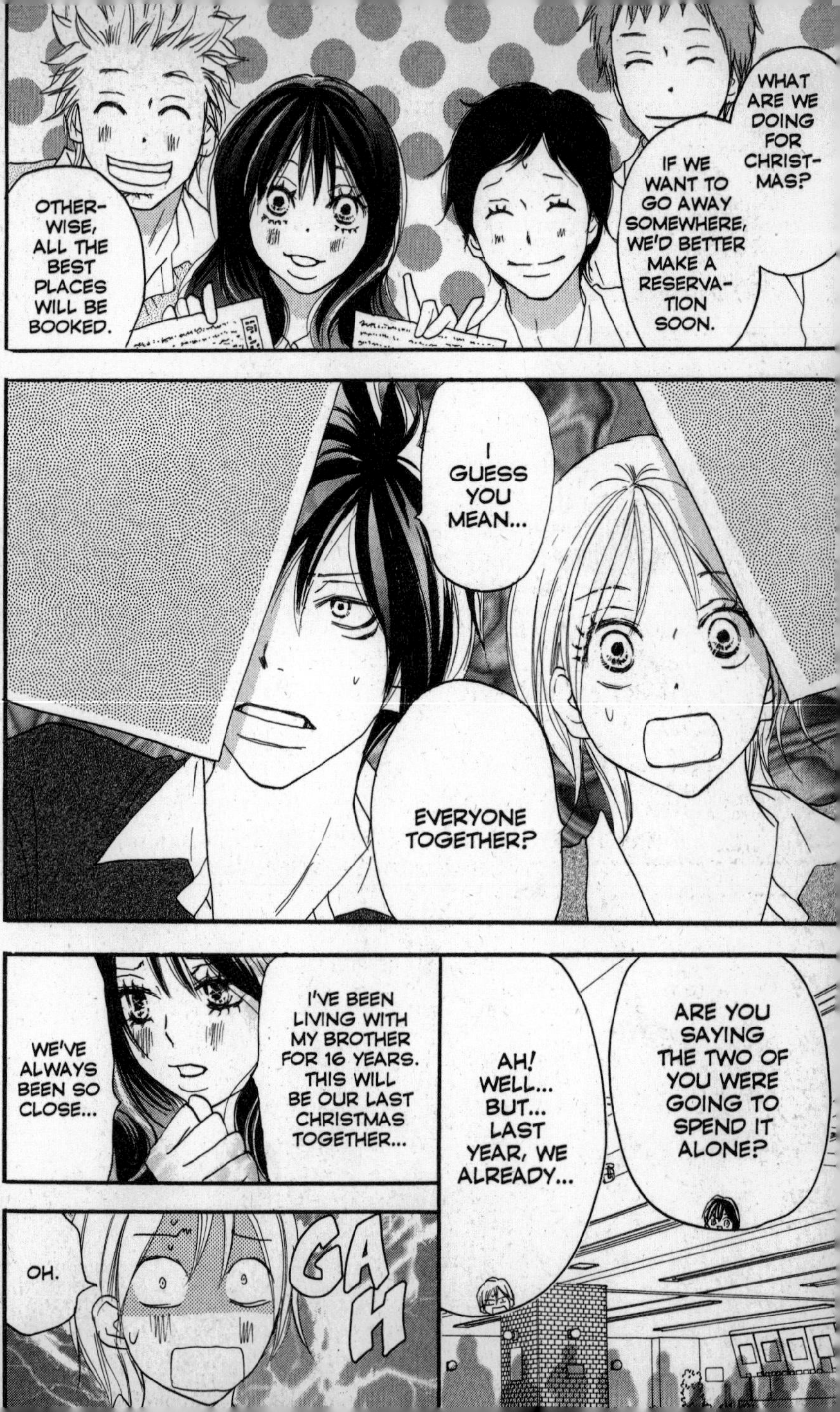
WHAT ARE WE DOING FOR CHRISTMAS?
IF WE WANT TO GO AWAY SOMEWHERE, WE'D BETTER MAKE A RESERVATION SOON.
OTHERWISE, ALL THE BEST PLACES WILL BE BOOKED.
I GUESS YOU MEAN...
EVERYONE TOGETHER?
ARE YOU SAYING THE TWO OF YOU WERE GOING TO SPEND IT ALONE?
AH! WELL... BUT... LAST YEAR, WE ALREADY...
I'VE BEEN LIVING WITH MY BROTHER FOR 16 YEARS. THIS WILL BE OUR LAST CHRISTMAS TOGETHER...
WE'VE ALWAYS BEEN SO CLOSE...
GAH
OH.

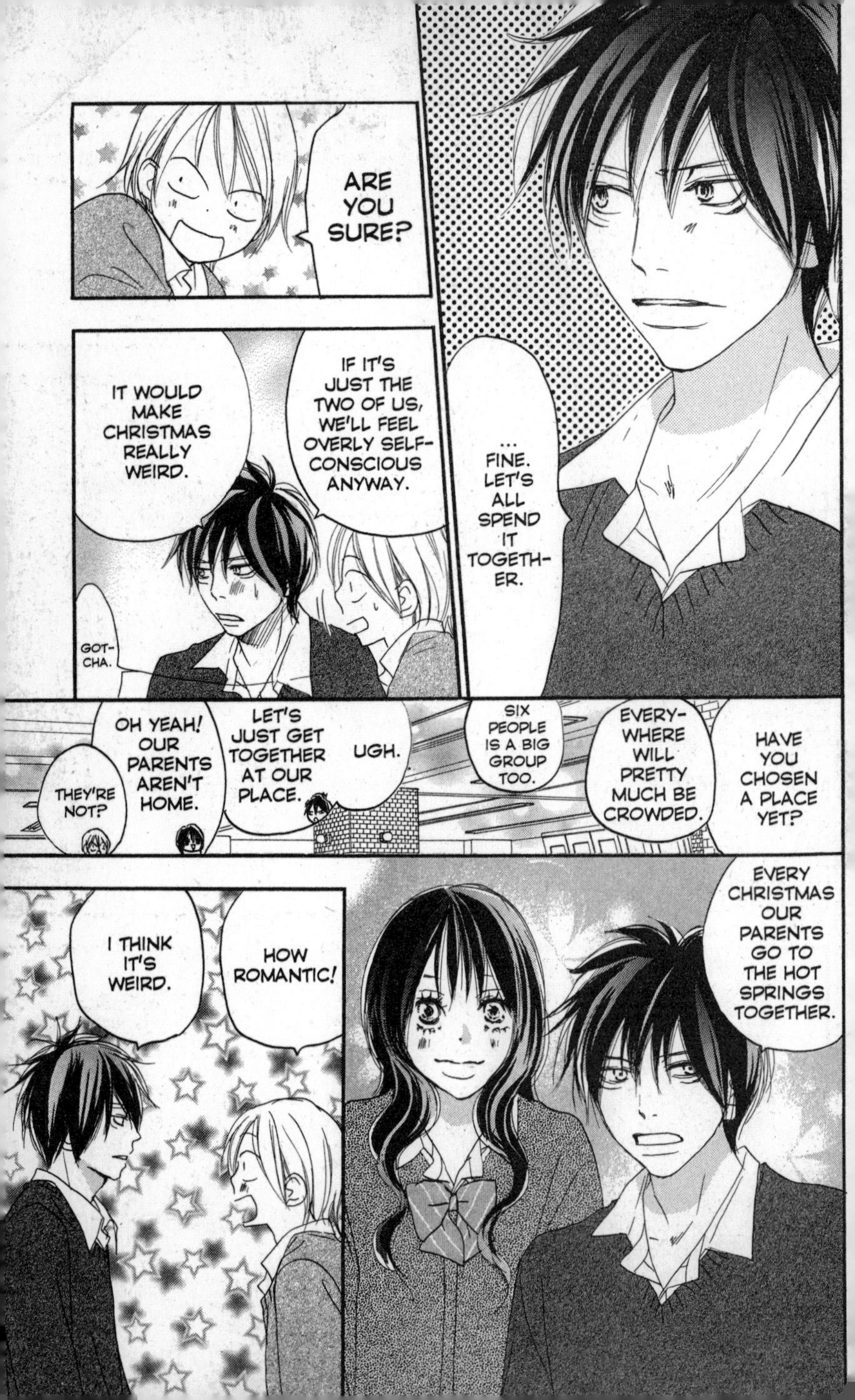
... FINE. LET'S ALL SPEND IT TOGETH-ER.
ARE YOU SURE?
IF IT'S JUST THE TWO OF US, WE'LL FEEL OVERLY SELF-CONSCIOUS ANYWAY.
IT WOULD MAKE CHRISTMAS REALLY WEIRD.
GOT-CHA.
HAVE YOU CHOSEN A PLACE YET?
EVERY-WHERE WILL PRETTY MUCH BE CROWDED.
SIX PEOPLE IS A BIG GROUP TOO.
UGH.
LET'S JUST GET TOGETHER AT OUR PLACE.
OH YEAH! OUR PARENTS AREN'T HOME.
THEY'RE NOT?
EVERY CHRISTMAS OUR PARENTS GO TO THE HOT SPRINGS TOGETHER.
HOW ROMANTIC!
I THINK IT'S WEIRD.

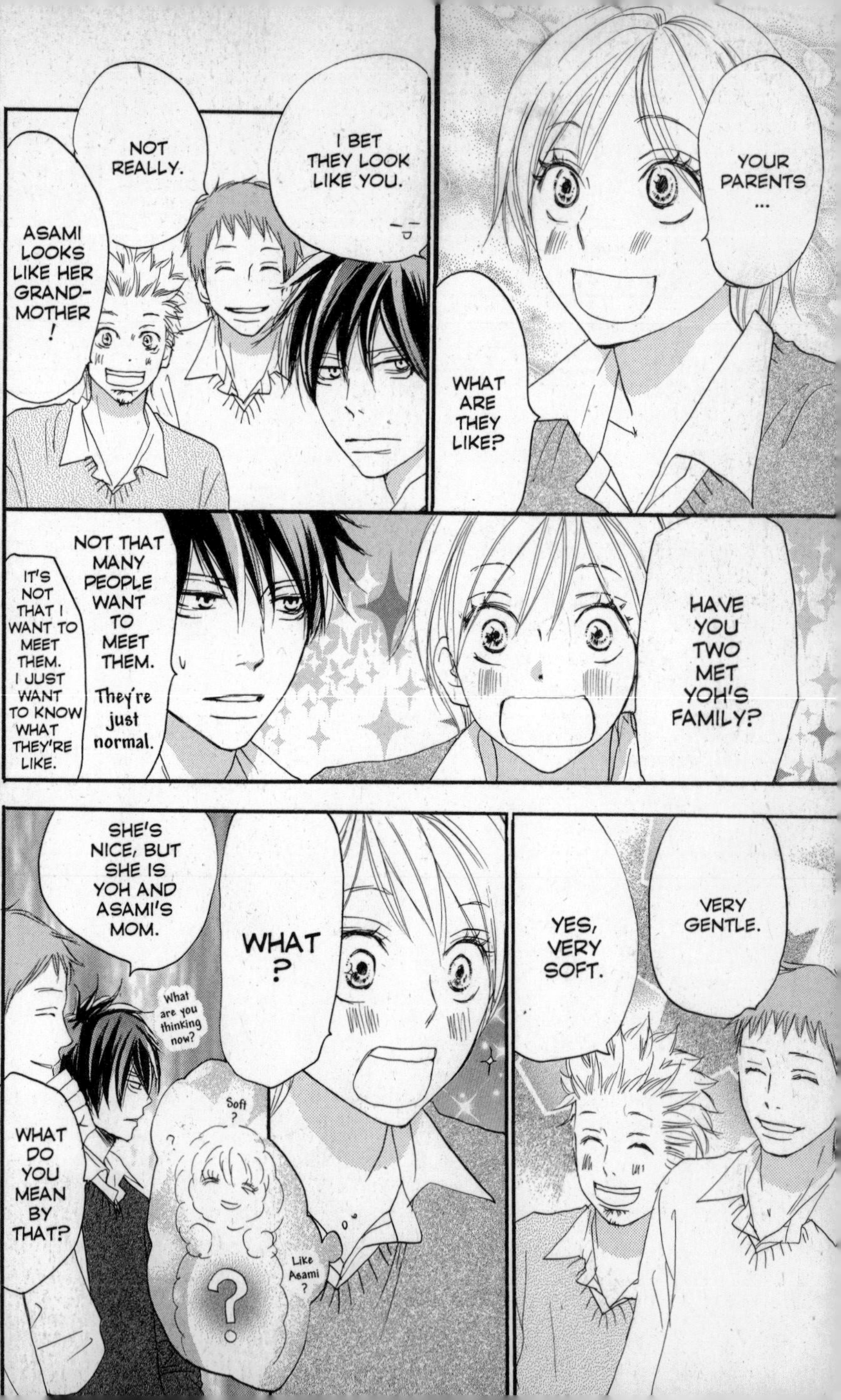
YOUR PARENTS ...
WHAT ARE THEY LIKE?
I BET THEY LOOK LIKE YOU.
NOT REALLY.
ASAMI LOOKS LIKE HER GRAND-MOTHER!
HAVE YOU TWO MET YOH'S FAMILY?
NOT THAT MANY PEOPLE WANT TO MEET THEM.
They're just normal.
IT'S NOT THAT I WANT TO MEET THEM. I JUST WANT TO KNOW WHAT THEY'RE LIKE.
VERY GENTLE.
YES, VERY SOFT.
WHAT?
SHE'S NICE, BUT SHE IS YOH AND ASAMI'S MOM.
What are you thinking now?
Soft?
Like Asami?
WHAT DO YOU MEAN BY THAT?

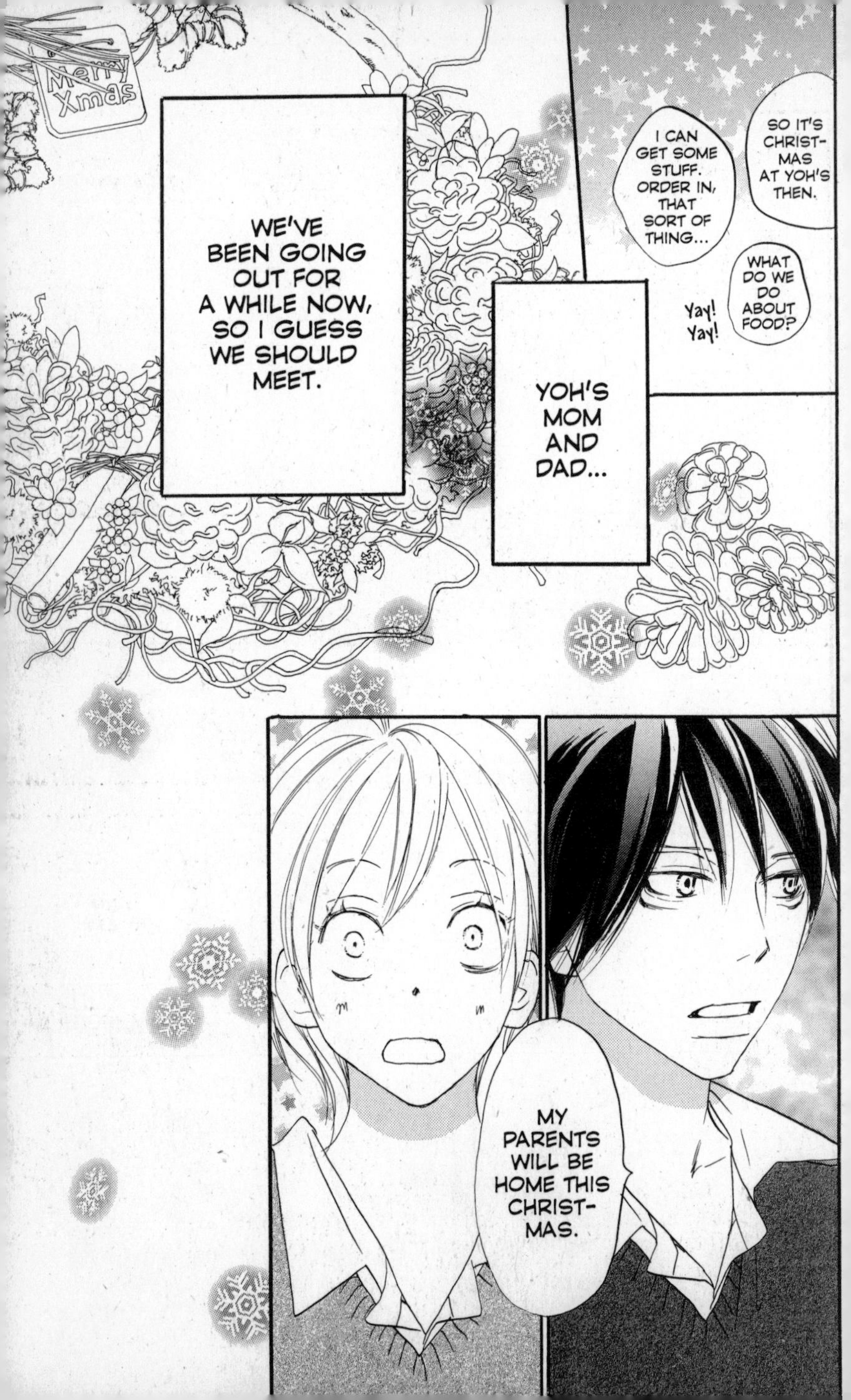
SO IT'S CHRISTMAS AT YOH'S THEN.
WHAT DO WE DO ABOUT FOOD?
I CAN GET SOME STUFF. ORDER IN, THAT SORT OF THING...
Yay! Yay!
MY PARENTS WILL BE HOME THIS CHRISTMAS.
YOH'S MOM AND DAD...
WE'VE BEEN GOING OUT FOR A WHILE NOW, SO I GUESS WE SHOULD MEET.
Merry Xmas

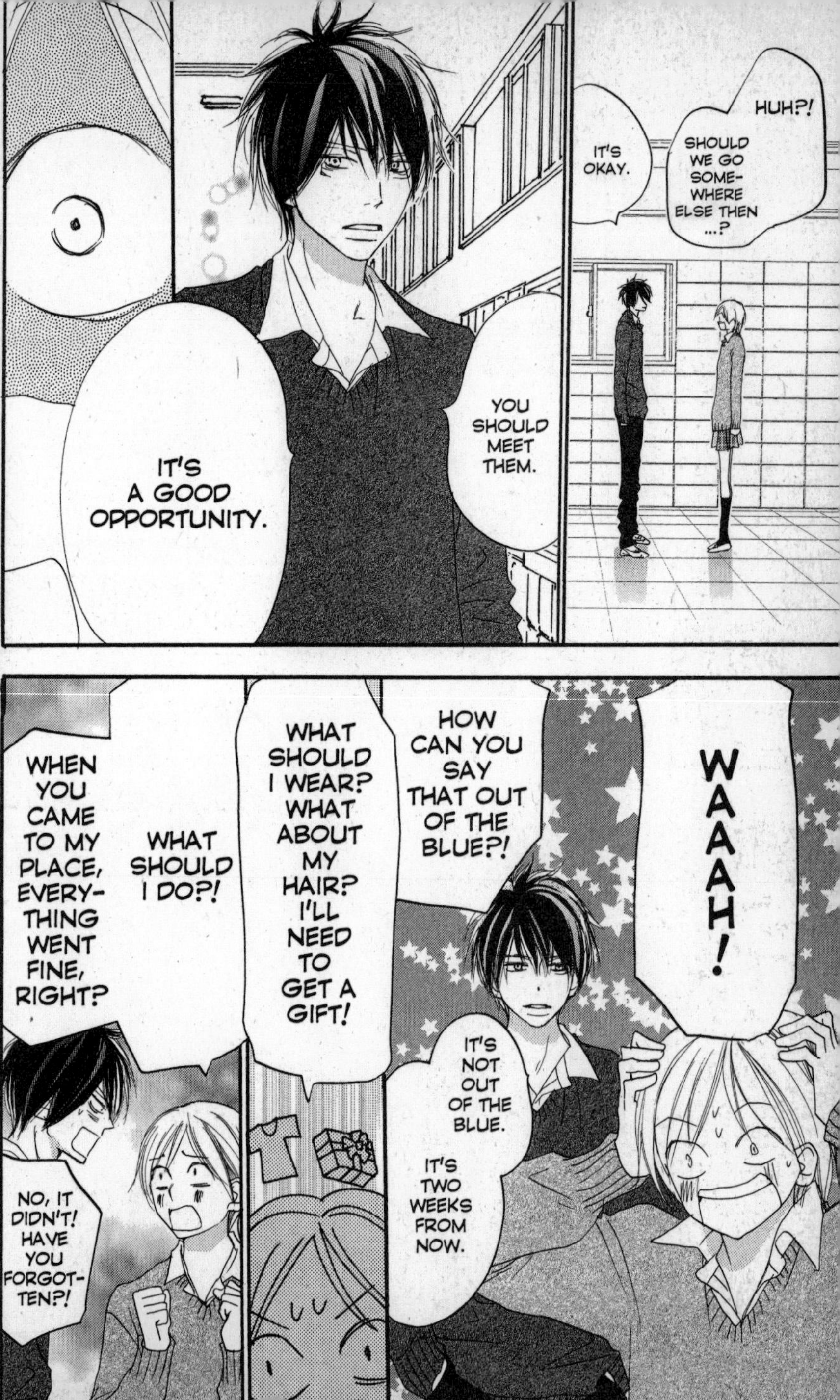
HUH?!
SHOULD WE GO SOMEWHERE ELSE THEN ...?
IT'S OKAY.
YOU SHOULD MEET THEM.
IT'S A GOOD OPPORTUNITY.
WAAAH!
HOW CAN YOU SAY THAT OUT OF THE BLUE?!
IT'S NOT OUT OF THE BLUE.
IT'S TWO WEEKS FROM NOW.
WHAT SHOULD I WEAR? WHAT ABOUT MY HAIR? I'LL NEED TO GET A GIFT!
WHAT SHOULD I DO?!
WHEN YOU CAME TO MY PLACE, EVERYTHING WENT FINE, RIGHT?
NO, IT DIDN'T! HAVE YOU FORGOTTEN?!

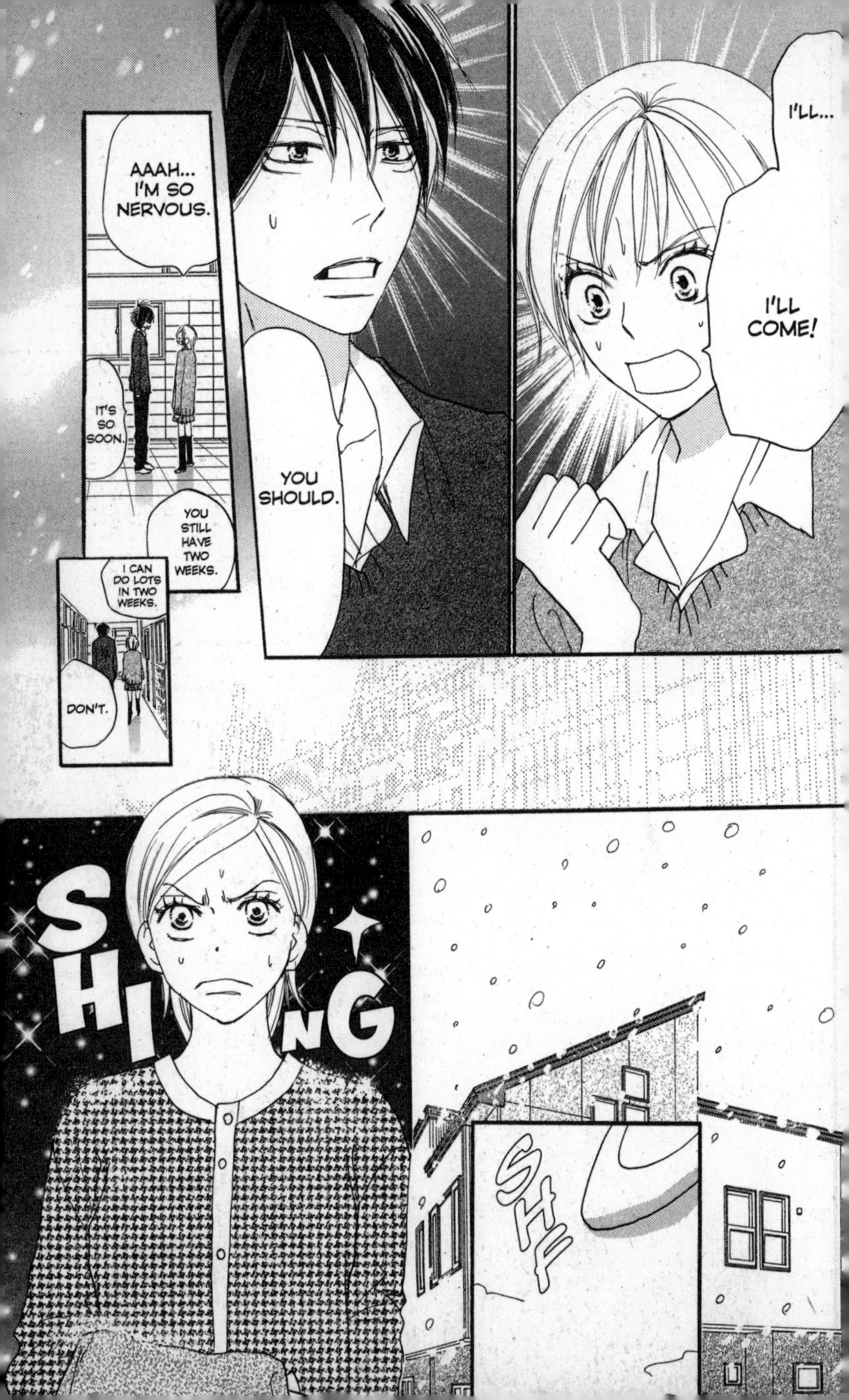
I'LL...
I'LL COME!
YOU SHOULD.
AAAH... I'M SO NERVOUS.
IT'S SO SOON.
YOU STILL HAVE TWO WEEKS.
I CAN DO LOTS IN TWO WEEKS.
DON'T.
SHF
SHING

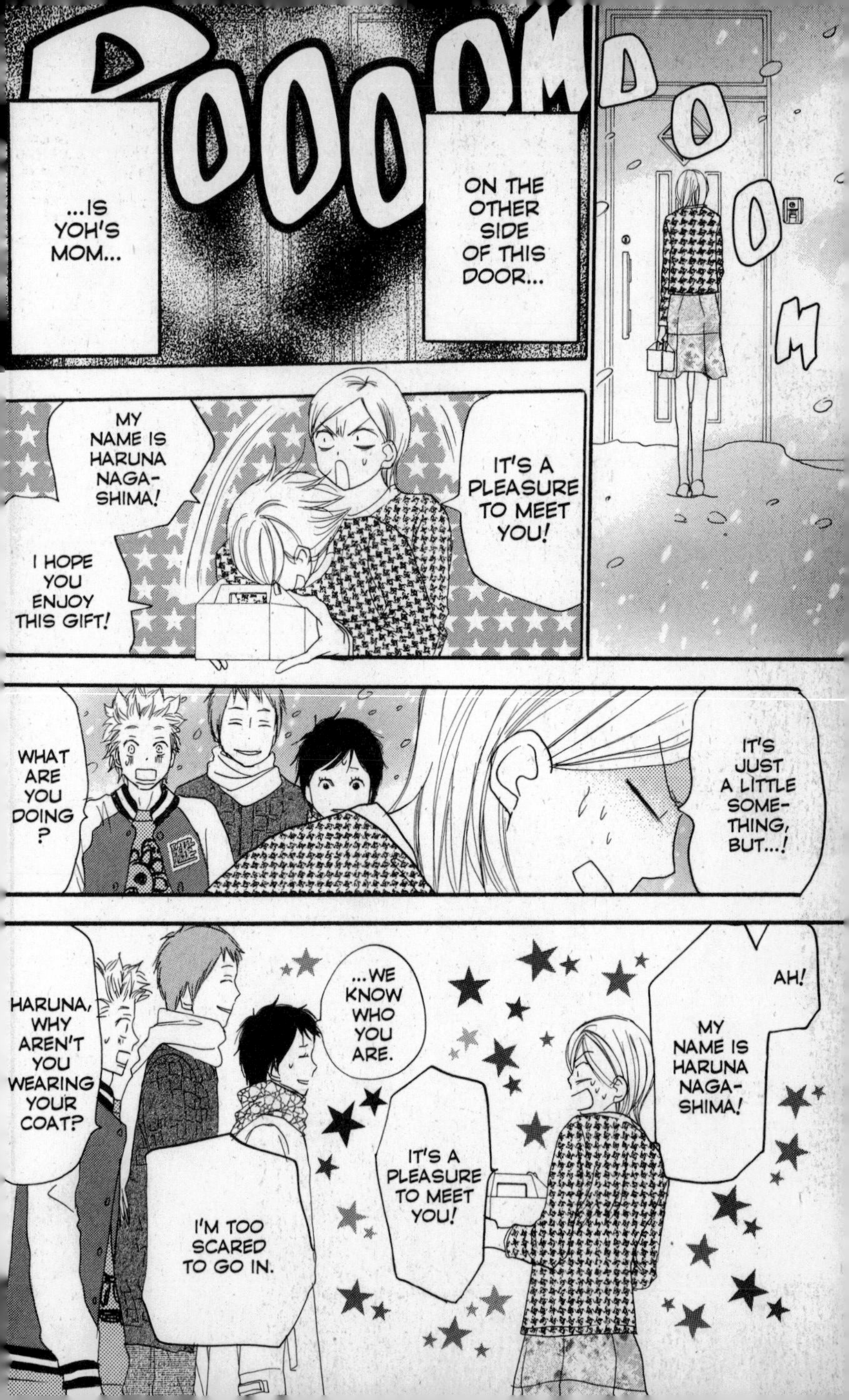
DOOOOM
DOOM
ON THE OTHER SIDE OF THIS DOOR...
...IS YOH'S MOM...
IT'S A PLEASURE TO MEET YOU!
MY NAME IS HARUNA NAGA-SHIMA!
I HOPE YOU ENJOY THIS GIFT!
IT'S JUST A LITTLE SOME-THING, BUT...!
WHAT ARE YOU DOING?
AH!
MY NAME IS HARUNA NAGA-SHIMA!
IT'S A PLEASURE TO MEET YOU!
...WE KNOW WHO YOU ARE.
HARUNA, WHY AREN'T YOU WEARING YOUR COAT?
I'M TOO SCARED TO GO IN.

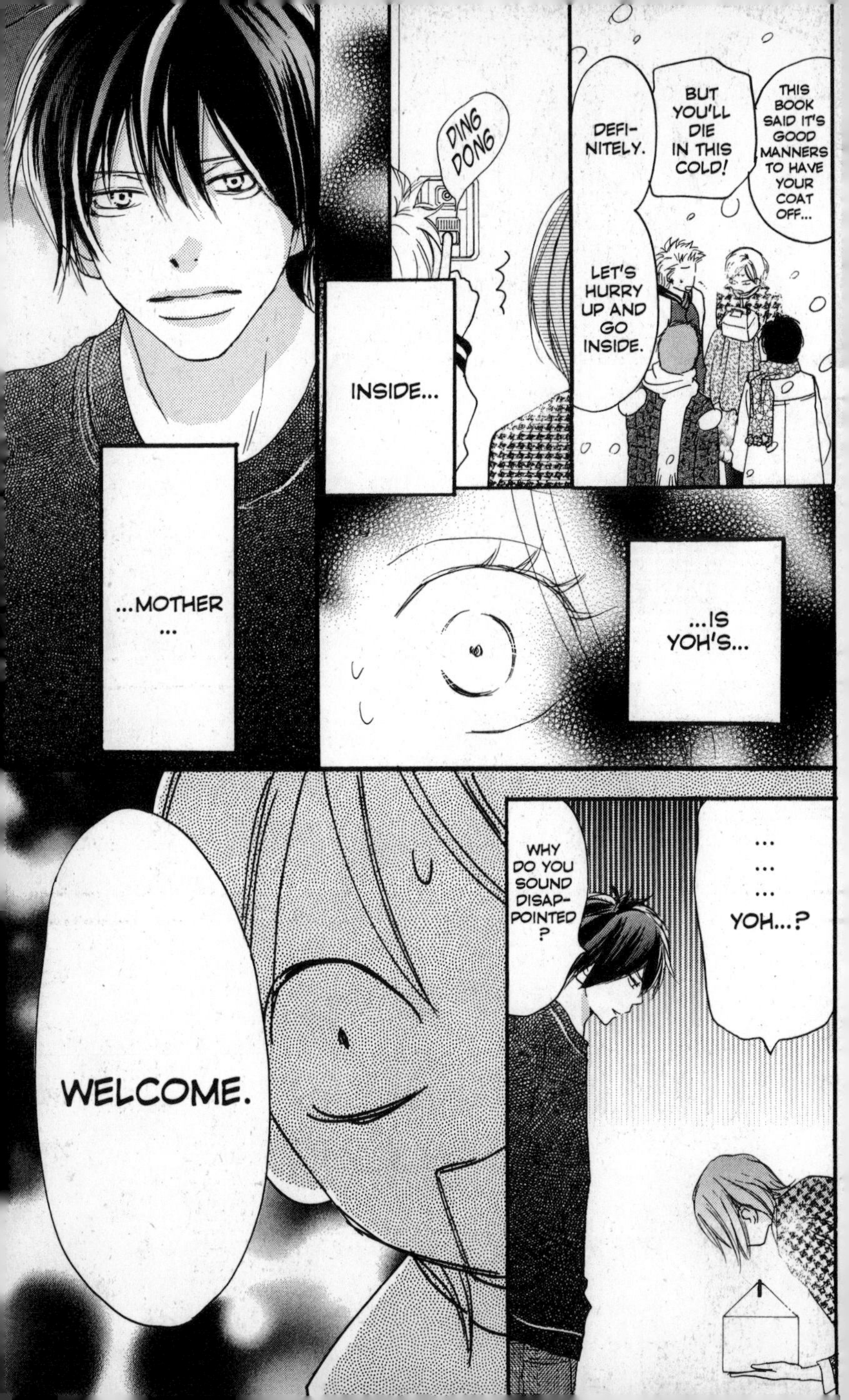

THIS BOOK SAID IT'S GOOD MANNERS TO HAVE YOUR COAT OFF...
BUT YOU'LL DIE IN THIS COLD!
DEFINITELY.
LET'S HURRY UP AND GO INSIDE.
DING DONG
INSIDE...
...IS YOH'S...
...MOTHER ...
... ... YOH...?
WHY DO YOU SOUND DISAPPOINTED?
WELCOME.

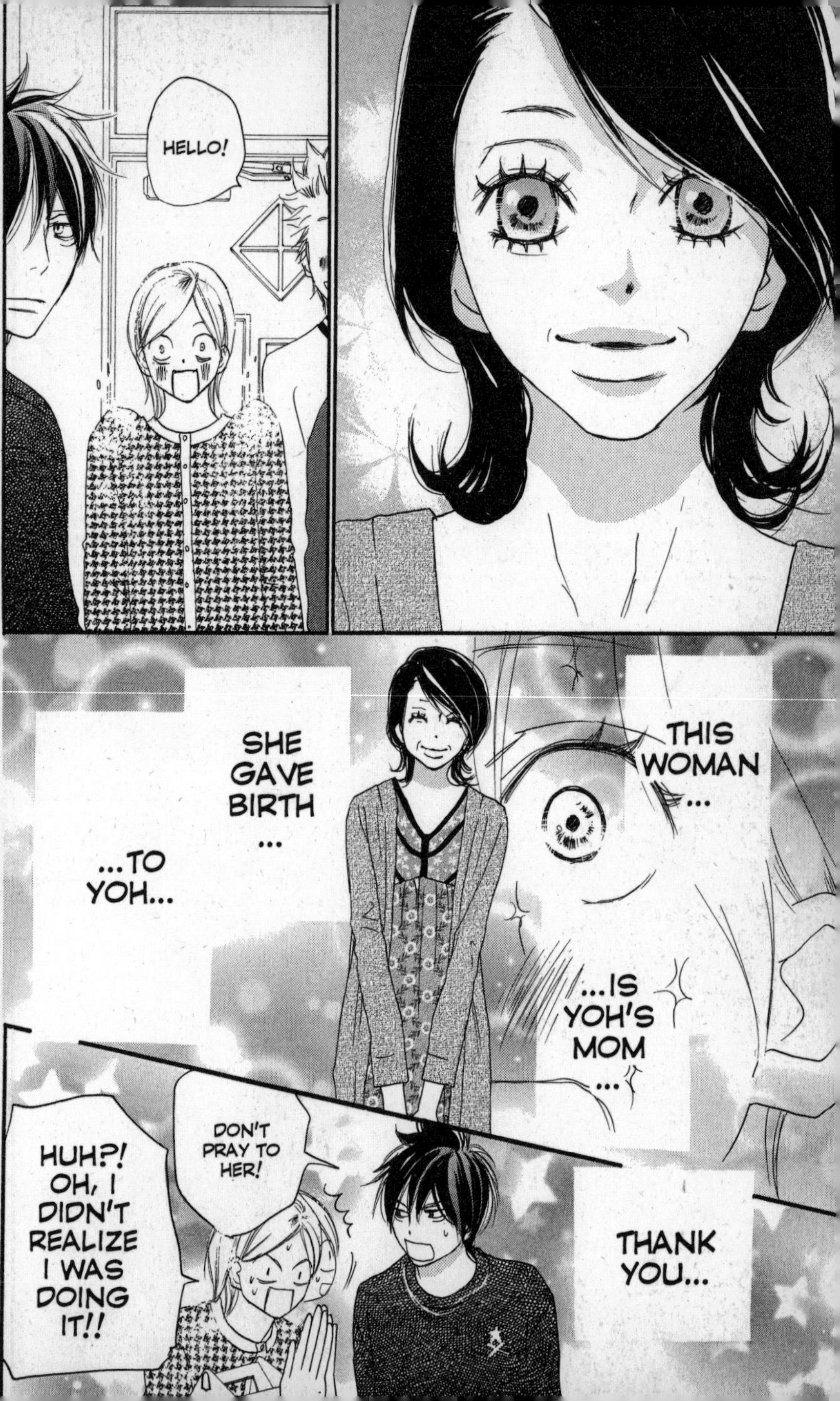
HELLO!
THIS WOMAN...
...IS YOH'S MOM...
SHE GAVE BIRTH...
...TO YOH...
THANK YOU...
DON'T PRAY TO HER!
HUH?! OH, I DIDN'T REALIZE I WAS DOING IT!!

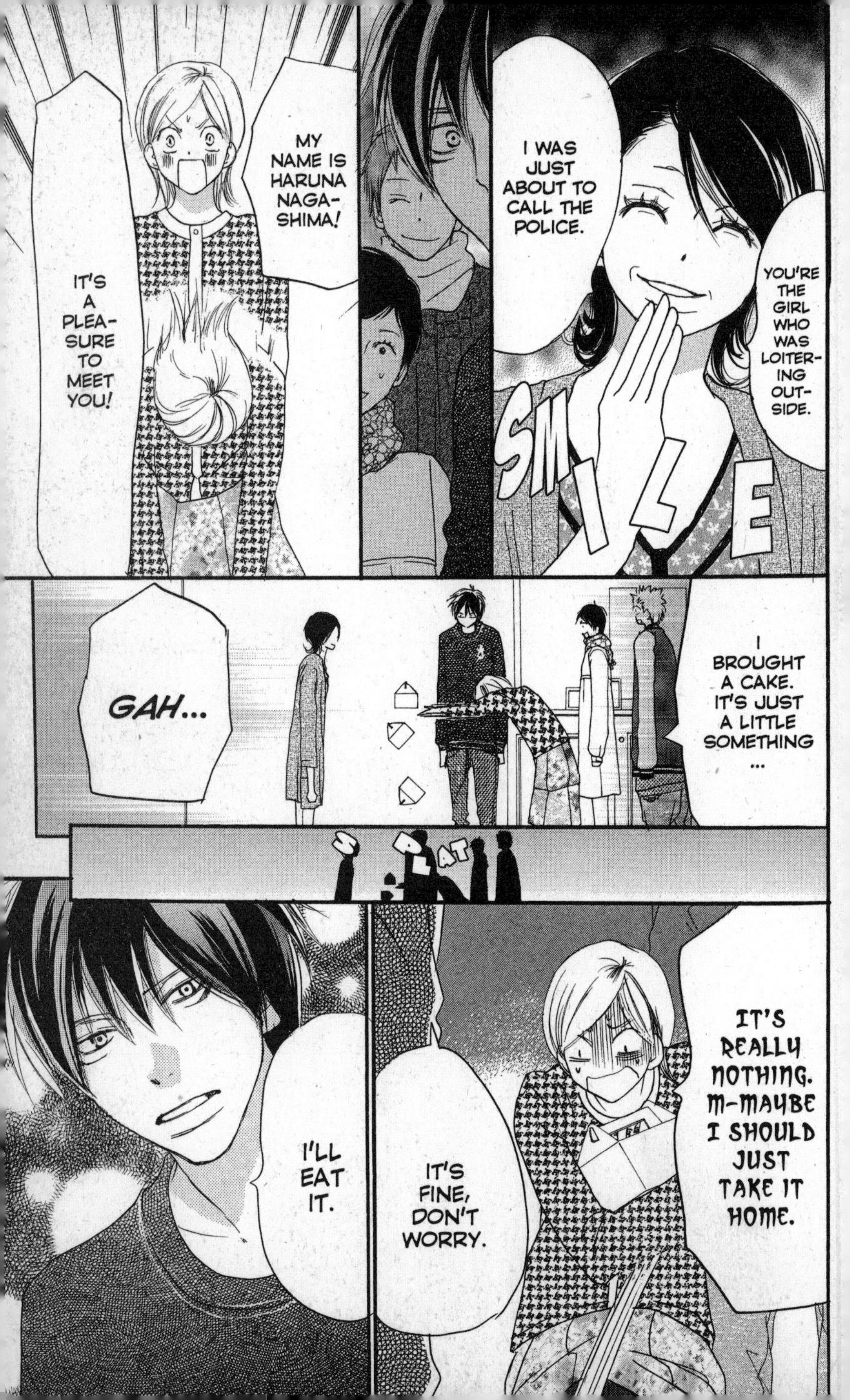
YOU'RE THE GIRL WHO WAS LOITERING OUTSIDE.
I WAS JUST ABOUT TO CALL THE POLICE.
SMILE
MY NAME IS HARUNA NAGASHIMA!
IT'S A PLEASURE TO MEET YOU!
I BROUGHT A CAKE. IT'S JUST A LITTLE SOMETHING...
GAH...
SPLAT
IT'S REALLY NOTHING. M-MAYBE I SHOULD JUST TAKE IT HOME.
IT'S FINE, DON'T WORRY.
I'LL EAT IT.

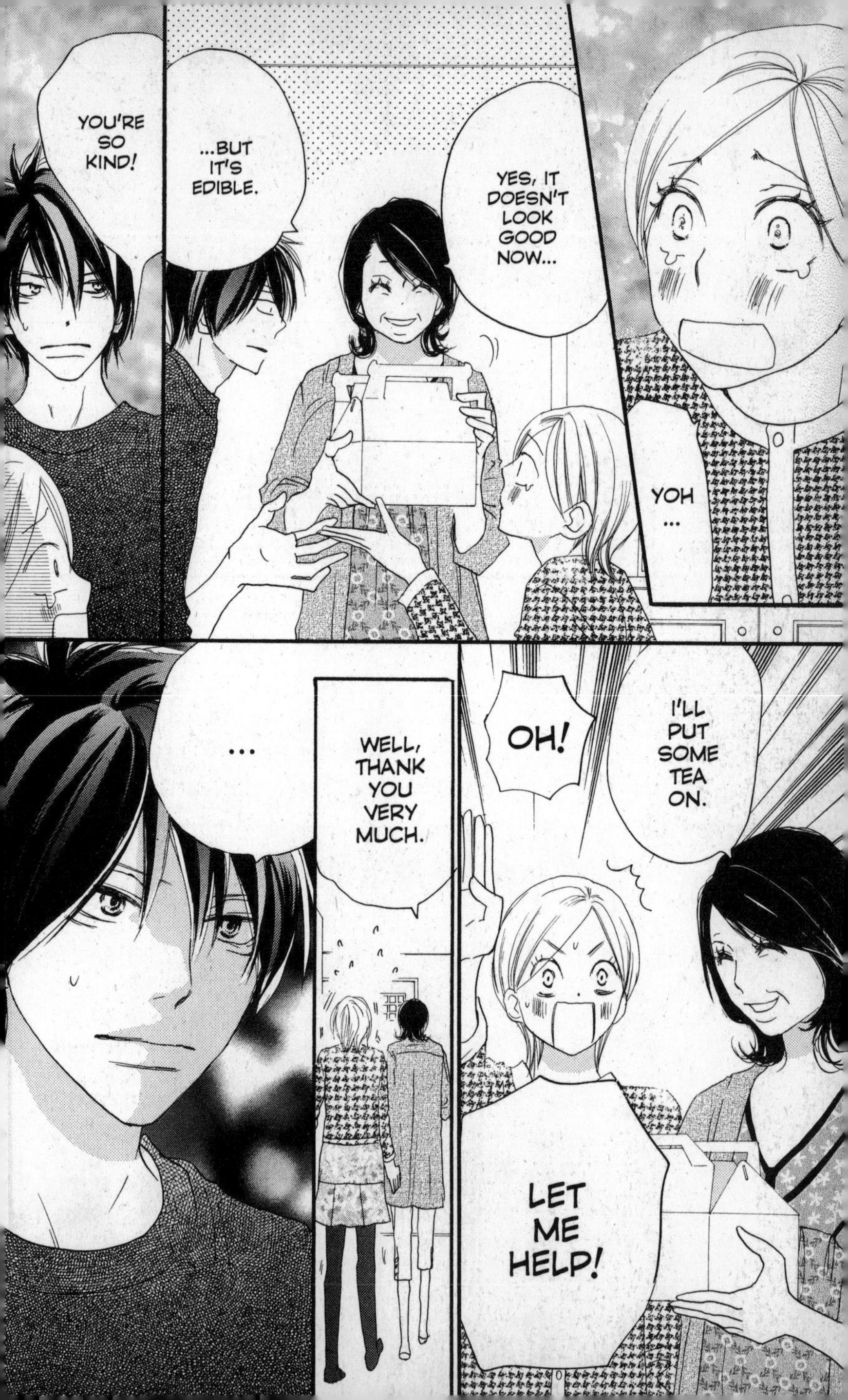
YOH ...
YES, IT DOESN'T LOOK GOOD NOW...
...BUT IT'S EDIBLE.
YOU'RE SO KIND!
I'LL PUT SOME TEA ON.
OH!
LET ME HELP!
WELL, THANK YOU VERY MUCH.
...

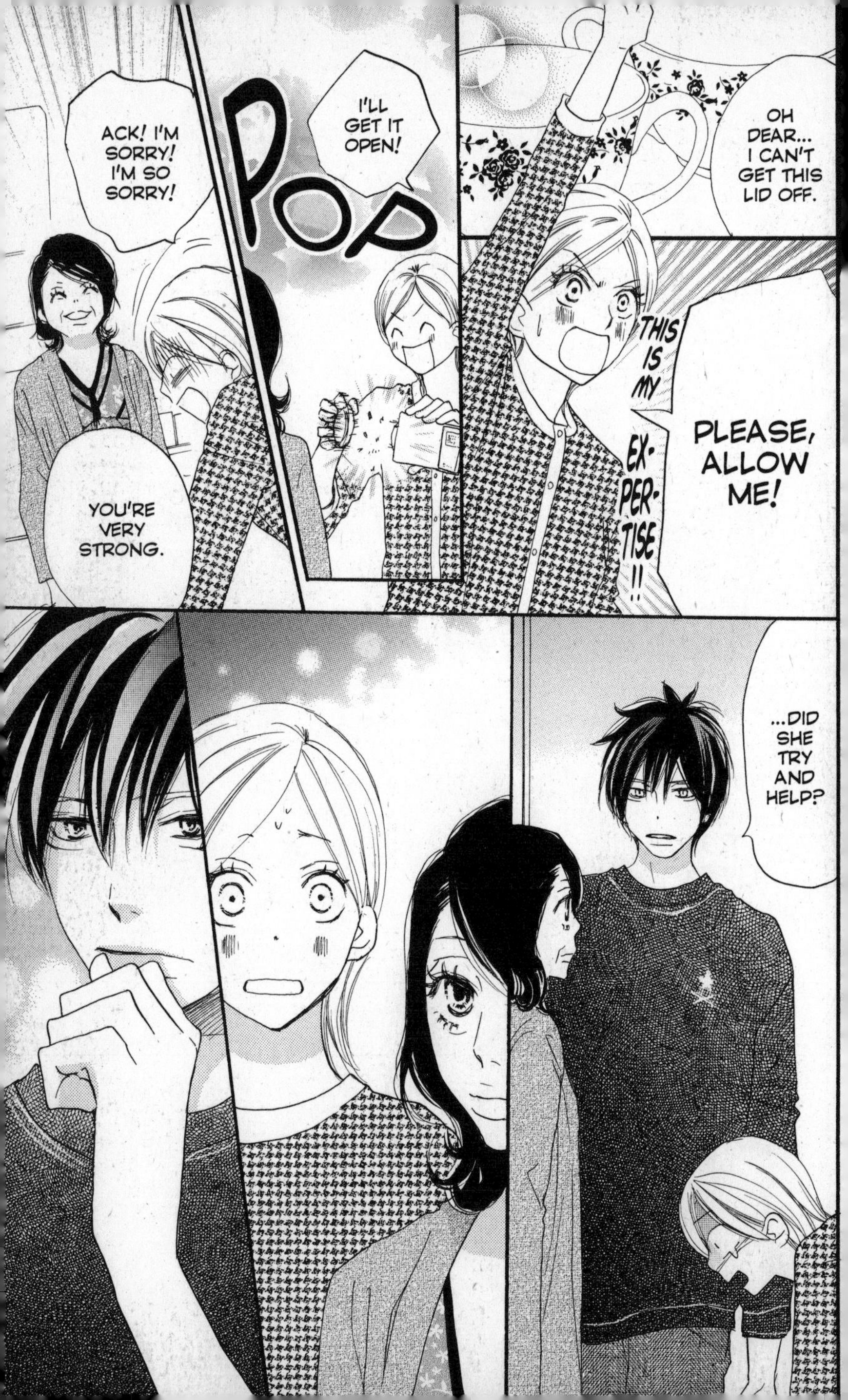
OH DEAR... I CAN'T GET THIS LID OFF.
PLEASE, ALLOW ME!
THIS IS MY EXPERTISE!!
I'LL GET IT OPEN!
POP
ACK! I'M SORRY! I'M SO SORRY!
YOU'RE VERY STRONG.
...DID SHE TRY AND HELP?

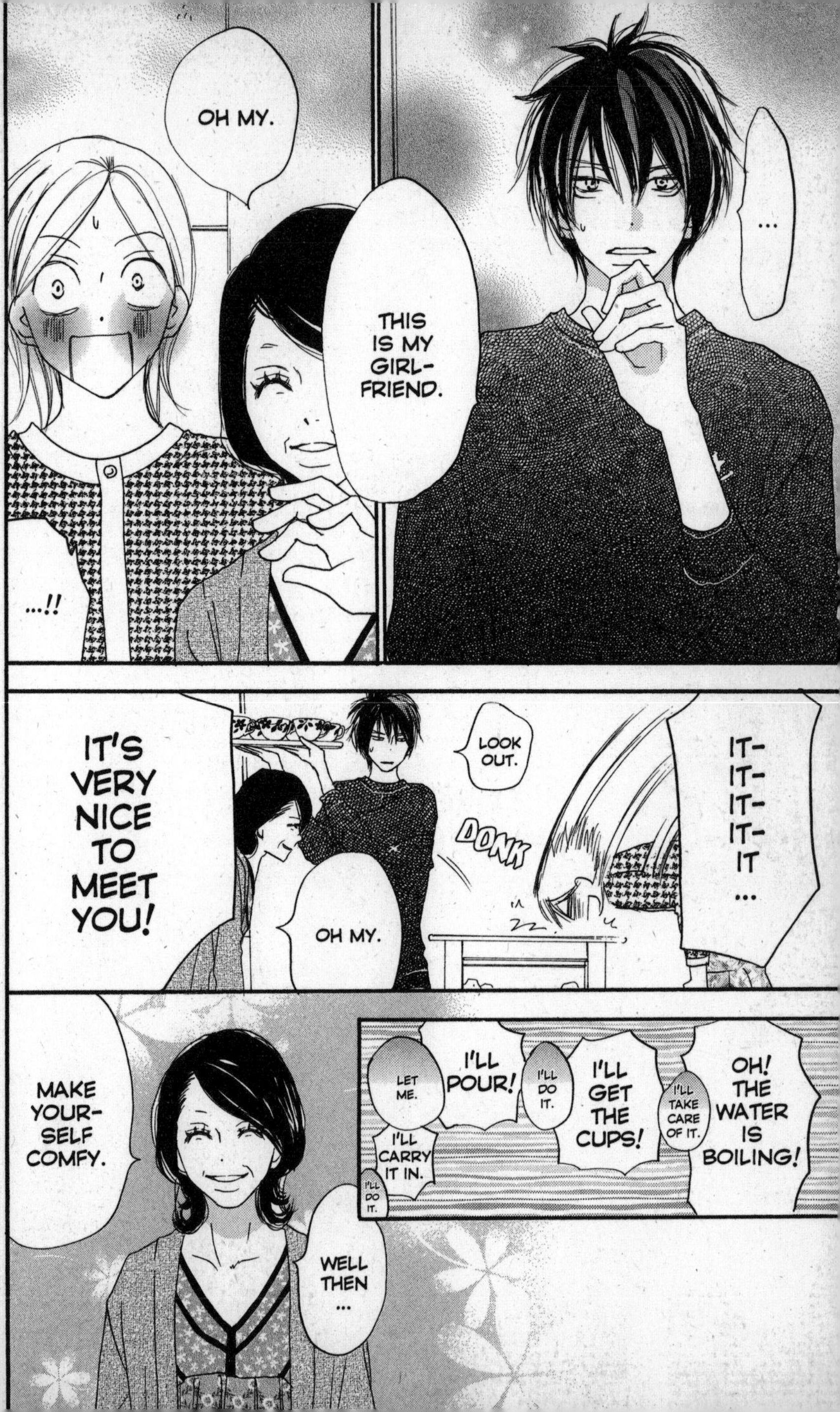
...
THIS IS MY GIRL-FRIEND.
OH MY.
...!!
IT-IT-IT-IT-IT ...
LOOK OUT.
DONK
OH MY.
IT'S VERY NICE TO MEET YOU!
OH! THE WATER IS BOILING!
I'LL TAKE CARE OF IT.
I'LL GET THE CUPS!
I'LL DO IT.
I'LL POUR!
LET ME.
I'LL CARRY IT IN.
I'LL DO IT.
MAKE YOUR-SELF COMFY.
WELL THEN ...

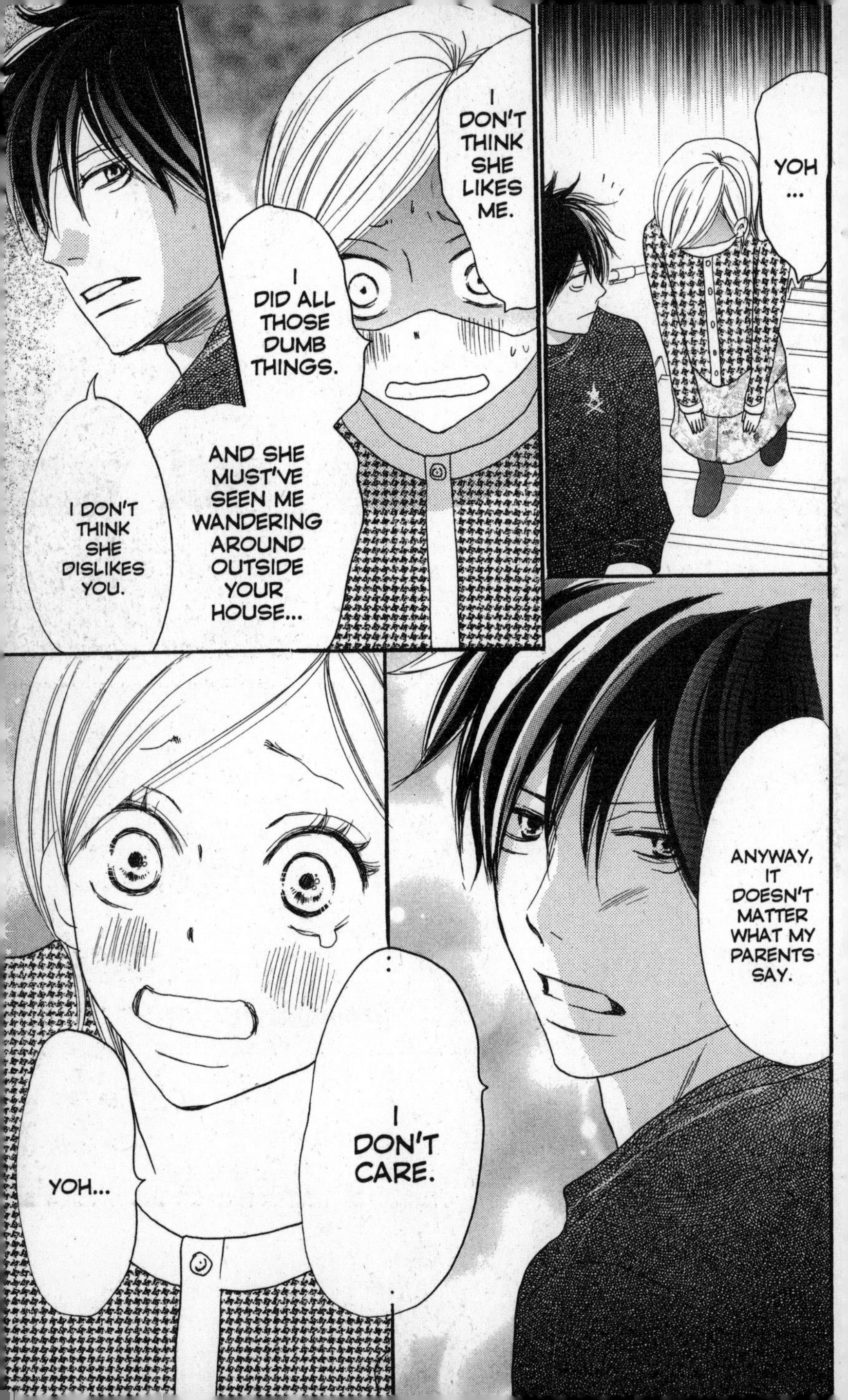
YOH ...
I DON'T THINK SHE LIKES ME.
I DID ALL THOSE DUMB THINGS.
AND SHE MUST'VE SEEN ME WANDERING AROUND OUTSIDE YOUR HOUSE...
I DON'T THINK SHE DISLIKES YOU.
ANYWAY, IT DOESN'T MATTER WHAT MY PARENTS SAY.
I DON'T CARE.
YOH...

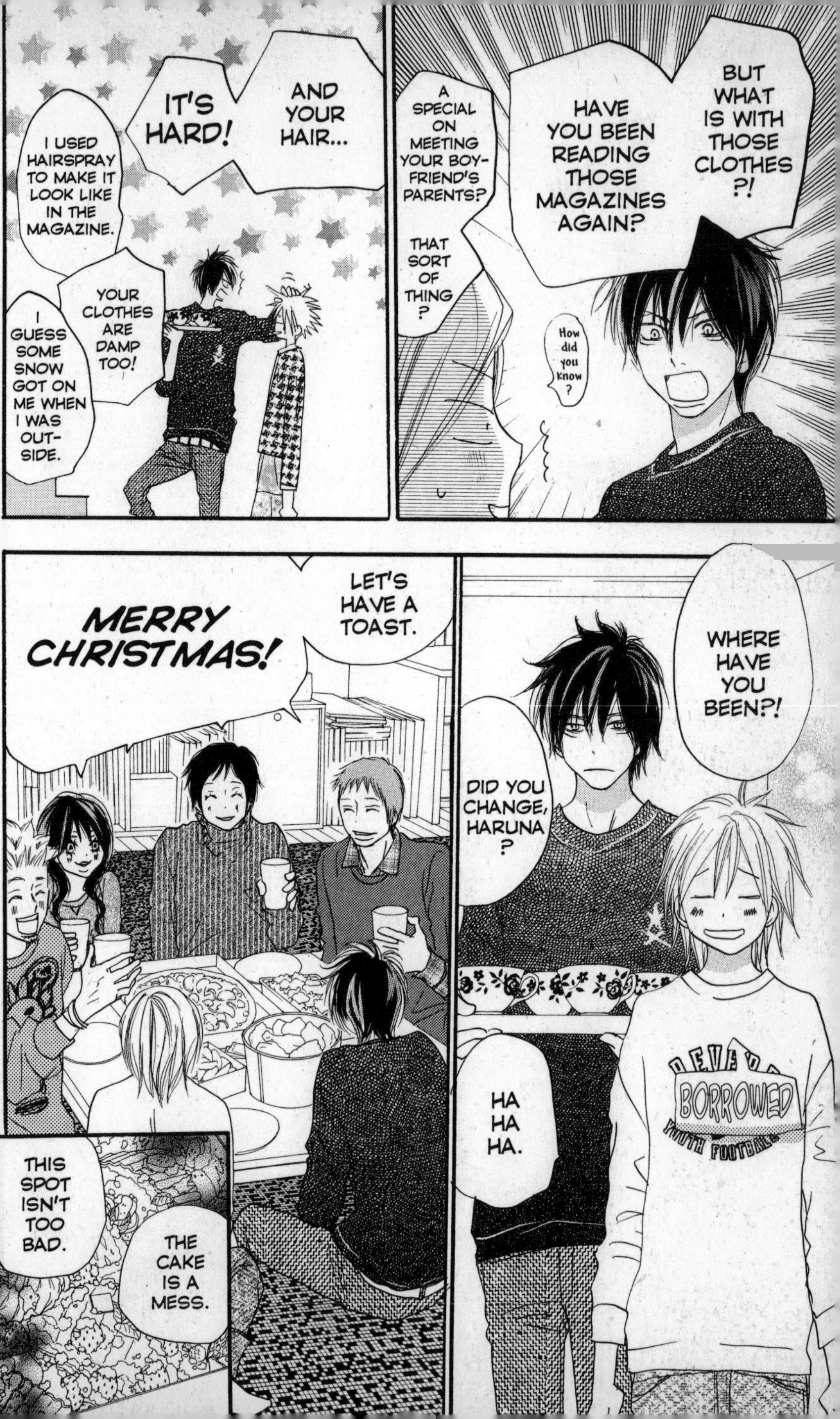
BUT WHAT IS WITH THOSE CLOTHES?!
HAVE YOU BEEN READING THOSE MAGAZINES AGAIN?
A SPECIAL ON MEETING YOUR BOY-FRIEND'S PARENTS?
THAT SORT OF THING?
How did you know?
AND YOUR HAIR...
IT'S HARD!
I USED HAIRSPRAY TO MAKE IT LOOK LIKE IN THE MAGAZINE.
YOUR CLOTHES ARE DAMP TOO!
I GUESS SOME SNOW GOT ON ME WHEN I WAS OUT-SIDE.
WHERE HAVE YOU BEEN?!
DID YOU CHANGE, HARUNA?
BORROWED
HA HA HA.
LET'S HAVE A TOAST.
MERRY CHRISTMAS!
THIS SPOT ISN'T TOO BAD.
THE CAKE IS A MESS.

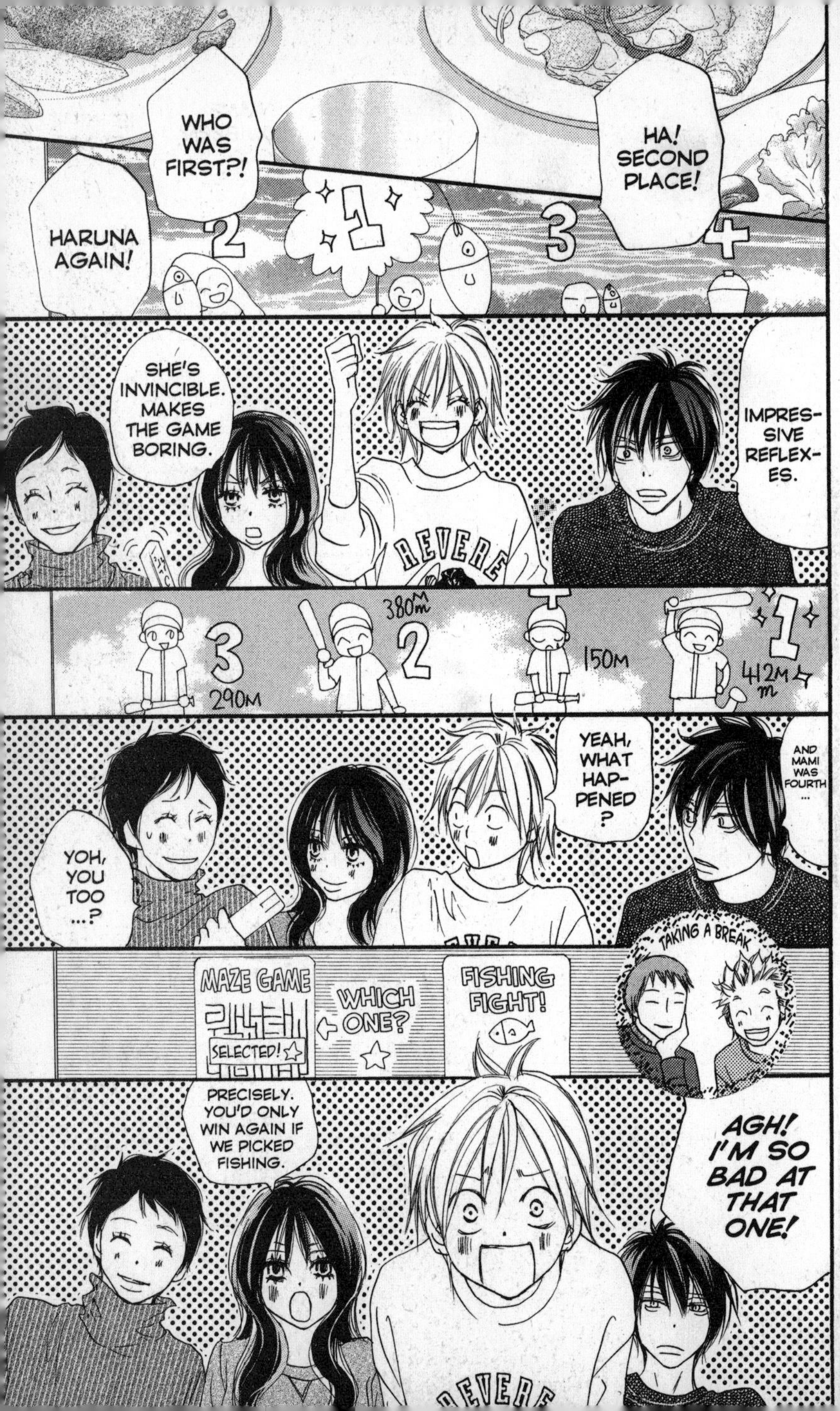
HA! SECOND PLACE!
WHO WAS FIRST?!
HARUNA AGAIN!
IMPRESSIVE REFLEXES.
SHE'S INVINCIBLE. MAKES THE GAME BORING.
412M
150M
380M
290M
AND MAMI WAS FOURTH...
YEAH, WHAT HAPPENED?
YOH, YOU TOO...?
TAKING A BREAK
FISHING FIGHT!
WHICH ONE?
MAZE GAME
SELECTED!
AGH! I'M SO BAD AT THAT ONE!
PRECISELY. YOU'D ONLY WIN AGAIN IF WE PICKED FISHING.

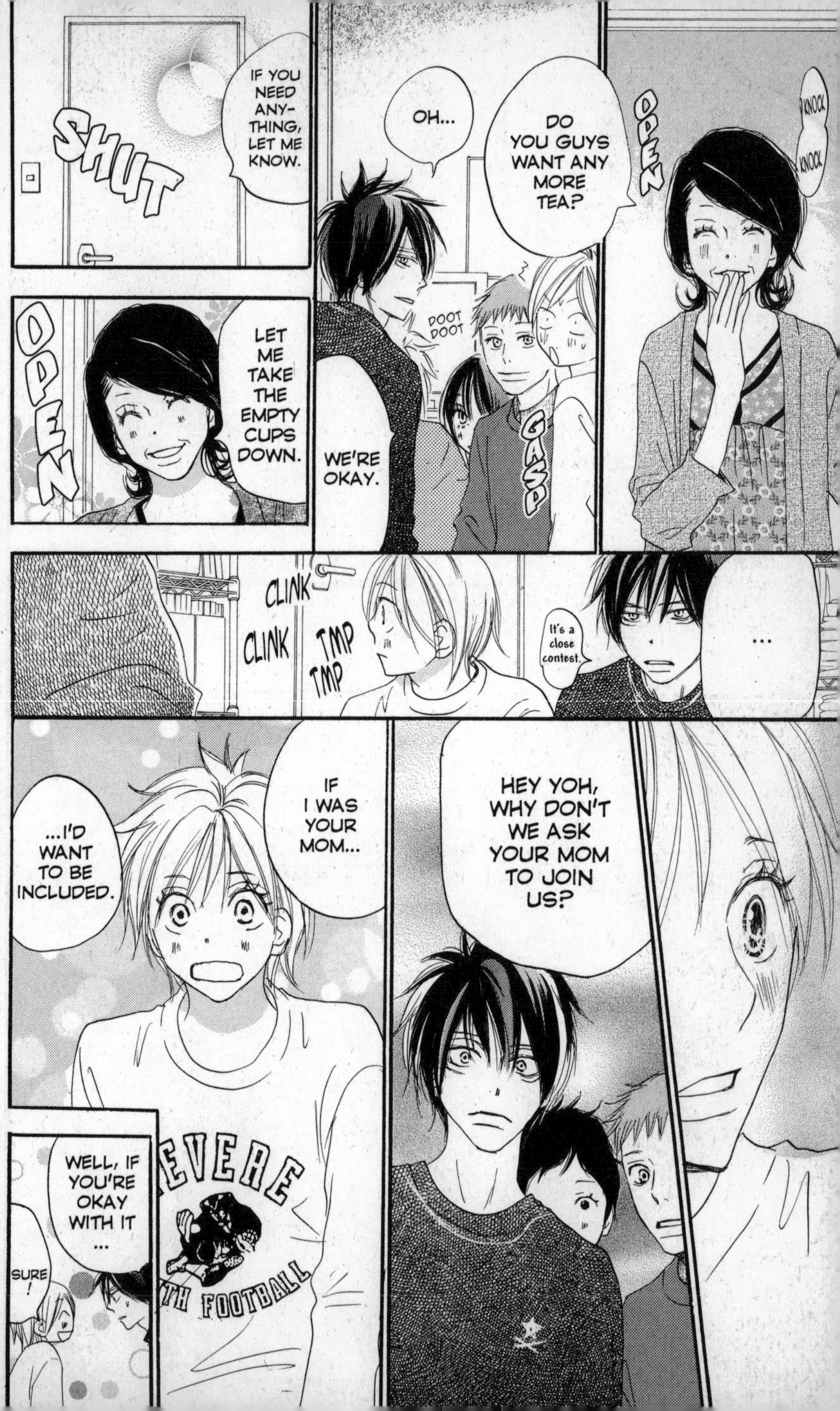
KNOCK KNOCK
OPEN
DO YOU GUYS WANT ANY MORE TEA?
OH...
DOOT DOOT
GASP
WE'RE OKAY.
SHUT
IF YOU NEED ANYTHING, LET ME KNOW.
OPEN
LET ME TAKE THE EMPTY CUPS DOWN.
...
It's a close contest.
CLINK
CLINK
TMP TMP
HEY YOH, WHY DON'T WE ASK YOUR MOM TO JOIN US?
IF I WAS YOUR MOM...
...I'D WANT TO BE INCLUDED.
WELL, IF YOU'RE OKAY WITH IT ...
SURE!

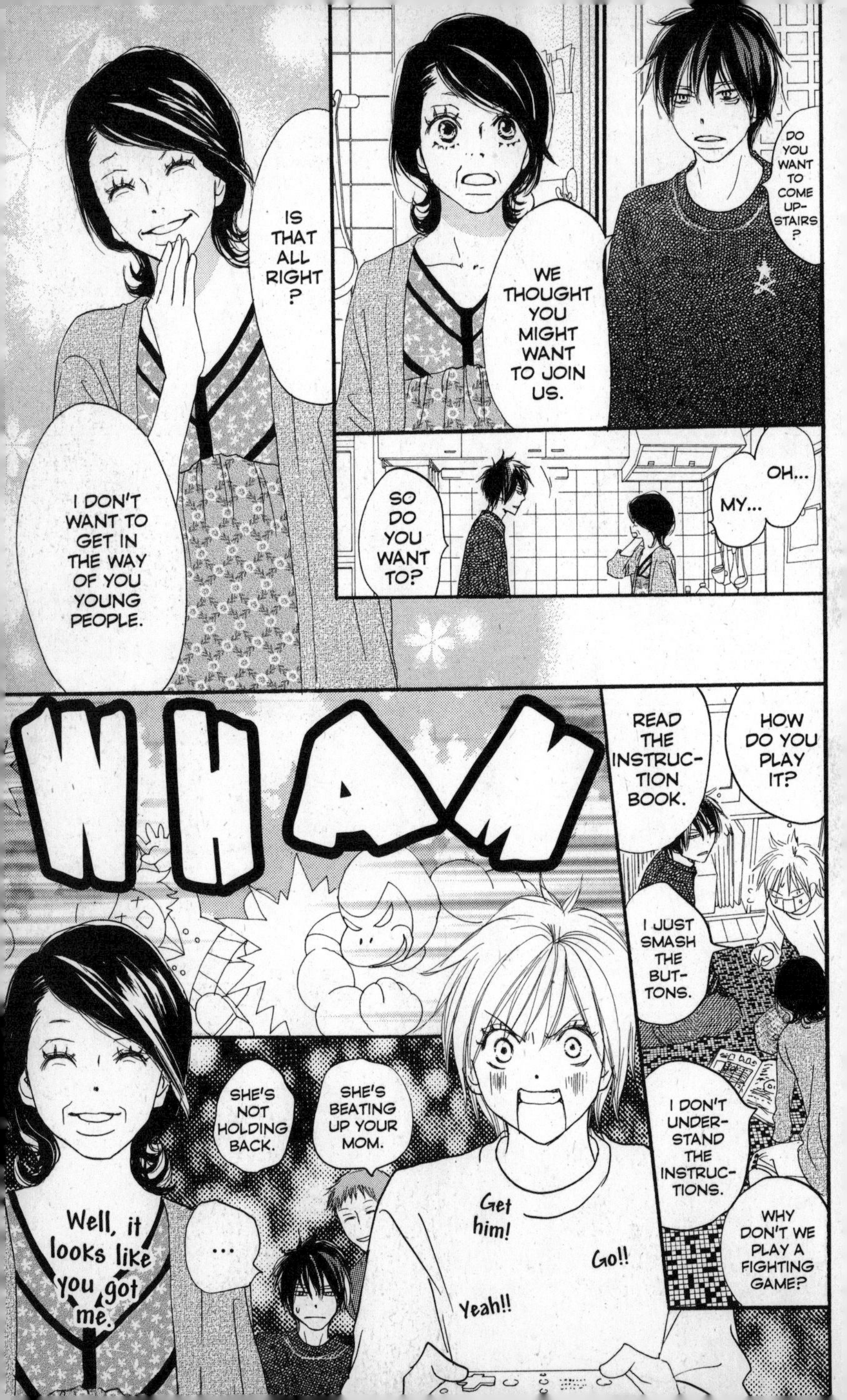
DO YOU WANT TO COME UP-STAIRS?
WE THOUGHT YOU MIGHT WANT TO JOIN US.
OH... MY...
SO DO YOU WANT TO?
IS THAT ALL RIGHT?
I DON'T WANT TO GET IN THE WAY OF YOU YOUNG PEOPLE.
HOW DO YOU PLAY IT?
READ THE INSTRUC-TION BOOK.
I JUST SMASH THE BUT-TONS.
I DON'T UNDER-STAND THE INSTRUC-TIONS.
WHY DON'T WE PLAY A FIGHTING GAME?
WHAM
SHE'S BEATING UP YOUR MOM.
SHE'S NOT HOLDING BACK.
Get him!
Go!!
Yeah!!
...
Well, it looks like you got me.

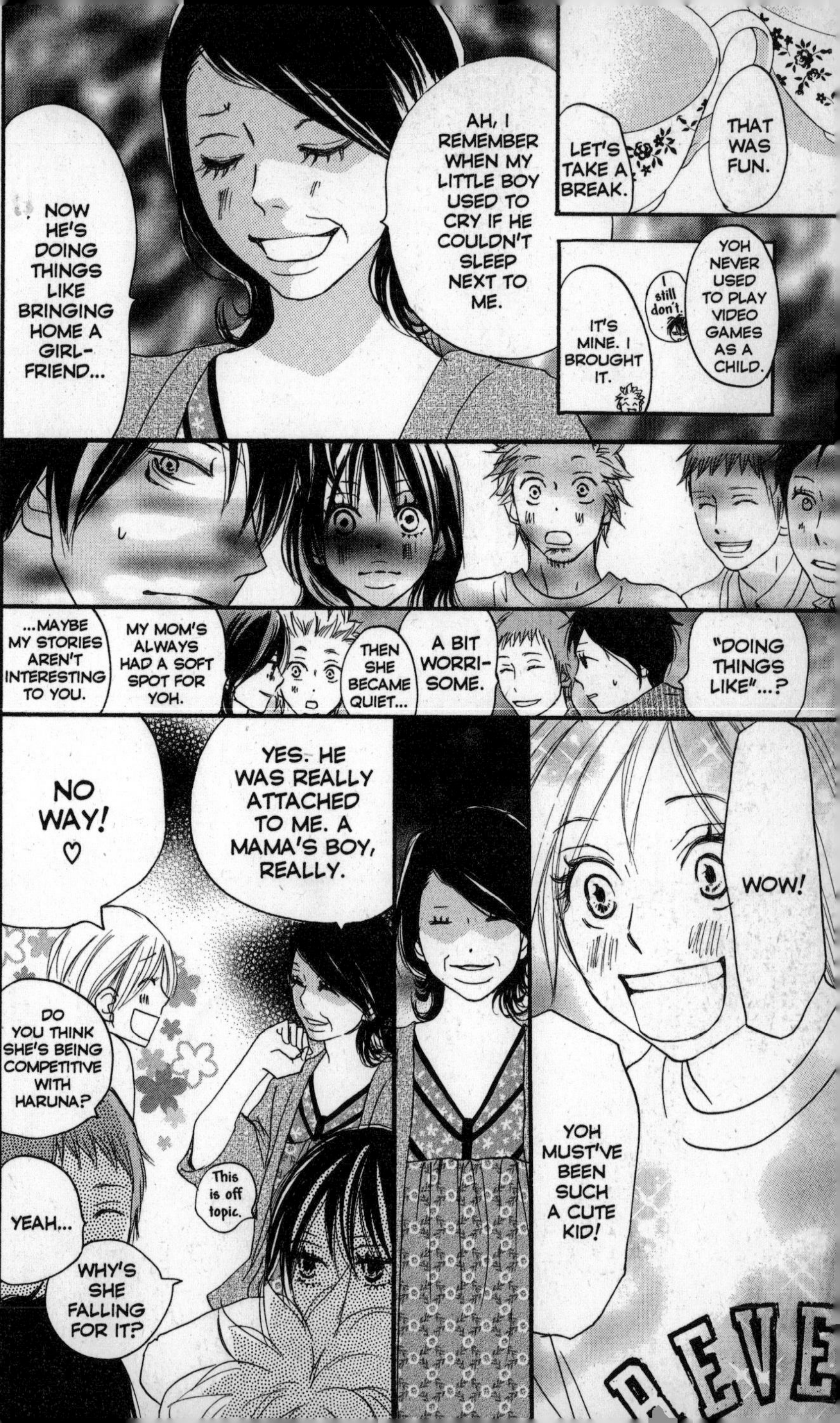
THAT WAS FUN.
LET'S TAKE A BREAK.
YOH NEVER USED TO PLAY VIDEO GAMES AS A CHILD.
I still don't.
IT'S MINE. I BROUGHT IT.
AH, I REMEMBER WHEN MY LITTLE BOY USED TO CRY IF HE COULDN'T SLEEP NEXT TO ME.
NOW HE'S DOING THINGS LIKE BRINGING HOME A GIRL-FRIEND...
"DOING THINGS LIKE"...?
A BIT WORRI-SOME.
THEN SHE BECAME QUIET...
MY MOM'S ALWAYS HAD A SOFT SPOT FOR YOH.
...MAYBE MY STORIES AREN'T INTERESTING TO YOU.
WOW!
YOH MUST'VE BEEN SUCH A CUTE KID!
YES. HE WAS REALLY ATTACHED TO ME. A MAMA'S BOY, REALLY.
NO WAY! ♡
DO YOU THINK SHE'S BEING COMPETITIVE WITH HARUNA?
This is off topic.
YEAH...
WHY'S SHE FALLING FOR IT?

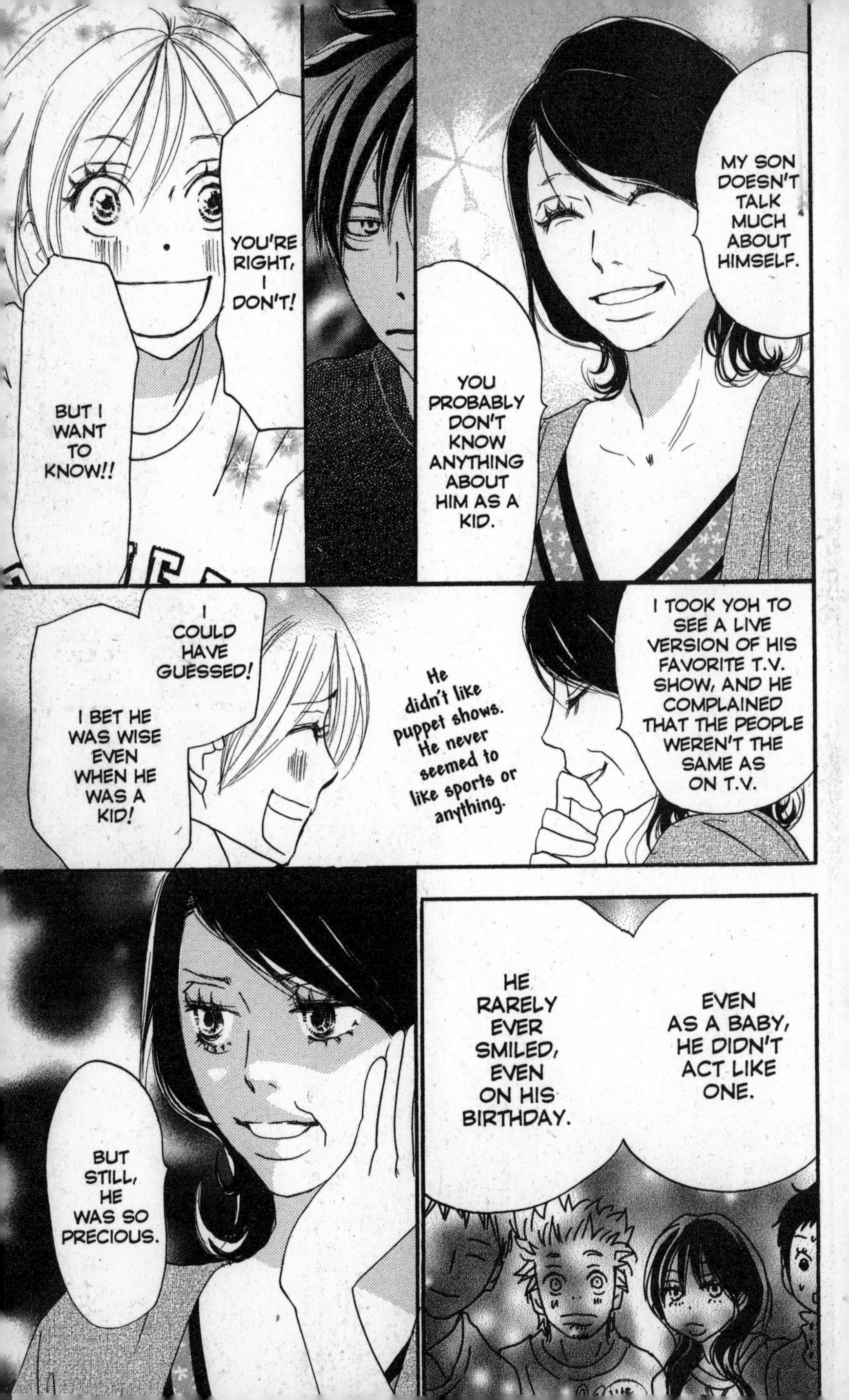
MY SON DOESN'T TALK MUCH ABOUT HIMSELF.
YOU PROBABLY DON'T KNOW ANYTHING ABOUT HIM AS A KID.
YOU'RE RIGHT, I DON'T!
BUT I WANT TO KNOW!!
I TOOK YOH TO SEE A LIVE VERSION OF HIS FAVORITE T.V. SHOW, AND HE COMPLAINED THAT THE PEOPLE WEREN'T THE SAME AS ON T.V.
He didn't like puppet shows. He never seemed to like sports or anything.
I COULD HAVE GUESSED!
I BET HE WAS WISE EVEN WHEN HE WAS A KID!
EVEN AS A BABY, HE DIDN'T ACT LIKE ONE.
HE RARELY EVER SMILED, EVEN ON HIS BIRTHDAY.
BUT STILL, HE WAS SO PRECIOUS.

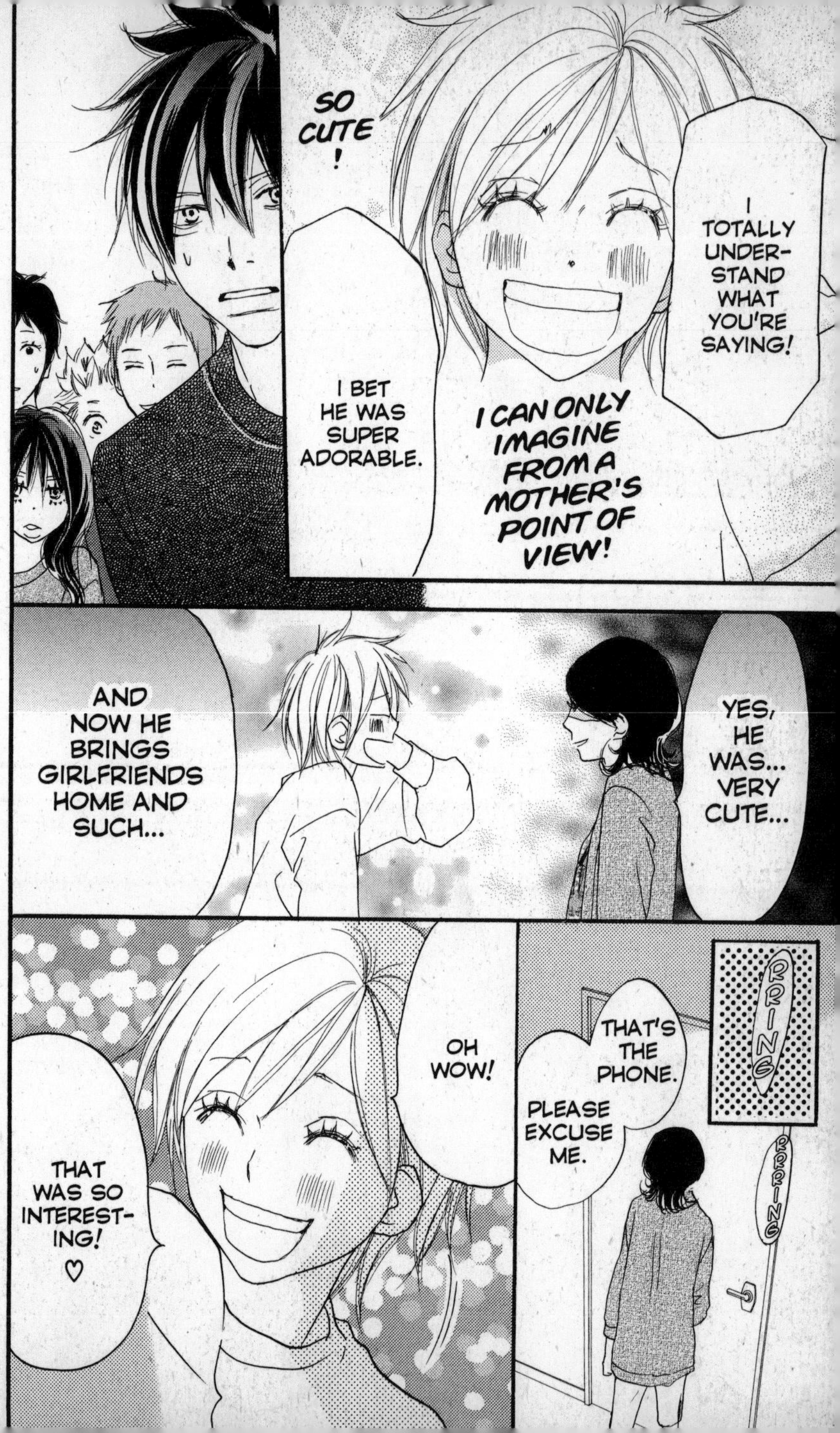
I TOTALLY UNDER-STAND WHAT YOU'RE SAYING!
SO CUTE!
I CAN ONLY IMAGINE FROM A MOTHER'S POINT OF VIEW!
I BET HE WAS SUPER ADORABLE.
YES, HE WAS... VERY CUTE...
AND NOW HE BRINGS GIRLFRIENDS HOME AND SUCH...
RRING
THAT'S THE PHONE.
PLEASE EXCUSE ME.
RRRING
OH WOW!
THAT WAS SO INTEREST-ING! ♡

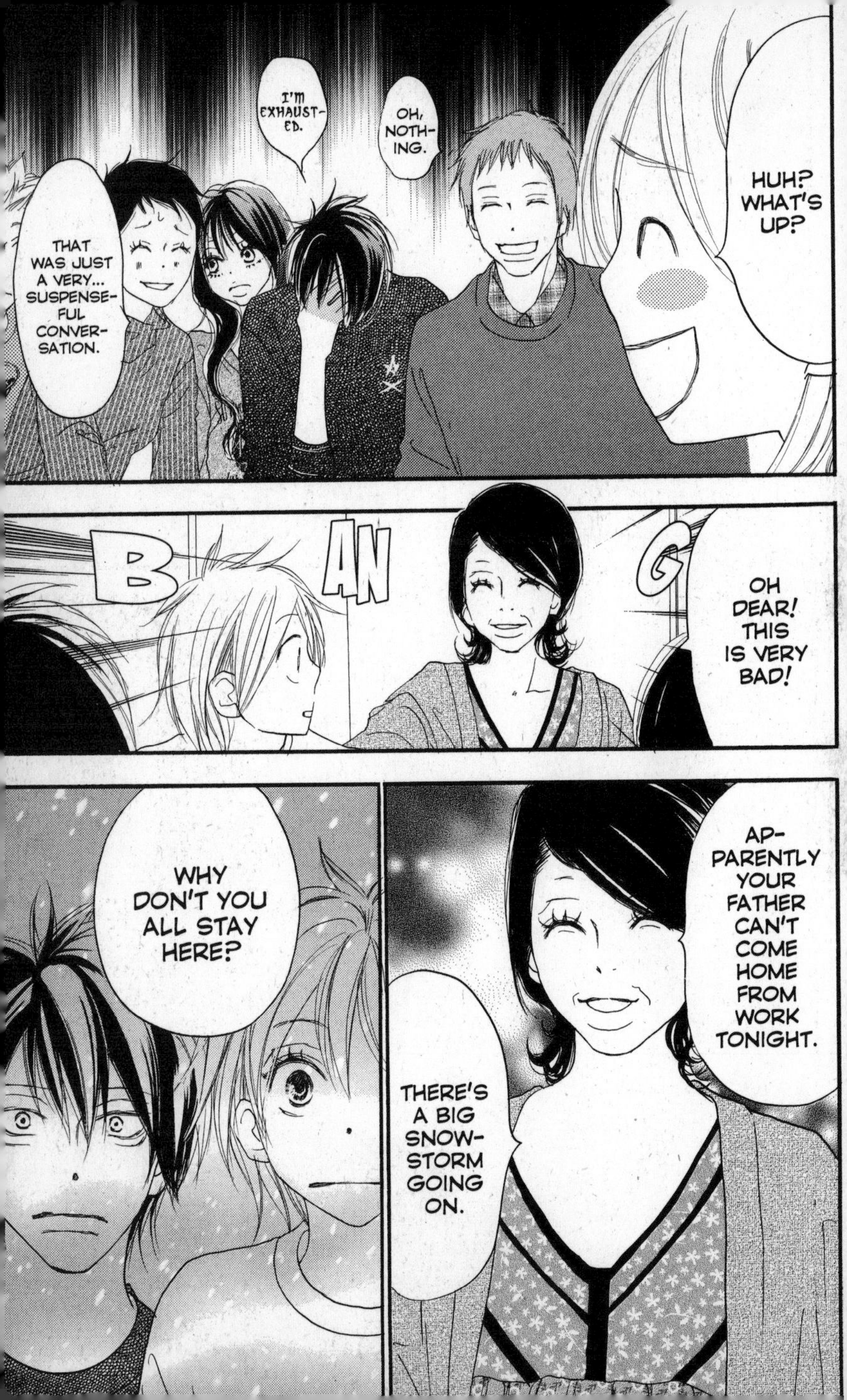
HUH? WHAT'S UP?
OH, NOTH-ING.
I'M EXHAUST-ED.
THAT WAS JUST A VERY... SUSPENSE-FUL CONVER-SATION.
BANG
OH DEAR! THIS IS VERY BAD!
AP-PARENTLY YOUR FATHER CAN'T COME HOME FROM WORK TONIGHT.
THERE'S A BIG SNOW-STORM GOING ON.
WHY DON'T YOU ALL STAY HERE?

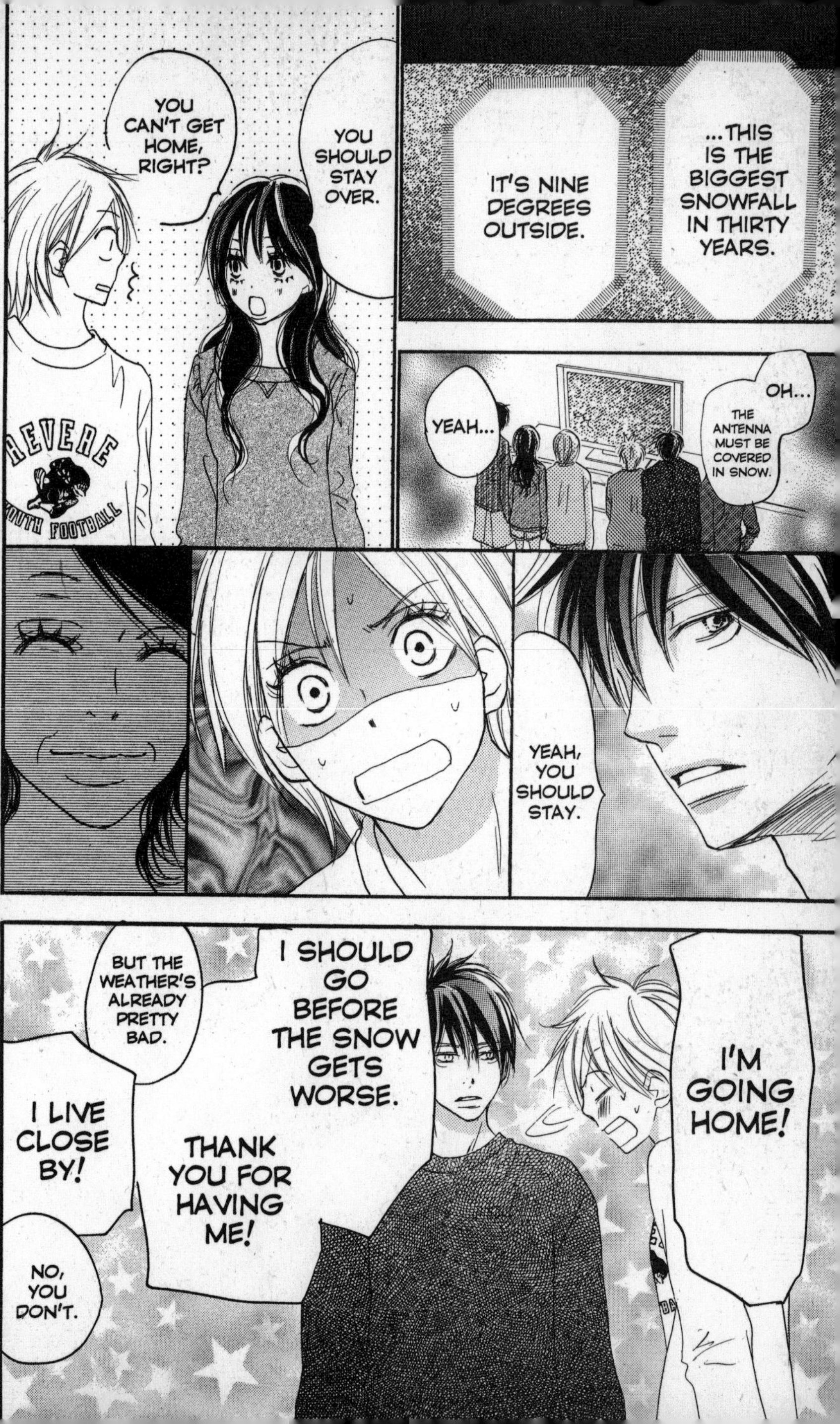
...THIS IS THE BIGGEST SNOWFALL IN THIRTY YEARS.
IT'S NINE DEGREES OUTSIDE.
OH... THE ANTENNA MUST BE COVERED IN SNOW.
YEAH...
YOU SHOULD STAY OVER.
YOU CAN'T GET HOME, RIGHT?
REVERE YOUTH FOOTBALL
YEAH, YOU SHOULD STAY.
I'M GOING HOME!
I SHOULD GO BEFORE THE SNOW GETS WORSE.
BUT THE WEATHER'S ALREADY PRETTY BAD.
THANK YOU FOR HAVING ME!
I LIVE CLOSE BY!
NO, YOU DON'T.

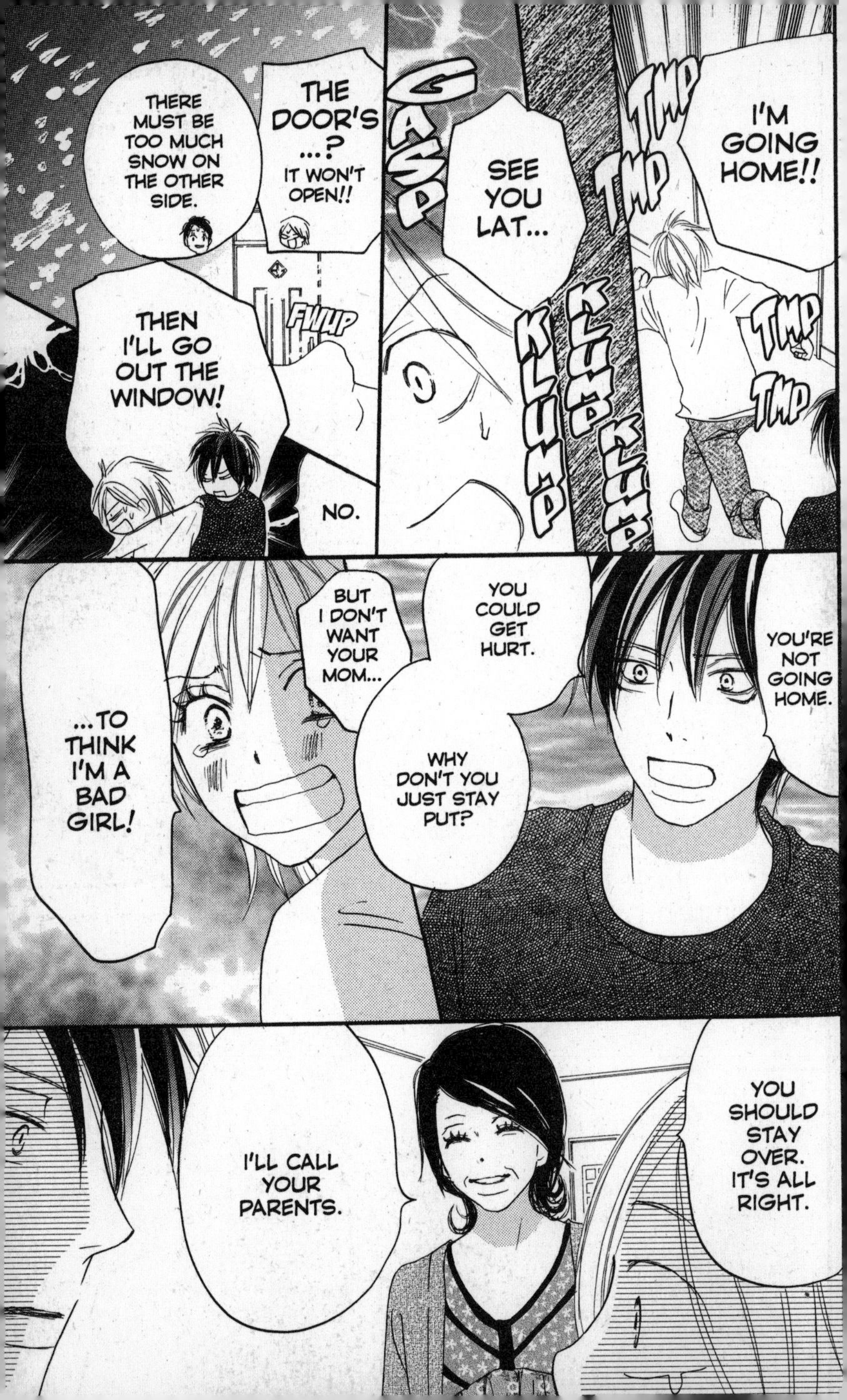
TMP
TMP
I'M GOING HOME!!
TMP
TMP
GASP
SEE YOU LAT...
KLUMP
KLUMP
KLUMP
THE DOOR'S ...? IT WON'T OPEN!!
THERE MUST BE TOO MUCH SNOW ON THE OTHER SIDE.
FWUP
THEN I'LL GO OUT THE WINDOW!
NO.
YOU'RE NOT GOING HOME.
YOU COULD GET HURT.
WHY DON'T YOU JUST STAY PUT?
BUT I DON'T WANT YOUR MOM...
...TO THINK I'M A BAD GIRL!
YOU SHOULD STAY OVER. IT'S ALL RIGHT.
I'LL CALL YOUR PARENTS.

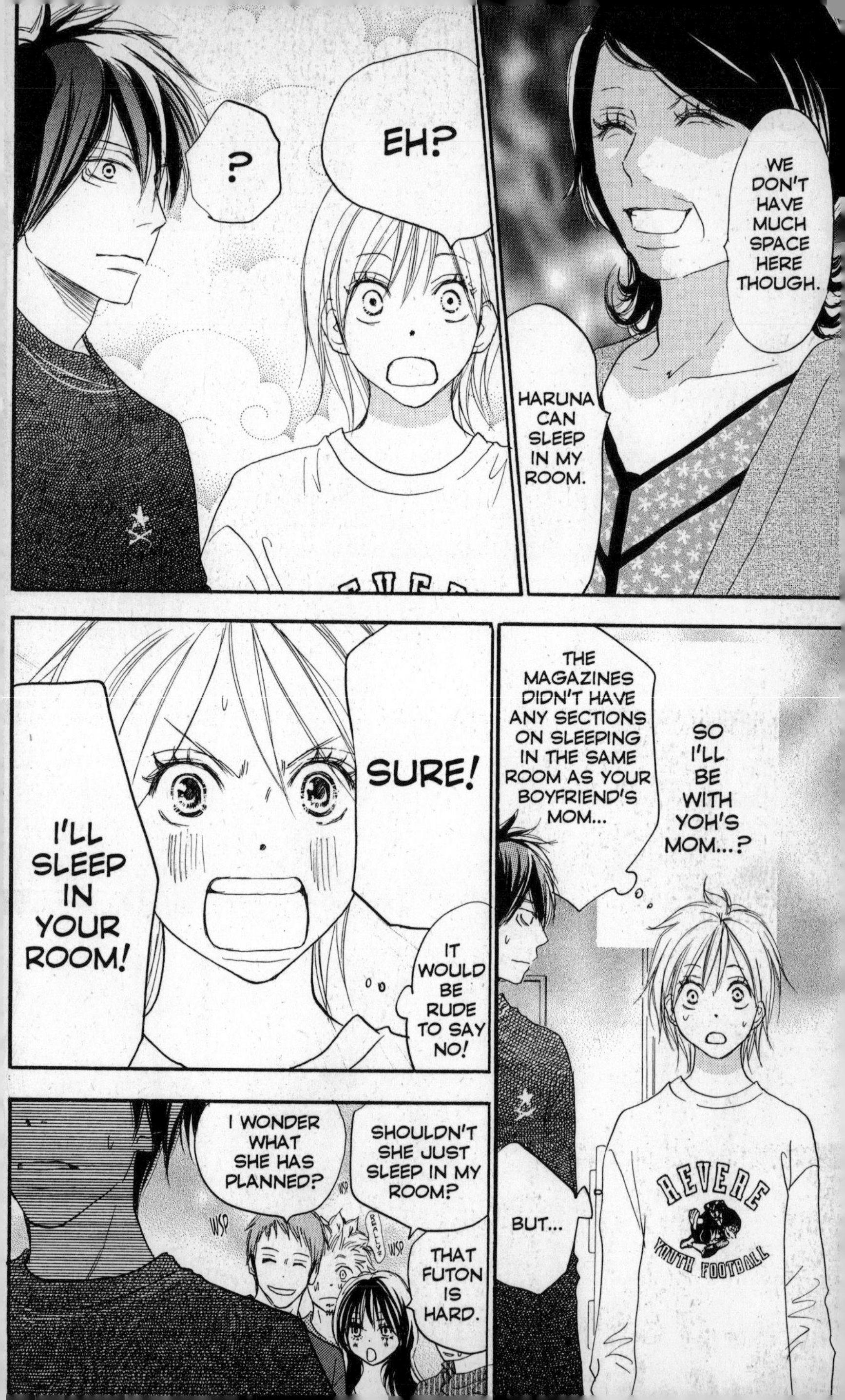
WE DON'T HAVE MUCH SPACE HERE THOUGH.
HARUNA CAN SLEEP IN MY ROOM.
EH?
?
THE MAGAZINES DIDN'T HAVE ANY SECTIONS ON SLEEPING IN THE SAME ROOM AS YOUR BOYFRIEND'S MOM...
SO I'LL BE WITH YOH'S MOM...?
BUT...
SURE!
IT WOULD BE RUDE TO SAY NO!
I'LL SLEEP IN YOUR ROOM!
SHOULDN'T SHE JUST SLEEP IN MY ROOM?
I WONDER WHAT SHE HAS PLANNED?
WSP
REALLY?
WSP
WSP
THAT FUTON IS HARD.

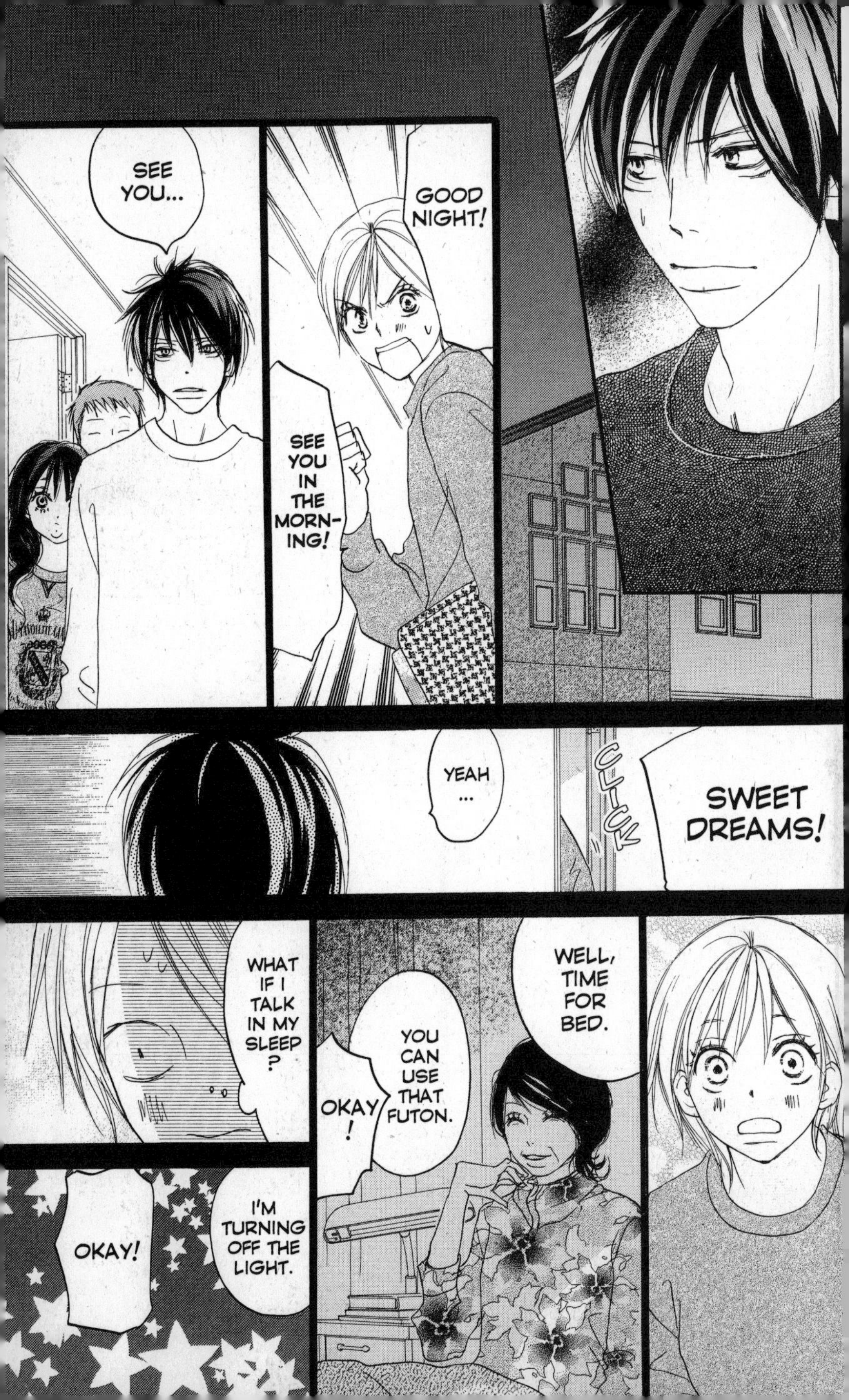
GOOD NIGHT!
SEE YOU IN THE MORNING!
SEE YOU...
SWEET DREAMS!
CLICK
YEAH...
WELL, TIME FOR BED.
YOU CAN USE THAT FUTON.
OKAY!
WHAT IF I TALK IN MY SLEEP?
I'M TURNING OFF THE LIGHT.
OKAY!

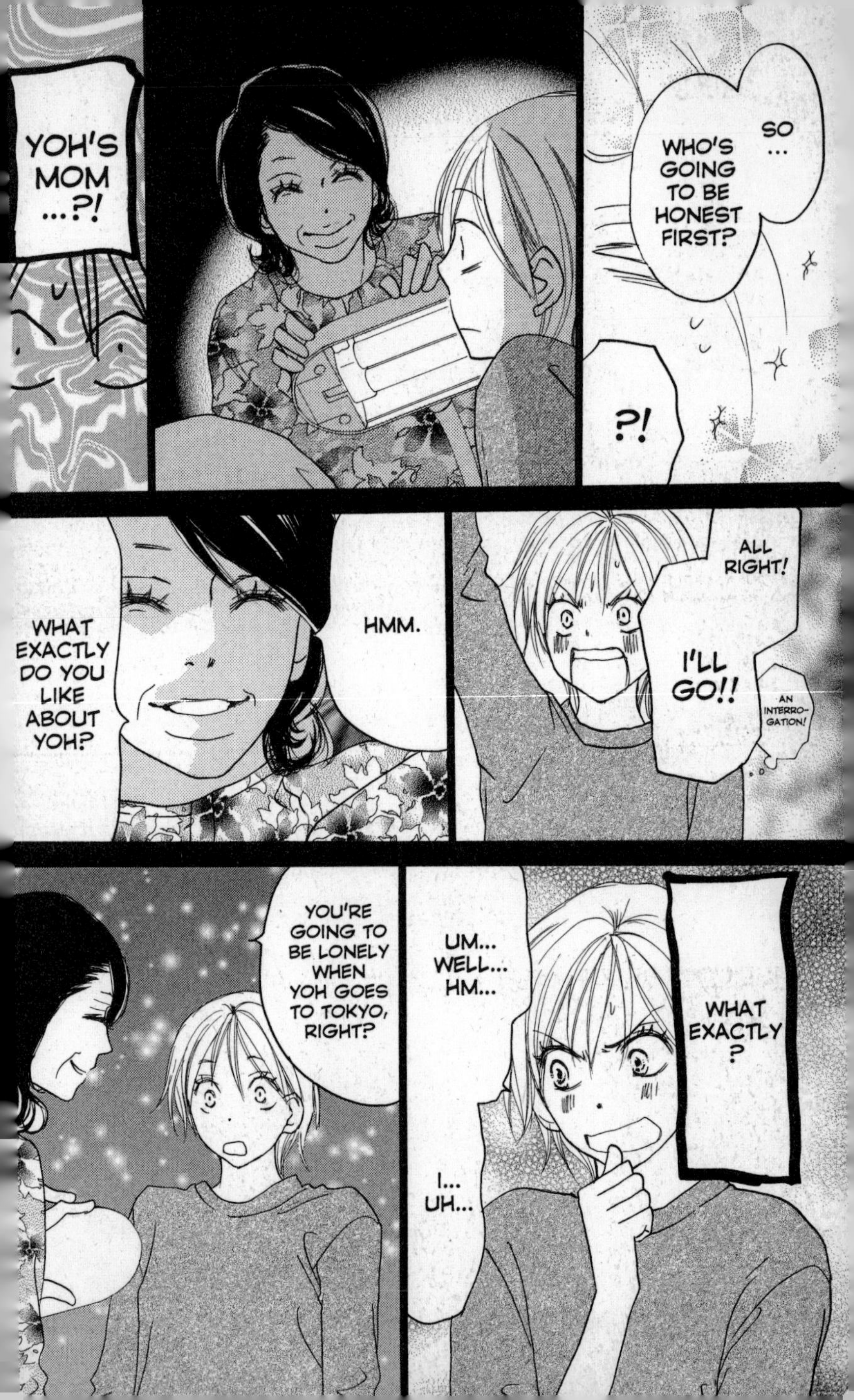
SO... WHO'S GOING TO BE HONEST FIRST?
?!
YOH'S MOM ...?!
ALL RIGHT! I'LL GO!!
AN INTERROGATION!
HMM.
WHAT EXACTLY DO YOU LIKE ABOUT YOH?
WHAT EXACTLY?
UM... WELL... HM...
I... UH...
YOU'RE GOING TO BE LONELY WHEN YOH GOES TO TOKYO, RIGHT?

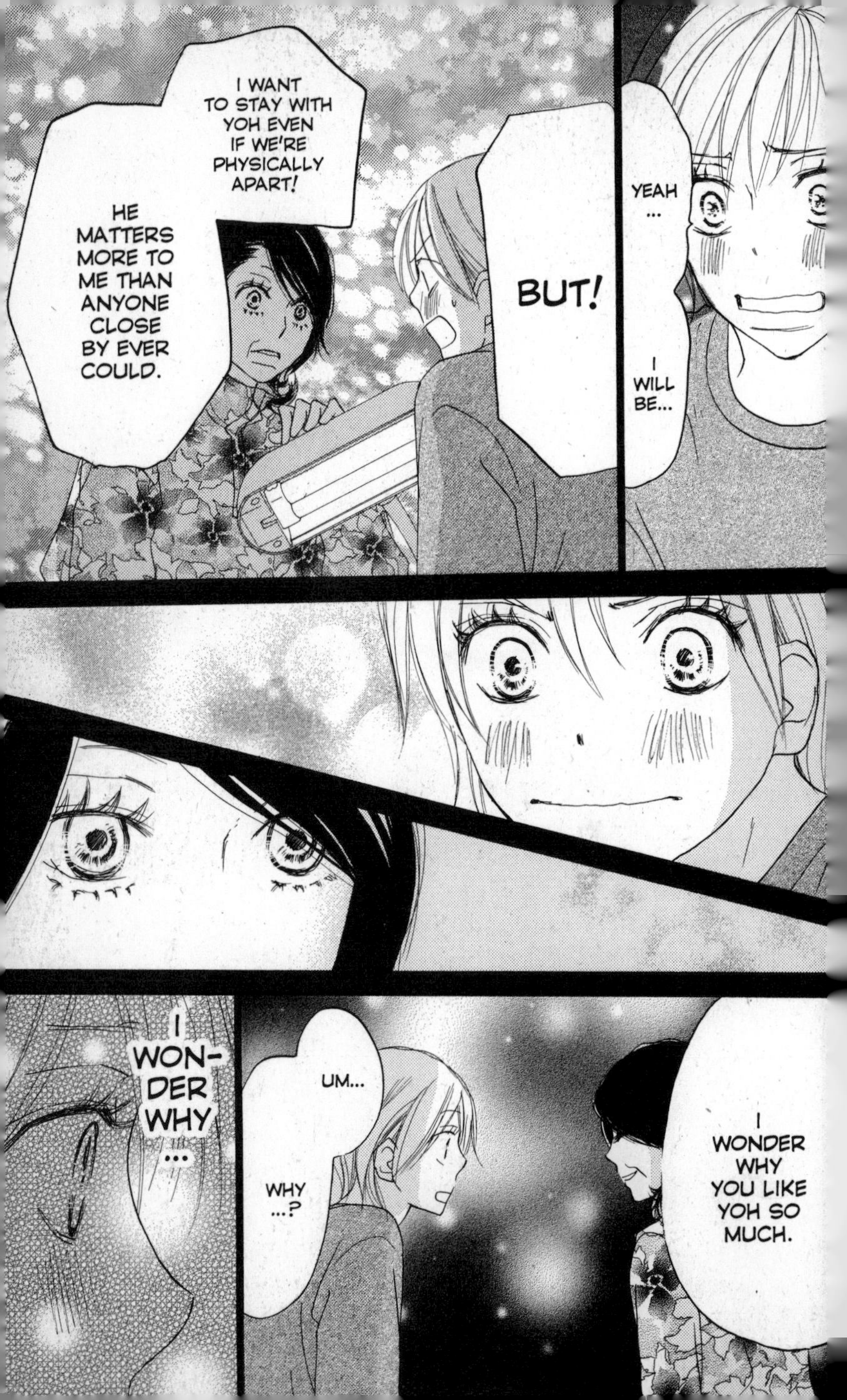
YEAH ...
I WILL BE...
BUT!
I WANT TO STAY WITH YOH EVEN IF WE'RE PHYSICALLY APART!
HE MATTERS MORE TO ME THAN ANYONE CLOSE BY EVER COULD.
I WONDER WHY YOU LIKE YOH SO MUCH.
UM...
WHY ...?
I WONDER WHY ...

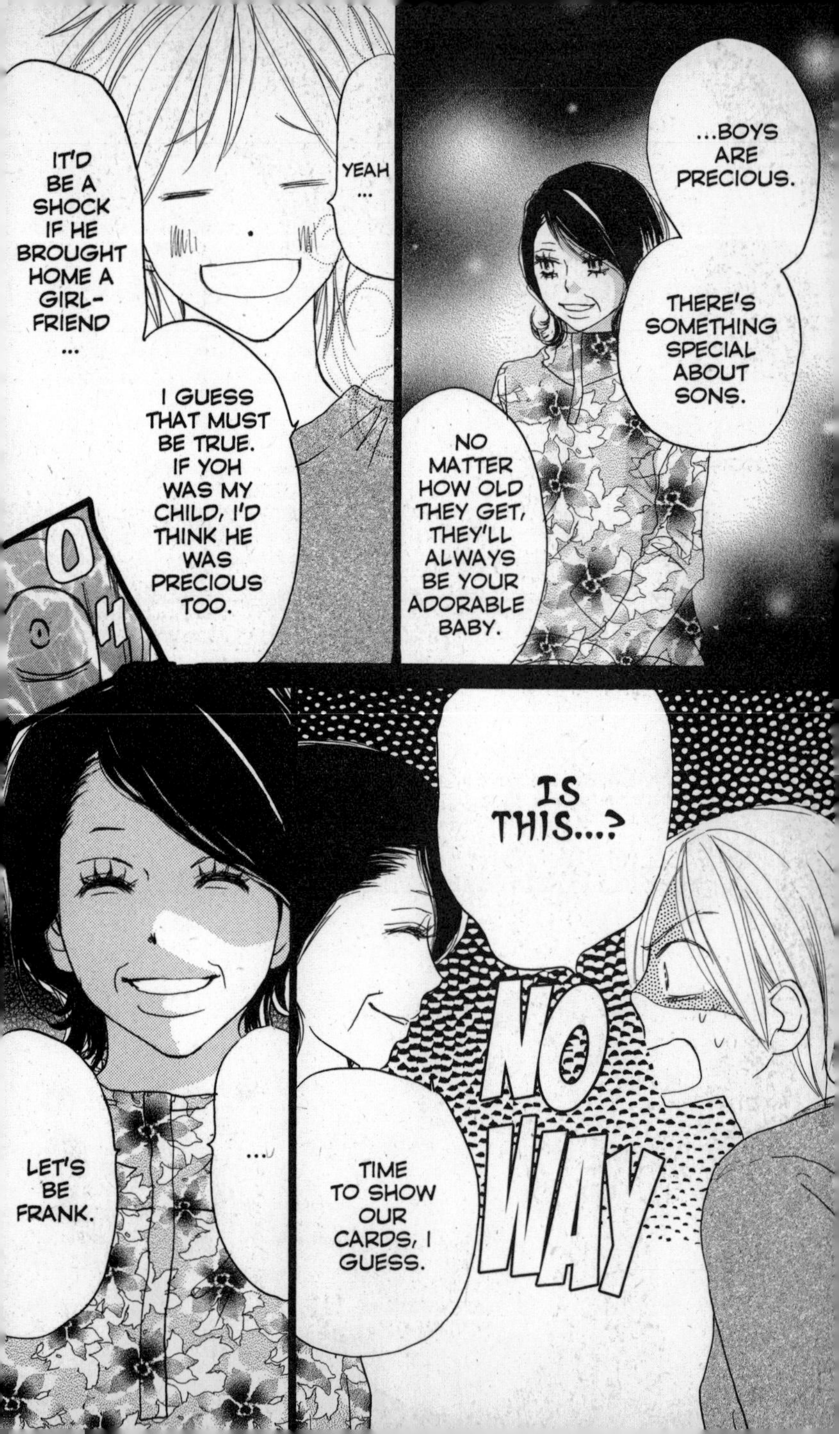
...BOYS ARE PRECIOUS.
THERE'S SOMETHING SPECIAL ABOUT SONS.
NO MATTER HOW OLD THEY GET, THEY'LL ALWAYS BE YOUR ADORABLE BABY.
YEAH ...
IT'D BE A SHOCK IF HE BROUGHT HOME A GIRL-FRIEND ...
I GUESS THAT MUST BE TRUE. IF YOH WAS MY CHILD, I'D THINK HE WAS PRECIOUS TOO.
OH
IS THIS...?
NO WAY
TIME TO SHOW OUR CARDS, I GUESS.
...
LET'S BE FRANK.

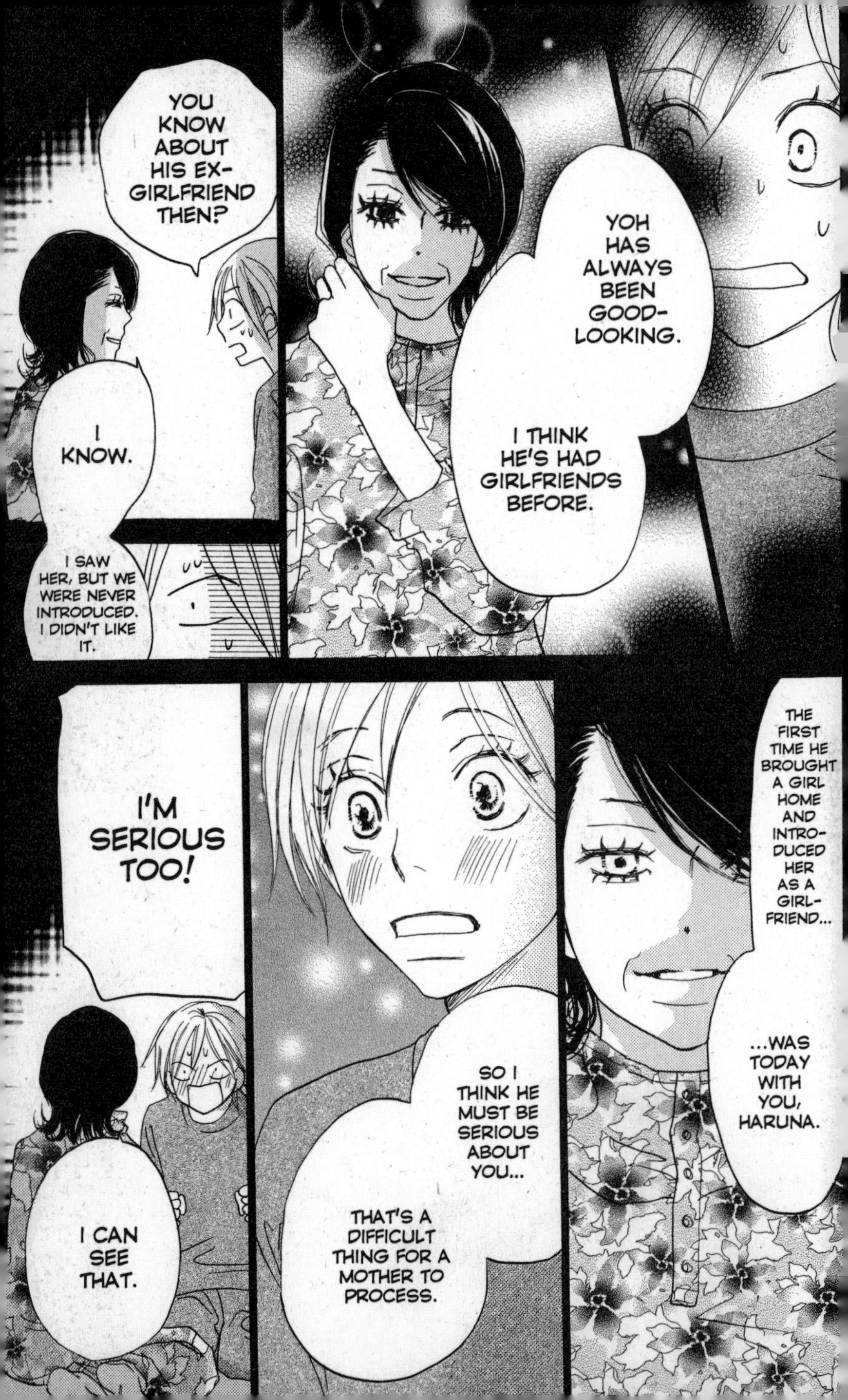
YOH HAS ALWAYS BEEN GOOD-LOOKING.
I THINK HE'S HAD GIRLFRIENDS BEFORE.
YOU KNOW ABOUT HIS EX-GIRLFRIEND THEN?
I KNOW.
I SAW HER, BUT WE WERE NEVER INTRODUCED. I DIDN'T LIKE IT.
THE FIRST TIME HE BROUGHT A GIRL HOME AND INTRODUCED HER AS A GIRLFRIEND...
...WAS TODAY WITH YOU, HARUNA.
SO I THINK HE MUST BE SERIOUS ABOUT YOU...
THAT'S A DIFFICULT THING FOR A MOTHER TO PROCESS.
I'M SERIOUS TOO!
I CAN SEE THAT.

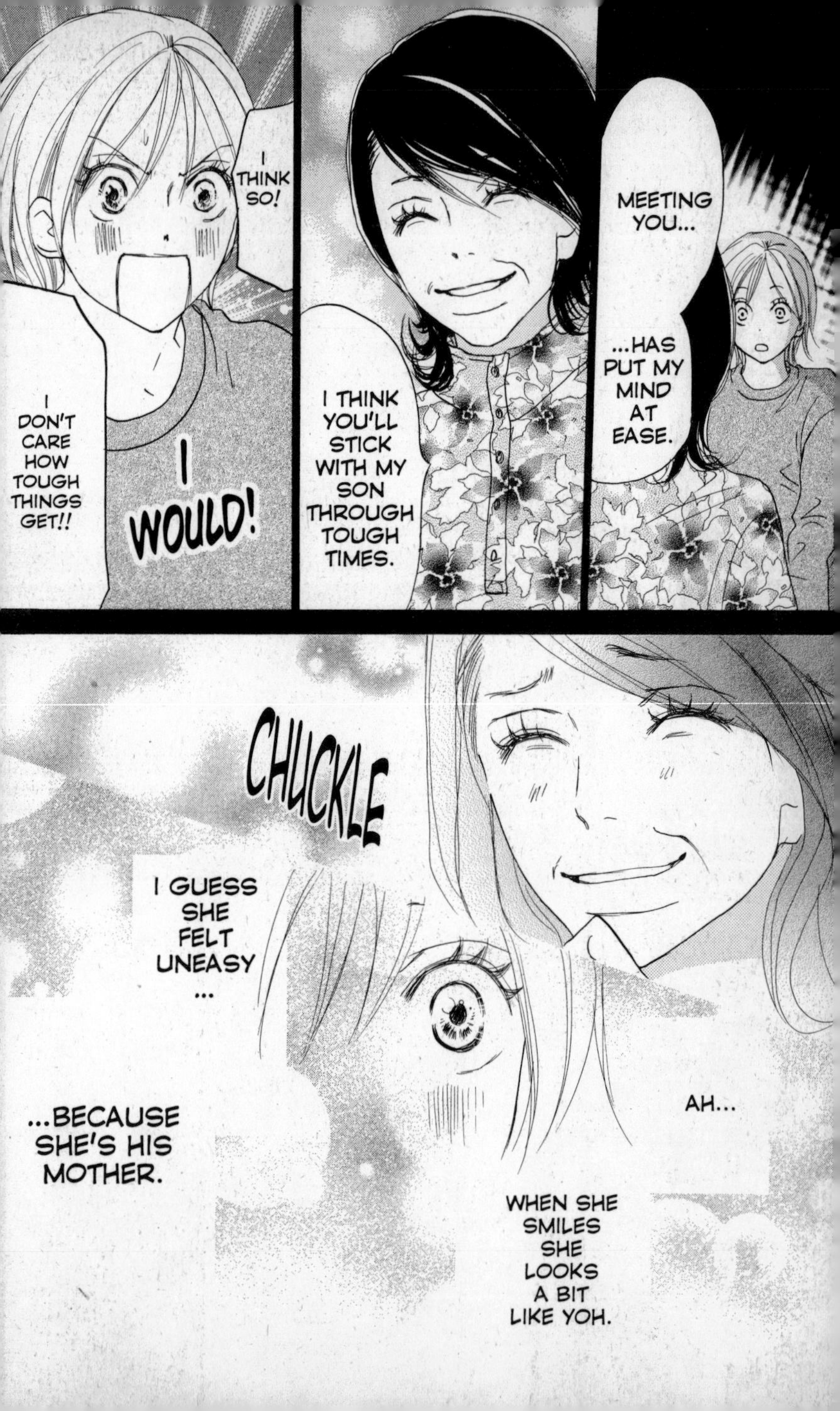
MEETING YOU...
...HAS PUT MY MIND AT EASE.
I THINK YOU'LL STICK WITH MY SON THROUGH TOUGH TIMES.
I THINK SO!
I WOULD!
I DON'T CARE HOW TOUGH THINGS GET!!
CHUCKLE
AH...
WHEN SHE SMILES SHE LOOKS A BIT LIKE YOH.
I GUESS SHE FELT UNEASY...
...BECAUSE SHE'S HIS MOTHER.

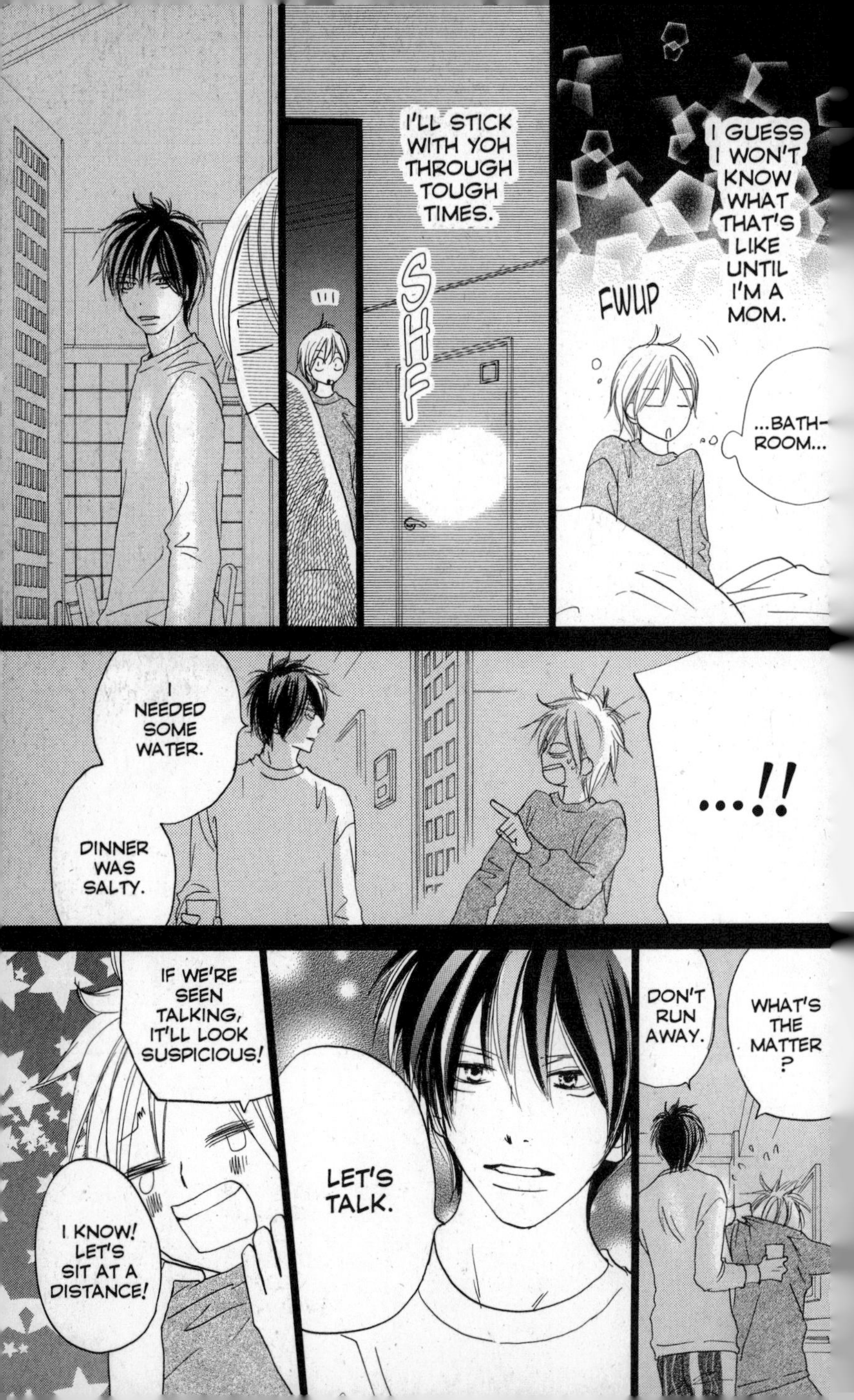
I GUESS I WON'T KNOW WHAT THAT'S LIKE UNTIL I'M A MOM.
FWUP
...BATH-ROOM...
I'LL STICK WITH YOH THROUGH TOUGH TIMES.
SHF
...!!
I NEEDED SOME WATER.
DINNER WAS SALTY.
WHAT'S THE MATTER?
DON'T RUN AWAY.
LET'S TALK.
IF WE'RE SEEN TALKING, IT'LL LOOK SUSPICIOUS!
I KNOW! LET'S SIT AT A DISTANCE!

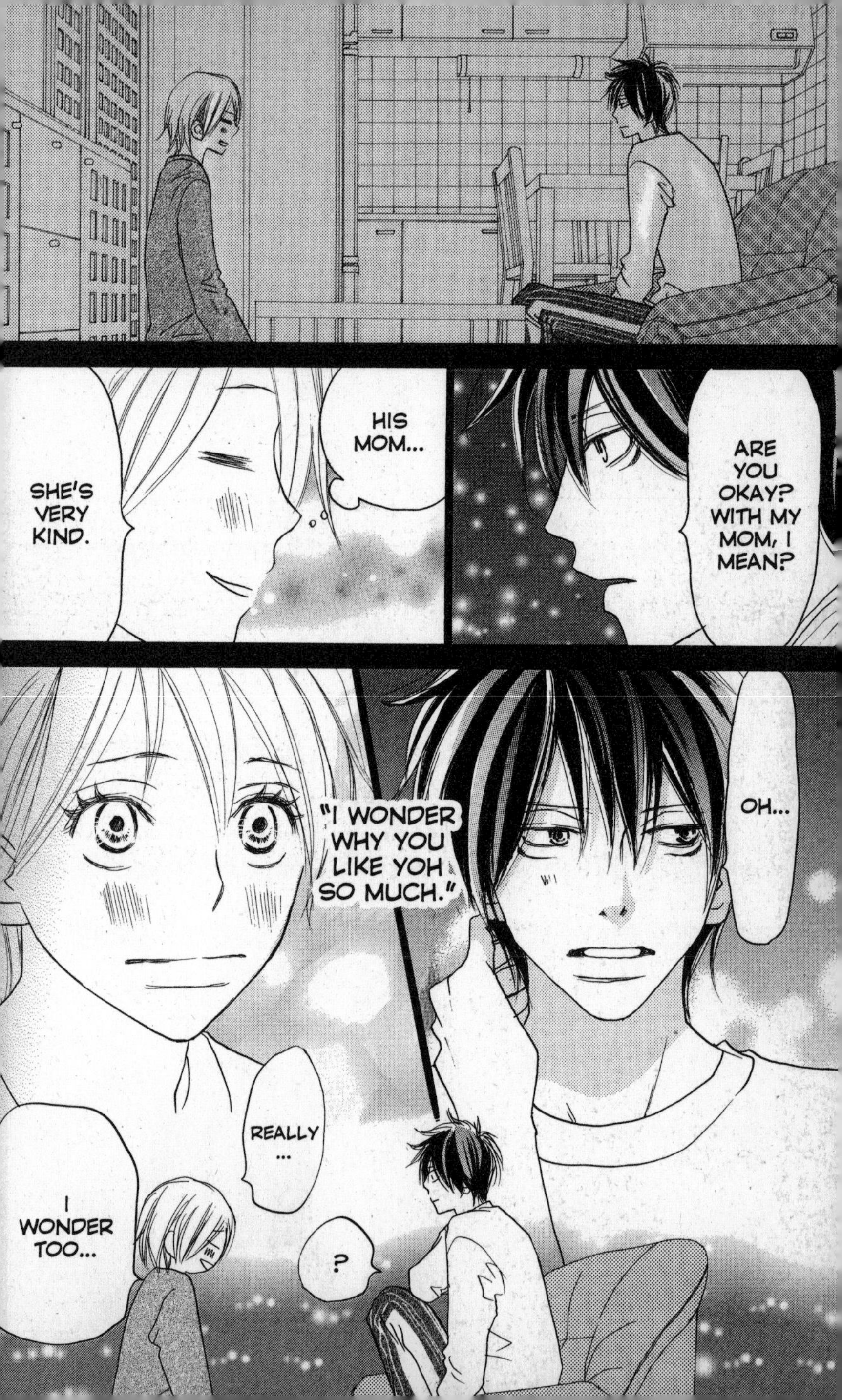
ARE YOU OKAY? WITH MY MOM, I MEAN?
HIS MOM...
SHE'S VERY KIND.
OH...
"I WONDER WHY YOU LIKE YOH SO MUCH."
REALLY ...
?
I WONDER TOO...

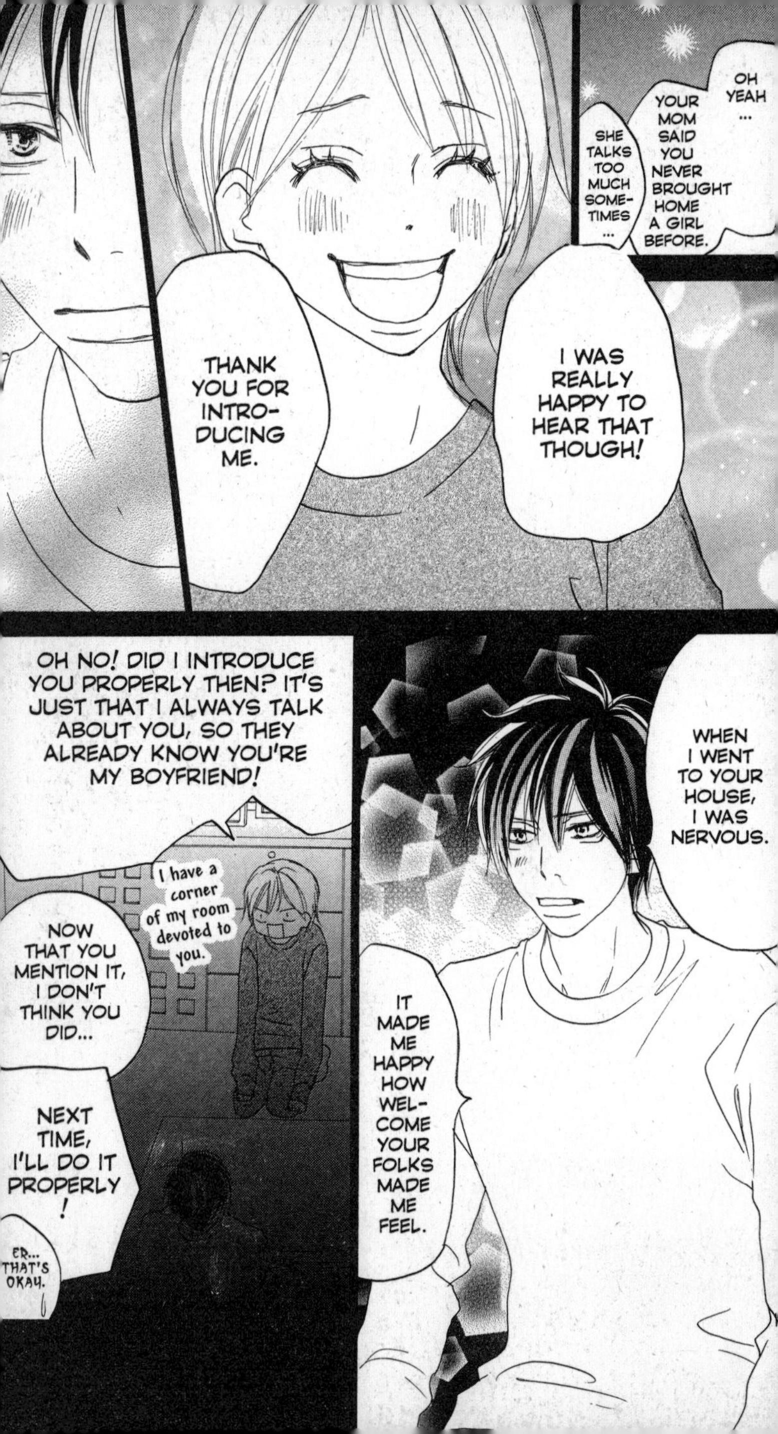
OH YEAH ...
YOUR MOM SAID YOU NEVER BROUGHT HOME A GIRL BEFORE.
SHE TALKS TOO MUCH SOME-TIMES ...
I WAS REALLY HAPPY TO HEAR THAT THOUGH!
THANK YOU FOR INTRO-DUCING ME.
WHEN I WENT TO YOUR HOUSE, I WAS NERVOUS.
IT MADE ME HAPPY HOW WEL-COME YOUR FOLKS MADE ME FEEL.
OH NO! DID I INTRODUCE YOU PROPERLY THEN? IT'S JUST THAT I ALWAYS TALK ABOUT YOU, SO THEY ALREADY KNOW YOU'RE MY BOYFRIEND!
I have a corner of my room devoted to you.
NOW THAT YOU MENTION IT, I DON'T THINK YOU DID...
NEXT TIME, I'LL DO IT PROPERLY!
ER... THAT'S OKAY.

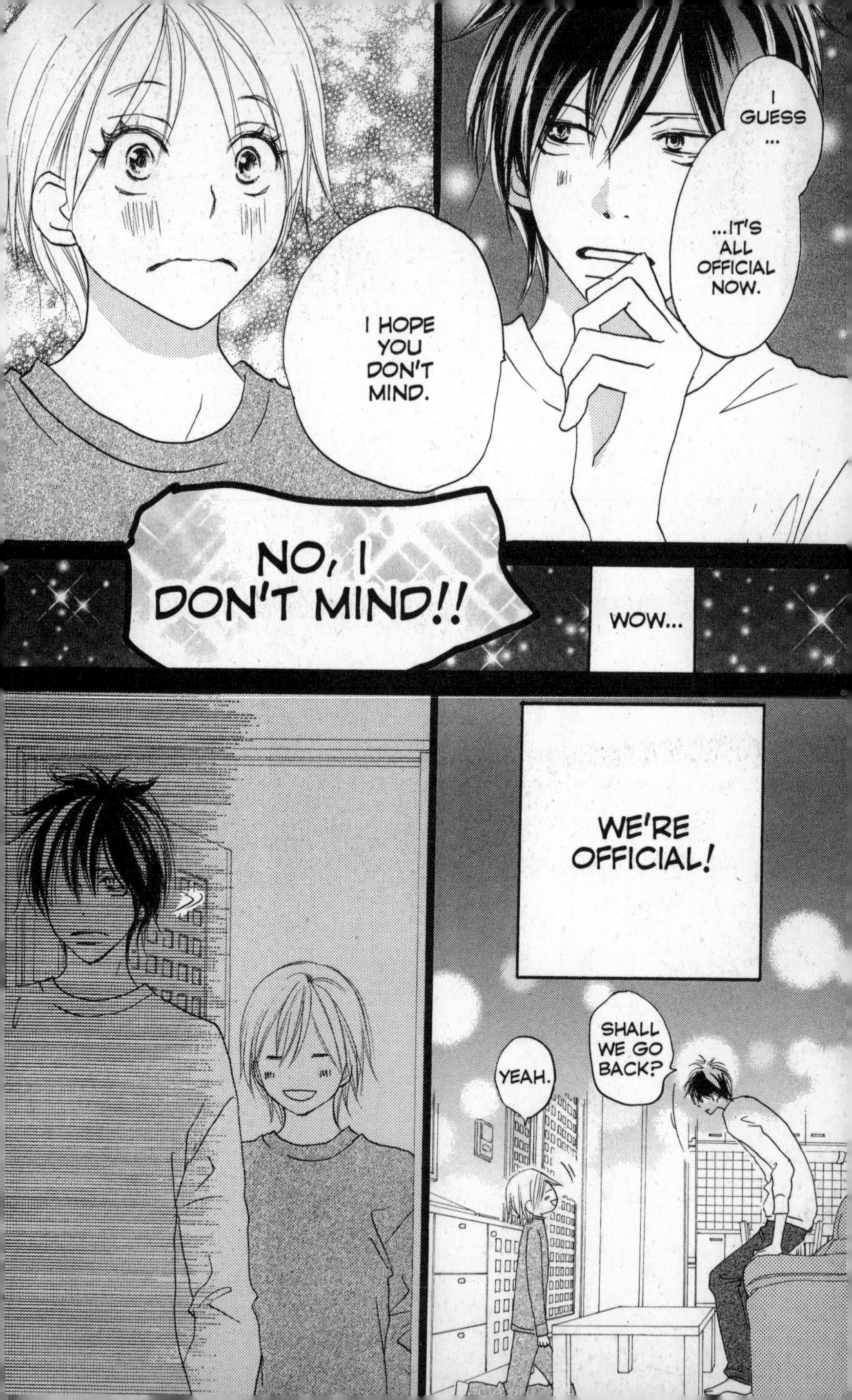
I GUESS ...
...IT'S ALL OFFICIAL NOW.
I HOPE YOU DON'T MIND.
NO, I DON'T MIND!!
WOW...
WE'RE OFFICIAL!
SHALL WE GO BACK?
YEAH.

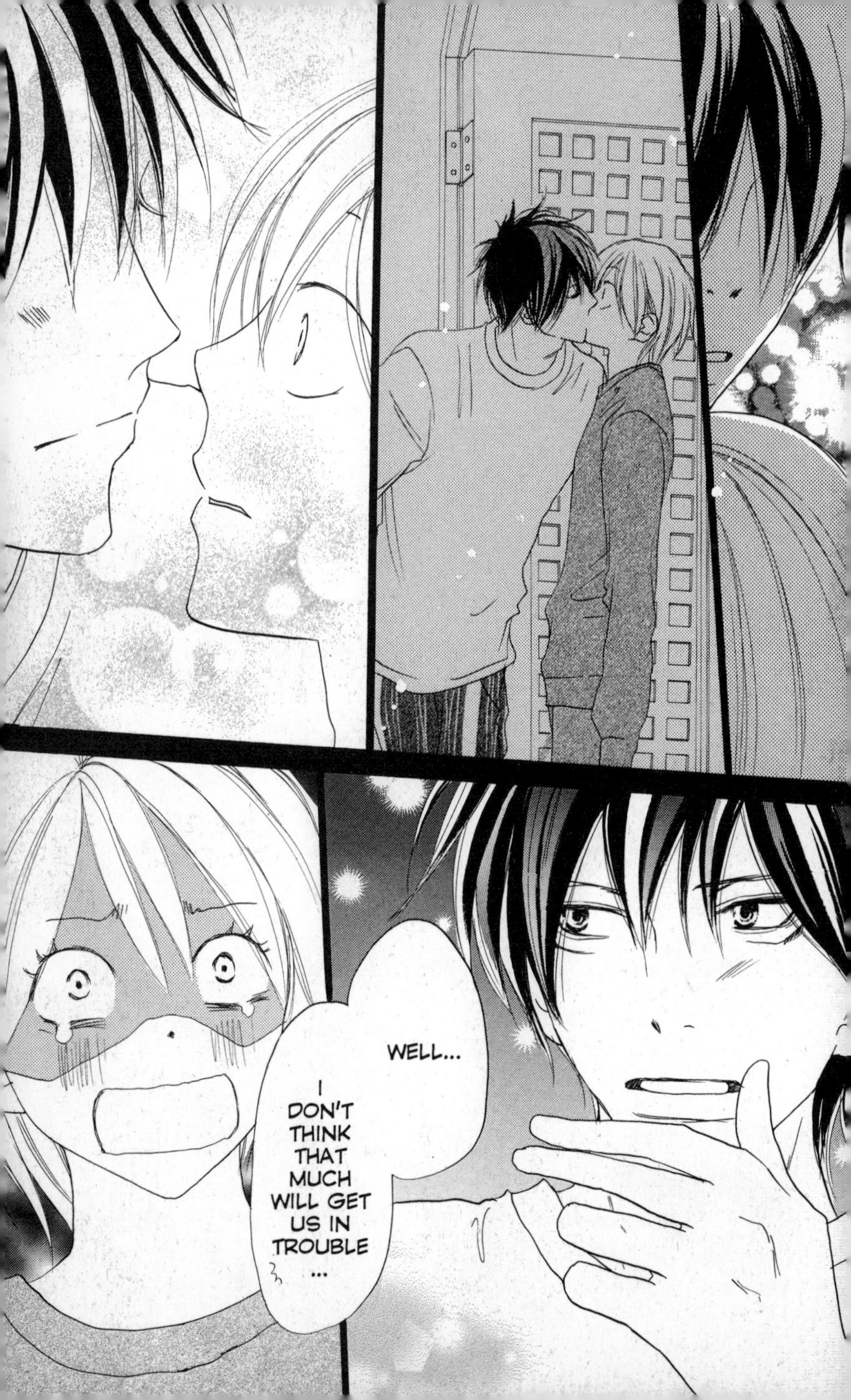
WELL...
I DON'T THINK THAT MUCH WILL GET US IN TROUBLE ...

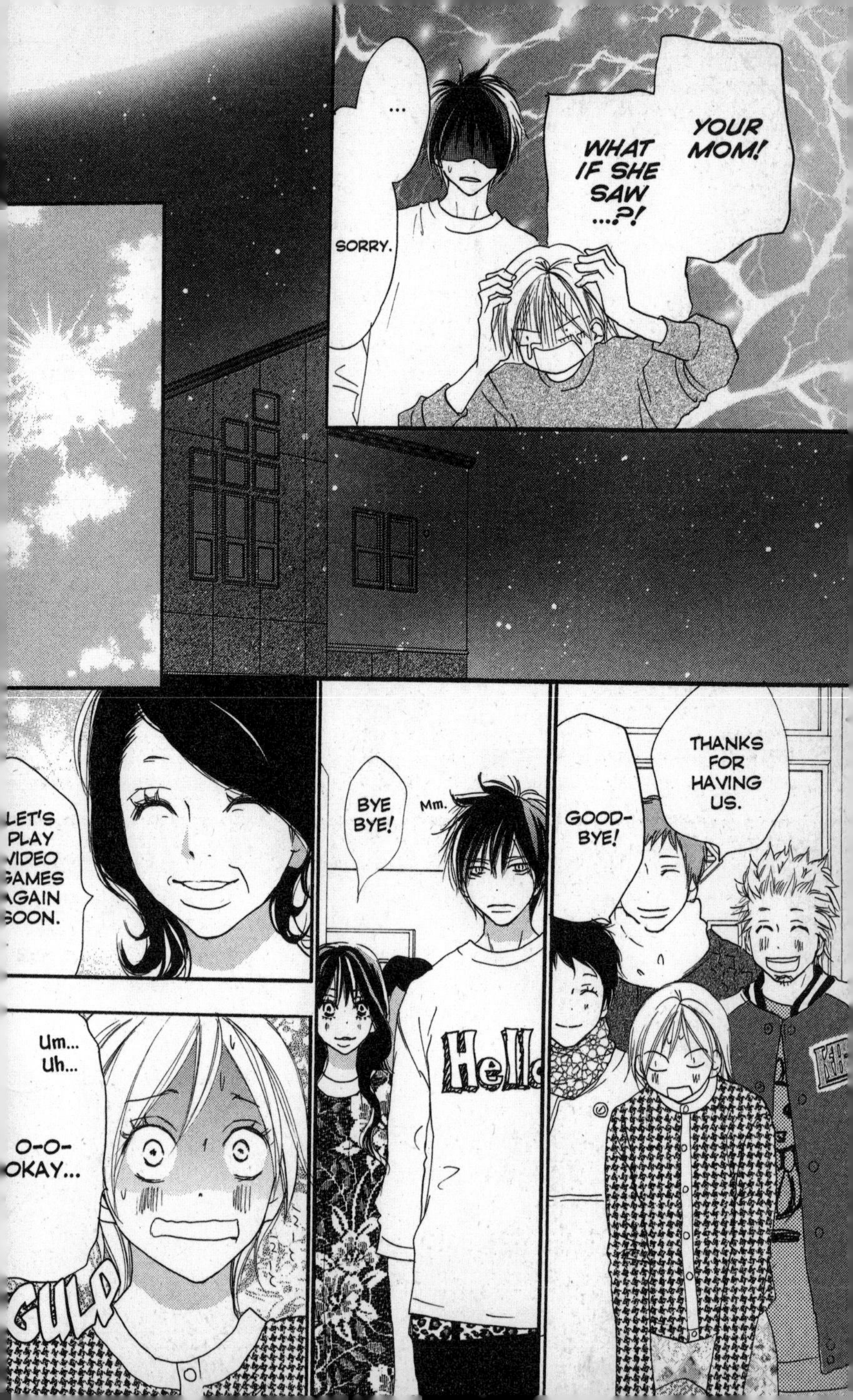
YOUR MOM! WHAT IF SHE SAW ...?!
...
SORRY.
THANKS FOR HAVING US.
GOOD-BYE!
Mm.
BYE BYE!
LET'S PLAY VIDEO GAMES AGAIN SOON.
Um... Uh...
O-O-OKAY...
GULP

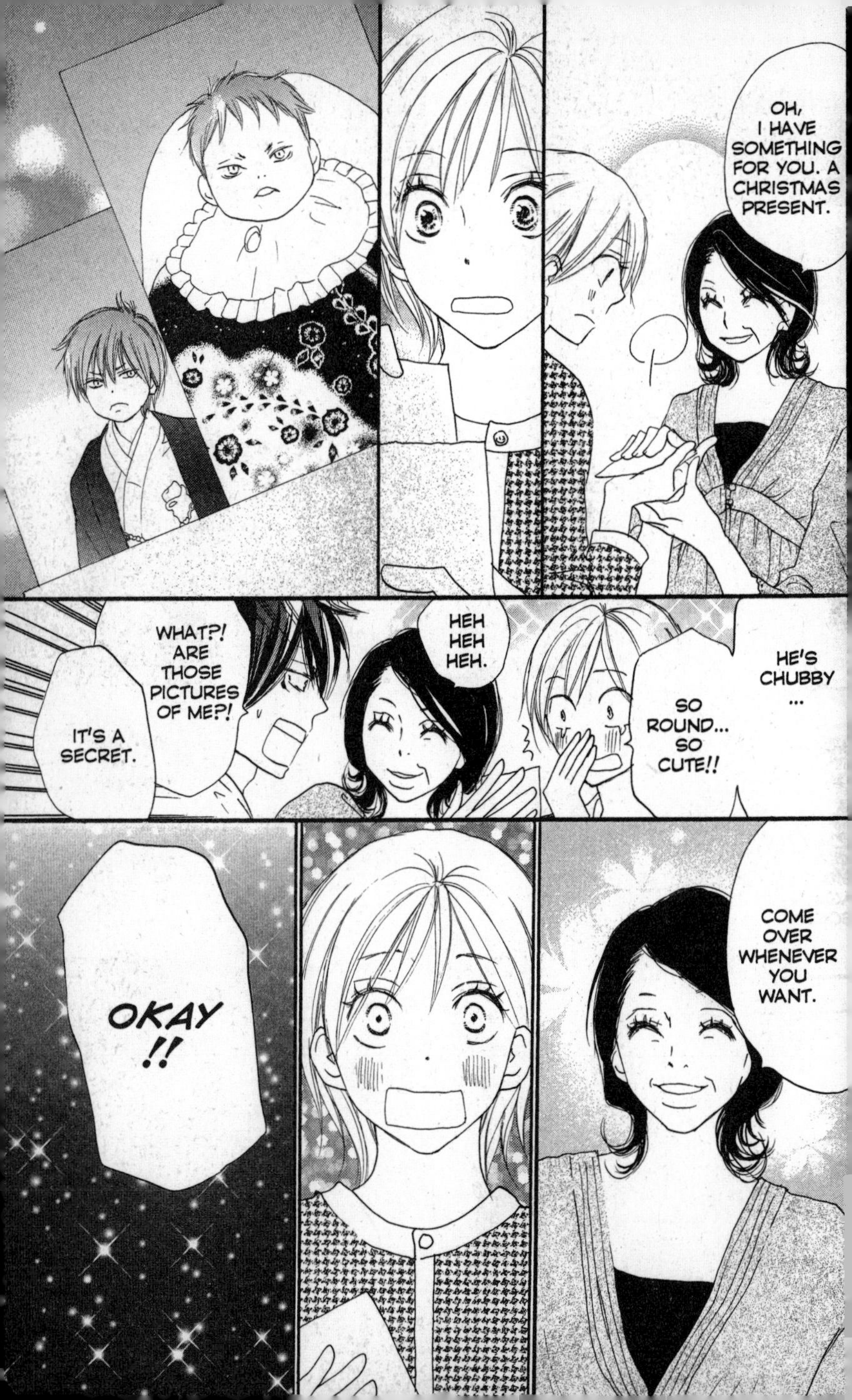
OH, I HAVE SOMETHING FOR YOU. A CHRISTMAS PRESENT.
HE'S CHUBBY ...
SO ROUND... SO CUTE!!
HEH HEH HEH.
WHAT?! ARE THOSE PICTURES OF ME?!
IT'S A SECRET.
COME OVER WHENEVER YOU WANT.
OKAY !!

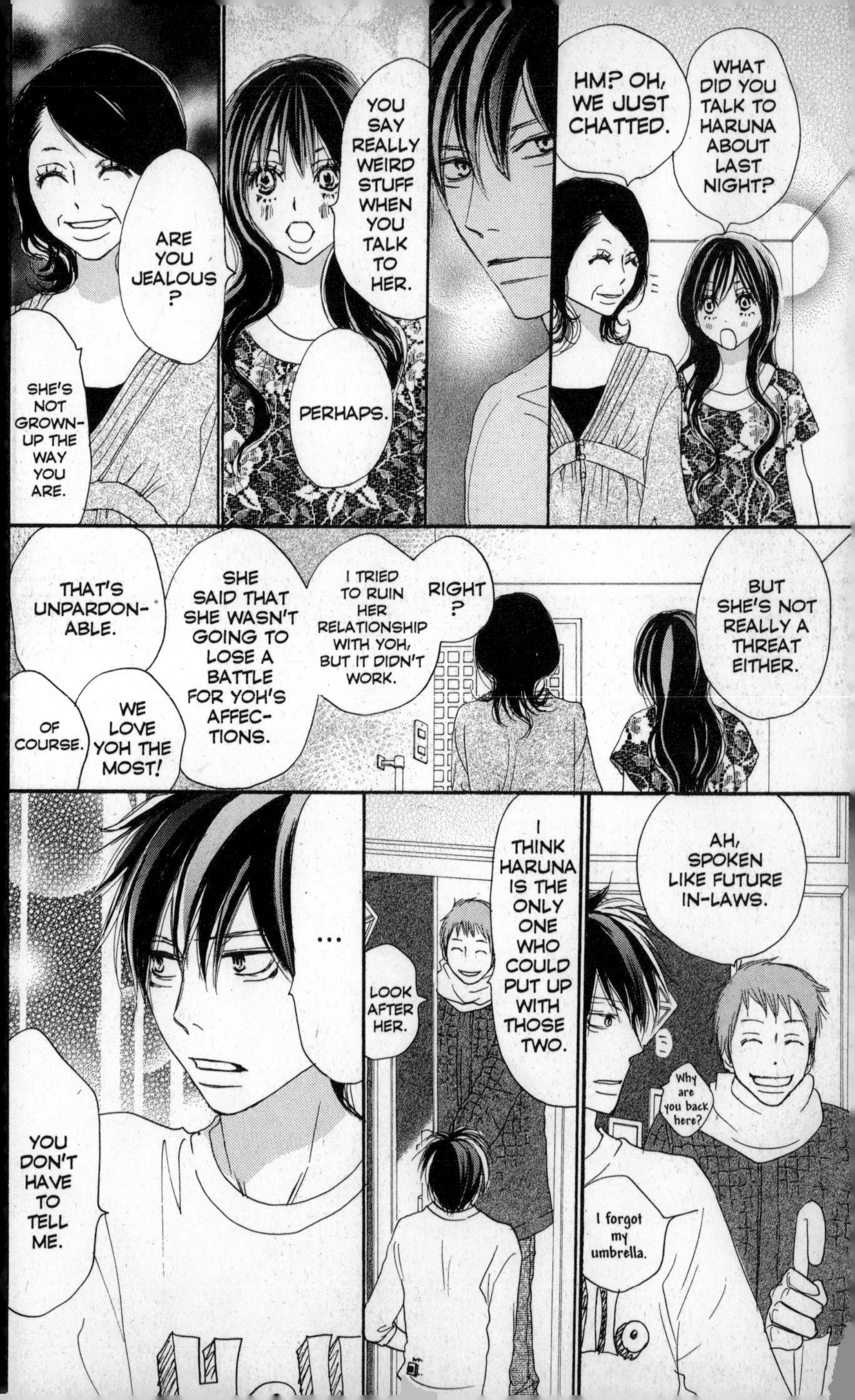
WHAT DID YOU TALK TO HARUNA ABOUT LAST NIGHT?
HM? OH, WE JUST CHATTED.
YOU SAY REALLY WEIRD STUFF WHEN YOU TALK TO HER.
PERHAPS.
ARE YOU JEALOUS?
SHE'S NOT GROWN-UP THE WAY YOU ARE.
BUT SHE'S NOT REALLY A THREAT EITHER.
RIGHT?
I TRIED TO RUIN HER RELATIONSHIP WITH YOH, BUT IT DIDN'T WORK.
SHE SAID THAT SHE WASN'T GOING TO LOSE A BATTLE FOR YOH'S AFFECTIONS.
THAT'S UNPARDONABLE.
WE LOVE YOH THE MOST!
OF COURSE.
AH, SPOKEN LIKE FUTURE IN-LAWS.
Why are you back here?
I forgot my umbrella.
I THINK HARUNA IS THE ONLY ONE WHO COULD PUT UP WITH THOSE TWO.
LOOK AFTER HER.
...
YOU DON'T HAVE TO TELL ME.

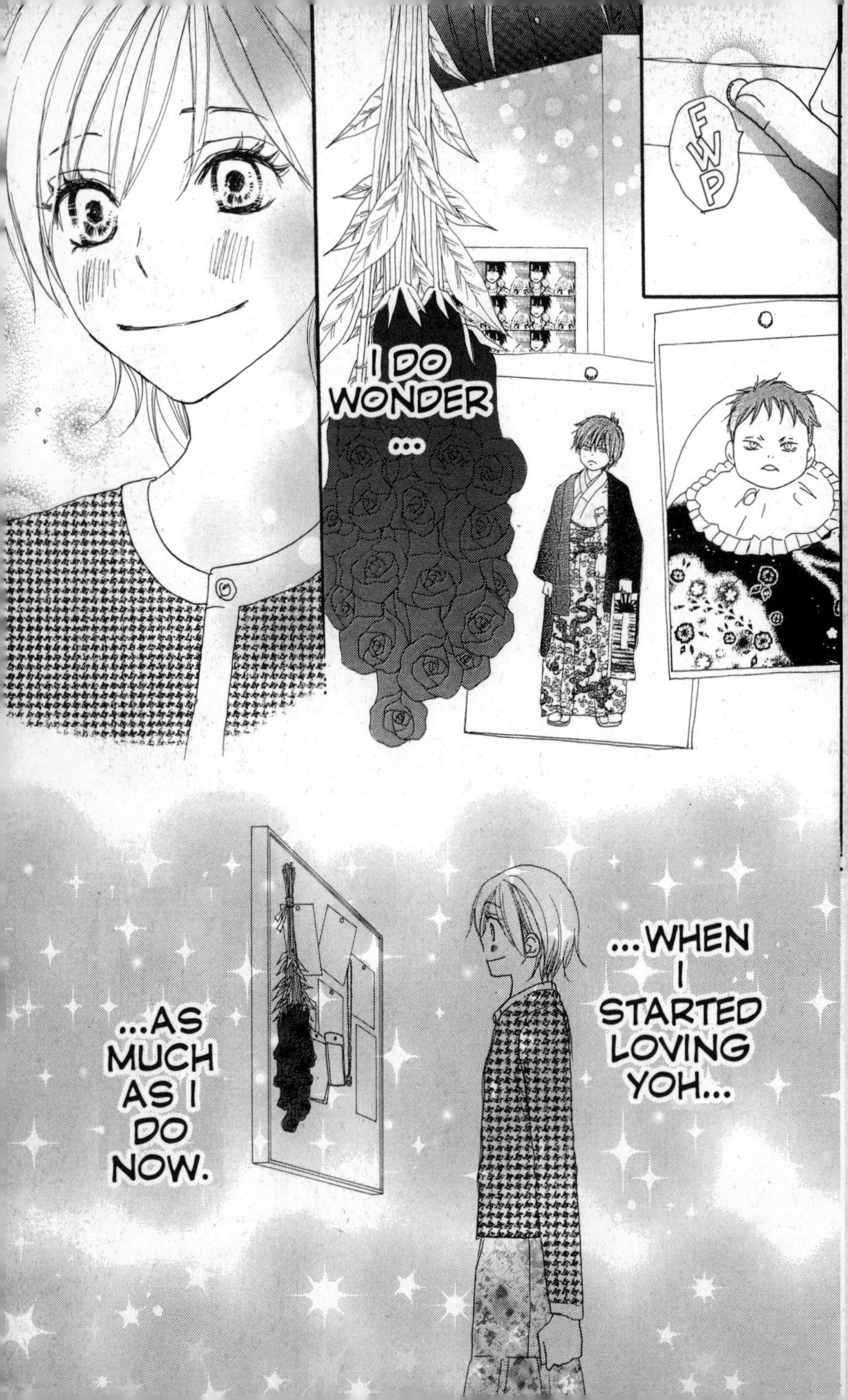
FWP
I DO WONDER...
...WHEN I STARTED LOVING YOH...
...AS MUCH AS I DO NOW.

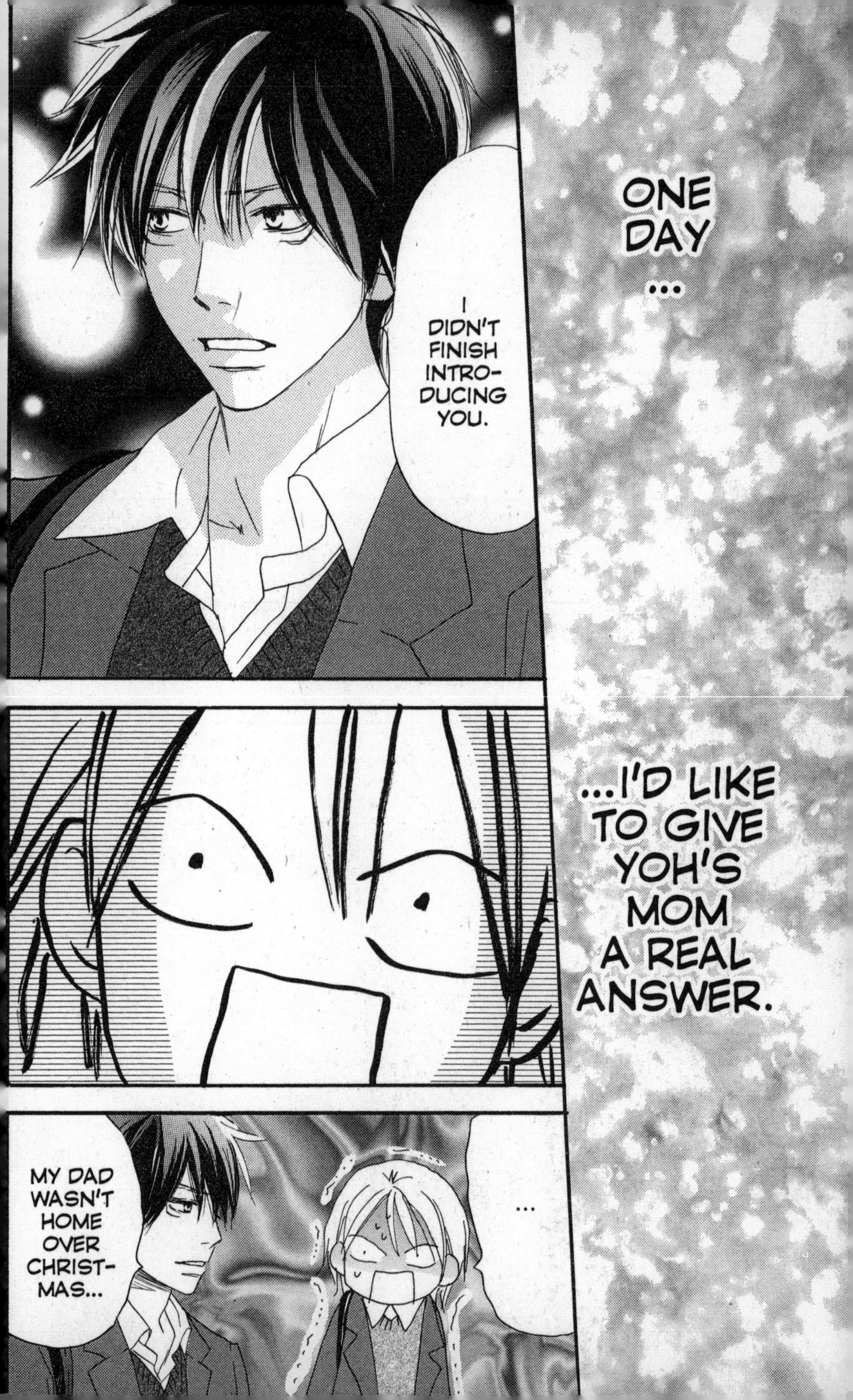
ONE DAY ...
...I'D LIKE TO GIVE YOH'S MOM A REAL ANSWER.
I DIDN'T FINISH INTRO-DUCING YOU.
...
MY DAD WASN'T HOME OVER CHRIST-MAS...

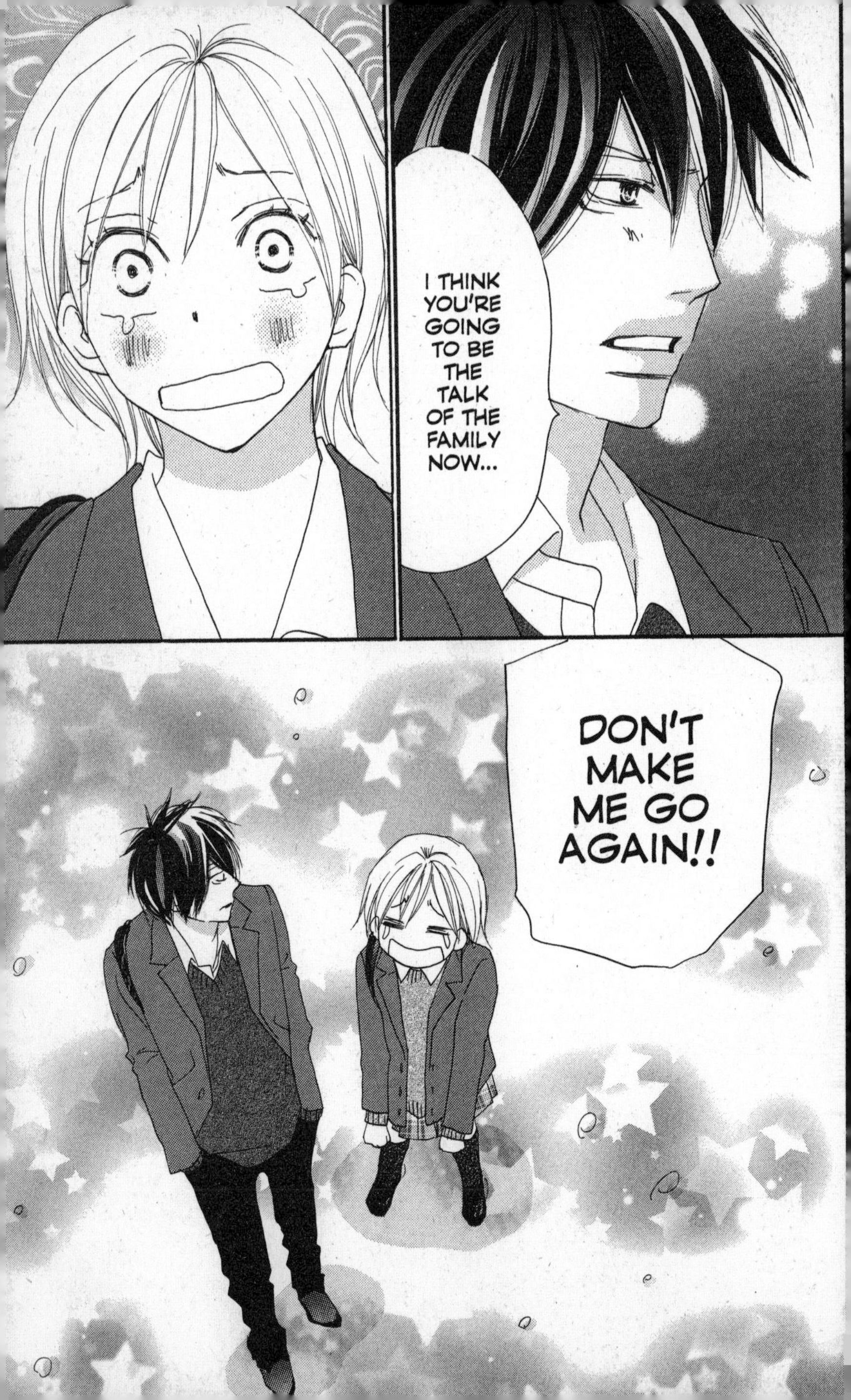
I THINK YOU'RE GOING TO BE THE TALK OF THE FAMILY NOW...
DON'T MAKE ME GO AGAIN!!

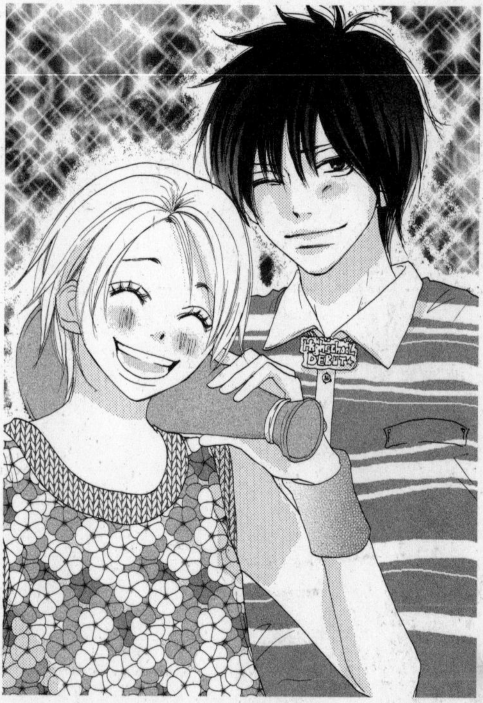
High school DEBUT

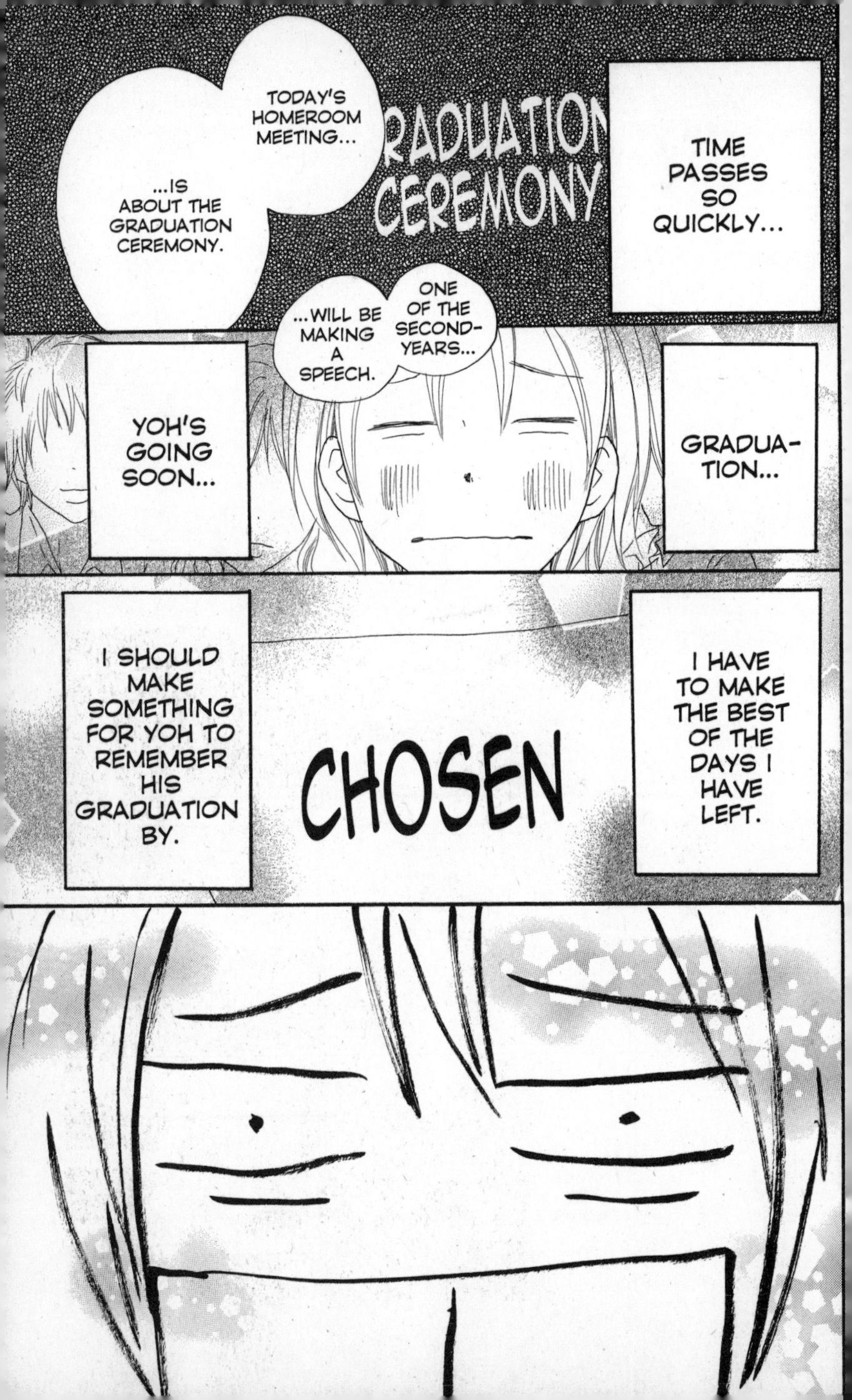
TIME PASSES SO QUICKLY...
RADUATION CEREMONY
TODAY'S HOMEROOM MEETING...
...IS ABOUT THE GRADUATION CEREMONY.
ONE OF THE SECOND-YEARS...
...WILL BE MAKING A SPEECH.
GRADUA-TION...
YOH'S GOING SOON...
I HAVE TO MAKE THE BEST OF THE DAYS I HAVE LEFT.
CHOSEN
I SHOULD MAKE SOMETHING FOR YOH TO REMEMBER HIS GRADUATION BY.

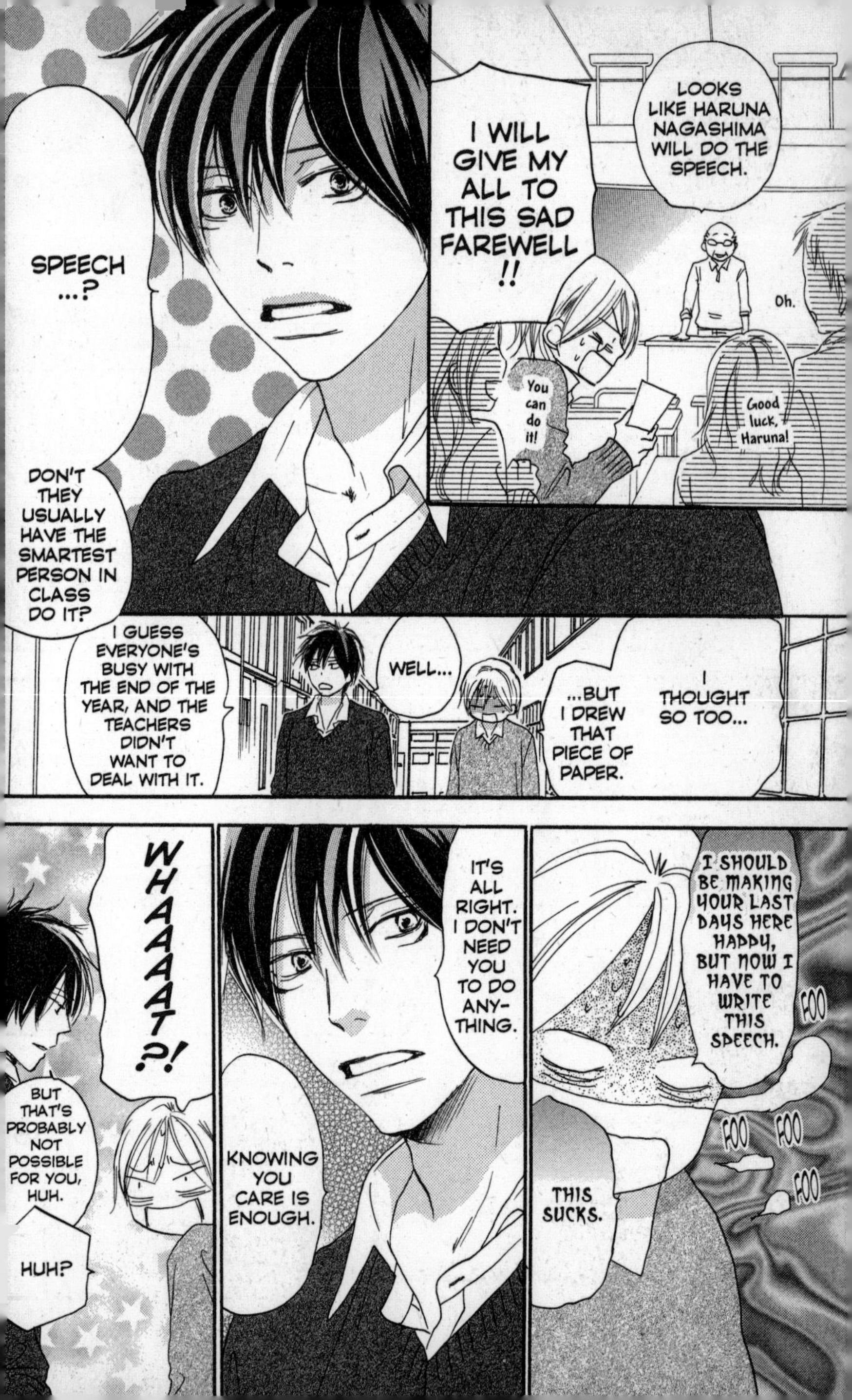
LOOKS LIKE HARUNA NAGASHIMA WILL DO THE SPEECH.
Oh.
Good luck, Haruna!
I WILL GIVE MY ALL TO THIS SAD FAREWELL!!
You can do it!
SPEECH ...?
DON'T THEY USUALLY HAVE THE SMARTEST PERSON IN CLASS DO IT?
I THOUGHT SO TOO...
...BUT I DREW THAT PIECE OF PAPER.
WELL...
I GUESS EVERYONE'S BUSY WITH THE END OF THE YEAR, AND THE TEACHERS DIDN'T WANT TO DEAL WITH IT.
I SHOULD BE MAKING YOUR LAST DAYS HERE HAPPY, BUT NOW I HAVE TO WRITE THIS SPEECH.
FOO
FOO FOO
FOO
THIS SUCKS.
IT'S ALL RIGHT. I DON'T NEED YOU TO DO ANY-THING.
KNOWING YOU CARE IS ENOUGH.
WHAAAAT?!
BUT THAT'S PROBABLY NOT POSSIBLE FOR YOU, HUH.
HUH?

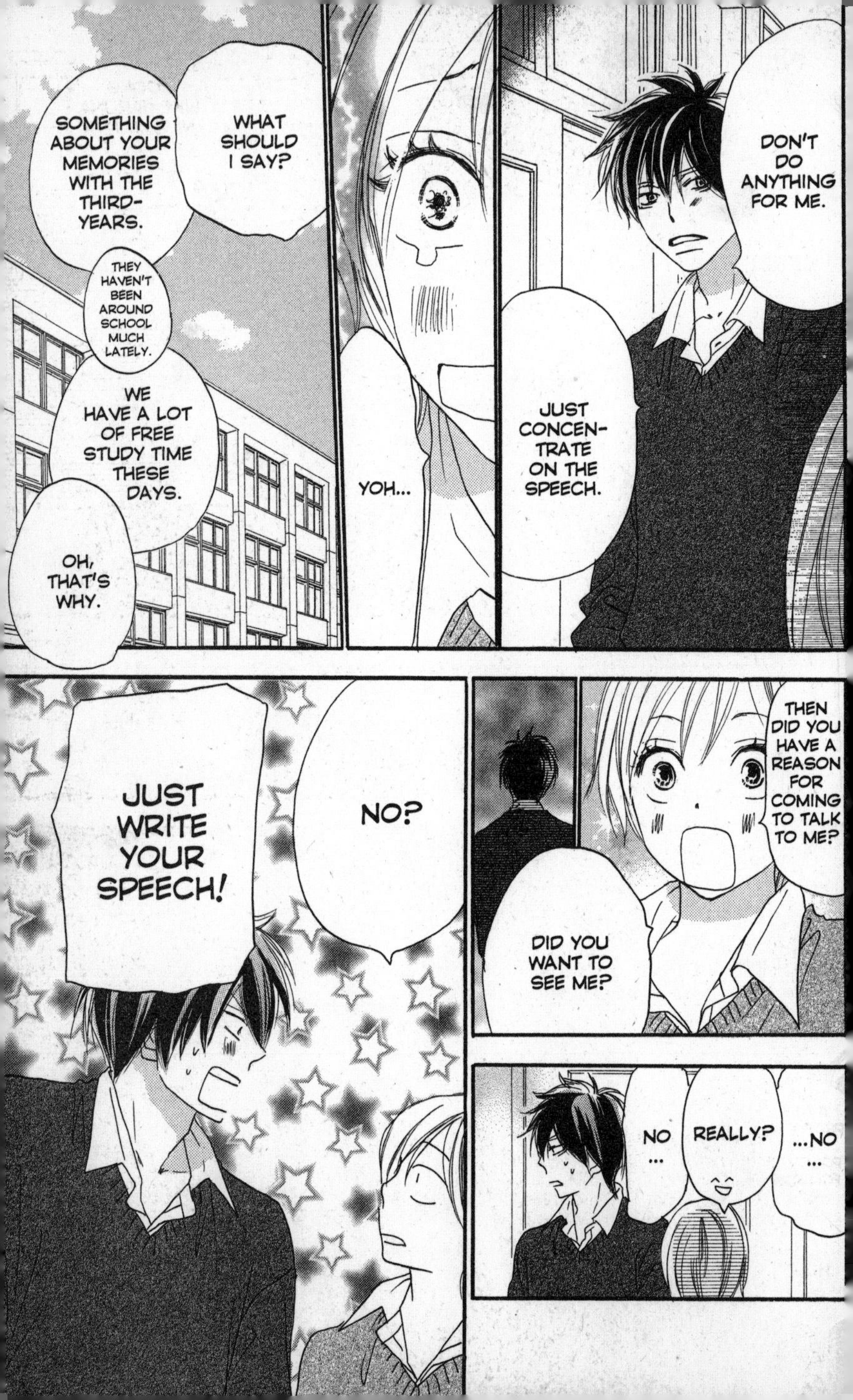
DON'T DO ANYTHING FOR ME.
JUST CONCENTRATE ON THE SPEECH.
YOH...
WHAT SHOULD I SAY?
SOMETHING ABOUT YOUR MEMORIES WITH THE THIRD-YEARS.
THEY HAVEN'T BEEN AROUND SCHOOL MUCH LATELY.
WE HAVE A LOT OF FREE STUDY TIME THESE DAYS.
OH, THAT'S WHY.
THEN DID YOU HAVE A REASON FOR COMING TO TALK TO ME?
DID YOU WANT TO SEE ME?
...NO ...
REALLY?
NO ...
NO?
JUST WRITE YOUR SPEECH!

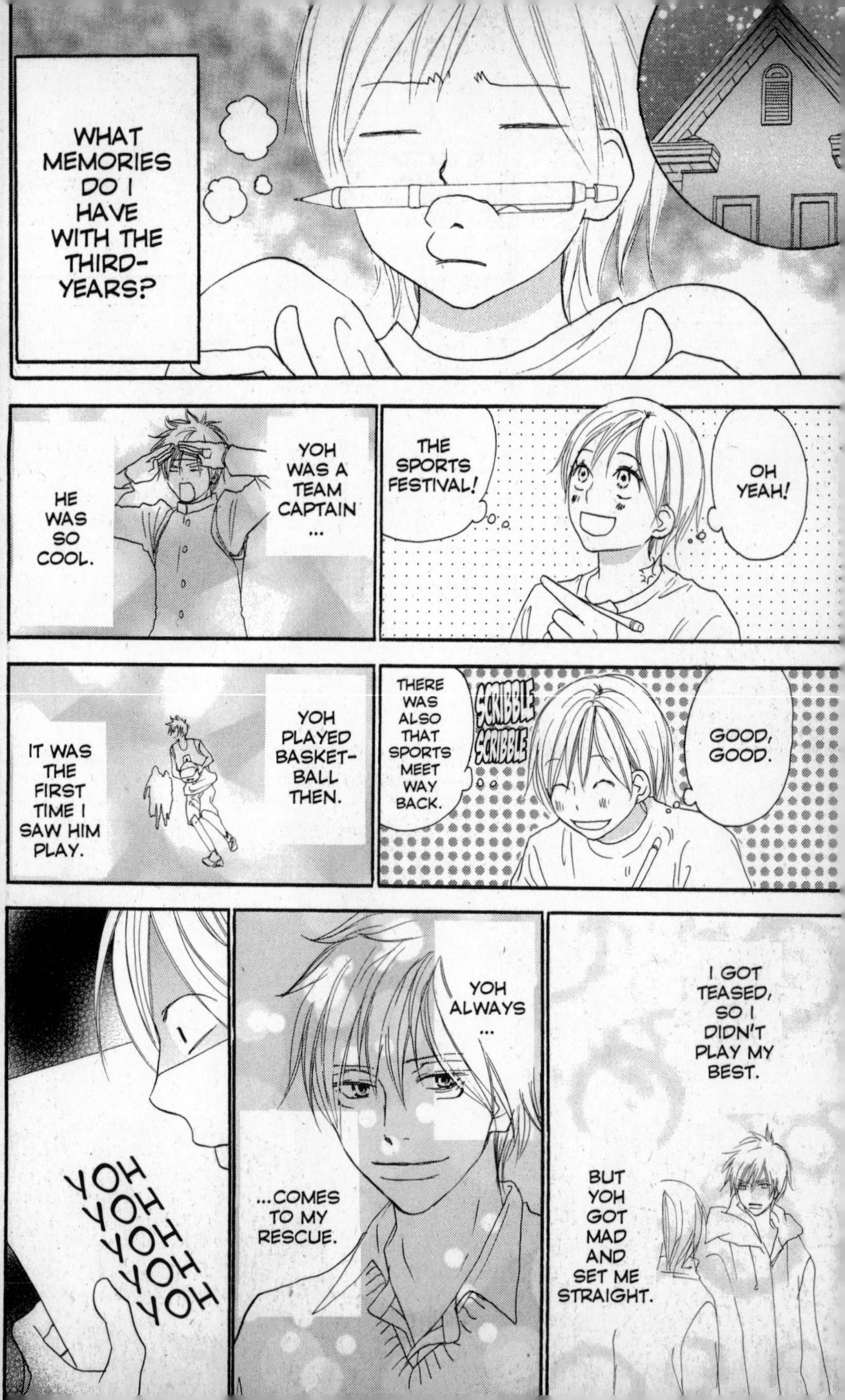
WHAT MEMORIES DO I HAVE WITH THE THIRD-YEARS?
OH YEAH!
THE SPORTS FESTIVAL!
YOH WAS A TEAM CAPTAIN ...
HE WAS SO COOL.
GOOD, GOOD.
SCRIBBLE SCRIBBLE
THERE WAS ALSO THAT SPORTS MEET WAY BACK.
YOH PLAYED BASKET-BALL THEN.
IT WAS THE FIRST TIME I SAW HIM PLAY.
I GOT TEASED, SO I DIDN'T PLAY MY BEST.
BUT YOH GOT MAD AND SET ME STRAIGHT.
YOH ALWAYS ...
...COMES TO MY RESCUE.
YOH YOH YOH YOH YOH

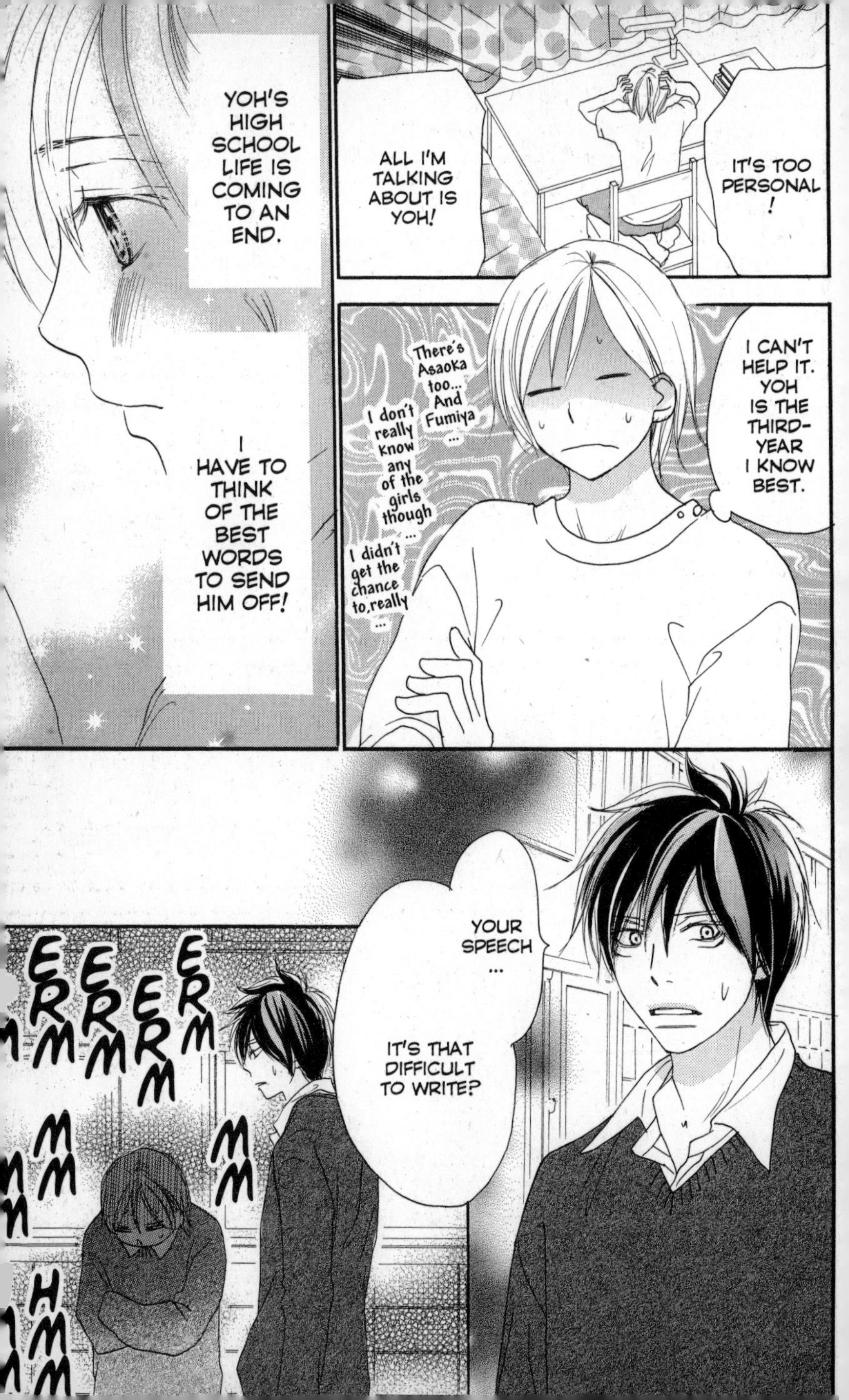
IT'S TOO PERSONAL!
ALL I'M TALKING ABOUT IS YOH!
I CAN'T HELP IT. YOH IS THE THIRD-YEAR I KNOW BEST.
There's Asaoka too... And Fumiya...
I don't really know any of the girls though...
I didn't get the chance to, really...
YOH'S HIGH SCHOOL LIFE IS COMING TO AN END.
I HAVE TO THINK OF THE BEST WORDS TO SEND HIM OFF!
YOUR SPEECH...
IT'S THAT DIFFICULT TO WRITE?
ERM ERRM ERM ERM
MM MM
HMM

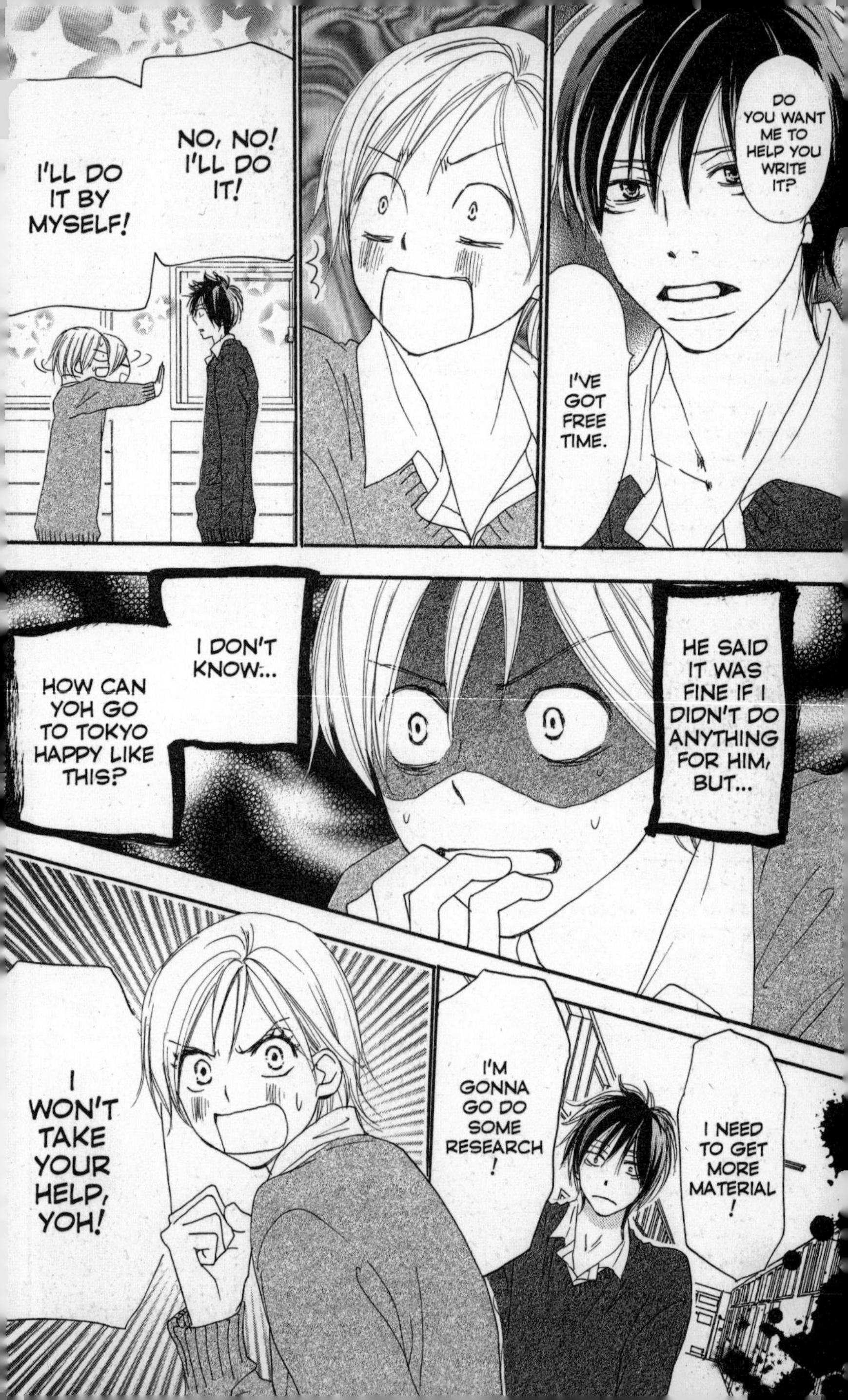
DO YOU WANT ME TO HELP YOU WRITE IT?
I'VE GOT FREE TIME.
NO, NO! I'LL DO IT!
I'LL DO IT BY MYSELF!
HE SAID IT WAS FINE IF I DIDN'T DO ANYTHING FOR HIM, BUT...
I DON'T KNOW...
HOW CAN YOH GO TO TOKYO HAPPY LIKE THIS?
I NEED TO GET MORE MATERIAL!
I'M GONNA GO DO SOME RESEARCH!
I WON'T TAKE YOUR HELP, YOH!

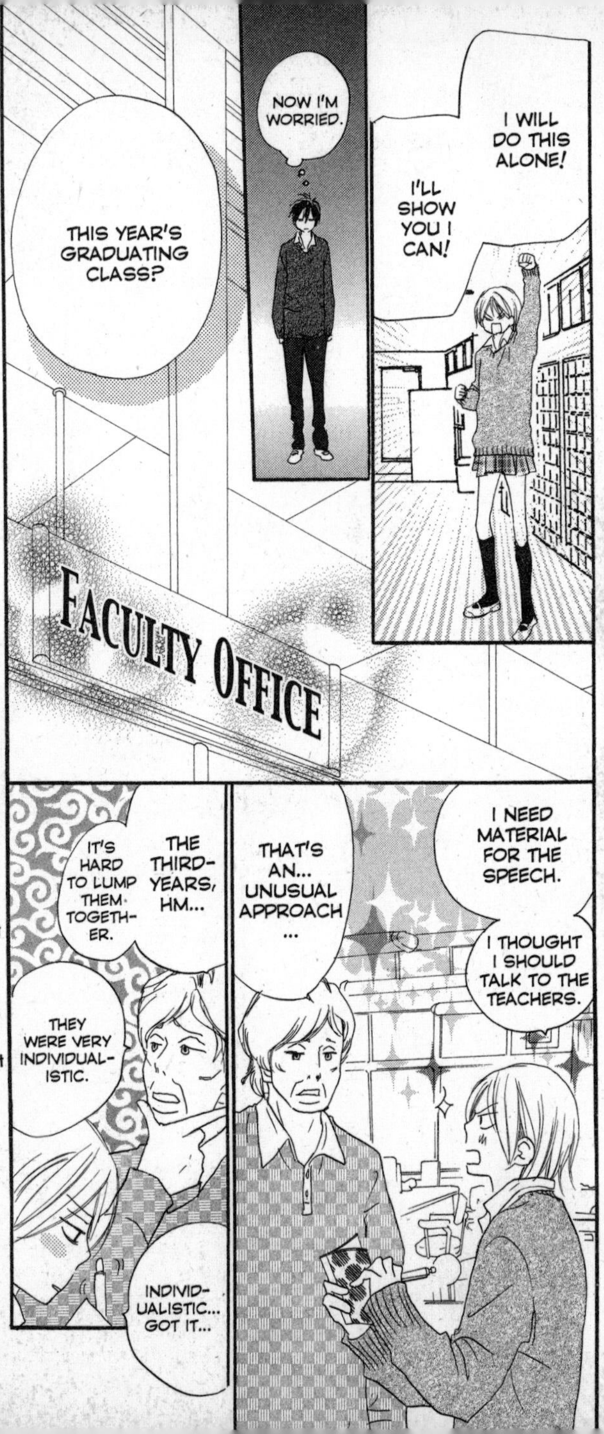
I WILL DO THIS ALONE!
I'LL SHOW YOU I CAN!
NOW I'M WORRIED.
THIS YEAR'S GRADUATING CLASS?
FACULTY OFFICE
I NEED MATERIAL FOR THE SPEECH.
I THOUGHT I SHOULD TALK TO THE TEACHERS.
THAT'S AN... UNUSUAL APPROACH ...
THE THIRD-YEARS, HM...
IT'S HARD TO LUMP THEM TOGETH-ER.
THEY WERE VERY INDIVIDUAL-ISTIC.
INDIVID-UALISTIC... GOT IT...

2 Last!

Thank you to the editors! I'm sorry I forgot my notes so often. I'm sorry I forgot to write notes even. I'm sorry I went to bed early and ignored calls after nine o'clock. I'm sorry for my six o'clock emails.

I also want to thank the designers for the title pages. Thank you for all your hard work on the covers as well. Sorry if I made things hard. (As a result, one of the characters on the original volume 12 cover was squashed. Here she is. ↓)

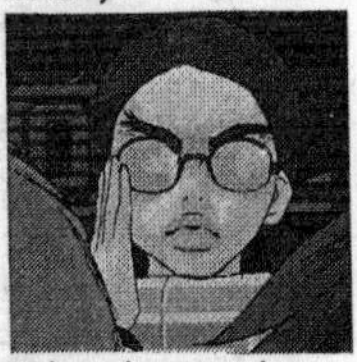

It doesn't matter how many years have passed. I still can't draw well. The bodies are always out of proportion. I'm sorry you had to tell me!

The room I'm sitting in is too cold, so I'm sorry if my handwriting is difficult to read!

Sorry again and thank you! I have so much to say!

Thank you so much!!

One last big thank you!

I'm sure we'll meet again. I hope there will be an announcement for my readers soon!

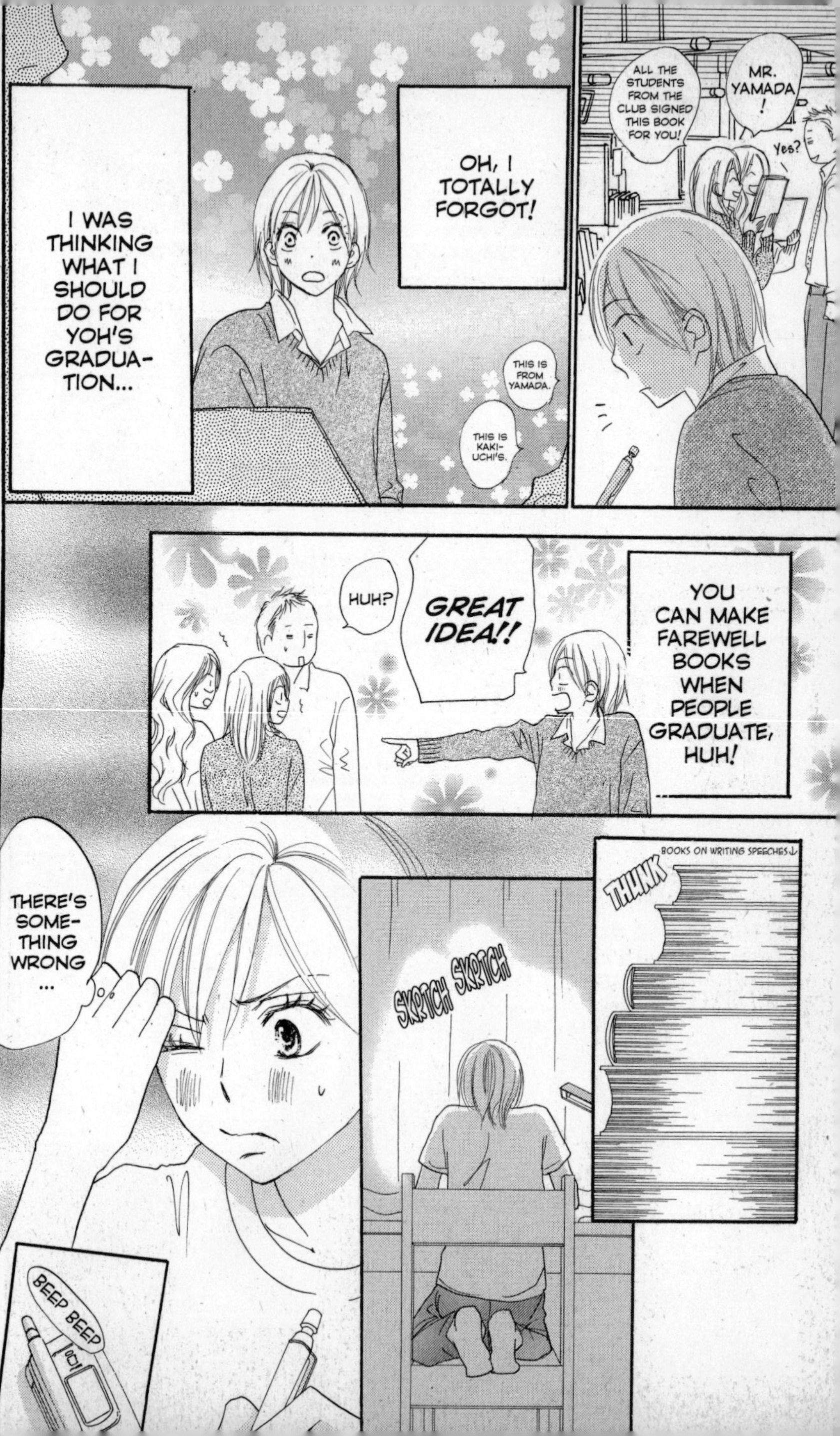
MR. YAMADA!
ALL THE STUDENTS FROM THE CLUB SIGNED THIS BOOK FOR YOU!
Yes?
OH, I TOTALLY FORGOT!
THIS IS FROM YAMADA.
THIS IS KAKI-UCHI'S.
I WAS THINKING WHAT I SHOULD DO FOR YOH'S GRADUA-TION...
YOU CAN MAKE FAREWELL BOOKS WHEN PEOPLE GRADUATE, HUH!
GREAT IDEA!!
HUH?
BOOKS ON WRITING SPEECHES↓
THUNK
SKRTCH SKRTCH
THERE'S SOME-THING WRONG ...
BEEP BEEP

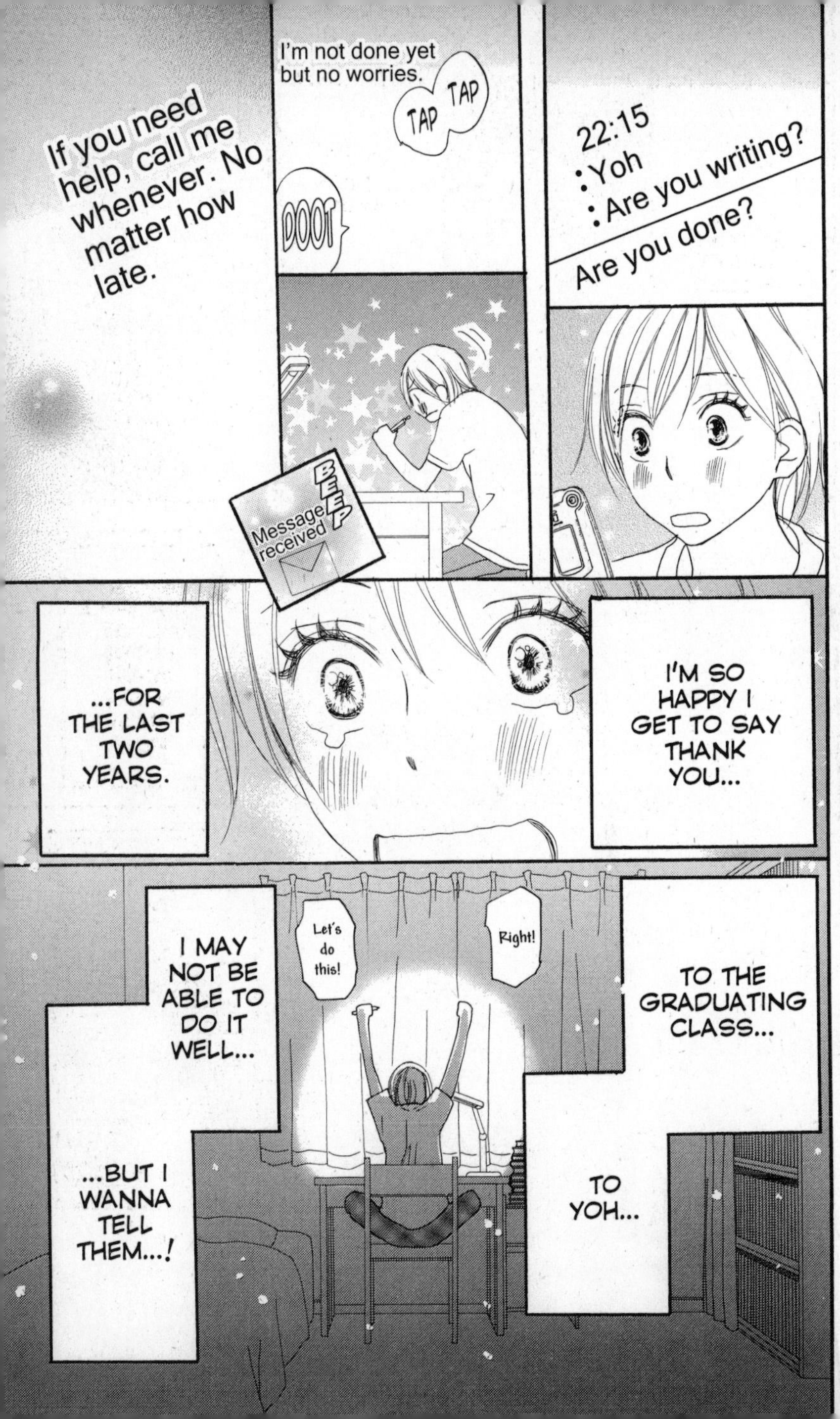
22:15
•Yoh
•Are you writing?
Are you done?
I'm not done yet but no worries.
TAP TAP
DOOT
BEEP
Message received
If you need help, call me whenever. No matter how late.
I'M SO HAPPY I GET TO SAY THANK YOU...
...FOR THE LAST TWO YEARS.
TO THE GRADUATING CLASS...
TO YOH...
Right!
Let's do this!
I MAY NOT BE ABLE TO DO IT WELL...
...BUT I WANNA TELL THEM...!

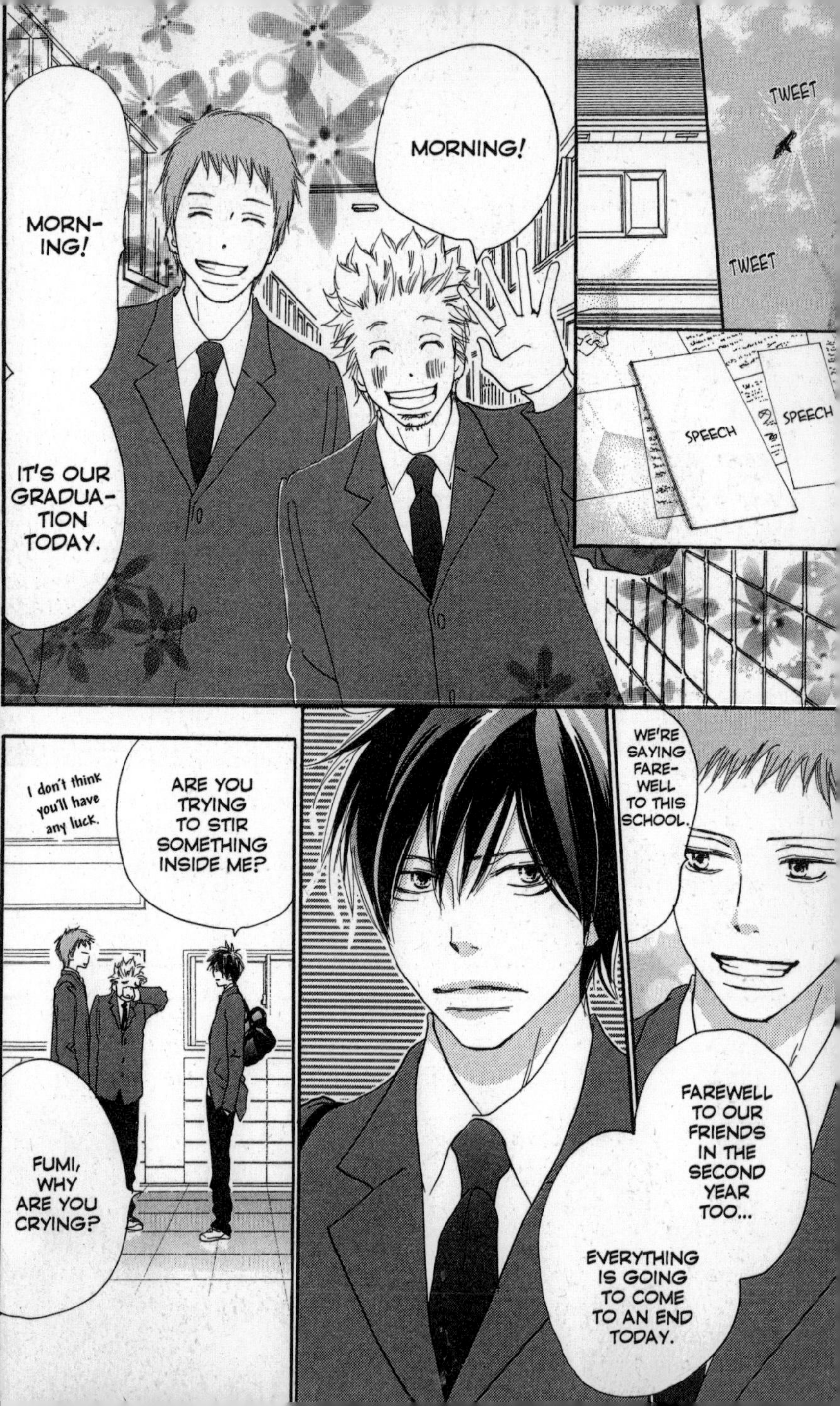
TWEET
TWEET
SPEECH
SPEECH
MORNING!
MORN-ING!
IT'S OUR GRADUA-TION TODAY.
WE'RE SAYING FARE-WELL TO THIS SCHOOL.
FAREWELL TO OUR FRIENDS IN THE SECOND YEAR TOO...
EVERYTHING IS GOING TO COME TO AN END TODAY.
ARE YOU TRYING TO STIR SOMETHING INSIDE ME?
I don't think you'll have any luck.
FUMI, WHY ARE YOU CRYING?

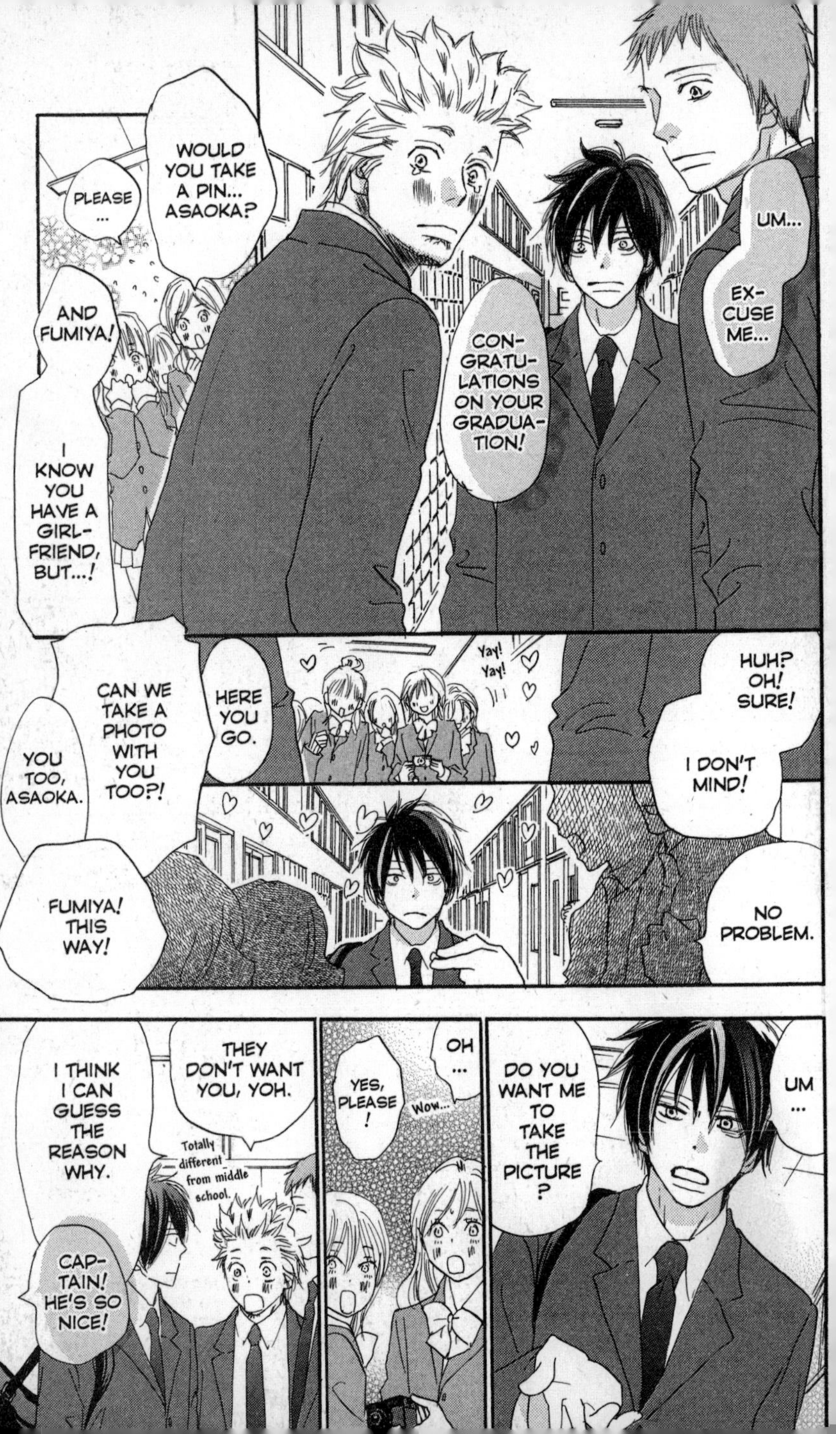
UM... EXCUSE ME...
CONGRATULATIONS ON YOUR GRADUATION!
WOULD YOU TAKE A PIN... ASAOKA?
PLEASE ...
AND FUMIYA!
I KNOW YOU HAVE A GIRLFRIEND, BUT...!
HUH? OH! SURE!
I DON'T MIND!
Yay! Yay!
HERE YOU GO.
CAN WE TAKE A PHOTO WITH YOU TOO?!
YOU TOO, ASAOKA.
NO PROBLEM.
FUMIYA! THIS WAY!
UM ...
DO YOU WANT ME TO TAKE THE PICTURE?
OH ...
YES, PLEASE!
Wow...
THEY DON'T WANT YOU, YOH.
I THINK I CAN GUESS THE REASON WHY.
Totally different from middle school.
CAPTAIN! HE'S SO NICE!

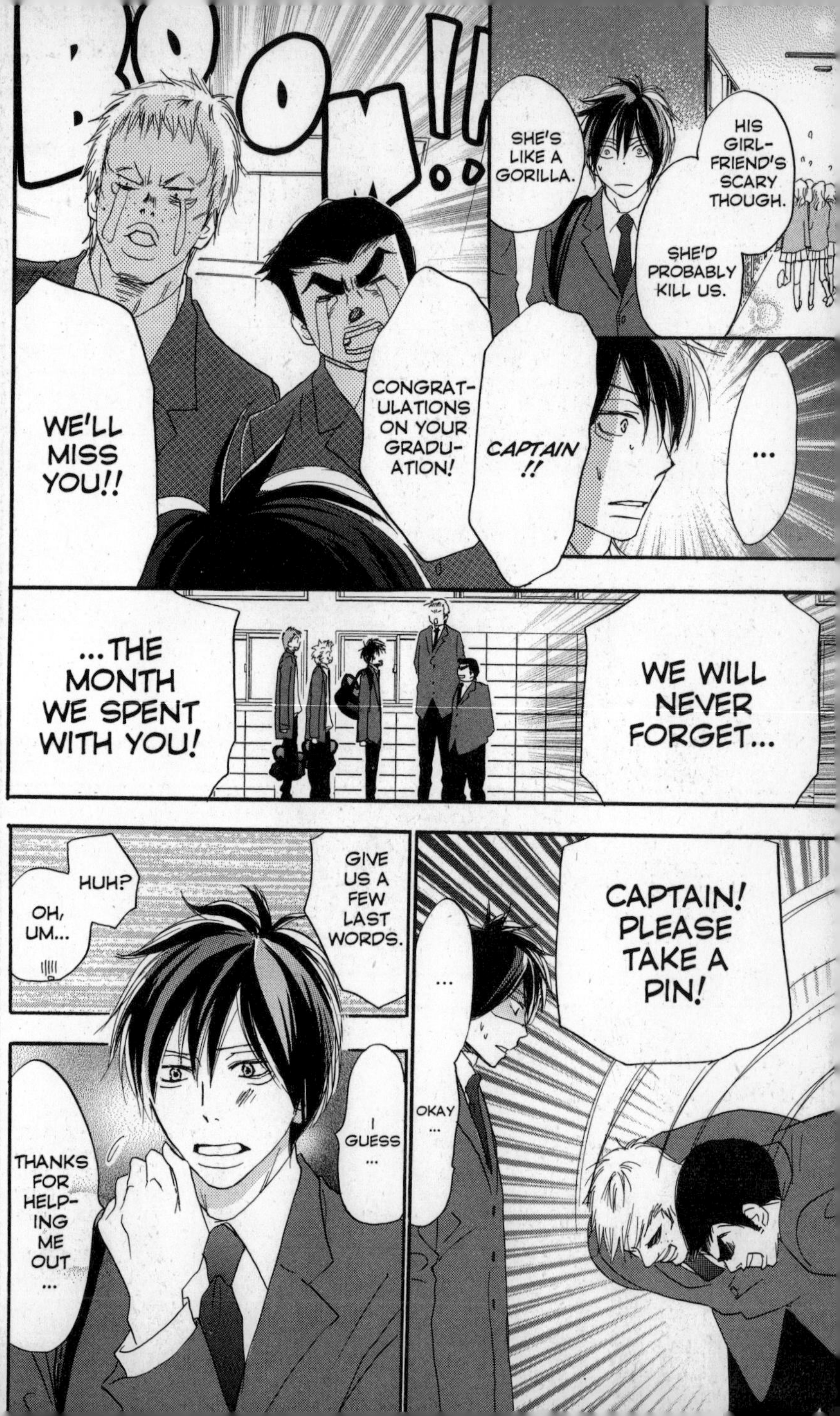
HIS GIRL-FRIEND'S SCARY THOUGH.
SHE'D PROBABLY KILL US.
SHE'S LIKE A GORILLA.
...
CAPTAIN!!
CONGRAT-ULATIONS ON YOUR GRADU-ATION!
BOOM!!
WE'LL MISS YOU!!
WE WILL NEVER FORGET...
...THE MONTH WE SPENT WITH YOU!
CAPTAIN! PLEASE TAKE A PIN!
...
OKAY...
GIVE US A FEW LAST WORDS.
HUH?
OH, UM...
I GUESS...
THANKS FOR HELP-ING ME OUT...

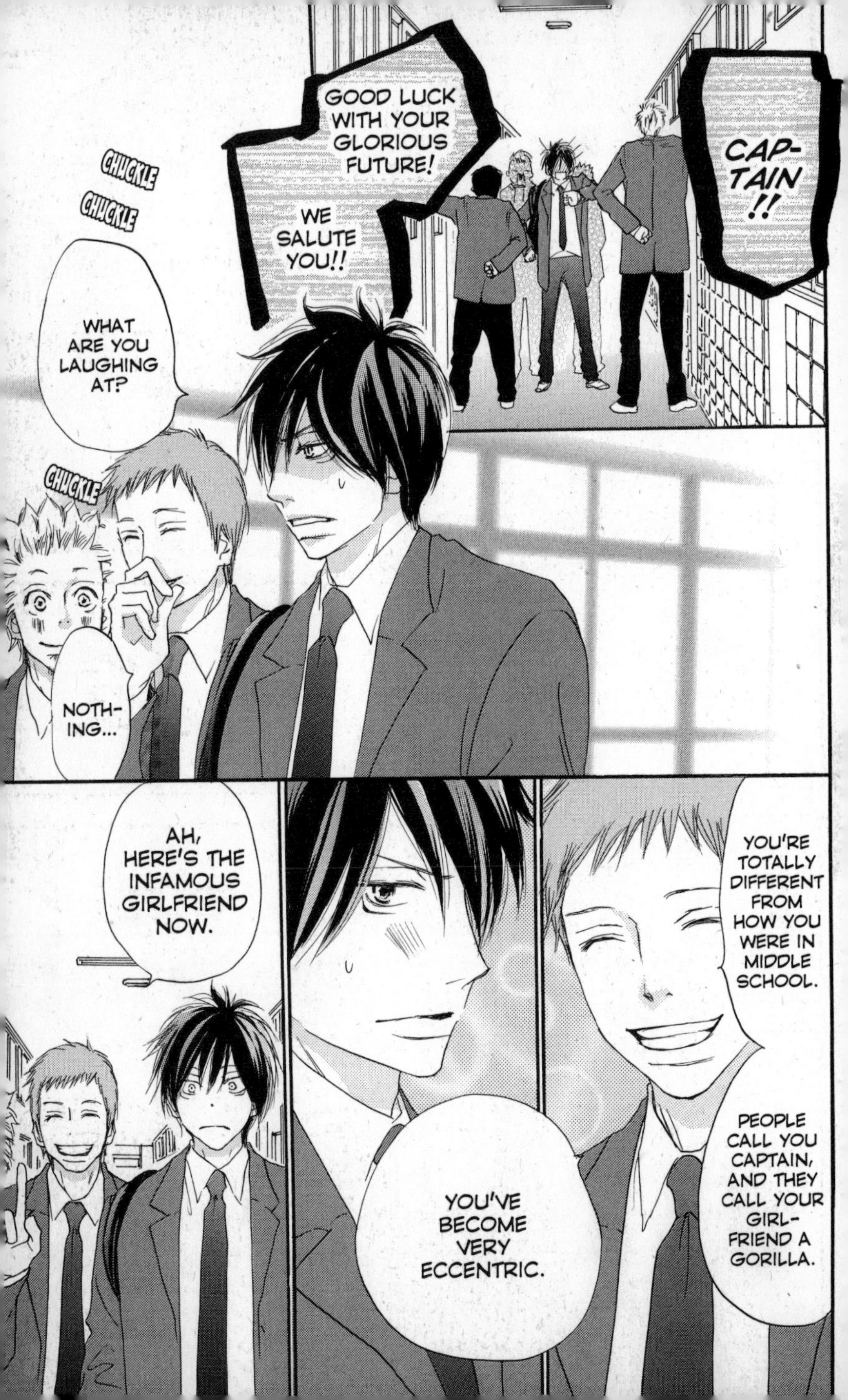
CAP-TAIN!!
GOOD LUCK WITH YOUR GLORIOUS FUTURE!
WE SALUTE YOU!!
CHUCKLE
CHUCKLE
WHAT ARE YOU LAUGHING AT?
CHUCKLE
NOTH-ING...
YOU'RE TOTALLY DIFFERENT FROM HOW YOU WERE IN MIDDLE SCHOOL.
PEOPLE CALL YOU CAPTAIN, AND THEY CALL YOUR GIRL-FRIEND A GORILLA.
YOU'VE BECOME VERY ECCENTRIC.
AH, HERE'S THE INFAMOUS GIRLFRIEND NOW.

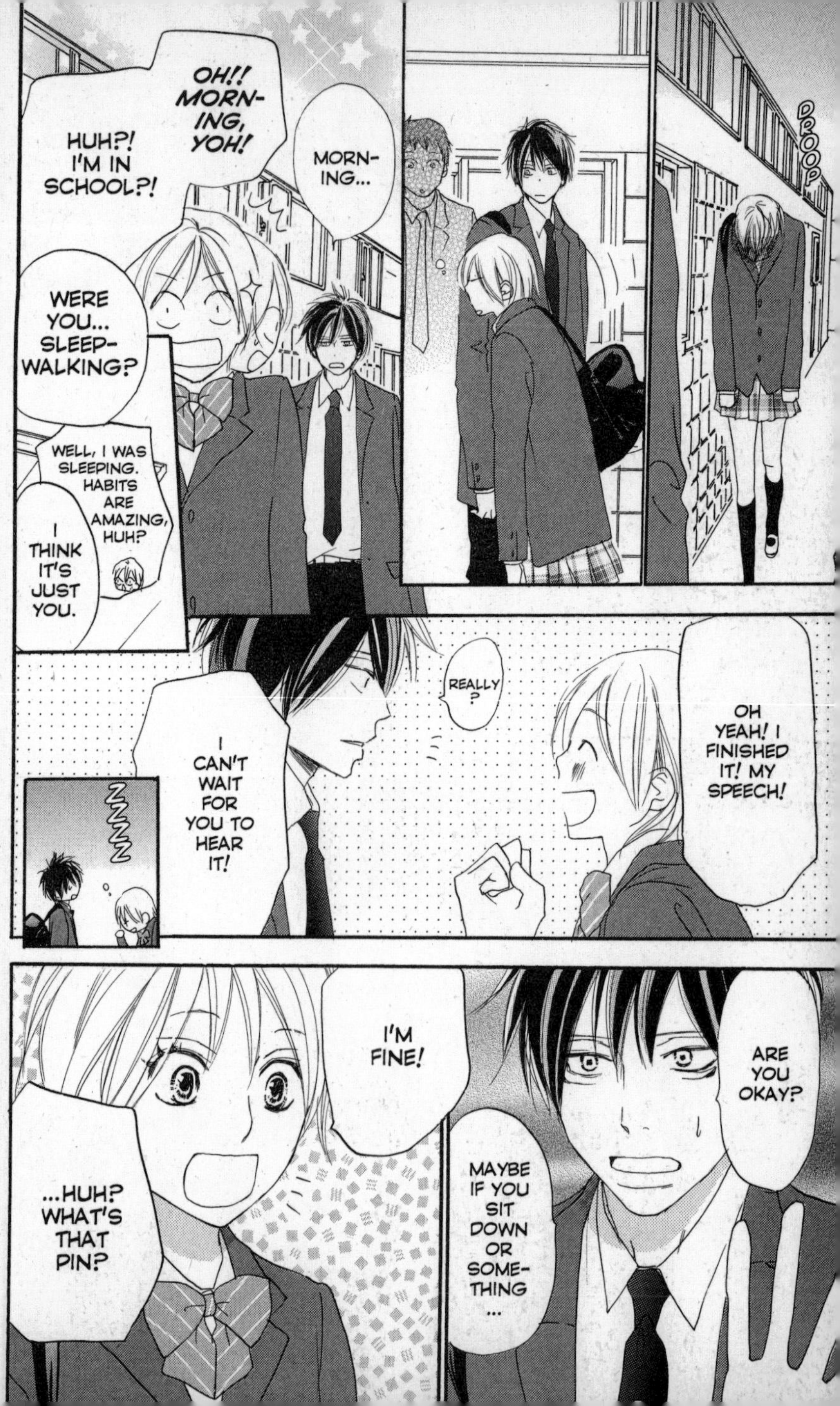
DROOP
OH!! MORNING, YOH!
MORNING...
HUH?! I'M IN SCHOOL?!
WERE YOU... SLEEPWALKING?
WELL, I WAS SLEEPING. HABITS ARE AMAZING, HUH?
I THINK IT'S JUST YOU.
OH YEAH! I FINISHED IT! MY SPEECH!
REALLY?
I CAN'T WAIT FOR YOU TO HEAR IT!
ZZZZ
ARE YOU OKAY?
MAYBE IF YOU SIT DOWN OR SOMETHING...
I'M FINE!
...HUH? WHAT'S THAT PIN?

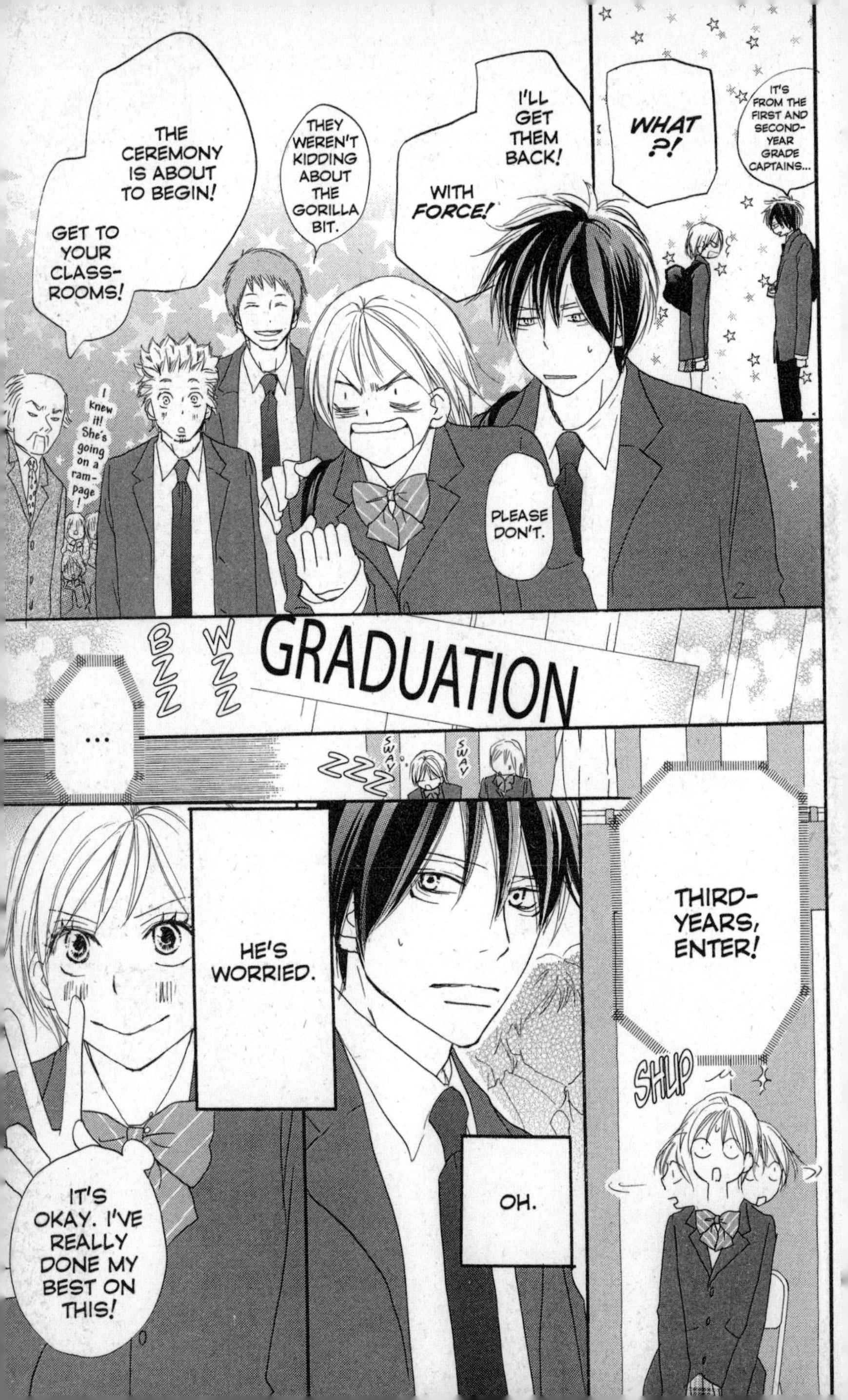
IT'S FROM THE FIRST AND SECOND-YEAR GRADE CAPTAINS...
WHAT ?!
I'LL GET THEM BACK!
WITH FORCE!
THEY WEREN'T KIDDING ABOUT THE GORILLA BIT.
THE CEREMONY IS ABOUT TO BEGIN!
GET TO YOUR CLASS-ROOMS!
I knew it! She's going on a ram-page!
PLEASE DON'T.
GRADUATION
BZZZ
WZZZ
...
SWAY
SWAY
ZZZ
THIRD-YEARS, ENTER!
SHUP
OH.
HE'S WORRIED.
IT'S OKAY. I'VE REALLY DONE MY BEST ON THIS!

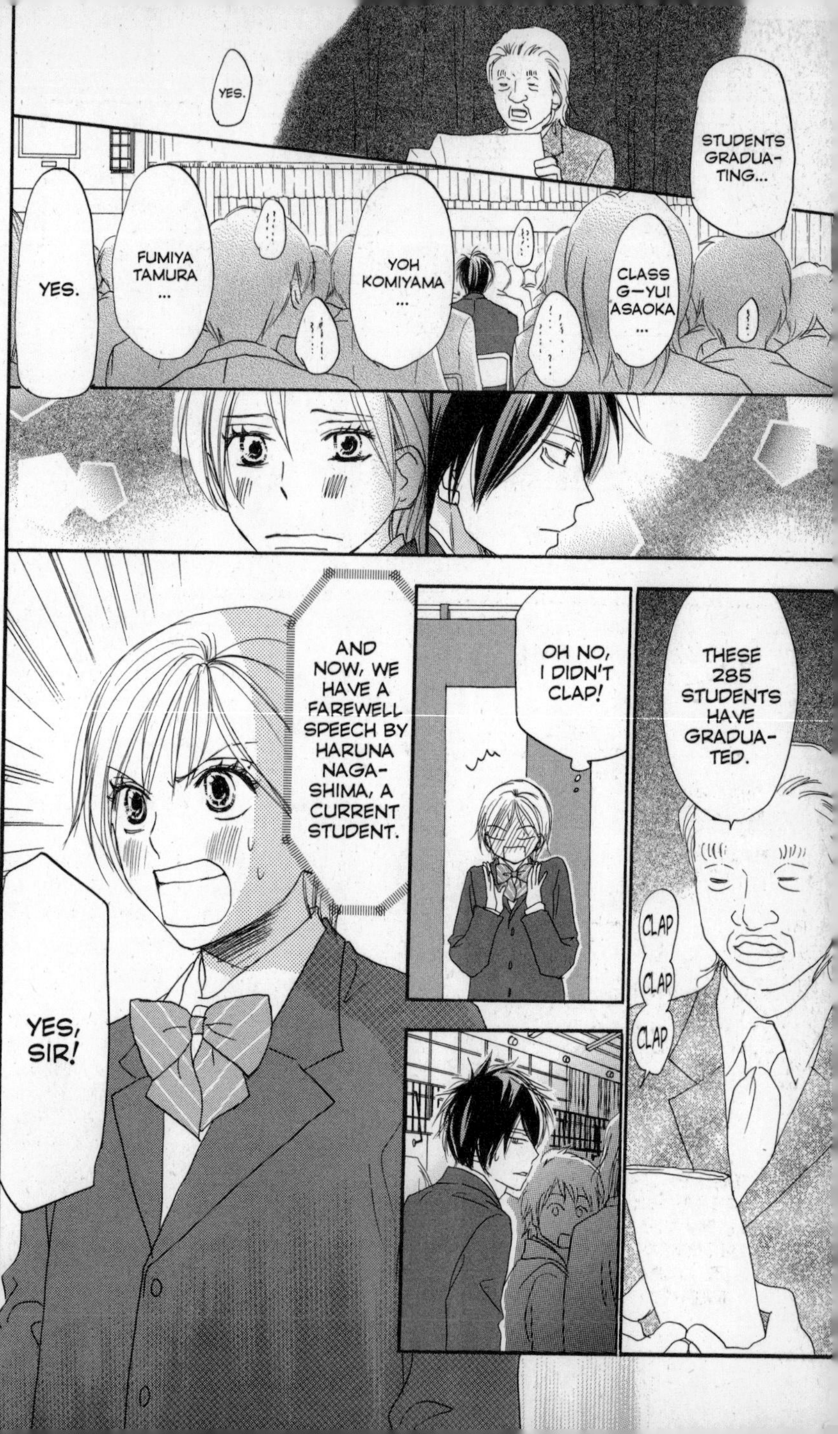

STUDENTS GRADUATING...
YES.
CLASS G—YUI ASAOKA ...
YOH KOMIYAMA ...
FUMIYA TAMURA ...
YES.
THESE 285 STUDENTS HAVE GRADUATED.
CLAP
CLAP
CLAP
OH NO, I DIDN'T CLAP!
AND NOW, WE HAVE A FAREWELL SPEECH BY HARUNA NAGASHIMA, A CURRENT STUDENT.
YES, SIR!

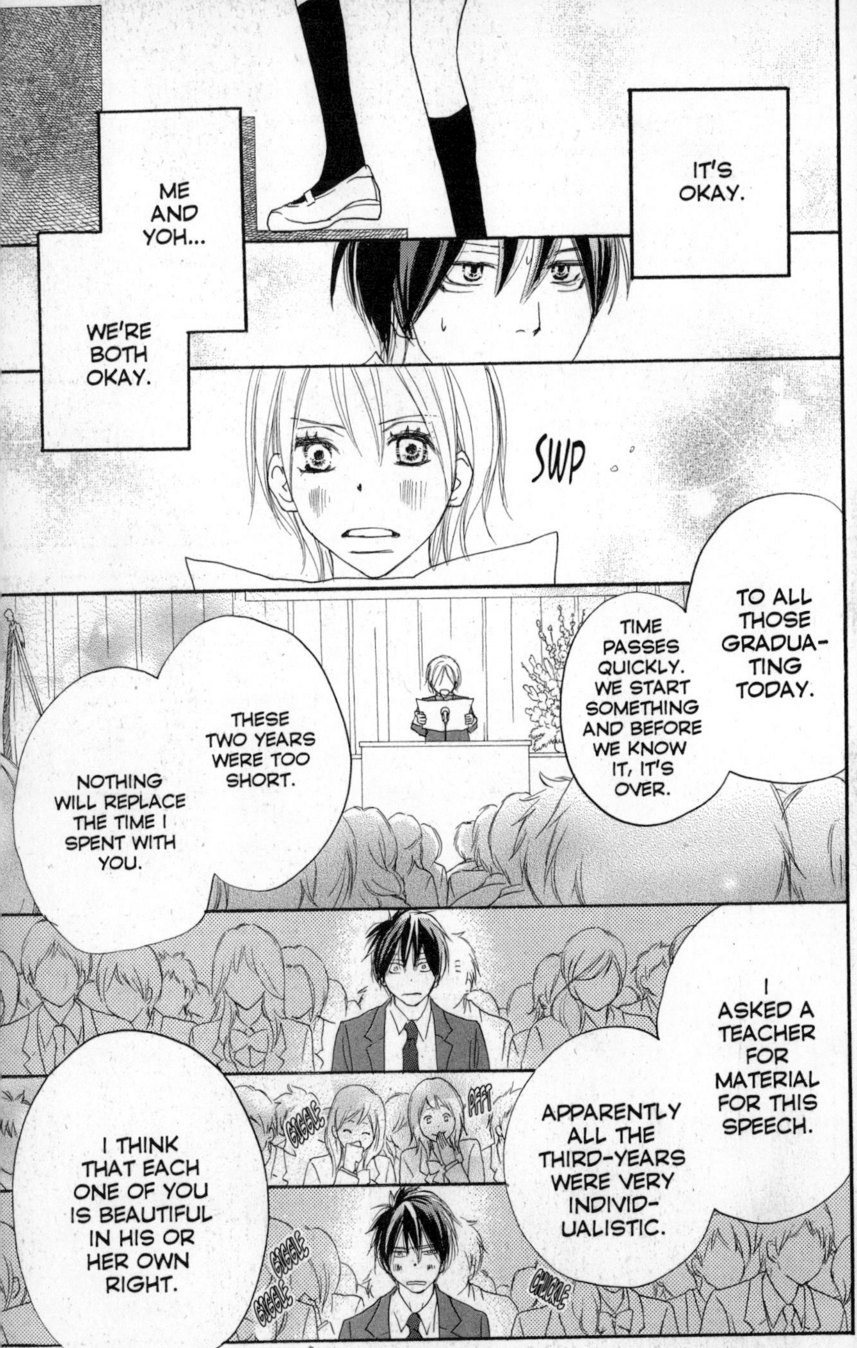
IT'S OKAY.
ME AND YOH...
WE'RE BOTH OKAY.
SWP
TO ALL THOSE GRADUATING TODAY.
TIME PASSES QUICKLY. WE START SOMETHING AND BEFORE WE KNOW IT, IT'S OVER.
THESE TWO YEARS WERE TOO SHORT.
NOTHING WILL REPLACE THE TIME I SPENT WITH YOU.
I ASKED A TEACHER FOR MATERIAL FOR THIS SPEECH.
APPARENTLY ALL THE THIRD-YEARS WERE VERY INDIVIDUALISTIC.
PFFT
GIGGLE
I THINK THAT EACH ONE OF YOU IS BEAUTIFUL IN HIS OR HER OWN RIGHT.
CHUCKLE
GIGGLE
GIGGLE

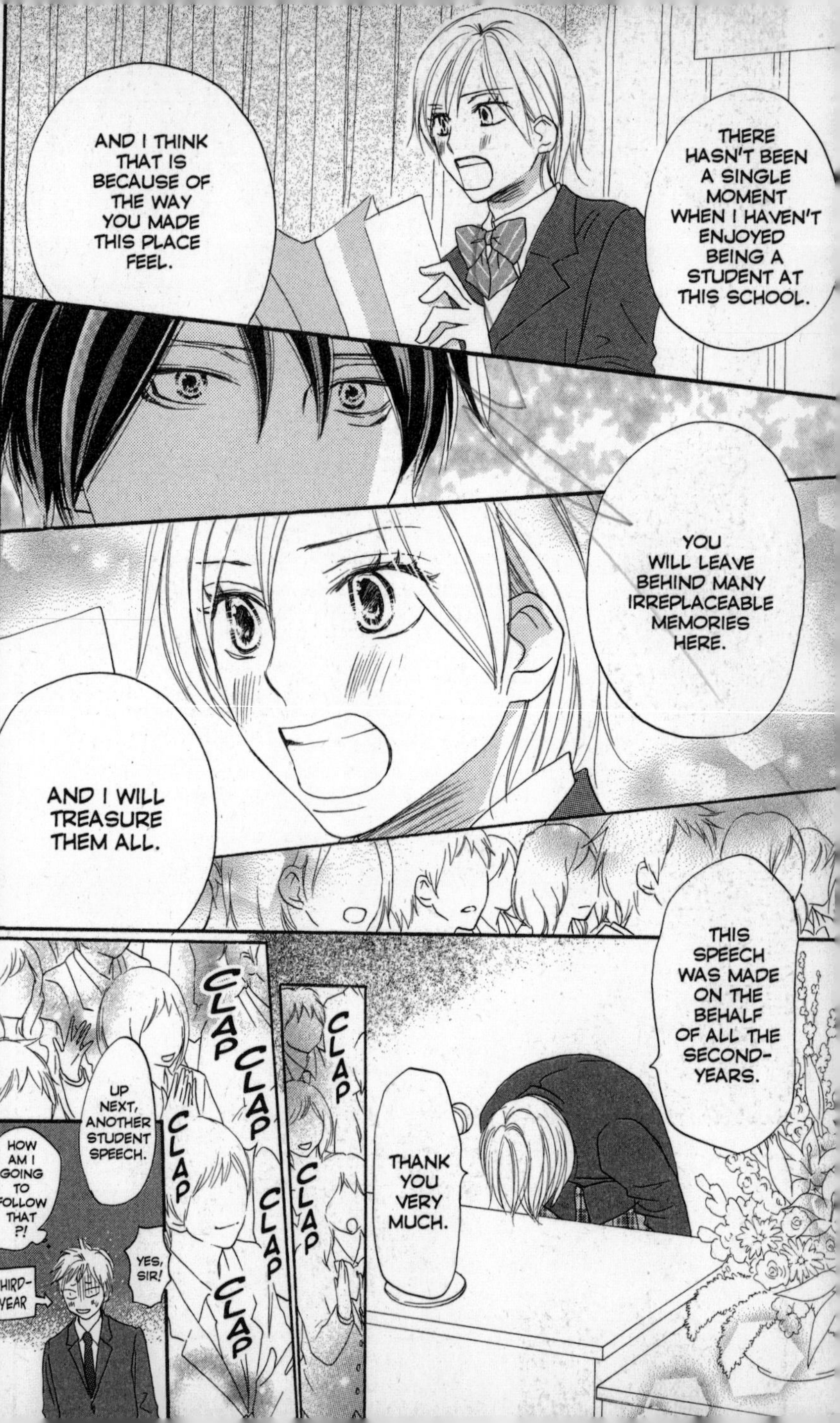
THERE HASN'T BEEN A SINGLE MOMENT WHEN I HAVEN'T ENJOYED BEING A STUDENT AT THIS SCHOOL.
AND I THINK THAT IS BECAUSE OF THE WAY YOU MADE THIS PLACE FEEL.
YOU WILL LEAVE BEHIND MANY IRREPLACEABLE MEMORIES HERE.
AND I WILL TREASURE THEM ALL.
THIS SPEECH WAS MADE ON THE BEHALF OF ALL THE SECOND-YEARS.
THANK YOU VERY MUCH.
CLAP CLAP
CLAP CLAP CLAP
CLAP CLAP CLAP CLAP
UP NEXT, ANOTHER STUDENT SPEECH.
YES, SIR!
HOW AM I GOING TO FOLLOW THAT?!
THIRD-YEAR

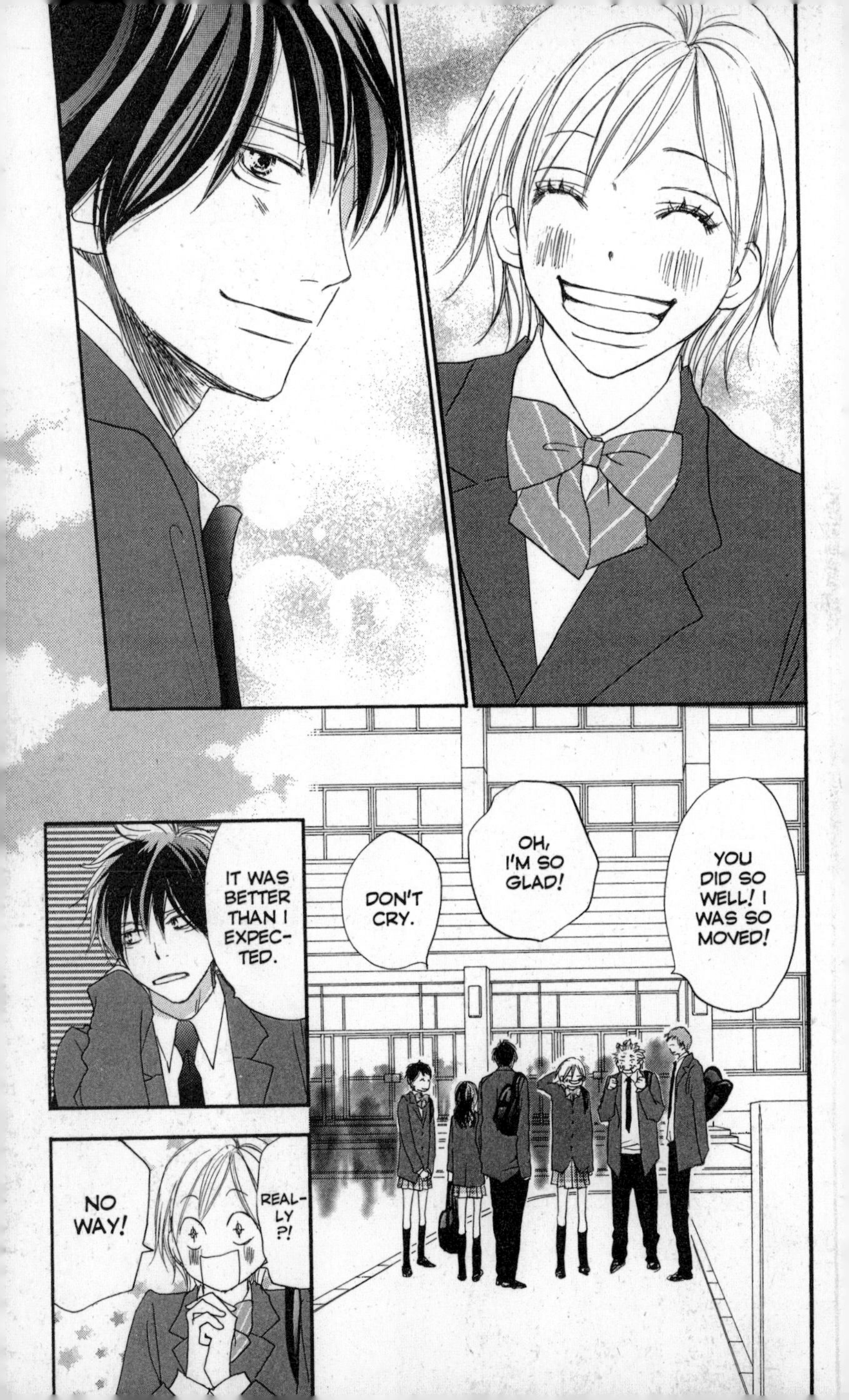
YOU DID SO WELL! I WAS SO MOVED!
OH, I'M SO GLAD!
DON'T CRY.
IT WAS BETTER THAN I EXPECTED.
REAL-LY?!
NO WAY!

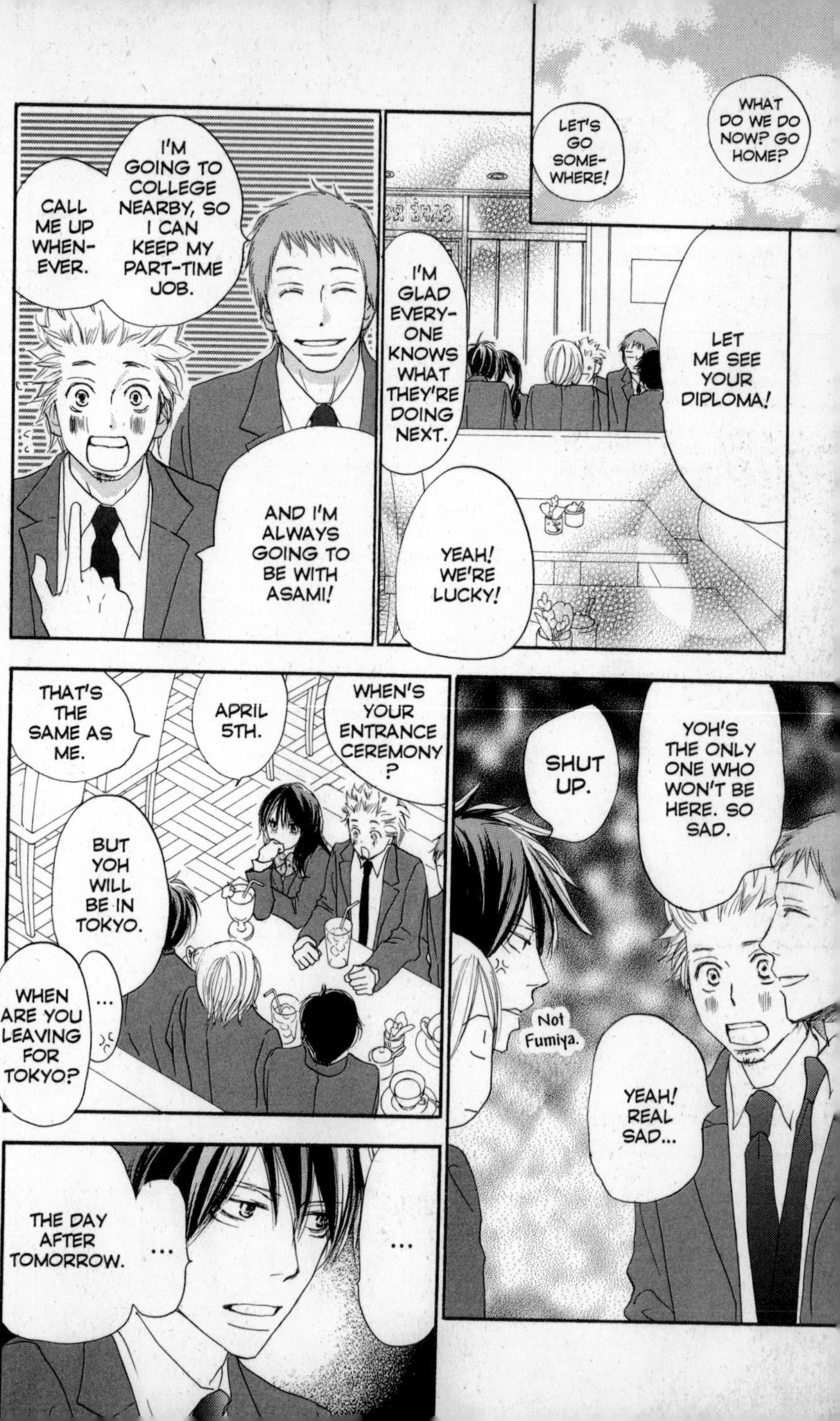
WHAT DO WE DO NOW? GO HOME?
LET'S GO SOME-WHERE!
LET ME SEE YOUR DIPLOMA!
I'M GLAD EVERY-ONE KNOWS WHAT THEY'RE DOING NEXT.
YEAH! WE'RE LUCKY!
I'M GOING TO COLLEGE NEARBY, SO I CAN KEEP MY PART-TIME JOB.
CALL ME UP WHEN-EVER.
AND I'M ALWAYS GOING TO BE WITH ASAMI!
YOH'S THE ONLY ONE WHO WON'T BE HERE. SO SAD.
SHUT UP.
Not Fumiya.
YEAH! REAL SAD...
WHEN'S YOUR ENTRANCE CEREMONY?
APRIL 5TH.
THAT'S THE SAME AS ME.
BUT YOH WILL BE IN TOKYO.
...
WHEN ARE YOU LEAVING FOR TOKYO?
...
...
THE DAY AFTER TOMORROW.

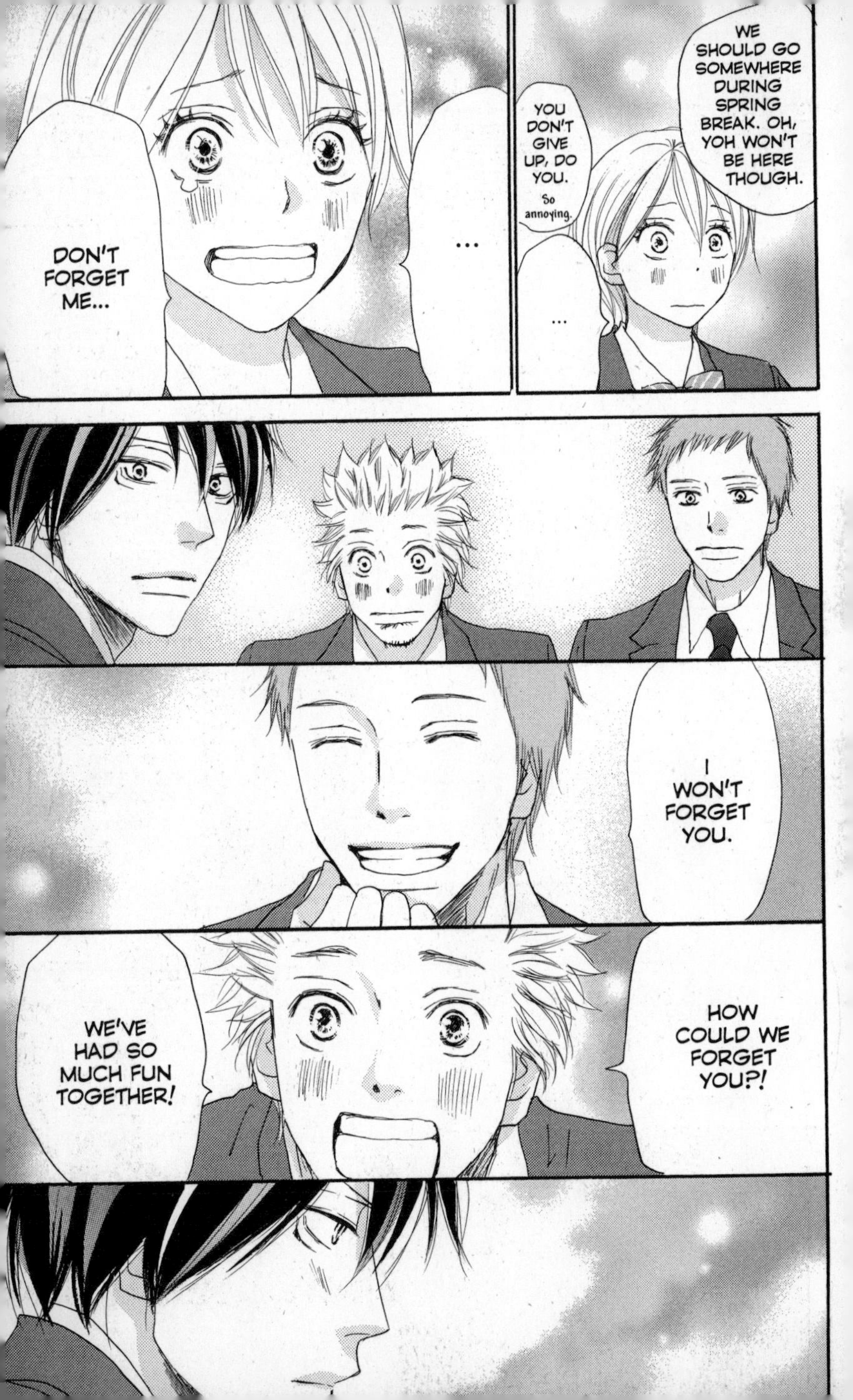
WE SHOULD GO SOMEWHERE DURING SPRING BREAK. OH, YOH WON'T BE HERE THOUGH.
YOU DON'T GIVE UP, DO YOU.
So annoying.
...
...
DON'T FORGET ME...
I WON'T FORGET YOU.
HOW COULD WE FORGET YOU?!
WE'VE HAD SO MUCH FUN TOGETHER!

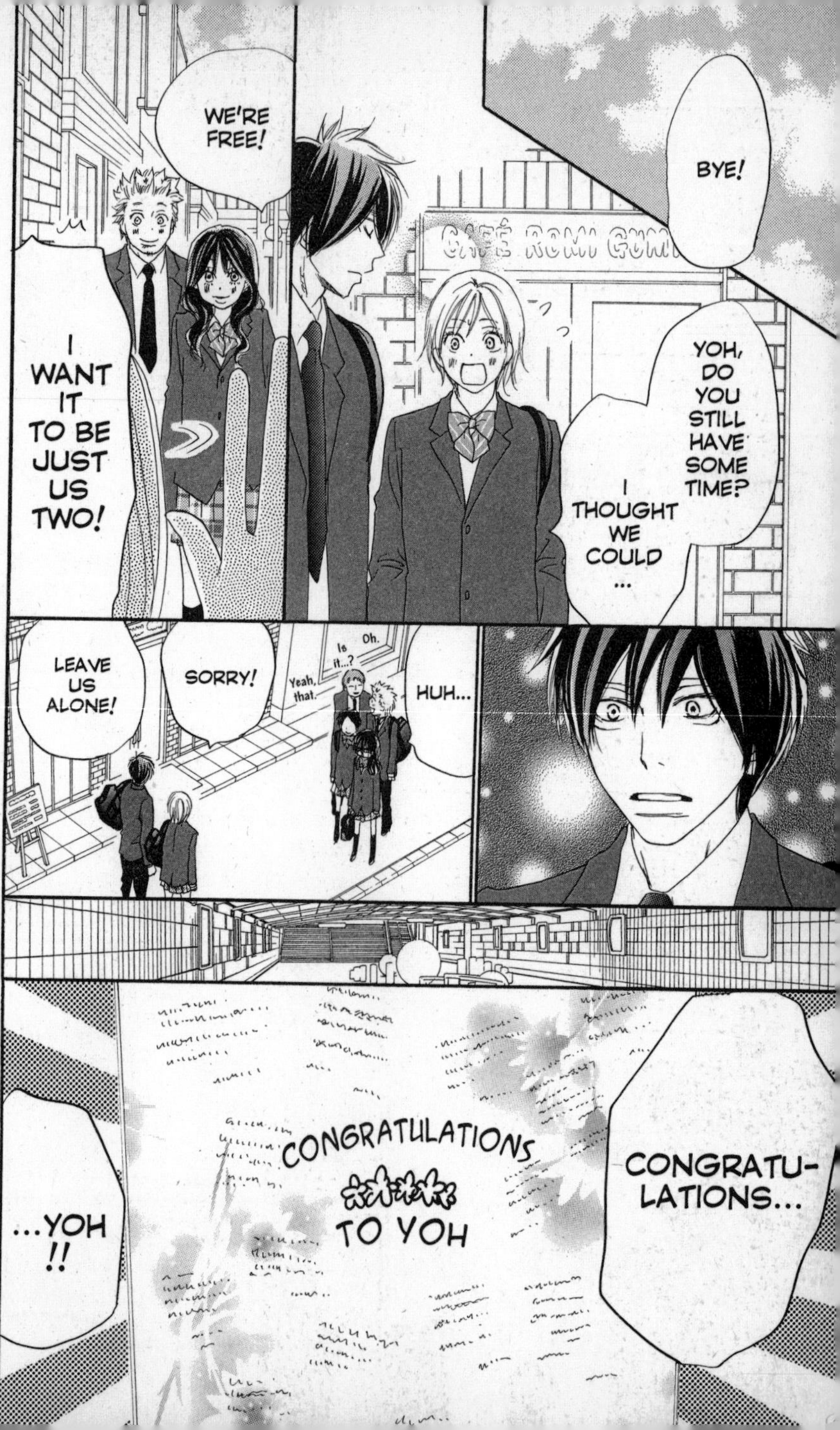
BYE!
YOH, DO YOU STILL HAVE SOME TIME?
I THOUGHT WE COULD ...
WE'RE FREE!
I WANT IT TO BE JUST US TWO!
HUH...
Oh.
Is it...?
Yeah, that.
SORRY!
LEAVE US ALONE!
CONGRATU-LATIONS...
CONGRATULATIONS
TO YOH
...YOH !!

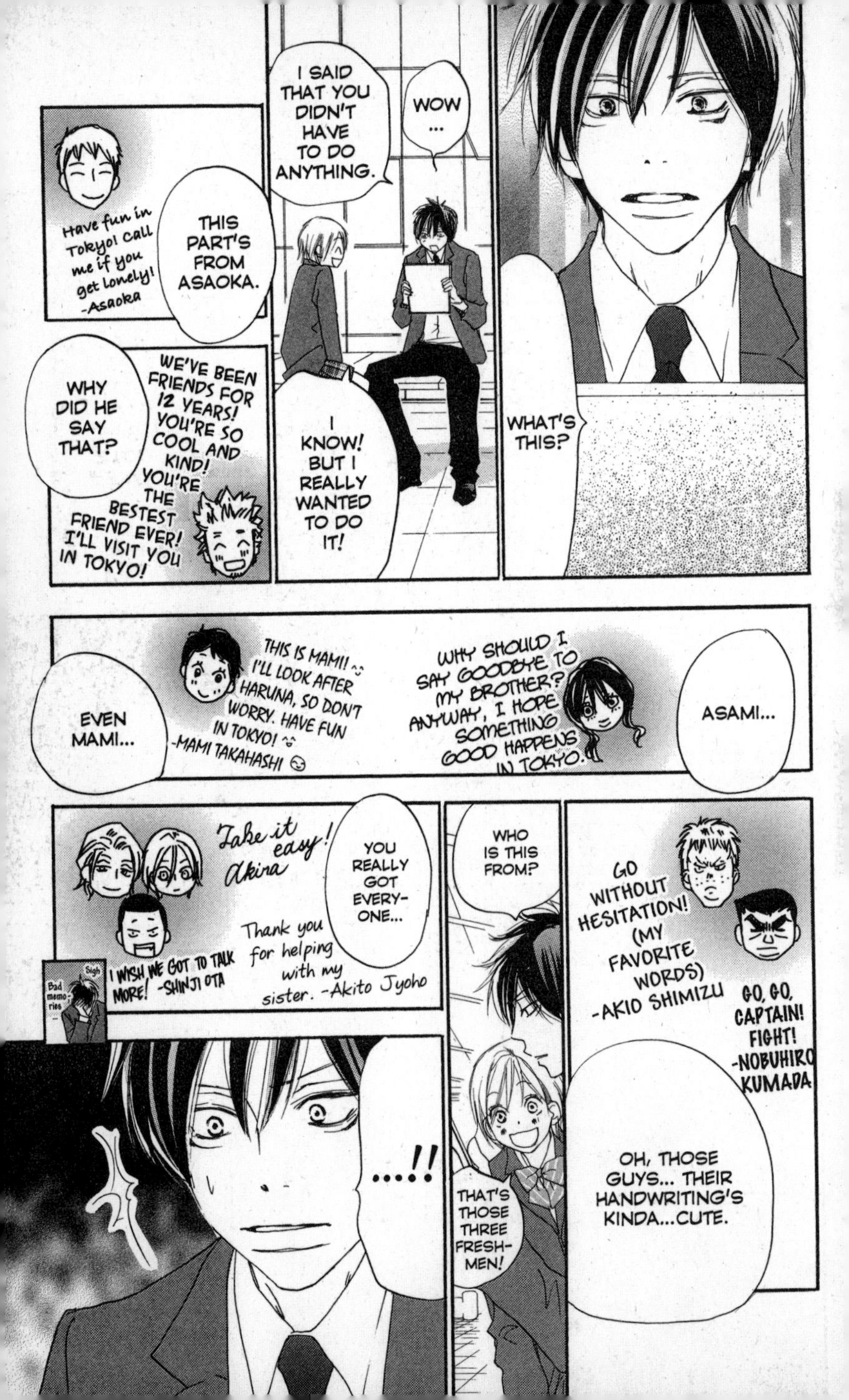
WHAT'S THIS?
WOW...
I SAID THAT YOU DIDN'T HAVE TO DO ANYTHING.
I KNOW! BUT I REALLY WANTED TO DO IT!
THIS PART'S FROM ASAOKA.
Have fun in Tokyo! Call me if you get lonely! -Asaoka
WE'VE BEEN FRIENDS FOR 12 YEARS! YOU'RE SO COOL AND KIND! YOU'RE THE BESTEST FRIEND EVER! I'LL VISIT YOU IN TOKYO!
WHY DID HE SAY THAT?
ASAMI...
WHY SHOULD I SAY GOODBYE TO MY BROTHER? ANYWAY, I HOPE SOMETHING GOOD HAPPENS IN TOKYO.
THIS IS MAMI! I'LL LOOK AFTER HARUNA, SO DON'T WORRY. HAVE FUN IN TOKYO! -MAMI TAKAHASHI
EVEN MAMI...
GO WITHOUT HESITATION! (MY FAVORITE WORDS) -AKIO SHIMIZU
GO, GO, CAPTAIN! FIGHT! -NOBUHIRO KUMADA
OH, THOSE GUYS... THEIR HANDWRITING'S KINDA...CUTE.
WHO IS THIS FROM?
THAT'S THOSE THREE FRESHMEN!
YOU REALLY GOT EVERYONE...
Take it easy! Akira
Thank you for helping with my sister. -Akito Jyoho
I WISH WE GOT TO TALK MORE! -SHINJI OTA
Sigh
Bad memories...
...!!

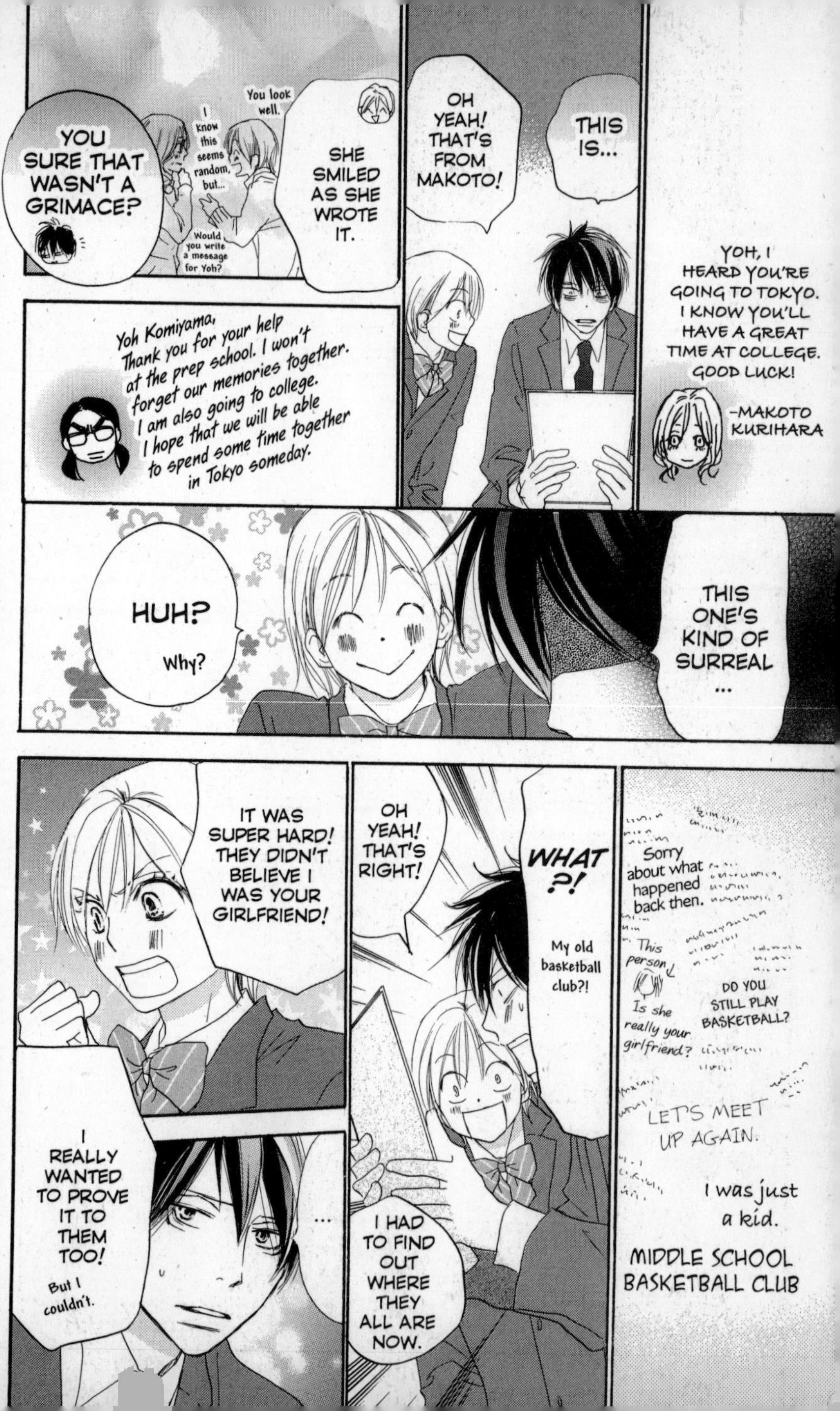
THIS IS...
YOH, I HEARD YOU'RE GOING TO TOKYO. I KNOW YOU'LL HAVE A GREAT TIME AT COLLEGE. GOOD LUCK!
-MAKOTO KURIHARA
OH YEAH! THAT'S FROM MAKOTO!
SHE SMILED AS SHE WROTE IT.
You look well.
I know this seems random, but...
Would you write a message for Yoh?
YOU SURE THAT WASN'T A GRIMACE?
Yoh Komiyama, Thank you for your help at the prep school. I won't forget our memories together. I am also going to college. I hope that we will be able to spend some time together in Tokyo someday.
THIS ONE'S KIND OF SURREAL ...
HUH?
Why?
Sorry about what happened back then.
This person
Is she really your girlfriend?
DO YOU STILL PLAY BASKETBALL?
LET'S MEET UP AGAIN.
I was just a kid.
MIDDLE SCHOOL BASKETBALL CLUB
WHAT ?!
My old basketball club?!
OH YEAH! THAT'S RIGHT!
I HAD TO FIND OUT WHERE THEY ALL ARE NOW.
...
IT WAS SUPER HARD! THEY DIDN'T BELIEVE I WAS YOUR GIRLFRIEND!
I REALLY WANTED TO PROVE IT TO THEM TOO!
But I couldn't.

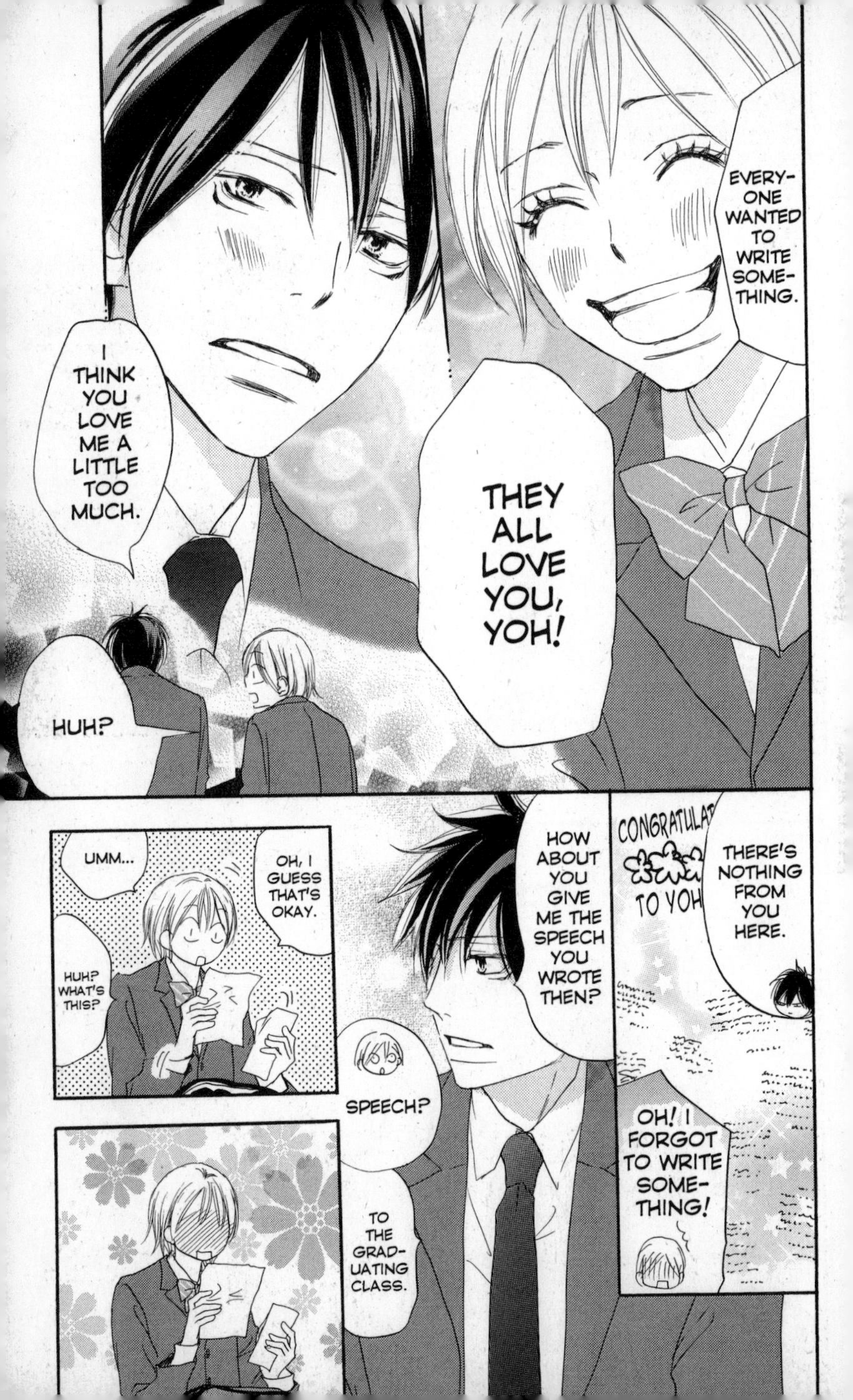
EVERYONE WANTED TO WRITE SOMETHING.
THEY ALL LOVE YOU, YOH!
I THINK YOU LOVE ME A LITTLE TOO MUCH.
HUH?
CONGRATULA
TO YOH
THERE'S NOTHING FROM YOU HERE.
OH! I FORGOT TO WRITE SOMETHING!
HOW ABOUT YOU GIVE ME THE SPEECH YOU WROTE THEN?
SPEECH?
TO THE GRADUATING CLASS.
OH, I GUESS THAT'S OKAY.
UMM...
HUH? WHAT'S THIS?

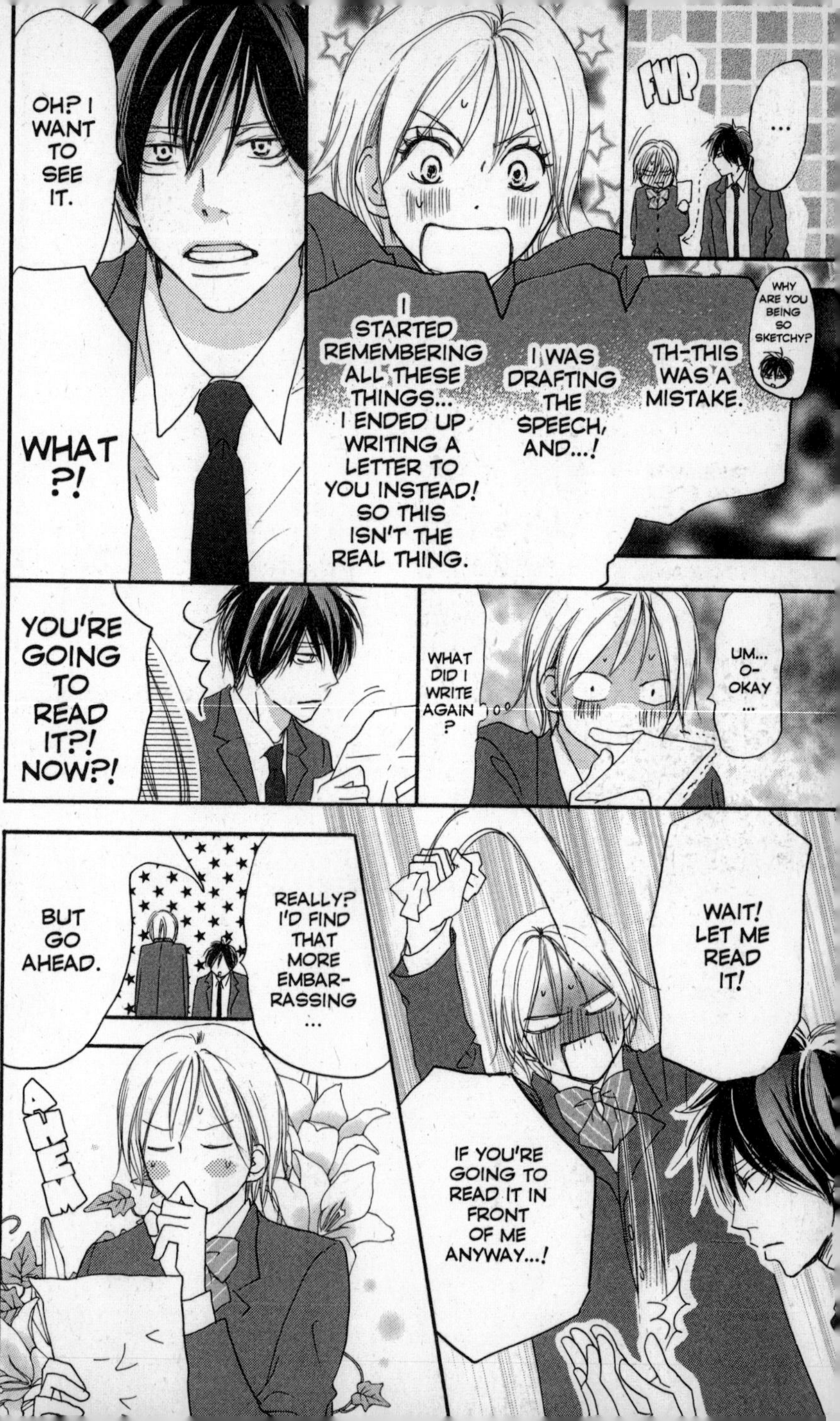
FWP
...
WHY ARE YOU BEING SO SKETCHY?
TH-THIS WAS A MISTAKE.
I WAS DRAFTING THE SPEECH, AND...!
I STARTED REMEMBERING ALL THESE THINGS... I ENDED UP WRITING A LETTER TO YOU INSTEAD! SO THIS ISN'T THE REAL THING.
OH? I WANT TO SEE IT.
WHAT?!
UM... O-OKAY ...
WHAT DID I WRITE AGAIN ?
YOU'RE GOING TO READ IT?! NOW?!
WAIT! LET ME READ IT!
IF YOU'RE GOING TO READ IT IN FRONT OF ME ANYWAY...!
REALLY? I'D FIND THAT MORE EMBARRASSING ...
BUT GO AHEAD.
AHEM

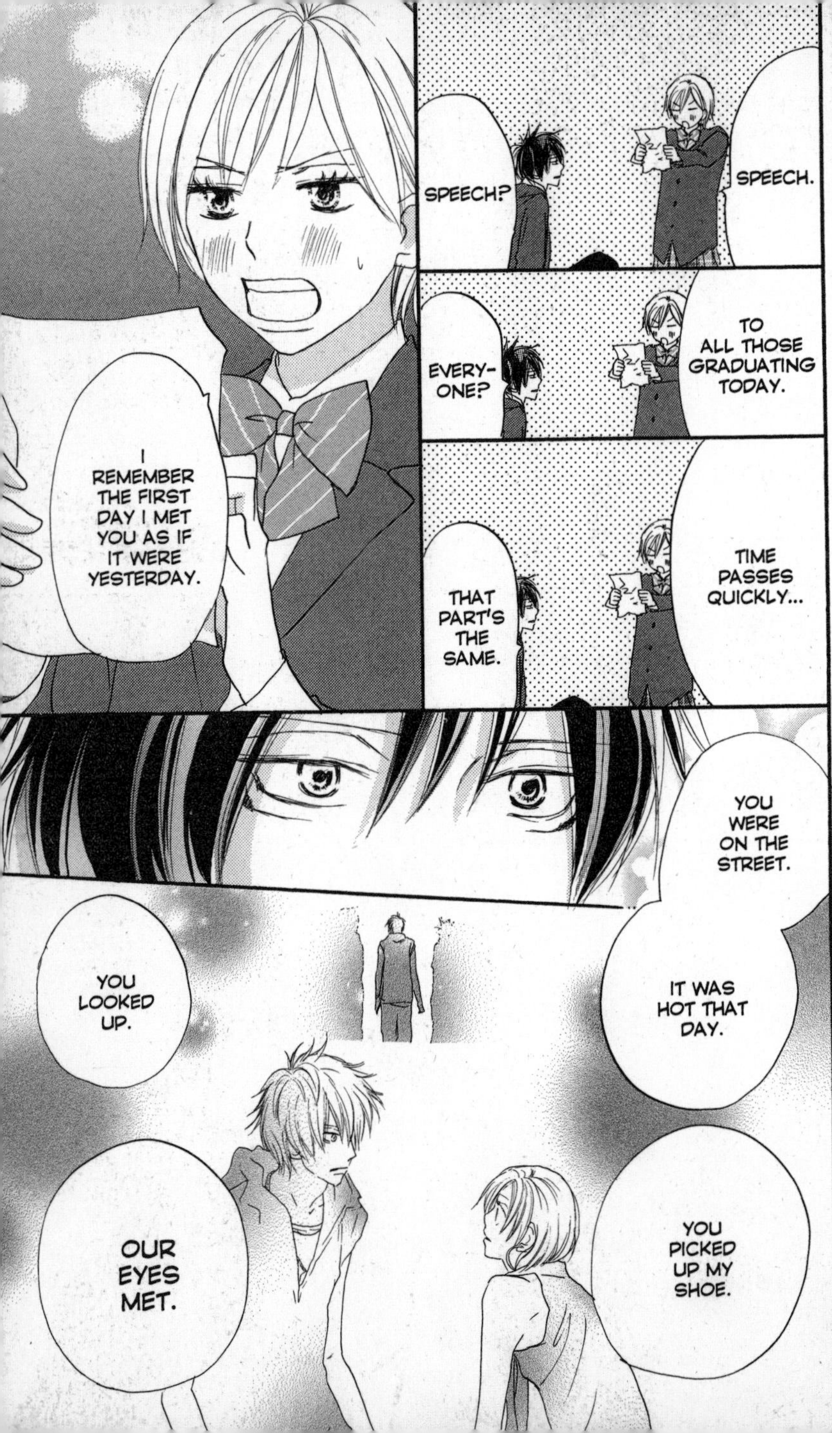
SPEECH.
SPEECH?
TO ALL THOSE GRADUATING TODAY.
EVERY-ONE?
TIME PASSES QUICKLY...
THAT PART'S THE SAME.
I REMEMBER THE FIRST DAY I MET YOU AS IF IT WERE YESTERDAY.
YOU WERE ON THE STREET.
IT WAS HOT THAT DAY.
YOU LOOKED UP.
YOU PICKED UP MY SHOE.
OUR EYES MET.

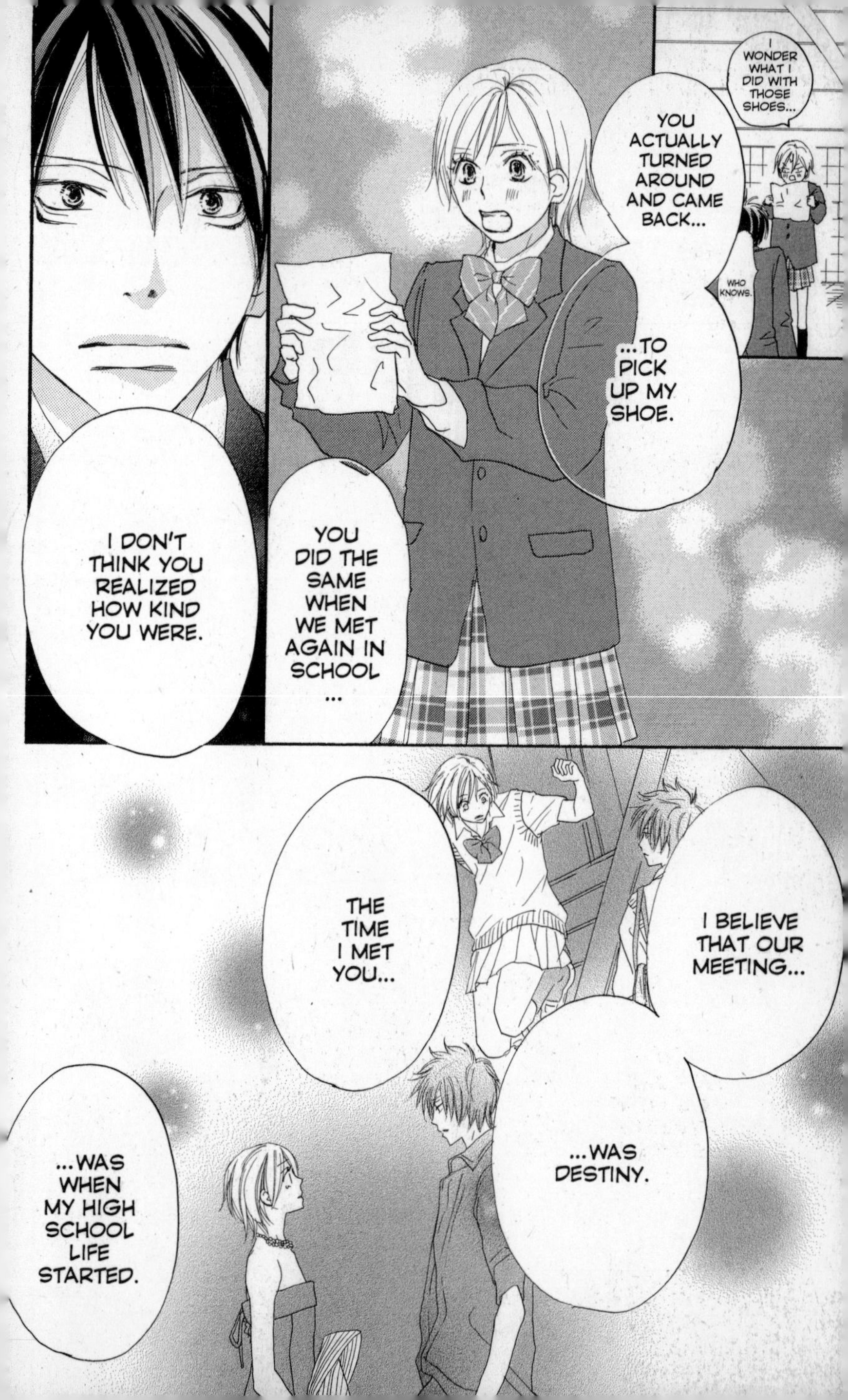
I WONDER WHAT I DID WITH THOSE SHOES...
WHO KNOWS.
YOU ACTUALLY TURNED AROUND AND CAME BACK...
...TO PICK UP MY SHOE.
YOU DID THE SAME WHEN WE MET AGAIN IN SCHOOL...
I DON'T THINK YOU REALIZED HOW KIND YOU WERE.
I BELIEVE THAT OUR MEETING...
...WAS DESTINY.
THE TIME I MET YOU...
...WAS WHEN MY HIGH SCHOOL LIFE STARTED.

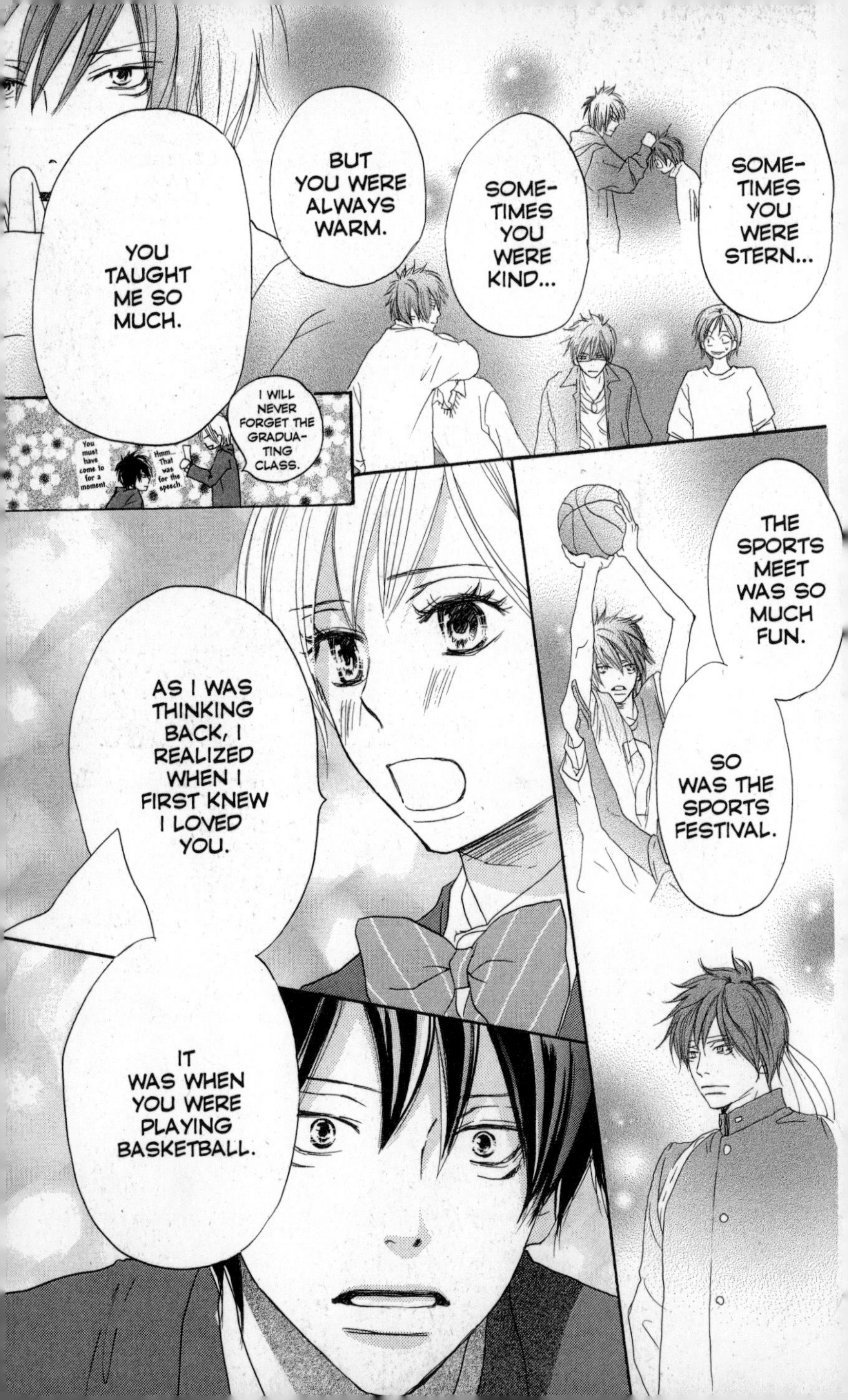
SOMETIMES YOU WERE STERN...
SOMETIMES YOU WERE KIND...
BUT YOU WERE ALWAYS WARM.
YOU TAUGHT ME SO MUCH.
I WILL NEVER FORGET THE GRADUATING CLASS.
Hmm... That was for the speech.
You must have come to for a moment.
THE SPORTS MEET WAS SO MUCH FUN.
SO WAS THE SPORTS FESTIVAL.
AS I WAS THINKING BACK, I REALIZED WHEN I FIRST KNEW I LOVED YOU.
IT WAS WHEN YOU WERE PLAYING BASKETBALL.

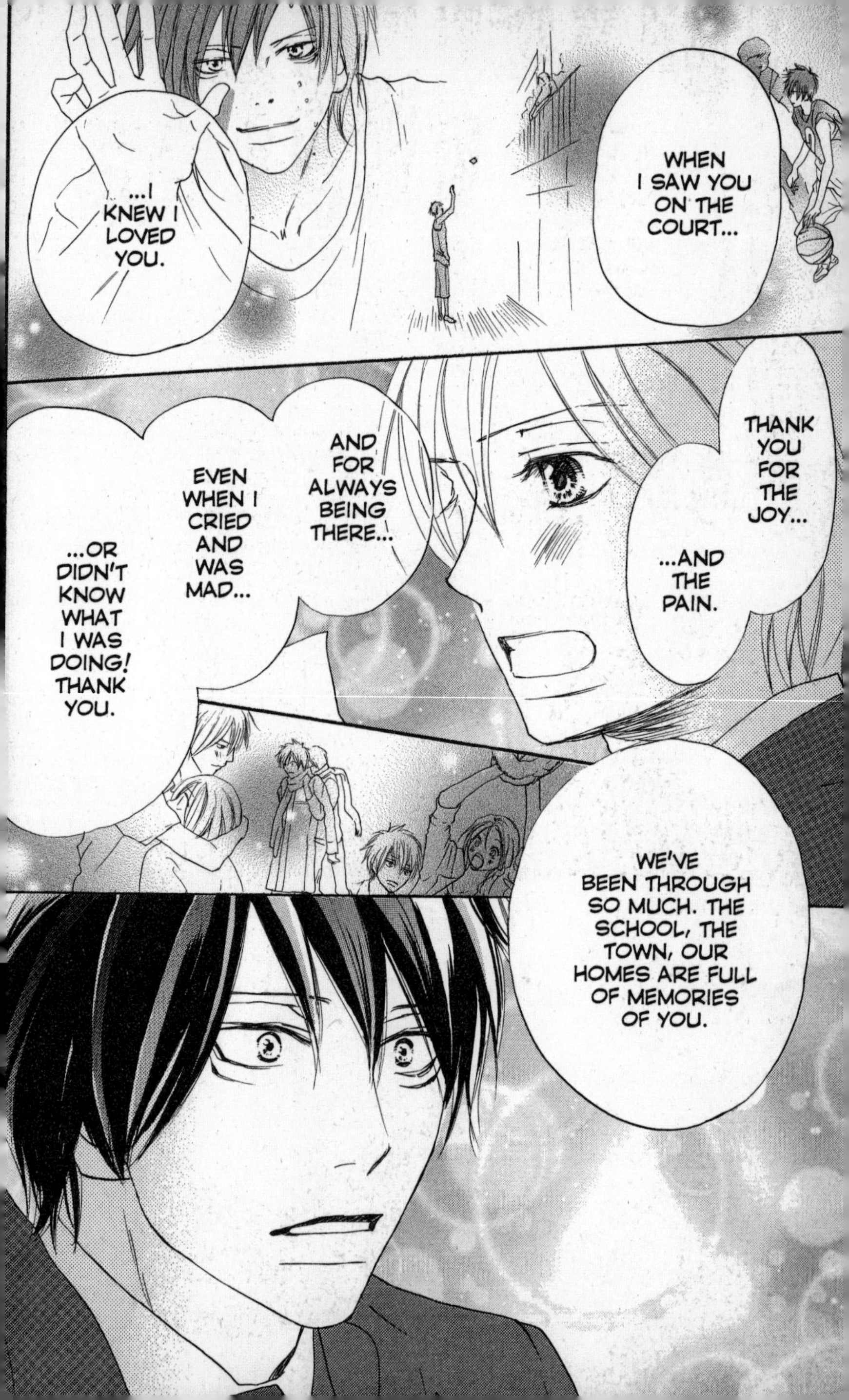
WHEN I SAW YOU ON THE COURT...
...I KNEW I LOVED YOU.
THANK YOU FOR THE JOY...
...AND THE PAIN.
AND FOR ALWAYS BEING THERE...
EVEN WHEN I CRIED AND WAS MAD...
...OR DIDN'T KNOW WHAT I WAS DOING! THANK YOU.
WE'VE BEEN THROUGH SO MUCH. THE SCHOOL, THE TOWN, OUR HOMES ARE FULL OF MEMORIES OF YOU.

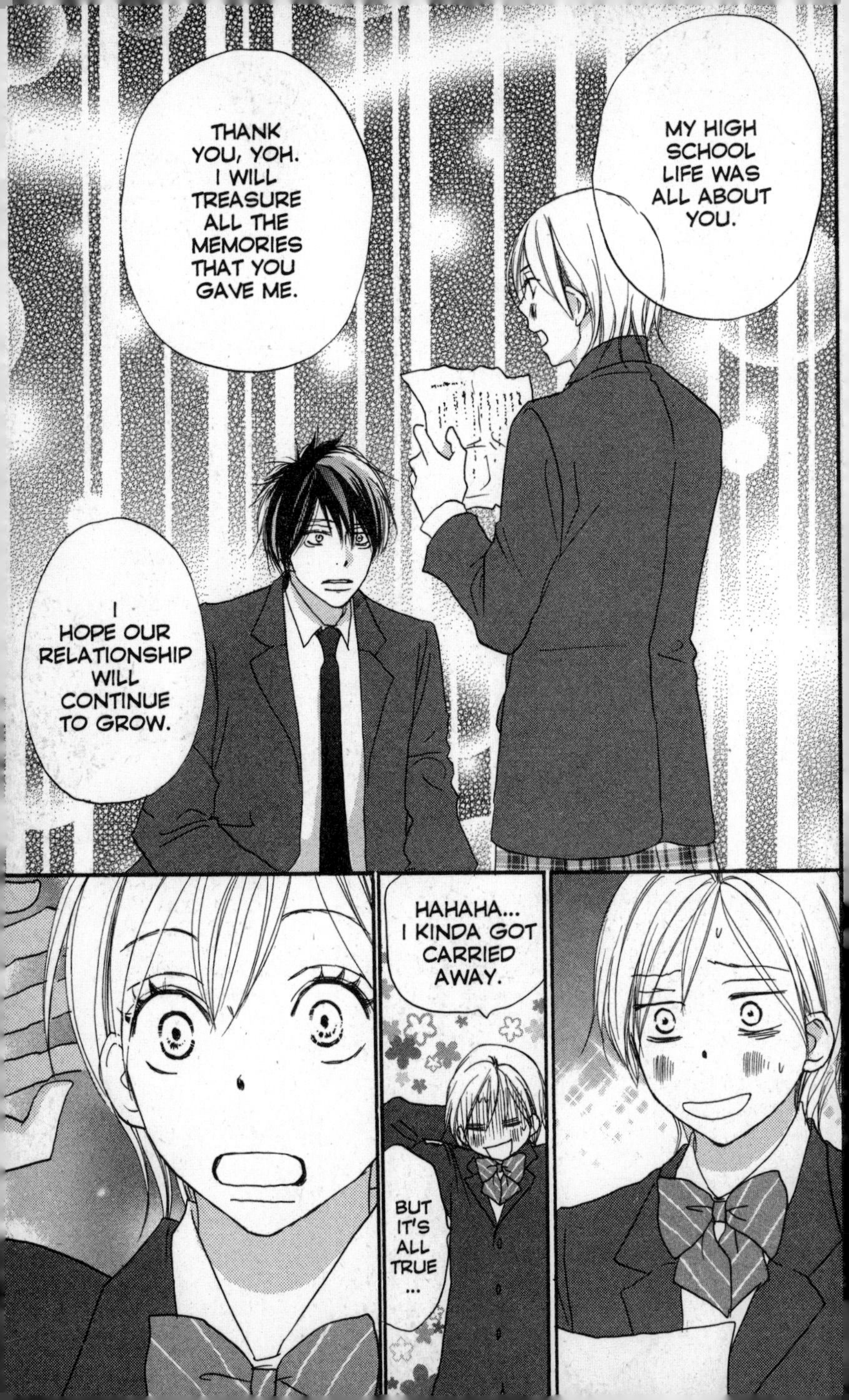
MY HIGH SCHOOL LIFE WAS ALL ABOUT YOU.
THANK YOU, YOH. I WILL TREASURE ALL THE MEMORIES THAT YOU GAVE ME.
I HOPE OUR RELATIONSHIP WILL CONTINUE TO GROW.
HAHAHA... I KINDA GOT CARRIED AWAY.
BUT IT'S ALL TRUE ...

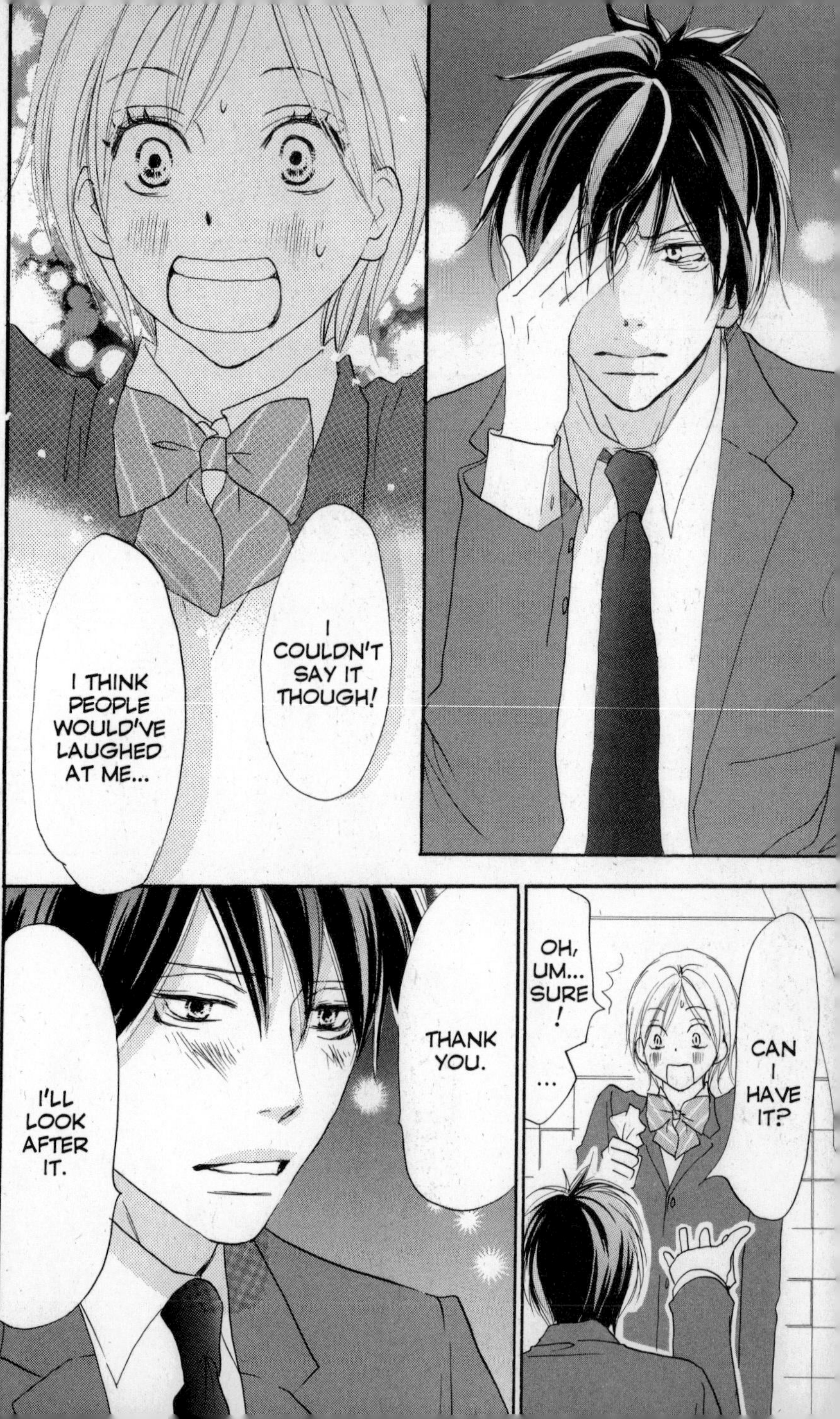
I COULDN'T SAY IT THOUGH!
I THINK PEOPLE WOULD'VE LAUGHED AT ME...
CAN I HAVE IT?
OH, UM... SURE!
...
THANK YOU.
I'LL LOOK AFTER IT.

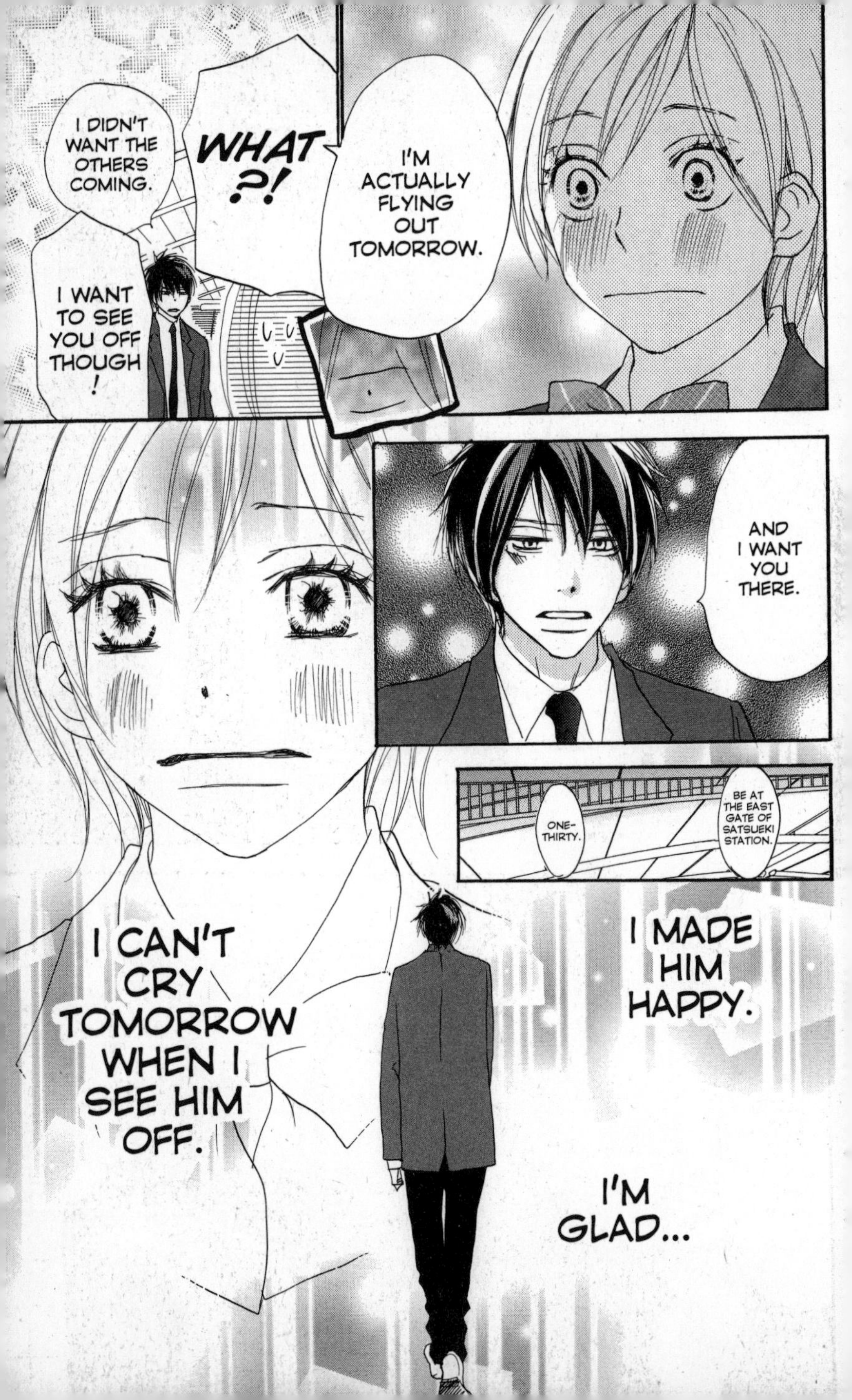
I'M ACTUALLY FLYING OUT TOMORROW.
WHAT?!
I DIDN'T WANT THE OTHERS COMING.
I WANT TO SEE YOU OFF THOUGH!
AND I WANT YOU THERE.
BE AT THE EAST GATE OF SATSUEKI STATION.
ONE-THIRTY.
I MADE HIM HAPPY.
I'M GLAD...
I CAN'T CRY TOMORROW WHEN I SEE HIM OFF.

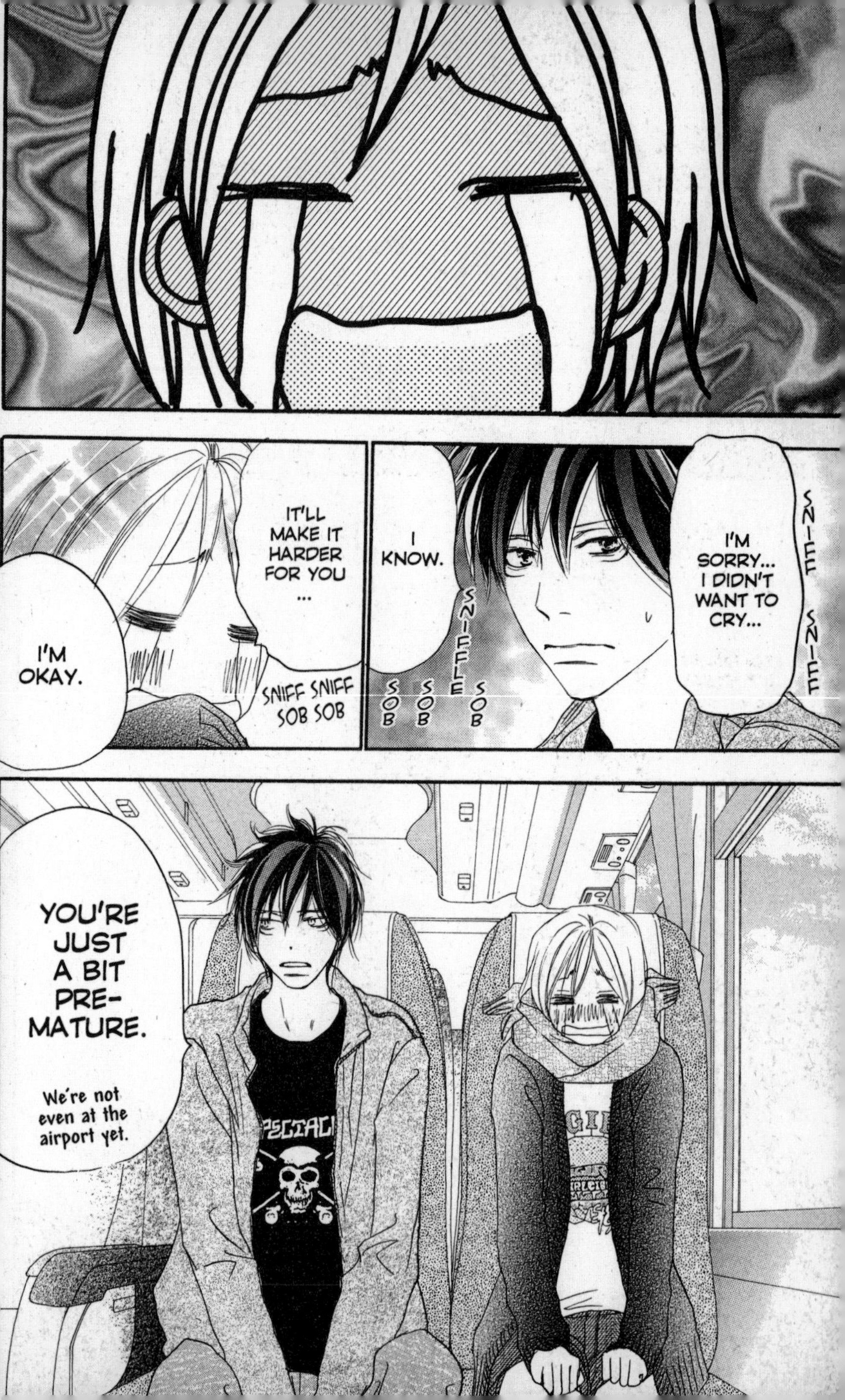
I'M SORRY... I DIDN'T WANT TO CRY...
SNIFF SNIFF
SNIFFLE
SOB SOB SOB
I KNOW.
IT'LL MAKE IT HARDER FOR YOU ...
SNIFF SNIFF SOB SOB
I'M OKAY.
YOU'RE JUST A BIT PRE-MATURE.
We're not even at the airport yet.

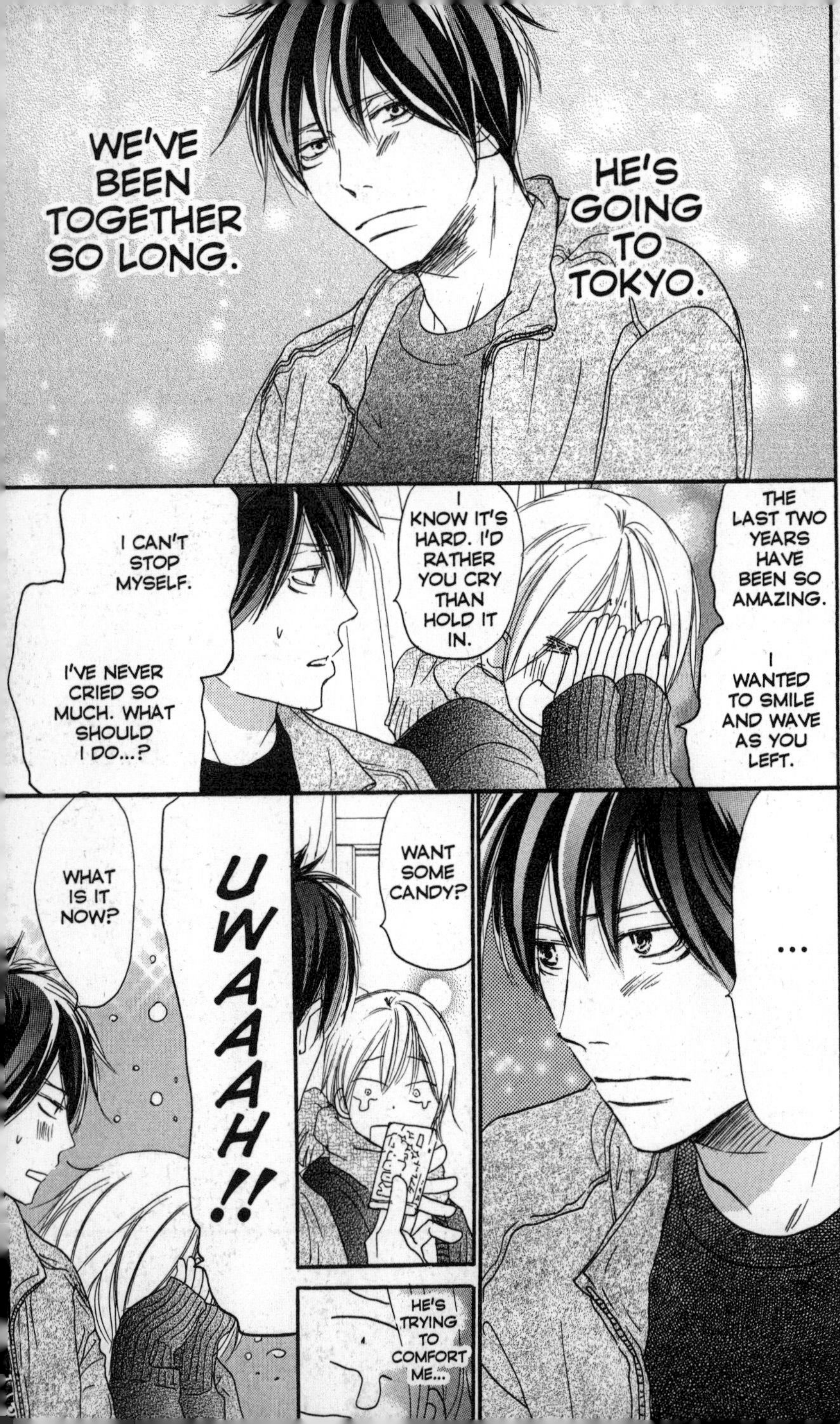
HE'S GOING TO TOKYO.
WE'VE BEEN TOGETHER SO LONG.
THE LAST TWO YEARS HAVE BEEN SO AMAZING.
I WANTED TO SMILE AND WAVE AS YOU LEFT.
I KNOW IT'S HARD. I'D RATHER YOU CRY THAN HOLD IT IN.
I CAN'T STOP MYSELF.
I'VE NEVER CRIED SO MUCH. WHAT SHOULD I DO...?
...
WANT SOME CANDY?
HE'S TRYING TO COMFORT ME...
UWAAAAH!!
WHAT IS IT NOW?

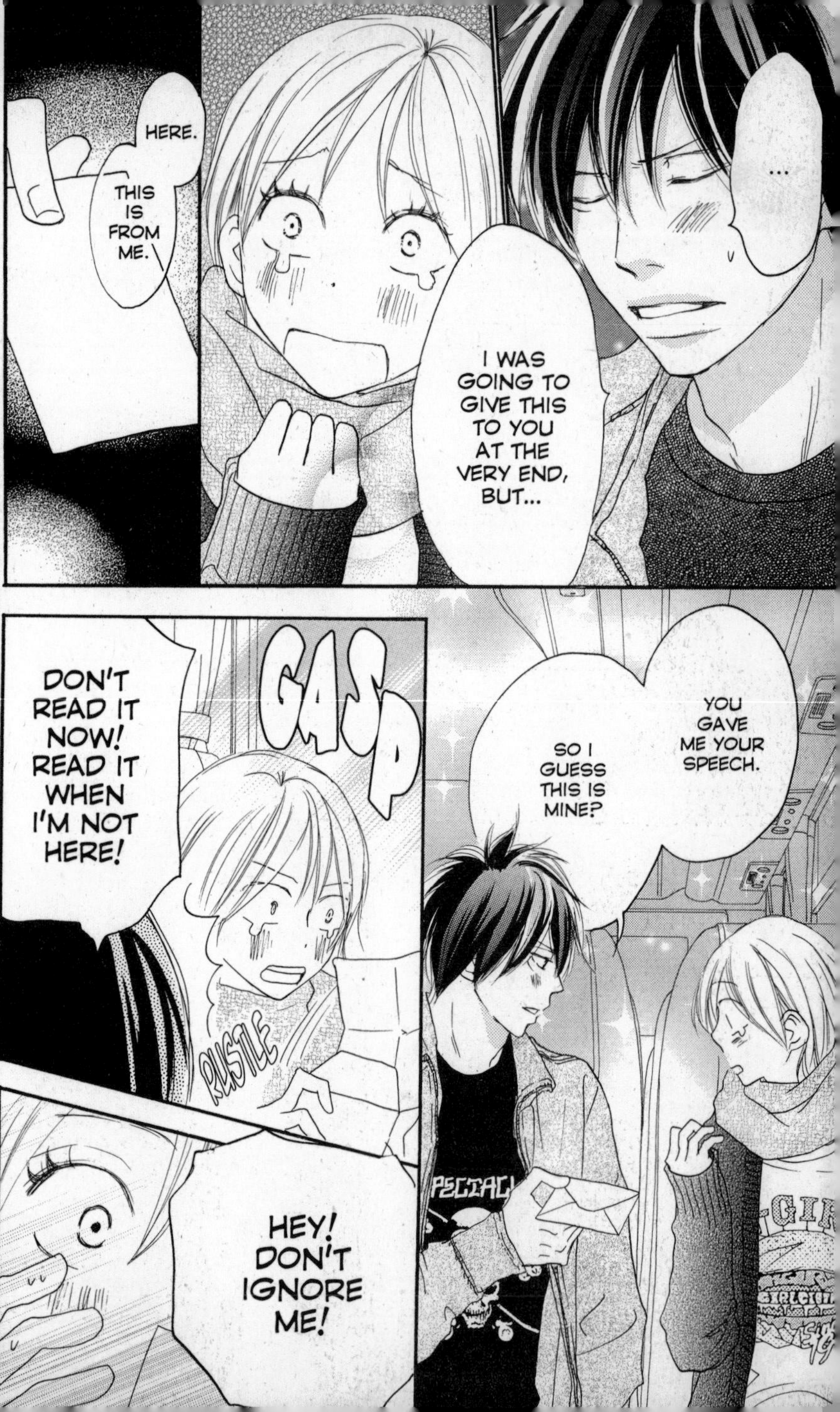
...
I WAS GOING TO GIVE THIS TO YOU AT THE VERY END, BUT...
HERE.
THIS IS FROM ME.
YOU GAVE ME YOUR SPEECH.
SO I GUESS THIS IS MINE?
GASP
DON'T READ IT NOW! READ IT WHEN I'M NOT HERE!
RUSTLE
HEY! DON'T IGNORE ME!

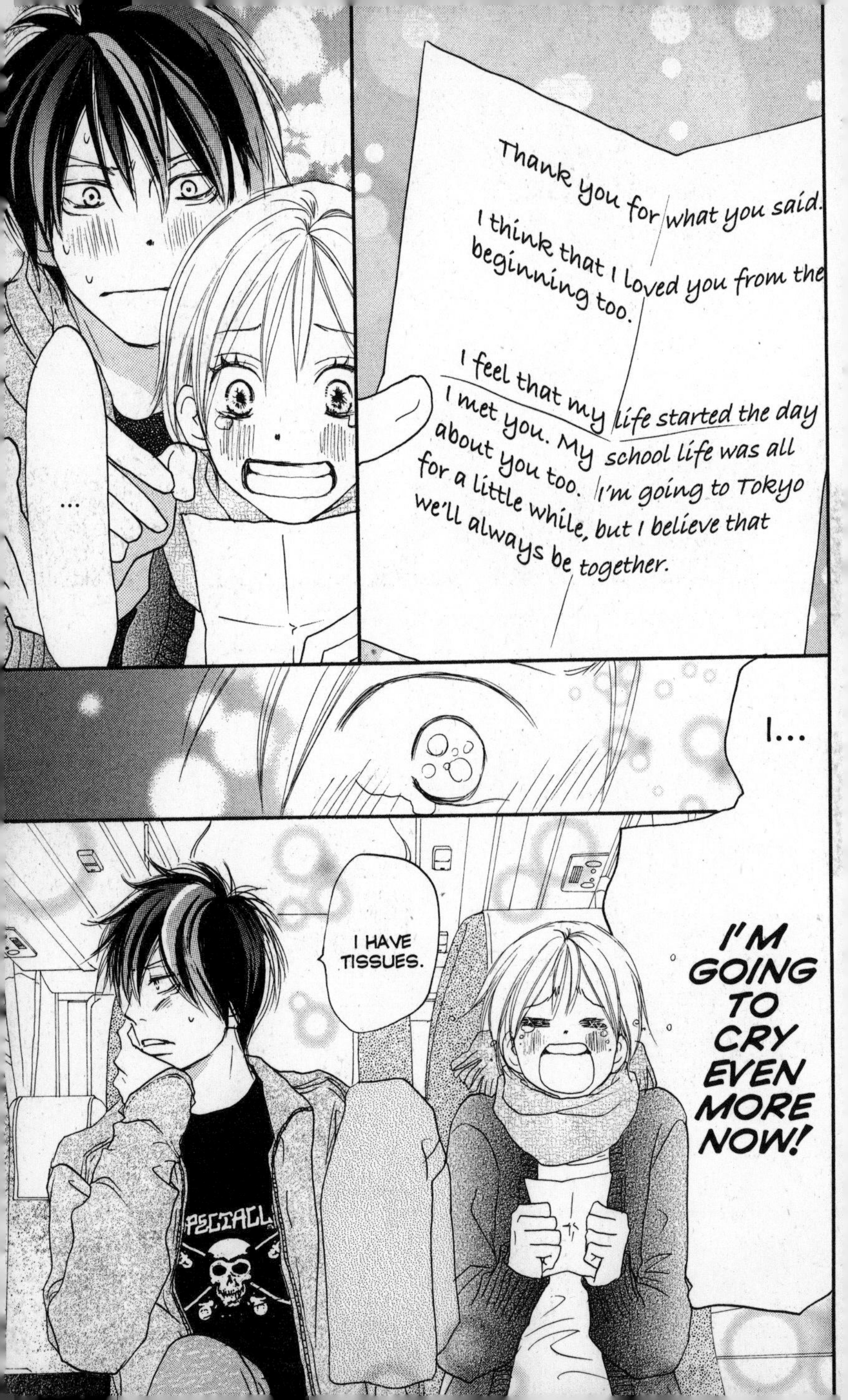
Thank you for what you said.
I think that I loved you from the beginning too.
I feel that my life started the day I met you. My school life was all about you too. I'm going to Tokyo for a little while, but I believe that we'll always be together.
...
I...
I'M GOING TO CRY EVEN MORE NOW!
I HAVE TISSUES.

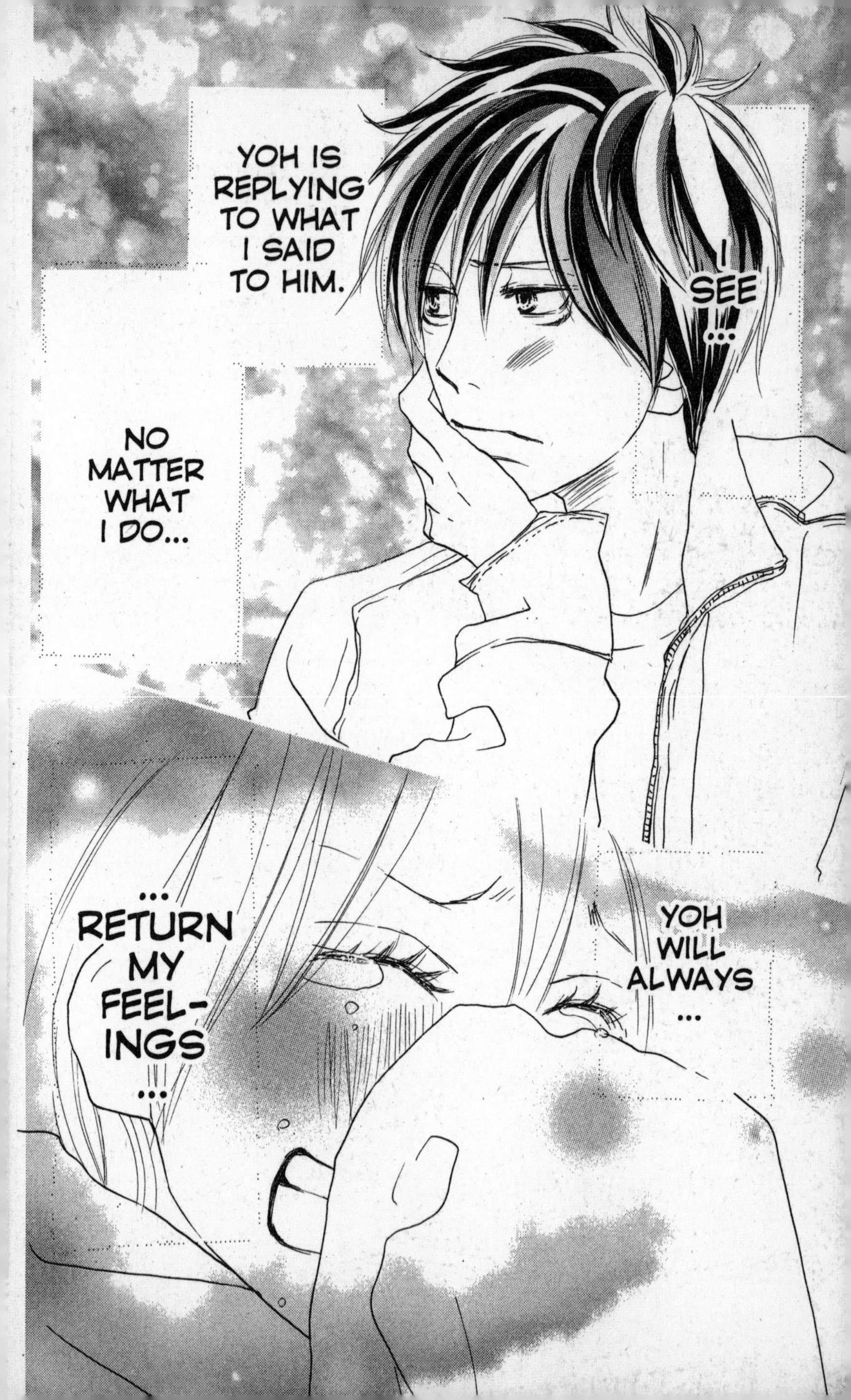
I SEE ...
YOH IS REPLYING TO WHAT I SAID TO HIM.
NO MATTER WHAT I DO...
YOH WILL ALWAYS ...
... RETURN MY FEEL-INGS ...

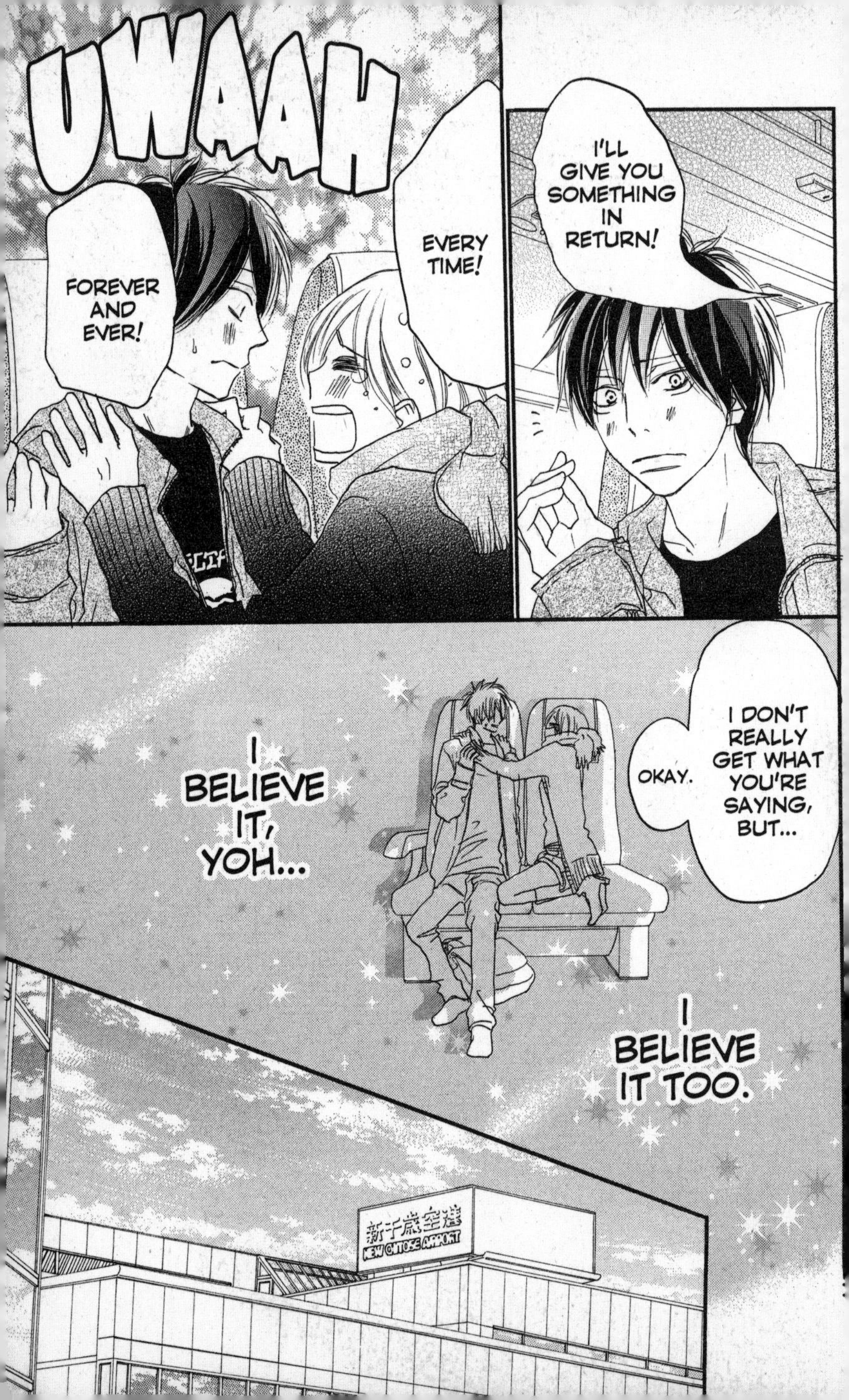
I'LL GIVE YOU SOMETHING IN RETURN!
EVERY TIME!
UWAAH
FOREVER AND EVER!
I DON'T REALLY GET WHAT YOU'RE SAYING, BUT...
OKAY.
I BELIEVE IT, YOH...
I BELIEVE IT TOO.
新千歳空港
NEW CHITOSE AIRPORT

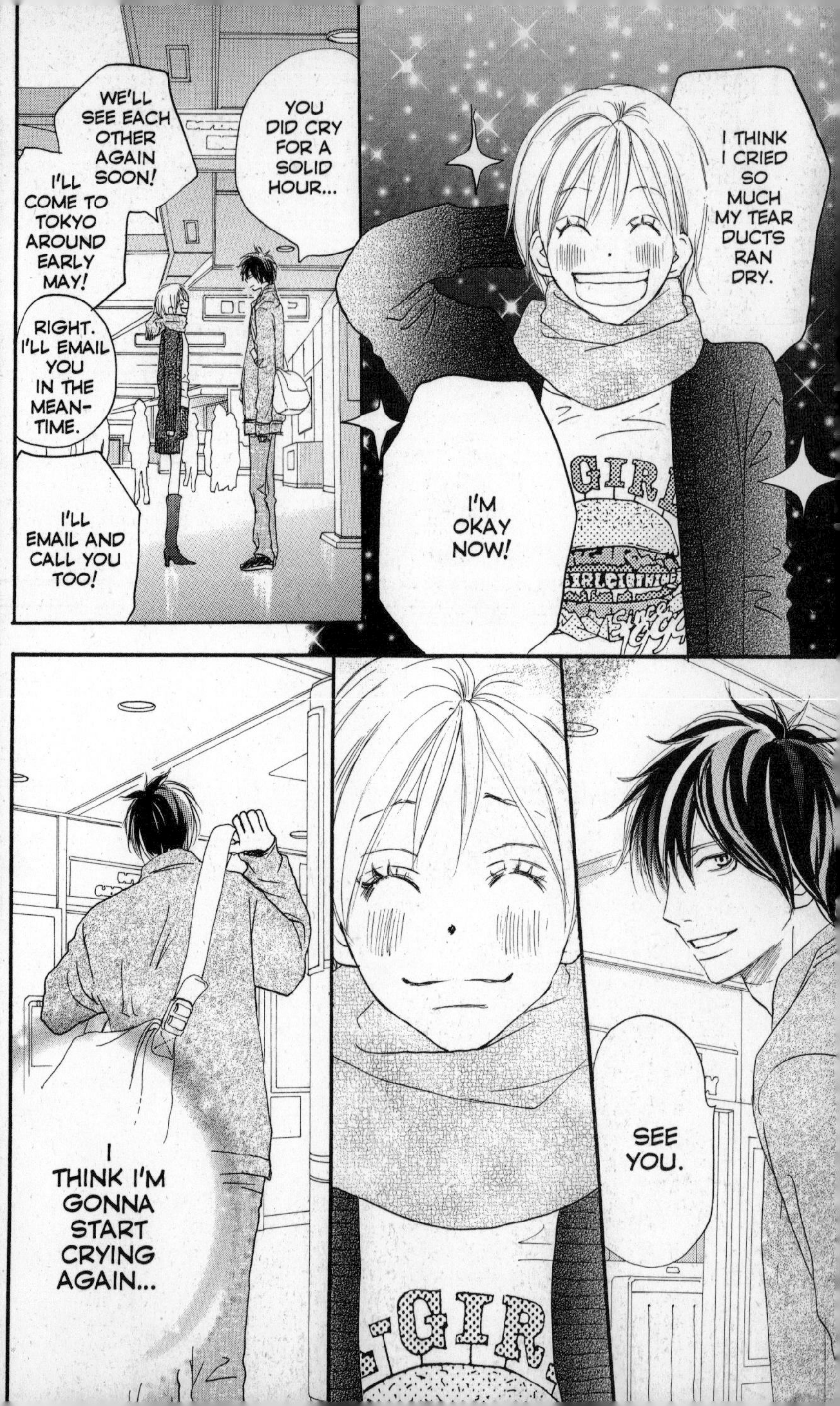
I THINK I CRIED SO MUCH MY TEAR DUCTS RAN DRY.
I'M OKAY NOW!
YOU DID CRY FOR A SOLID HOUR...
WE'LL SEE EACH OTHER AGAIN SOON!
I'LL COME TO TOKYO AROUND EARLY MAY!
RIGHT. I'LL EMAIL YOU IN THE MEAN-TIME.
I'LL EMAIL AND CALL YOU TOO!
SEE YOU.
I THINK I'M GONNA START CRYING AGAIN...

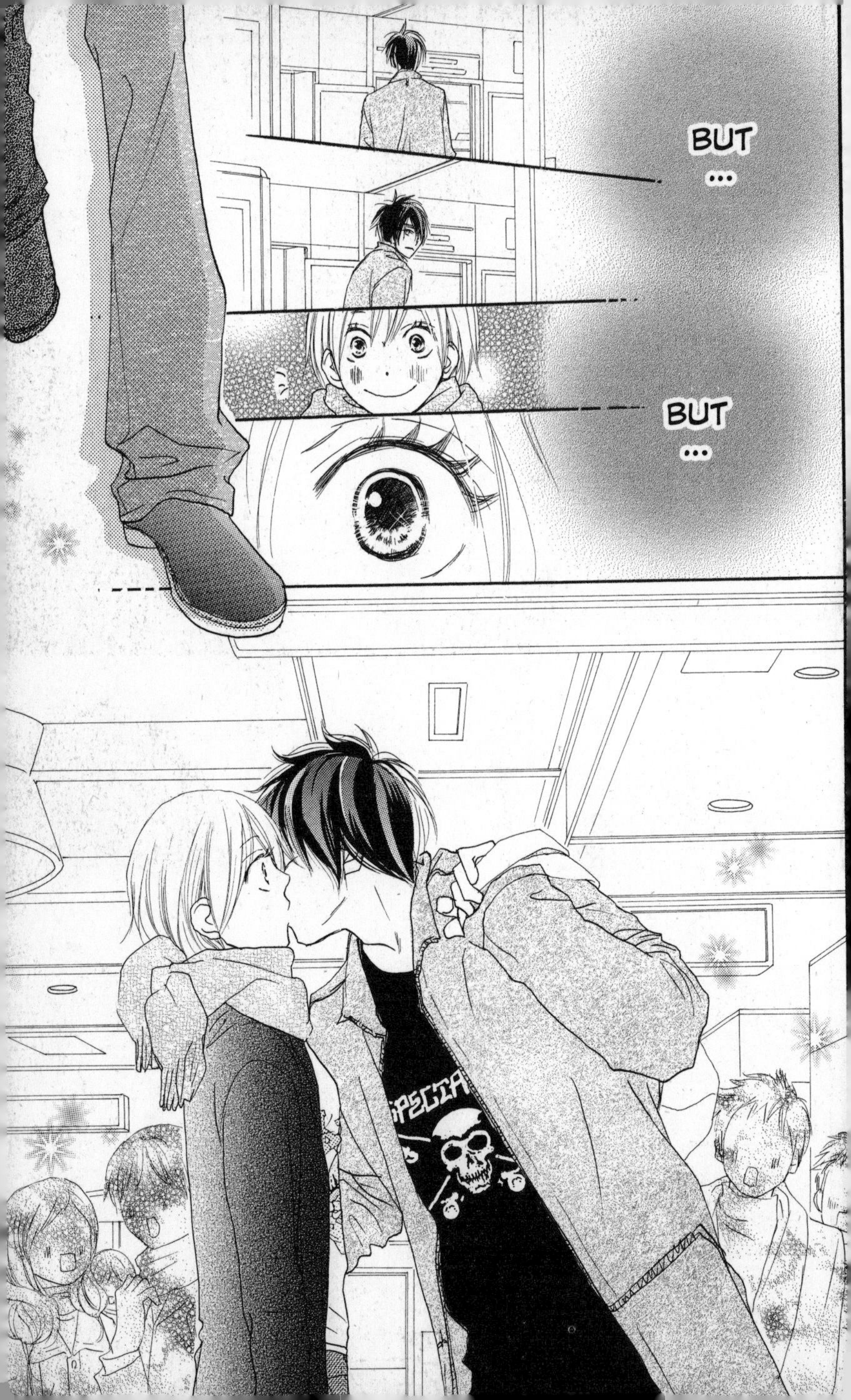
BUT ...
BUT ...

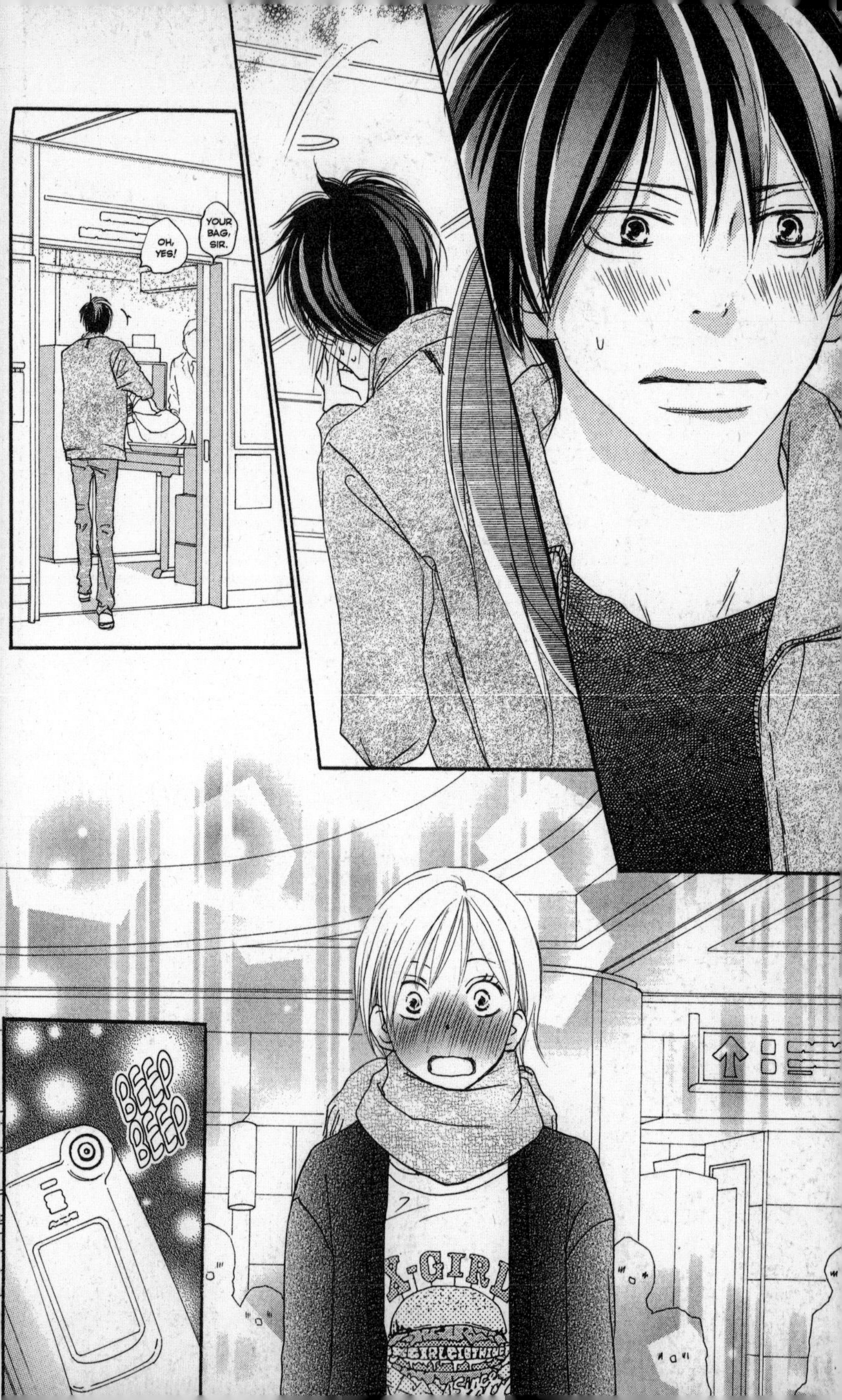
YOUR BAG, SIR.
OH, YES!
BEEP BEEP

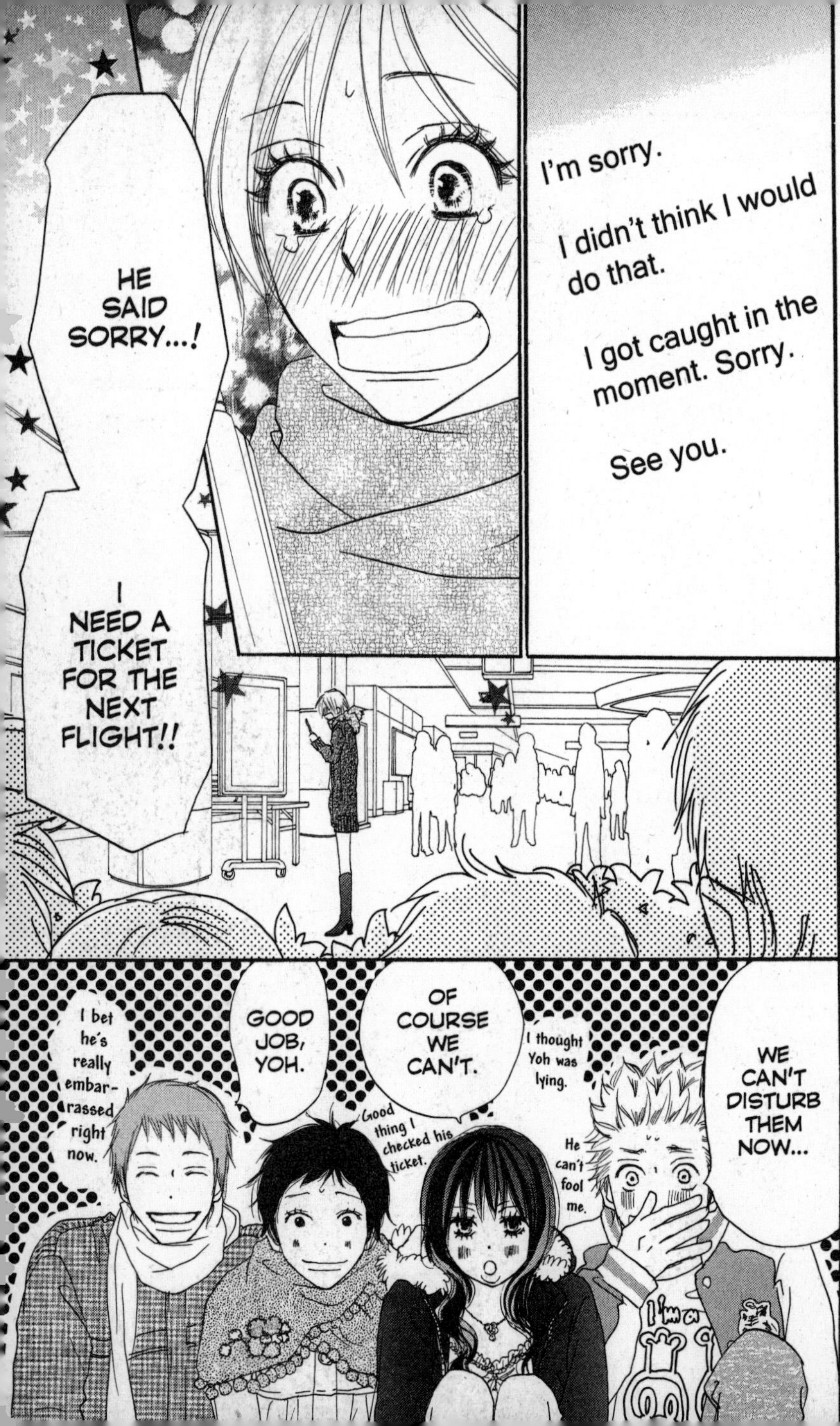
I'm sorry.
I didn't think I would do that.
I got caught in the moment. Sorry.
See you.
HE SAID SORRY...!
I NEED A TICKET FOR THE NEXT FLIGHT!!
WE CAN'T DISTURB THEM NOW...
He can't fool me.
I thought Yoh was lying.
OF COURSE WE CAN'T.
Good thing I checked his ticket.
GOOD JOB, YOH.
I bet he's really embar-rassed right now.

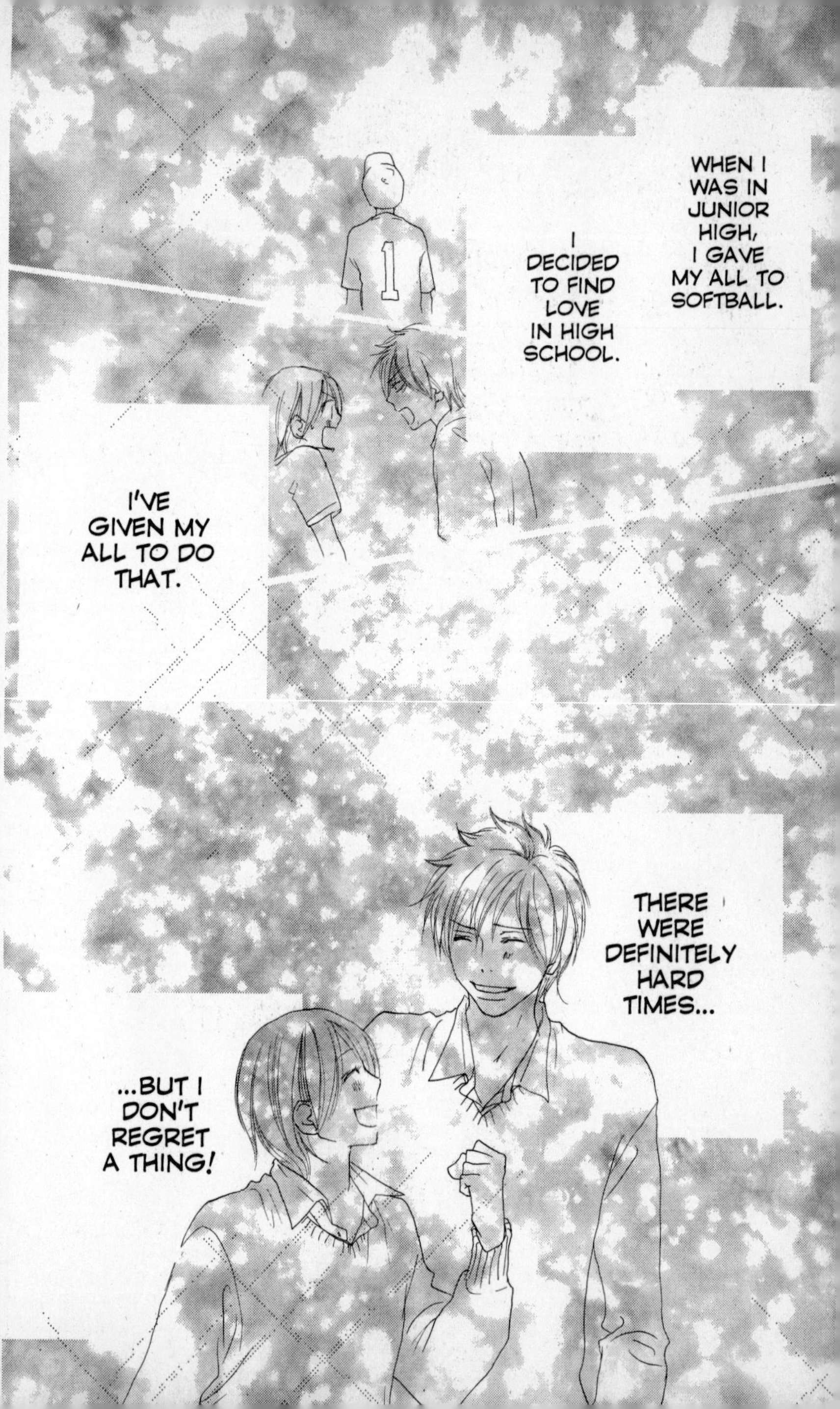
WHEN I WAS IN JUNIOR HIGH, I GAVE MY ALL TO SOFTBALL.
I DECIDED TO FIND LOVE IN HIGH SCHOOL.
I'VE GIVEN MY ALL TO DO THAT.
THERE WERE DEFINITELY HARD TIMES...
...BUT I DON'T REGRET A THING!

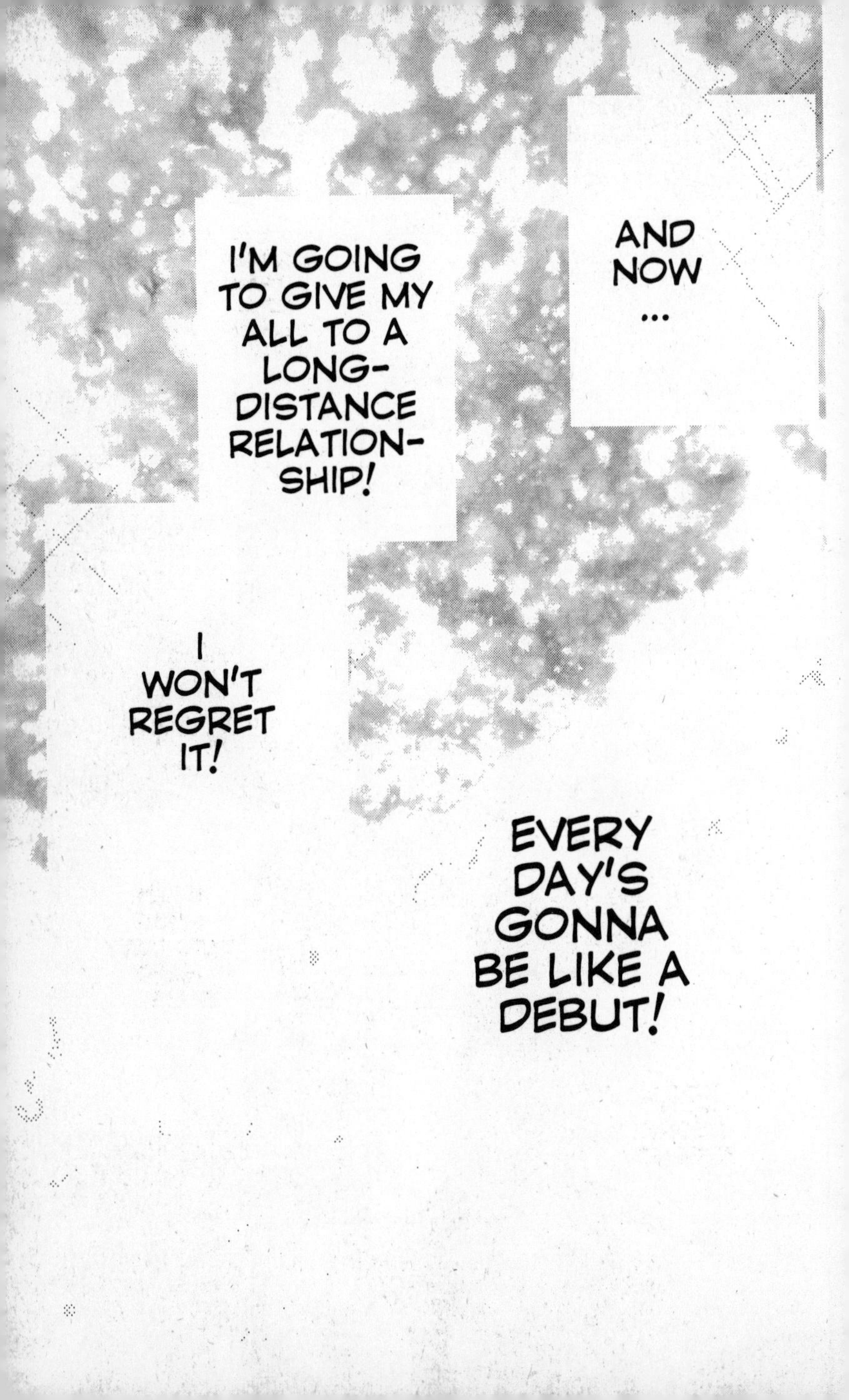
AND NOW ...
I'M GOING TO GIVE MY ALL TO A LONG-DISTANCE RELATION-SHIP!
I WON'T REGRET IT!
EVERY DAY'S GONNA BE LIKE A DEBUT!

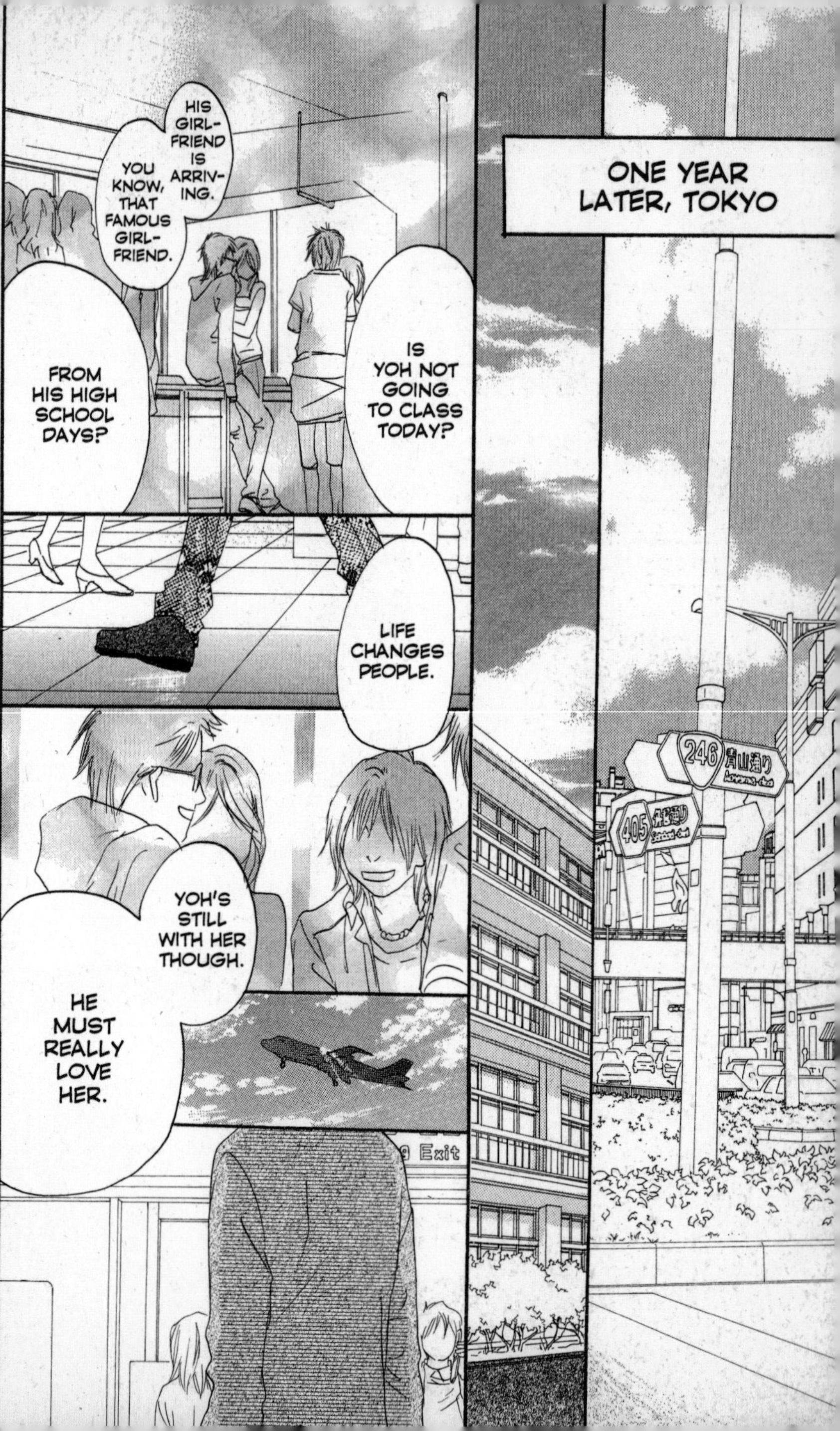
ONE YEAR LATER, TOKYO
246 青山通り
IS YOH NOT GOING TO CLASS TODAY?
HIS GIRL-FRIEND IS ARRIV-ING.
YOU KNOW, THAT FAMOUS GIRL-FRIEND.
FROM HIS HIGH SCHOOL DAYS?
LIFE CHANGES PEOPLE.
YOH'S STILL WITH HER THOUGH.
HE MUST REALLY LOVE HER.

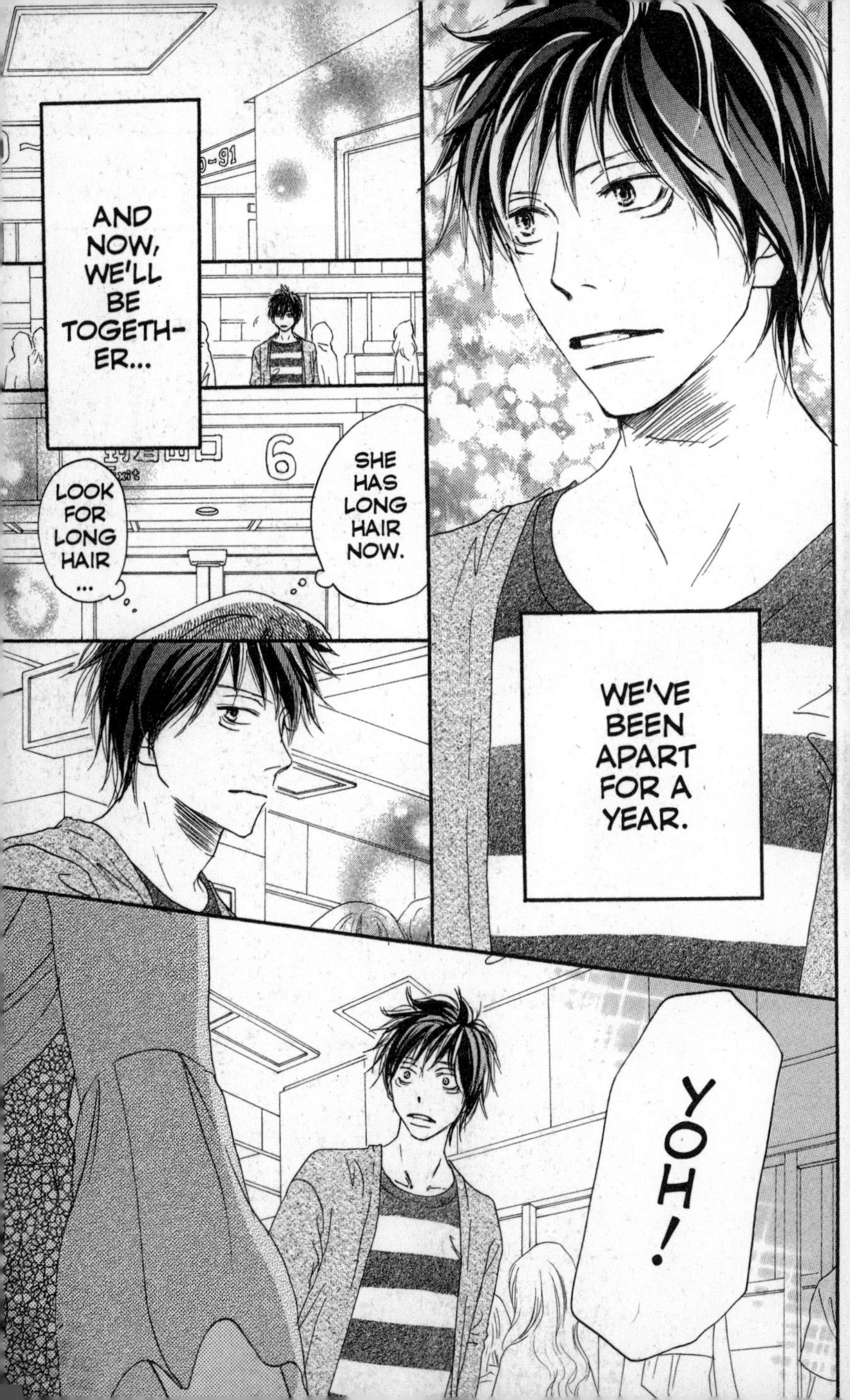
WE'VE BEEN APART FOR A YEAR.
AND NOW, WE'LL BE TOGETH-ER...
SHE HAS LONG HAIR NOW.
LOOK FOR LONG HAIR ...
YOH!

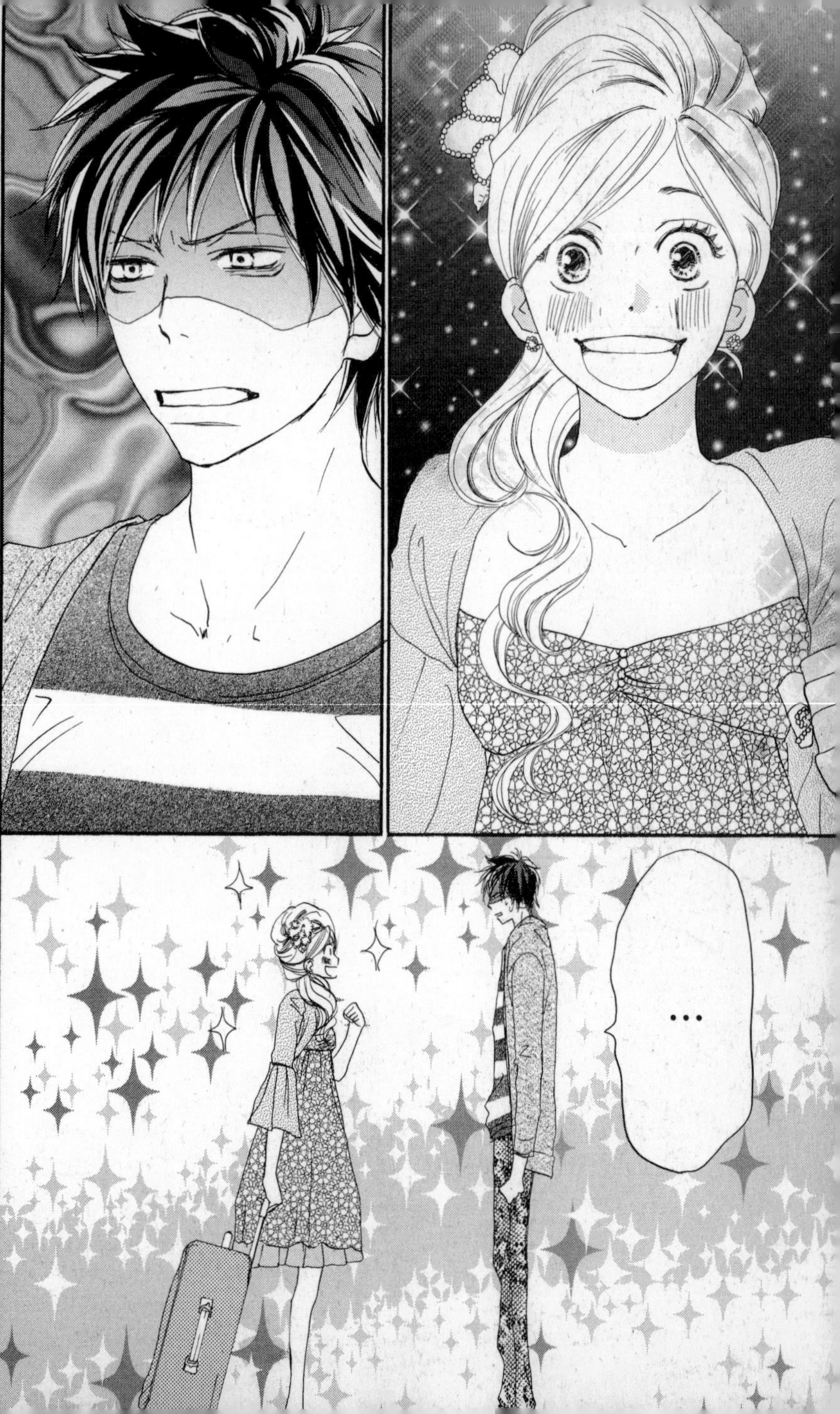
...

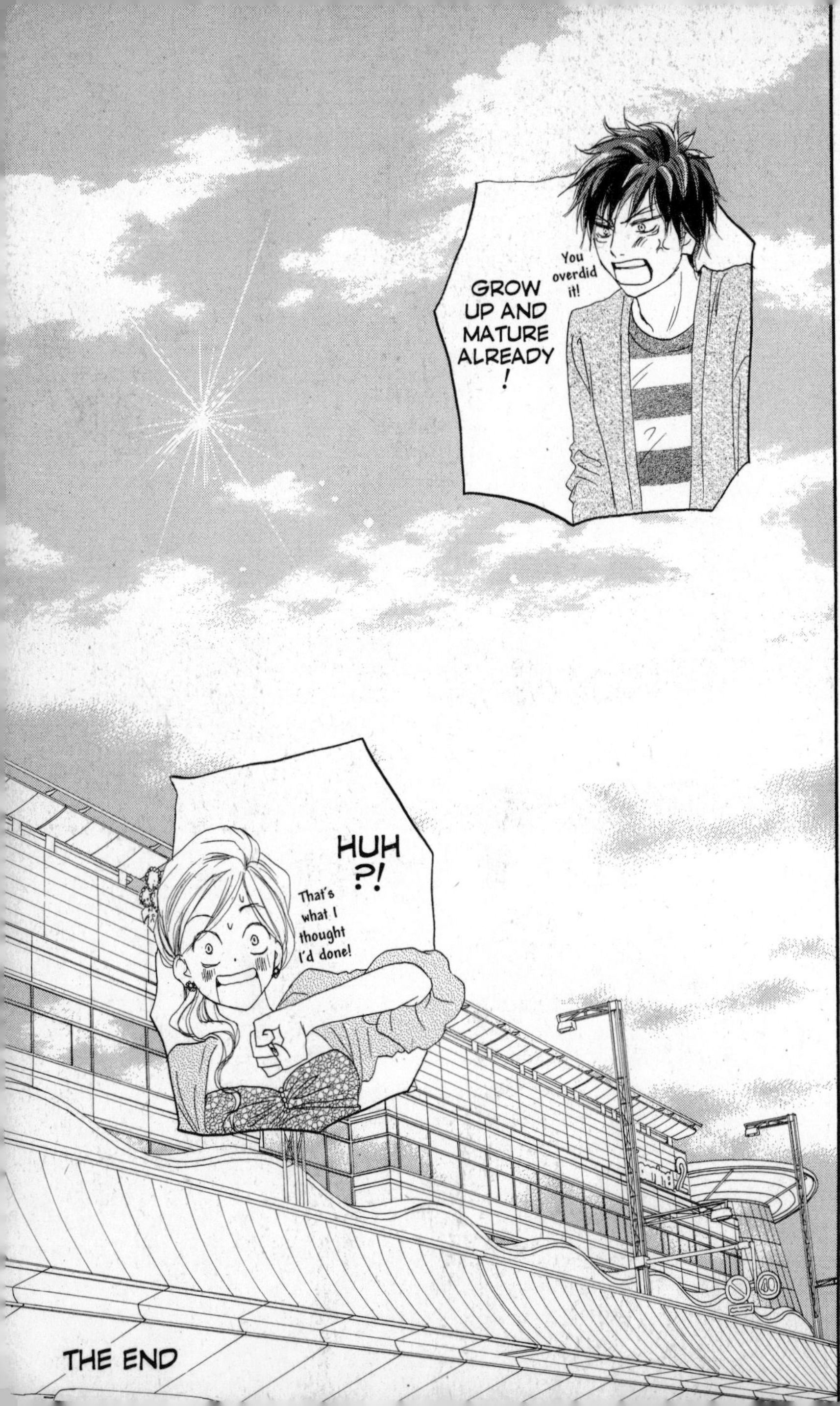
GROW UP AND MATURE ALREADY!
You overdid it!
HUH?!
That's what I thought I'd done!
THE END

This is the final volume. Thank you for all your support! I'm currently working on some special volumes. I do hope you take a look at them. Thank you for your letters and gifts too! I'm very happy!

– Kazune Kawahara

Kazune Kawahara is from Hokkaido Prefecture and was born on March 11th (a Pisces!). She made her manga debut at age 18 with *Kare no Ichiban Sukina Hito* (His Most Favorite Person). Her other works include *Sensei!*, serialized in *Bessatsu Margaret* magazine. Her hobby is interior redecorating.

HIGH SCHOOL DEBUT
VOL. 13
Shojo Beat Manga Edition

STORY & ART BY
KAZUNE KAWAHARA

Translation & Adaptation/Gemma Collinge
Touch-up Art & Lettering/Rina Mapa
Cover Design/Courtney Utt
Interior Design/Amy Martin
Editor/Amy Yu

VP, Production/Alvin Lu
VP, Sales & Product Marketing/Gonzalo Ferreyra
VP, Creative/Linda Espinosa
Publisher/Hyoe Narita

First published in Japan in 2003 by SHUEISHA Inc., Tokyo.
English translation rights arranged by SHUEISHA Inc.

Printed in Canada

Published by VIZ Media, LLC
P.O. Box 77010
San Francisco, CA 94107

10 9 8 7 6 5 4 3 2 1
First printing, February 2010

www.viz.com
www.shojobeat.com

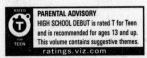

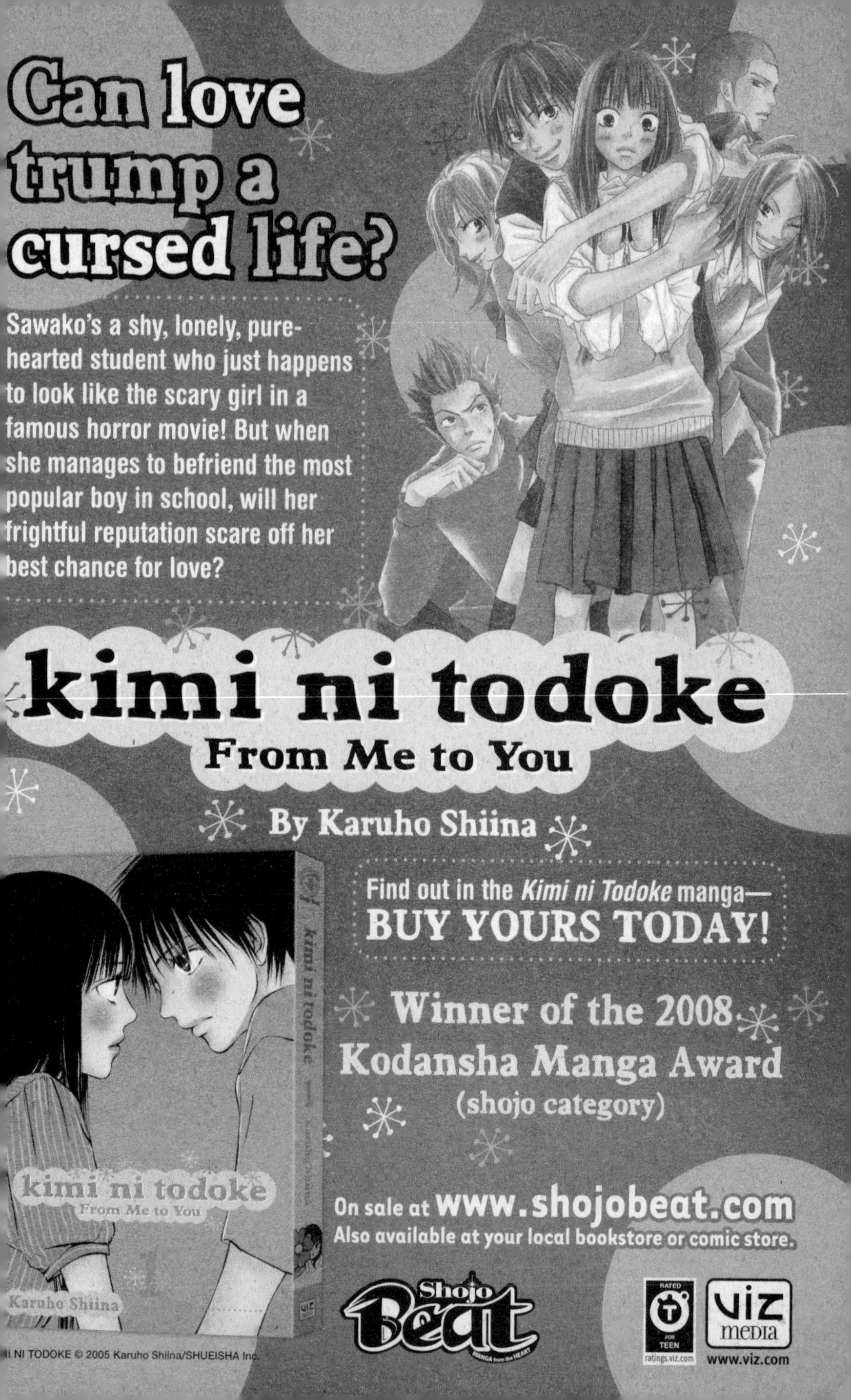
Can love trump a cursed life?
Sawako's a shy, lonely, pure-hearted student who just happens to look like the scary girl in a famous horror movie! But when she manages to befriend the most popular boy in school, will her frightful reputation scare off her best chance for love?
kimi ni todoke
From Me to You
By Karuho Shiina
Find out in the Kimi ni Todoke manga—
BUY YOURS TODAY!
Winner of the 2008 Kodansha Manga Award
(shojo category)
kimi ni todoke
From Me to You
Karuho Shiina
On sale at www.shojobeat.com
Also available at your local bookstore or comic store.
Shojo Beat
RATED T FOR TEEN
ratings.viz.com
VIZ media
www.viz.com
I NI TODOKE © 2005 Karuho Shiina/SHUEISHA Inc.

love ★ com

By Aya Nakahara

Class clown Risa and Ôtani join forces to find love

Manga available now